The Irish Abolitionist
Richard Madden and the Subversion of Empire

Leon Ó Broin

Translated and edited by
Mícheál Ó hAodha

NUASCÉALTA

An Maidíneach – Staraí na nÉireannach Aontaithe, by Leon Ó Broin, published by Sáirséal agus Dill, Dublin, 1971.

The original Irish-language rights for this work remain with Cló Iar-Chonnacht, Indreabhán, Co. na Gaillimhe.
www.cic.ie

Copyright © Leon Ó Broin, 1971.
English Translation © Mícheál Ó hAodha, 2014.
Annotated by Mícheál Ó hAodha

All rights reserved.
No part of this book may be reproduced in any form or by any means including electronic or mechanical photography, filming, recording or by any information storage and retrieval or video systems without prior permission from the publishers, Nuascéalta Teoranta.

www.nuascealta.com • info@nuascealta.com
Cover Illustration and Design: © Karen Dietrich, 2014.

Typesetting: Nuascéalta Teoranta.

ISBN-13: 978-1500942601
ISBN-10: 150094260X

INTRODUCTION

The story of the Irish who worked outside Ireland primarily and the Irish who worked as functionaries for the British colonial establishment and yet tried to remain true to their own personal and philosophical principles is a complex one. This is an aspect of the Irish experience that has witnessed a small surge of interest in more recent years. This is particularly true of the Irish who were "betwixt-and-between" in the latter half of the nineteenth century and the early twentieth century and who worked, often at the outer reaches of empire, where human rights violations were frequent and open. Madden was one of the first abolitionists from Ireland who identified the similarities between the Irish as oppressed at home and the many other nationalities he came across in the more remote regions of empire. People such as Madden had to mould their identity as circumstances dictated - chameleon-like - if they wanted to hold onto their jobs and feed their families. They eked out a living at the margins of power and relied on a hidden nexus of friends and supporters from within that establishment to protect them and ensure that when they were removed from one posting – as Madden frequently was – they found another. This is a very detailed book, and yet it is still never entirely clear who Madden's protectors were and why they were motivated to defend him from his biggest and far more powerful enemies. This is just one of the mysteries that will remain unsolved in relation to Madden, despite his profligate output in terms of his writings. This book on Madden is partly an exploration of how political power works and how the centre of power changes – and, so too the periphery – as depending on who is in the establishment. This is as true today as it ever was.

Given his refusal to remain silent on the treatment of

various enslaved peoples and minorities, both ethnic and religious – in Cuba, West Africa and in Australia to name but a few of his spheres of operation – the British establishment made frequent attempts to break Madden as an administrator, as a civil servant, and as a human being. Madden was an outsider, an Irish Catholic operating within a primarily British Protestant colonial administration and what he saw and experienced in many of his colonial postings horrified him; he wasn't shy to denounce oppression when he saw it. He suffered for his outspokenness, however, as he was transferred from one job to the next and lived and worked on four continents and in very harsh climates. Madden was tough, both psychologically and physically; he lived a long and full life. Administrator, medical doctor, writer, journalist, historian, human rights advocate – there was no end to his incredible array of talents. He was a renaissance man in his own way.

Mícheál Ó hAodha

CONTENTS

1	Madden's Youth	1
2	In Europe, Turkey and the Middle East	17
3	The Publication of Madden's First Book	46
4	Jamaica and the Anti-Slavery Movement	58
5	Cuba, Abolitionism and the Case of the *Amistad*	87
6	Madden's Religious "Conversion"	119
7	The Anti-Slavery Campaign on the Gold Coast	140
8	*The Lives of the United Irishmen*	175
9	*The Lives of the United Irishmen*: The Reviews	207
10	In Portugal for *The Morning Chronicle*	228
11	A Spell in Western Australia	268
12	Exile's Return: A Job in Ireland	321
13	Madden's Literary Career Takes a Prolific Turn	363
14	The Second Edition of the *Lives*	379
15	The End of the Road	401
	References	425
	About the Author	483
	About the Translator	483

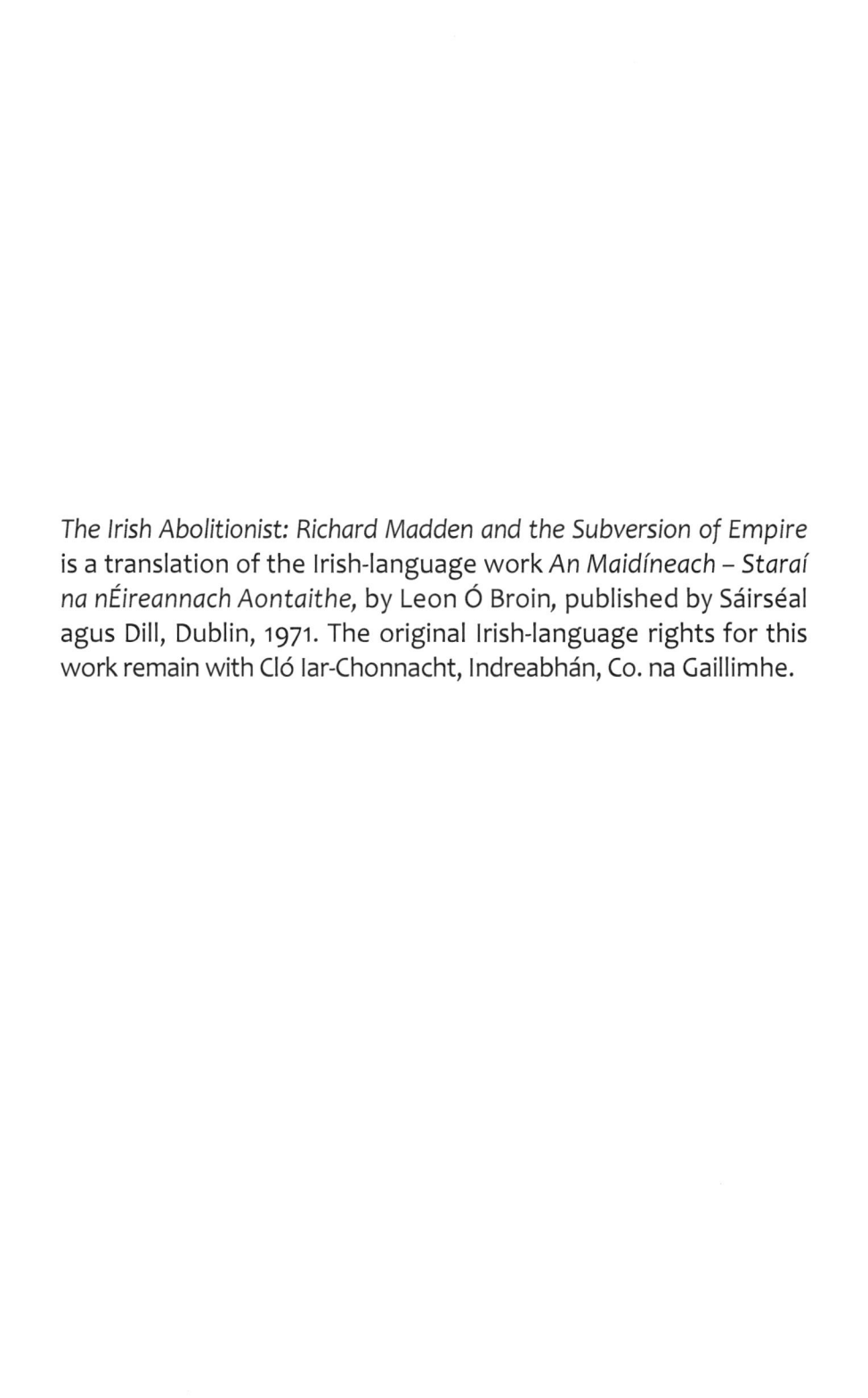

The Irish Abolitionist: Richard Madden and the Subversion of Empire is a translation of the Irish-language work *An Maidíneach – Staraí na nÉireannach Aontaithe,* by Leon Ó Broin, published by Sáirséal agus Dill, Dublin, 1971. The original Irish-language rights for this work remain with Cló Iar-Chonnacht, Indreabhán, Co. na Gaillimhe.

CHAPTER 1
MADDEN'S YOUTH

The subject of this book – Richard Robert Madden - used to work on this autobiography from time to time. Unfortunately, he didn't manage to finish it before his death in 1886, however. He was eighty-eight years of age when he died having lived a full life, a detailed description of which will be given here. He was such a busy man and involved with so many different social and political issues throughout his life that it is almost impossible to fully sketch his literary mind or his intellectual motivations. The part of his life that he did manage to record in print was published in 1891[1], an account that was bolstered by an appendix contributed by his son Dr. Thomas More Madden. That book gives a fairly good account of his early years, of his family background, so much so that it made it relatively easy for me to put together the first chapter or two of this book. It would not be inappropriate to assign the title "Madden of the United Irishmen" to the subject of this book for a number of reasons. It is likely that this would have been the title he would have chosen himself since it is largely as a consequence of his staunch defence of that movement that Madden's memory lives on. The first lines in his memoir make reference to the United Irishmen and the rebellion of 1798 was one of his abiding interests. His birth occurred during the rebellion, at the same time as his father's house in Wormwood Gate was being searched by the Provost of Dublin. While no fighting took place in Dublin itself, the plans for the rebellion were set in train only a short distance from Madden's house and following the arrest of the rebellion's leaders, the city was combed thoroughly by the British military. Here is Madden's description of what happened:

> *The ill-famed Major Sirr searched our house on the day that I was born – the 20th of August, 1798. He had a band of yeomen with him, evil thugs who terrified every Catholic, no matter how law-abiding, that they came across. Unopposed, they ransacked the bottom of our house before making their way to the door of my mother's room, where my father brought them to a halt. He put his life on the line before Major Sirr, himself, intervened to save him. He came running down the stairs just as the armed band was on the point of breaking into the room. "I know that Éamann Madden is a peaceful citizen," he said. To make a statement like that at this juncture was quite something, especially when the self-same statement referred to one of the few Catholic deputies, a figure mentioned who was mentioned in* The Memoirs of Wolfe Tone.[2]

His intervention was enough to save Madden's wife and child, although it must be said that the same child wasn't half as accommodating to the Bailiff when he got his chance to re-pay the compliment many years later. Major Sirr was no fool however. This was a period in Irish history when simply being a Catholic was enough to arouse suspicion. There were other reasons also for him to be doubtful of Éamann Madden's loyalty. The truth of the matter was that Madden Senior had once given protection to a man who was "on the run." Sirr had kept a close watch on this house from then on and when he arrested James Tandy in 1803 for his part in another attempted uprising, he also brought in Éamann Madden for questioning. Sirr questioned Madden about a certain dinner that had taken place in *The Smugglers*, a pub situated in Cooke Street, not far from Madden's house at 9 Wormwood Gate. The "information" that Éamann provided during this interrogation was of no value to the British authorities, however. If his memory of that evening served him correctly the crowd of men and women in attendance – (and there were some very "rough-looking" characters amongst them) – had all raised a glass to the health of the King and nobody amongst them had made any mention of a man named Napper Tandy[3]. As he gave this testimony, it was probably in the back of his mind that his own father had taken the oath of allegiance so as to hold avoid confiscation of their property, as had many other Catholic merchants of an earlier era.

The reference to "rough-looking" people was likely an indirect allusion to Madden senior's personal pride in his family's social status and genealogy. His son, Richard, was extremely proud and (even) boastful of his ancestors at times. According to a genealogical chart drawn up by Hart, he believed that he was the 130th descendant of Eoin Buach, the lord of Síl Amhaca[4] – (a man who had lived 2000 or 3000 years before the time of Christ – that is if he ever really existed at all!). This much *is* true however – the Madden family were big landowners at one point but most of their lands were taken from them so that by the end of the sixteenth century, they only had possession of the Barony of Longford in County Galway and the parish of Lusmagh in County Laois. They also owned a castle that straddled both sides of the river Shannon, a castle in the vicinity of which many battles against the English were fought. It was also the Maddens who founded a monastery near Meelick under the auspices of the Franciscans. When Madden examined the traditional lore of his forbears he came across many references to men and women of a peaceful disposition, ancestors who had a name for generosity and hospitality and who had built and decorated churches. Tradition has it that they were a family who had done their best to contribute to their local communities and imbued their neighbours with a love of God and a sense of humility. While tracing his genealogy Madden also discovered the names of many men who had fought and died bravely for their country and his researches revealed only one reference to somebody who had brought shame on the family. This was a man named Dónal Madden, an unscrupulous trickster who gained favour with the English king through treachery and thereby kept control of his lands. In fact, he had managed to hang onto his privileged position by attacking Dónal O'Sullivan Beare[5] as the latter's troops retreated after the rout at Kinsale. Dónal Madden's offspring would redeem the family name somewhat by remaining loyal to both the King and the Catholic cause. Many of his descendants also chose to go into exile or to serve in the ranks of foreign armies rather than to succumb to the colonial project.

Richard Madden's interest in family genealogy also threw up many other interesting gems of information. He discovered, for example, that a relative of his, a generation or two previously, had had a daughter who was married to Malachy Fallon, from Nathystown in County Roscommon. One would have been forgiven for thinking that this same Malachy Fallon had walked straight out of a Lever[6] novel. Éamann Madden had gone into business as a silk manufacturer in Merchant's Quay, Dublin, in or around the year 1760. The silk industry was one of the Ireland's primary industries at this juncture. In 1768 he had transferred his business to Wormswood Gate where he built a spacious new factory and a residence where he was to spend the next sixty years. He married twice. His first wife was Marie Duras, a sister of Edouard Duras, a rich factory-owner from Bordeaux. They had ten children between them, all of whom appeared to have died at a young age. Elizabeth Forde, whom he married in 1777, was his second wife. Eleven children were born as a result of this marriage, Richard Robert being the youngest. As far as we can ascertain, most of these children also died at a young age. Only two of the children outlived their mother and survived beyond the age of thirty, such were the high mortality rates of this era. In 1791, Mr. Duras died in

Bordeaux, prior to which he had named Edmund Madden as his executor of his will and his posthumous legate. The Revolutionary Government seized Duras' estate and despite Madden Senior's best efforts. He spent the best part of three months in France during the Terror and his own son Richard later managed to preserve two snippets of information from his father's notes as recorded at this critical time in the history of Europe. Madden Senior recounted that the journey from Dublin to Holyhead had taken 24 hours and that it took a further 37 hours to travel from Dover to Calais. He had also paid 406 francs to spend ten weeks in the *Hotel Angleterre* in Bordeaux. Shortly after his return to Ireland, Éamann had thrust himself headlong into the preparations for the Catholic Convention of 1792. This assembly saw Madden and four others chosen for a deputation that petitioned the English King regarding the grievances and oppression then being suffered by Irish Catholics.

The efforts of this deputation did see some initial progress when, for the first time, official documents which mentioned Catholics began to refer to them as "Catholics" or "Roman Catholics" as opposed to "Papists" or "persons professing the Popish religion." Shortly after this, the Relief Bill of 1793, was enacted. It is clear that Éamainn was an influential figure within the Irish Catholic community at this juncture and someone whose kindness, decency and piety was widely recognised. He had become a wealthy man prior to the Act of Union and shared his wealth generously with the poor. He also gave refuge to bishops and priests who were then being persecuted by the colonial regime. Elizabeth, his wife, was a cheerful and good-looking woman with a sunny disposition and it is not surprising that Bishop Delaney, Bishop McGowran, the Jesuit Doctor Betagh and Doctor Gahane, were all as fond of her as she was good to them. The poor had had a particular fondness for her and her own family found it difficult to describe adequately the extent to which they idealised her. Madden wrote the following concerning his mother:

> *Fondly-remembered by that person who was always at the tail-end of the brood (a reference to himself) - she never stopped praying for his well-being, and it was thanks to her*

prayers that saved him from that which was bad or dangerous...[7]

She was a true Christian in his view, a person who suffered greatly during the course of her life. We do know some of the crosses that she bore stoically: the death of so many of her children in infancy and the decline of her husband's business. We can be certain that she suffered when the few members of her family who survived into adulthood left their home place and the bosom of the family, a hurt exacerbated by the fact that she detected 'a certain waywardness' amongst some of them. She was a product of the Gaelic tradition and O'Carolan wrote a number of songs concerning her people, songs that Madden heard her singing in Irish, a language which he did not understand himself. Madden's childhood saw various relatives of his taking care of him at different points in time, as was then customary in Gaelic tradition:

A nobleman named Murphy undertook to raise the young Croppy. It wasn't long before he was doing his own thing and making a particular nuisance of himself when the era of the 'troubles' arrived. He spent about four years around Kilmainham, a time in which his fighting instincts were sharpened. This fiery aspect of his character could have been tamed if he had had a watchful guardian keeping an eye on him. He didn't take any part in Emmet's rebellion for reasons - he stated - that he would bring to the grave with him.[8]

Madden was five years of age at this juncture. Like most other city children, he had no knowledge of the countryside, which began only about a mile from his house, just beyond the gates of the Phoenix Park. His mind was formed in the life of the streets and in the regular movements of the river Liffey at the bottom of the hill. His world consisted of the huge buildings that surrounded him - the Four Courts, the two Cathedrals and the mysterious Temple of Saint Michan[9] with its nuns and mummified crusaders. His experiences were much the same as those of the average Dubliner or "Joe

Soap" of this period, one of whom was a friend of his by the name of Liam Bernard McCabe - or Barney McCabe as he was known to Madden. He lived only a short distance away from Madden at Ushers Quay and many's the hour he would have spent sitting in the nook of a window, keeping an incredulous eye on the crowds who gathered at the Four Courts. Not only was the countryside undiscovered territory for McCabe but he was also equally unaware of the existence of the Irish language, a language that was still spoken by a few million people in Ireland at this juncture. McCabe only realised that this language existed at all when a "Poor Scholar" called to his grandmother's door in Maynooth one day and neither he nor the servant girl who answered the door could understand what the man was saying. McCabe had to call his grandmother and when she saw who their caller was she brought him into the parlour where she placed both food and wine before him. She gave the "Poor Scholar" food and lodgings for a fortnight. He was a Kerry man who was on his way to Portugal to see whether he had a calling to the religious life. The Kerryman recited stories about ancient Ireland, stories which made such an impression on the young McCabe that he would recall them to mind even many years later and publish them in a book which he dedicated to Richard Madden. This particular "Poor Scholar" – a name named Micheal Mac Oireachtaigh - didn't have a vocation by all accounts and he later got a job as a reporter in London's House of Lords.

When the time came to attend school both Madden and Barney McCabe were initially sent to Peter Chaigneau in Usher Street, a man who is likely to have been related to the Chaigneaus who fled France during the Revolution. The only description that Madden has left of this school states that the boys there comprised "a select band", a group whose main source of diversion was "waging war" on other gangs of lads in the local area. He also mentions that a boy by the name of Joseph Augustine Wade refused to hang around with their group. Wade was a shy and quiet boy who had a particular interest in poetry and music. When Madden came across him again years later at a public dinner in London - in 1823 or 1824 - Wade had already established himself as a music teacher and a composer of note, composing such populist songs as *Meet me by Moonlight Alone*, a number that was so popular in its day that it would make the "Top Twenty" nowadays. Like many musicians of his era, Wade struggled to make a living from his art and by the time Madden ran into him again, he was already a hunched and worn-out individual, suffering the combined burdens of debt and poor health. Madden never did find out what became of Wade in his later years but he regretted afterwards that he hadn't helped publish the monograph entitled the *History of Music* - a work that Tom Moore[10] bought from Wade at one stage - and a work that Petrie[11] held in high regard. Having spent a while under the tutelage of Chaigneau, Madden was sent to a school run by the Reverend Doctor O'Farrell in Coldblow Lane in Donnybrook. This is a good distance from Wormwood Gate and it is likely that Madden lodged with relatives of his in Donnybrook. The third school that he attended was The Classical and Mercantile Academy, an establishment run by a Father Barnaby Murphy in North Anne's Street and a building which survived into the modern era, as situated opposite Saint Michan's Church. Newgate Prison was only a stone's throw from here. According to Doctor Meyler Ronan who has passed on, this latter school held a special place amongst the Catholic schools of the era, Father Barnaby Murphy boosting the school's finances through the publication of collections of his sermons.[12] By 1812, Madden was a student at the Classical and Mercantile Academy, as indicated by a description of his recorded when he was just 14 years of age. It was at this time also that he first visited Newgate Prison where the sound of a prisoner calling to him from behind a door fortified with iron bars, imprinted itself on his memory. The prisoner called Madden by name because he recognised him from a period that he had spent "in service" with Madden's father. The prisoner who had been sentenced to death requested that Madden's father plead for clemency on his behalf with then Viceroy. He was facing execution by hanging, a punishment that had been imposed on him for robbery.

Madden consulted with his cousin, Éamann Ó Broin and both of them went up to the hay-loft at the rear of the house in Wormwood Gate where they composed a memo to the then Viceroy, Duke Redmond. The memo was supposedly composed in the name of the prisoner's wife, "to whom numerous progeny was conceded." They tracked down each member of the jury and persuaded them to put their name to this memo, all except for the most senior juror. Then they presented the judge with a copy of the memo as he made his way into the Court one day. They then planned how best to ensure that the Viceroy also received a copy of this letter appealing for clemency. After much consideration, they thought of a girl whom they knew and who had a sister in service with the Duchess of Richmond. This girl helped them to ensure that their memo reached the Viceroy himself but the days ticked by and there was still no word to the prisoner.

On the day assigned for the execution both Madden and O'Byrne went to the prison in the early morning where they were horrified to see the gallows already prepared. Madden was so upset that he turned back and returned home again but O'Byrne stayed there and just before the time of execution he observed the sheriff's band of troops making their way to the prison where a cry went up from the waiting crowd: "A reprieve, a reprieve!" O'Byrne forced his way through the crowd and followed the sheriff's officers into the prison.

He actually saw the condemned man just a few moments after he heard that his death sentence had been rescinded at the last minute. The prisoner's first response was to push his big blackened hands out through the bars of the cell-door. "Ah, young man, is it yourself that is there?" he said before rubbing his neck with his left hand and exclaiming: "I never believed this neck was destined for the rope. Hurrah for Botany Bay!"[13] If either yourself or young Master Madden ever visit that country you will find me there as your friend" Although Master Madden did go to Australia many years later he never did get a chance to take this man up on his offer. He did however note the following in his papers as based on this whole tragic episode:

There is no human being too insignificant, of too humble a station in society, too feeble in his frame, too little acquainted with great people, to perform a service to humanity if he has only sufficient common sense to devise, and employ the means within his reach, together with sufficient energy to make the effort in a hopeful and enterprising spirit.[14]

To put the finishing touches to his education, Madden was sent to a school next to Stephen's Green, close to where an uncle of his mother's lived, a famous attorney by the name of Robert Leehane. Leehane, who had directed John Philpot Curran on his life's journey, was normally considered a "difficult" individual but he grew fond of young Madden, regarding him "a quiet retiring mope of a boy" and "a poor soft child" who needed looking after. It was on Lehane's advice that it was decided to send the boy to school in York Street and change his name from Richard to Robert. The school in York Street had a great reputation as an educational establishment and was run in a liberal spirit by Edmund Martin, then a government minister and a professor at Trinity College, Dublin. Unlike in other schools at this juncture, there was no discriminatory language used against Catholics at this school and when the Protestant scholars gathered together for their Christian doctrine classes every Saturday morning, the Catholic students would be sent home in order to receive their own instruction. Madden would subsequently compare this policy as respectful of all religious beliefs and the reverse which would happen in mixed schools in Ireland a few short years later. Madden was happy under Martin's tutelage and the afternoons often found him in his uncle's office on the Green, where he received a welcome every now and then from Curran. Curran was an idol of Madden's sometimes the young lad waited outside the Four Courts to see the renowned speech-maker. By this time, Curran had abandoned any scruples he might have had when he was younger and was employed as Master of the Rolls.[15] When he was seven years old Madden intimated to his family that he wished to become apprenticed to a famous Dublin surgeon named Keogh. To qualify as a surgeon in this era it was necessary for a prospective candidate to both practice and live with a particular surgeon-master, a condition of the apprenticeship that didn't appeal greatly to Madden, however. His father wasn't happy about the potential cost of an apprenticeship either while Madden's mother preferred that he live at home given that his health wasn't the best. Mr. Keogh provided a quick resolution to this dilemma however when he demanded the hefty sum of 250 pounds as his fee for the apprenticeship!

As other Dublin-based surgeons were equally expensive, Madden had no option but to apprentice himself to a chemist in the hope that his financial situation would improve in the meantime and that he could then switch to surgery. He therefore took the exam for chemists in the Apothecaries Hall, although he didn't actually tell his parents that he was taking this exam in case he failed. Jack Gifford, a sectarian and embittered Orangeman, was one of those on the exam board, a man who went by the nickname of "the dog in office":

> *I am a dog in office, both servile and mean,*
> *Who rose from wearing yellow hose, to wear a yellow chain,*
> *And a-grinning I will go - will go,*
> *And a-grinning I will go!*
> *What tho' my Madam Fortune has taken into tow*
> *The mendicants all swear I was whelped in Channel Row.*

Grattan referred to Gifford in less than glowing terms as:

> The hired traducer of his country, the excommunicated of his fellow citizens, the regal rebel, the unpunished ruffian, the

> agitator. In the city a firebrand; in the court a liar; in
> ⟨stree⟩ts a bully; in the field a coward.[16]

The exam went well until Madden was questioned about his age. He told the examination board that he was seventeen years of age but Gifford said he didn't believe him. Gifford's comment upset Madden and he shouted out: "I was born in 1798, a distinctive year in Irish history and one which you may recall yourself sir." When the other candidates heard this outburst they were sure that Madden's chances were gone. However, the chairman of the board stated that he was happy with Madden's qualifications. Madden then spent a while looking for a master with whom he could serve his apprenticeship before eventually finding a country doctor named Mr. Woods, based in Athboy, County Meath. Woods was looking for apprentices and was also only seeking a small fee for his services. Madden apprenticed himself to this doctor for the following five years. It seems likely that this was Madden's first taste of life outside Dublin and he probably didn't like much of what he saw.

What he saw and experienced in Athboy was probably a fairly representative picture of life in rural Ireland at this juncture. The Athboy area had a population of just under 7000 people then, and while a handful of them worked in the local flour mill, the only other means of livelihood in the area was working as an agricultural labourer, and there wasn't enough land available so that everybody could make a living from this. The lands in this area were owned by three men, the Earl of Darnley, Sir Francis Hopkins, General Bligh and Lord Trimleston, and the bulk of them were let out on lease. The tenant labourers generally had somewhere between two acres and twelve acres on which to eke out a subsistence living. The potato was the staple food of labourers and their families and the workers normally tried to sow enough potatoes in Spring-time so that they could survive those fallow periods when there was no work. When food was scarce, the parish priest would make representations with the wealthier landlord class, calling on them to help the poor who were all clothed in worn-out old clothes and rags. The tiny pay the workers received ensured that these fallow periods when the labourers had no food or harvest were common. In summer, the labourers earned eight pence a day and in the winter ten pence. In total, they earned between 10 pounds and 11 pounds a year. Their small houses were made of mud and were without either chimneys or windows. They paid between 1. 10. 0 and 3 pounds a year in rent and each mud-cabin had between three and five land plots adjacent to it. Sometimes they paid their rent with their labour. The only furniture they had were a few stools and other odd pieces and most of the tenants slept on straw that they scattered in the corner of the room. In at least fifty cabins, two families lived, including spouses and children.

There were also nearly eighty widows and their children living in the parish that Madden found himself living in. These widows survived on whatever work they could find and were almost always stretched with debt. Nearly a hundred other people were either too old or weak for work and were reliant on their families or neighbours to support them. There were also nearly another two hundred people on the side of the road seeking alms. No one was in immediate danger of dying from the hunger - the Great Hunger (Great Famine) had not yet happened - and yet the vast bulk of the Irish population, the people of Athboy included, were already in a very precarious state.

As resident doctor, Woods was very busy. The same can be said for Madden who worked as his apprentice between 1815 and 1819. There was no dispensary in the place until 1819. It was only then that the Earl of Darnley opened one in Athboy, a dispensary for which a special committee was appointed to gather subscriptions and one which received a grant from the High-Jury. From then onwards patients could visit the dispensary themselves, or, if unable to do so, the doctor or his assistant could call out to them on the recommendation of a member of the committee. In the absence of the most basic living conditions, fever was a frequent problem. Alcoholism was also a fast-growing problem in Athboy which was home to nineteen pubs and many illegal shebeens.

The doctor used to attend one of the landlords a man who, according to Madden, suffered from "a religious monomania of the same character as that of Lord George Gordon[17] of "no Popery" notoriety, heightened by spiritual agencies in the material form of whiskey." When Madden first accompanied Woods to see the landlord they were greeted by a string of curses and bluntly informed that they would receive no payment for their troubles. The landlord told them that it was the housekeepers who couldn't mind their own business that had let them in when he had ordered them to bring him more drink from the cellar, instead. As the doctor understood the type of person he was dealing with, he didn't mind telling a few lies. As he happened to be in the vicinity and was showing the area to his young friend, he couldn't have passed the house without calling in, he claimed. The doctor introduced Madden to Gordon, casually announcing that he was the grandson of Brazil Madden, Lord of Salamanca and the rightful heir to Clifden Castle in County Galway! He set himself down near the landlord who screamed:

> Don't examine my pulse please. Wipe that grave-looking countenance from your face and don't prescribe a purgative to clear the after-effects of the alcohol. Don't go outside the door and consult with the rest of the house either. And furthermore don't expect any fee from me, mister - aha - those who brought you here can pay you and they can swallow the purgative too if they wish.[18]

He gave them a mouthful then of what he thought of the Papists of the area and declared that the doctor was a Jesuit in the guise of a doctor, and a follower of the Antichrist. This angered the doctor who replied that the Jesuits had not made any bid for either the body or the soul of the landlord. As regards the Pope - it might be that he was the Antichrist - he didn't know, and he didn't really care - but there was one thing that was certain - The Pope hadn't come to Ireland to evict the tenants from their landholdings after the elections. And he wasn't going to let his tenants die in the ditches because they had voted against the landlords either. They were going on at one another like this until the landlord worked out that Madden was really a "Papist" and he went crazy altogether then. The doctor and his assistant had to leave in a hurry, afraid that Gordon might set his snarling dogs upon them. On completing his "time", Madden received a good recommendation from Woods. He was an honest person who frequently performed charitable acts, Woods vouched. Included in this recommendation was the fact that Madden had once saved a prisoner who had been sentenced to death, a prisoner who, upon his release, had carved out a new life for himself in Australia. In later years, Madden could embellish the history of his apprenticeship to Woods to his liking further when he heard that Woods had become a Catholic at the end of his life.

One incident that occurred at this time made such an impression on the young Madden that he recounted it in full years later to William Smith O'Brien in 1848 – citing it as an example of British Justice as it operated in Ireland. One of the local Meath gentry shot dead a local labouring man during an argument was let go free and didn't serve any punishment while a local labourer who shot at an aristocrat without hitting him was hanged. An aristocrat father and his son were involved in both cases. Both men had the same name – Sir Francis Hopkins - and Madden acted as an excellent witness in the first case where he didn't hesitate to refer to the killing of the labouring man as murder. A crowd of men happened to be drinking in a pub in Athboy after a hurling match when the argument took place and it was deemed that the murder occurred in "suspicious circumstances" i.e. Sir Francis had been intent on doling out his own form of "sapient justice" – an act of revenge that took place in the dark of the evening and included a belt around his waist into which two pistols were hidden.

On his way to the pub Madden overheard Sir Francis saying

that there were a group of blackguards in from the country who were planning some form of treachery and that there was a particularly bad individual amongst them named Denny Mangan. His curiosity got the better of Madden and he followed Sir Francis and his friends to the pub where they rushed in, pistols hand. The drinkers ran for cover but they were pursued and a number of shots were fired. One man was seriously injured and he was brought to Madden in the dispensary to see what could be done for him. At first it was thought that the injured man would survive and he was taken from the dispensary and "tried" before an illegal court. He was thrown into prison "with a ball of a Magistrate's pistol sticking in his spine." He died shortly afterwards – killed by a local Justice of the Peace!

CHAPTER 2
IN EUROPE, TURKEY AND THE MIDDLE EAST

Tuberculosis was a disease that affected many of Madden's family. Two of his brothers died from the disease while Madden was apprenticed in Athboy and he himself contracted tuberculosis having completed his apprenticeship in 1820. He kept the fact that he had contracted the disease from his mother and took medical advice from some doctors in Dublin. Then he headed for a warmer climate. Having received a small financial bequest, he was able to pay his passage from Cork to Bordeaux where he arrived with eleven guineas and a collection of Shakespeare's dramas as his sole possessions. He spent a few weeks looking for a job during which time he improved his French. In the end, he was forced to sell his Shakespeare collection because he was in debt. At one stage, he was readying himself to fight a duel (single combat) when it was alleged that he had scored a game of billiards unfairly. On another occasion he saved a man who was attempting to drown himself in a canal near the Bastille in Paris. Instead of expressing due gratitude, however, the Frenchman he pulled from the water blamed him for not recovering his hat from the water as well! "Of all mortals," Madden commented, "the Frenchman is the most unaccountable." While he had originally been thinking about going into business of some sort, it was while drying himself on the edge of the canal that day that he decided on a different path in life. He wanted to do something where he could put the valuable medical experience he had picked up to good use:

> I called into a chemist shop and enquired where I could find a job. I was directed to M. Planché on the Boulevard des Italiens. He was the chief-chemist in Paris at this time, and as he was seeking an assistant with English, I started working for him immediately that afternoon. I had a reasonable wage and had permission to service the hospitals. Nothing could disguise my happiness at this stroke of luck. Not alone could I continue with surgery, but I would also be free from hunger. Indeed, many were the louis that I earned from then on for performing minor operations.

Tom Moore was one of M. Planché's clients - "The glorious little Tommy Moore" was how Madden referred to him - and it gave him great pleasure to write a few lines of praise on a box of pills which he was prescribing for the poet. Madden wrote an interesting account of his life in M. Planché's shop. The widely-renowned chemist would spend half of the day in the laboratory and the other half dozing in a dark corner. His wife worked from morning till night, however. There were five other assistants in the pharmacy apart from Madden and the others picked on the "young Englishman" from day one. The situation got so bad that Madden ended up having to fight the toughest of them, little vulgar Gascon. He beat Gascon in this fight and from then on the other assistants showed him more respect. Madden needed various surgical instruments by then. The instruments cost sixty francs although he only had thirty francs with which to buy them. To source the money he decided to chance his luck on the red and black tables at the Palais Royal. He decided to bet all his money at the first attempt and to stop playing immediately if he was successful. He won money on his first attempt but didn't have the courage to leave the table at that stage....He left the casino some time later – completely broke! He didn't play the gambling tables ever again.

Madden was living in Paris for about six months when the disease in his lungs returned and Madden had to leave the city for the countryside again. He went to Marseilles first where he got some advice regarding his health from a Doctor Looby, an Irishman who had been living in that city for a long time. Madden decided to try and find work somewhere between Nice and Naples, a geographical region where there were many English people living for health reasons. He went to Nice but then decided for some reason to continue on southwards as far as Rome. He only just barely made it as far as Rome and by the time he arrived there he was very weak and coughing up blood. He thought he was dying but he managed to recover. He went sightseeing in the city and later visited Naples where he hoped to find work with a Doctor O'Reilly, a man who had the reputation for wealth and generosity. It took him five days to walk the full 150 miles in the absence of any transport as a consequence of a revolt then underway in the south of Italy, a revolt the Austrian army were attempting to quell. Doctor O'Reilly was as good as his reputation indicated and he hired Madden as an assistant:

> ...at a sufficient salary...with permission to attend the hospitals and the university...with the expectation of succeeding at the expiration of a year to share in the profits...[19]

Amongst the many upper-class patients who attended Dr. O'Reilly's clinic was Lord Charles Murray[20] who suffered from "periodical maniacal excesses." A fit of mania struck Murray one day while he was out walking with Madden. Murray was on the point of saying farewell to the Margravine von Anspach (whom they had come across on their walk) when Lord Charles announced in a haughty tone of voice: "Doctor, I am going to show the Margarvine how to climb into a carriage correctly."

With that, he walked slowly across to the carriage and took a run before jumping head first through the window of the carriage. When Madden opened the carriage door he found the young man lying prone in the back of the carriage, his head on the floor and his feet on the seat of the carriage-seat. Murray became agitated and got rough with Madden. Despite the fact that Murray was a younger and stronger man than the doctor's assistant, Madden managed to keep him subdued for an hour-and-a-half by which time the carriage had reached Naples. Madden had Murray pinned to the floor by the throat for the duration of that journey. Despite his best efforts, the young nobleman proved unable to shake Madden off, although he did manage at one point to kick out the front window of the carriage!

Barely a year had passed when Doctor O'Reilly recommended to a tubercular female patient of his that she bring Madden to Ireland with her as a helper for the journey by sea. The woman in question died before the ship reached port in London, however. Madden received 200 pounds payment for his services.

This payment left Madden in a very healthy financial state. He had more money now than he had ever had at any point previously in his life and it enabled him to winter in London where he attended a series of medical lectures at Saint George's Hospital. Having completed this next round of studies and running very short on funds again he returned to Naples where he went back into practice again with Doctor O'Reilly. He also continued his medical studies at the University in Naples and in the local hospitals. Within a very short time Madden found himself employed once again to accompany another young patient on the journey back to London, this time for a fee of 100 pounds. This is Madden's description of that awful journey:

> On the 21rst of April, 1823, we embarked on board a miserable schooner, entitled the Betsy of Plymouth. The captain was a man very loud in religious professions, which he unfortunately

discredited by being an intolerable drunkard. Our vessel was unseaworthy...and from the moment we were under weigh, throughout the voyage, the average leakage was some thirteen inches an hour. Abreast of Cadiz the north-west wind set in, and, owing to the drunkenness of our captain, we came within the influence of the trade winds before he thought of tacking. We were now daily approaching Madeira, and at one period, when only thirty miles distant from that island, and our provisions were getting scanty, in the course of the night we fell in with a German brig, with the master of which our captain exchanged his last tierce of salt beef for a cask of wine. A shift of wind at length took us back into the Bay of Biscay and matters now became rather alarming. We were on a short allowance of water - a pint a day, our biscuits were nearly out and, worst of all, my patient was sinking rapidly. The poor fellow was only in his twentieth year - a gentleman and a scholar...The disease in his lungs, long existing, rapidly progressed, and he died on the fiftieth day of our voyage...Believing it would be more gratifying to the feelings of his family that his remains be brought to England, and very much against the will of the crew of the vessel, I succeeded in embalming the body in a somewhat rough though effectual manner by means of common tar.[21]

The Betsy set anchor on the seventy-fifth day of the journey from Naples just outside Plymouth and Madden brought the remains of his companion to Rochester where he presented them to the man's relatives. Then he returned home to Ireland again. It was a full three years since he had last been home and he was very keen to see his friends and family again, particularly his mother. His journey from Liverpool to Dublin by boat was a rough one. He became ill and had to rush to a hotel on arrival in Dublin where he remained until his sickness cleared.

Even in so short a period as I had been absent, death had made no inconsiderable change amongst my acquaintances. My youthful companions were scattered over the kingdom, and of the few who remained, some, as I thought, received me coldly. My dear sister, Mrs. Cogan, whose affection and kindness was never interrupted through life, had become the mother of a family, my brothers were necessarily busily engaged in their several pursuits, and the infirmities of age were accumulating on my very good parents. It was the inevitable but nevertheless most afflicting experience of my life; the conviction felt for the first time that I was no longer a youth, and that home was no longer as home had been. I remained three weeks in Ireland, and then bade adieu, perhaps for ever, to the country which contained all that was dear to me on earth.[22]

Some of his friends were not particularly welcoming to him on this occasion, although it is not entirely clear why this was the case. Did it have something to do with his religious beliefs and the fact that he was thinking of changing his faith? He was anxious, and something was clearly was making him anxious at this juncture of his life and whatever it may have been he was clearly not very good at concealing it. He went back to London where he began to study surgery once more in Saint George's Hospital under the tutelage of Sir Benjamin Brodie. Madden paid for his studies from his own pocket and gained his Diploma in Surgery thereby qualifying as a member of the London College of Surgery. He became a fellow of the same College before earning his doctorate in Medicine from the University of Erlangen. He also secured a licence to practice pharmacy from the Pharmacists Society of London.

While studying in London he also earned four guineas a week working as a reporter on the *Morning Herald*, the newspaper founded by Henry Bate, "the fighting parson." The editor of the newspaper, Harry Thwaites, Madden described as follows:

...an exceedingly small statue of a man mounted on a lofty pedestal and very much diminished by elevation...[23]

Madden's first piece for the newspaper, which appeared in 1822, was a description of his journey to France and he followed this with a series of letters describing his travels in Italy and in the Levant.[24] While working at the *Morning Herald,* he also became a member of the *Eccentrics,* a club set up for members of "the Press, the Temple and the Stage" and a group which met regularly in a pub known as the *Shakespearian Tavern*. As soon as he received his various degrees, Madden returned to Naples. He was anticipating a return to Doctor O'Reilly's medical practice where a job had been promised to him. Unknown to Madden, however, O'Reilly was now sharing the practice with his son-in-law and so Madden was unable to get his old job back. The kindly doctor hired Madden to work in a district which the more prosperous English tourists frequented, however. It was here that Madden got to know Lord Blessington and his beautiful wife Sally Power. They loved Madden's linguistic abilities and his talent for conversation and found his sense of Irishness very attractive. After all, they were Irish themselves, in a manner of speaking.

Sally Power, or Margeurite Blessington as she was now known, was nine years younger than Madden, but she nevertheless related the horror story of her upbringing to him. She was the daughter of Éamann Power from Clonmel, who was a spendthrift and a drunkard. Power was a man who preferred the company of the aristocracy and became a Protestant in order to inveigle his way into their affections. He also accepted a judicial position from Dublin Castle and actively pursued and harassed the United Irishmen as much as he could during the 1798 revolt. While it is difficult to believe, he actually sold his daughter into marriage when she was just fifteen years of age, forcing her to marry a "dirty brute" named Maurice St. Leger Farmer the captain of a British infantry regiment, a man who beat her so badly that she left him and his madness behind and returned to live with her father. St. Leger Farmar was in a deranged state by then as a consequence of heavy drinking, debt and a generally debauched lifestyle. A short while prior to this, he was charged with a boy's murder but managed to be set free. On being let go free, St. Leger Farmer was informed that no further legal "concessions" would be made on his behalf should he commit a crime as serious as murder again.

Sally took this opportunity to flee to England with another army captain, a quiet and pleasant man named Thomas Jenkins, and they spent five happy years together. Rumour has it that he wasn't her only lover. Her ability to court "high society" and her incredible beauty meant that she wasn't long working her way back into the upper echelons of society again. Despite leaving Ireland in very poor circumstances, within a few short years she became one of the most learned and refined women in London's artistic circles. Eventually, she left Jenkins and was "snapped up" by the squint-eyed Lord Blessington - "Jenkins receiving adequate payment (10,000 pounds) for what can only be termed his storage charges."[25] Shortly after this Farmar had an accident where he fell from a very high window in his house and broke his neck. This meant that Blessington was now officially able to marry her. Lady Holland became a sort of a queen in her new domain – the queen of Holland House you could say. There were few noblewomen who were the social equal of her, the newly-elevated Lady Blessington. Her beauty and intelligence meant that it was almost "de rigeur" for the best-known aristocrats of her day to attend her gatherings at Gore House.

The parties held here were the most talked-about of this era and attracted some of the most important politicians of the day, including Palmerston, Castlereagh, Earl Grey, Canning, Erskine and Brougham. The best-known writers and artists were frequent guests also – the likes Thackeray, Moore, Dickens, Gall, Lawrence and Wilkie and the portrait of Lady Blessington - "the loveliest woman of the day" - painted by Lawrence caused quite a stir when first exhibited at the Royal Academy in 1821. The Blessingtons introduced Madden to some of their social circle and it was through them that he met the Abbé Campbell amongst others. The Abbé was chaplain to the Neapolitan residence in London for a while and was a gregarious and lively individual, a man who never refuted the allegation that it was he who had married Mrs. Fitzherbert and George the Fourth. Madden, for one, believed these rumours as he was certain that Mrs. Fitzherbert's religious scruples would not have allowed her to get married in the presence of a Church of England minister if she hadn't already been married in a Roman Catholic ceremony. What Madden didn't realise then was that the church regulations allowed for a Catholic getting married according to the Church of England rite at this juncture since the Acts of the General Council of Trent were never actually applied within Britain itself. Consequently, there was no canonical prohibition in relation to such a marriage.[26]

Lady Blessington and the dandy d'Orsay - who was twelve years her junior - were such close friends, that there any number of salacious rumours circulated concerning their relationship, and it may have been that some of these rumours were not without foundation. Madden himself never saw any evidence of impropriety and when he wrote his biography of Lady Blessington he avoided any reference to the "glaring d'Orsay scandal." When Charles Gavan Duffy later questioned him as to why he had omitted this aspect of Lady Blessington's life - "he shook his head and said there was no evidence in the papers submitted to him, and so he kept his peace."[27]

It may have been that Madden was something of an innocent in relation to this issue because it generally accepted today that there almost certainly was a love affair between Lady Blessington and D'Orsay. In fact, it is also said that a ménage á trois existed between D'Orsay, Lady Blessington and her husband, the Earl. D'Orsay[28] was the son of a French general who had earned his military title under Napoleon. When a friendship developed between the youthful and strapping Lady Blessington and D'Orsay the latter went to live with the Blessingtons and became part of their household, a household that also included Lady Blessington's sister, Evelyn, her sister's husband and their five children. Evelyn would later follow Sally's suit in having a complicated love life. She married one man, eloped with another and when the first man died, she married again and found herself a more secure foothold amongst the aristocracy. The various "tours "and adventures of this bohemian household were the "talk of high society" and the celebrities of their day, particularly those undertaken between the years 1822 and 1823. They spent nine weeks in Geneva where the poet Byron was then living and one story was worse than the next concerning their alleged debauched lifestyle. Byron was soon a regular member of their happy entourage, according to Madden. The poet thought the world of Lady Blessington's sharp and lively intellect and she eagerly reciprocated his friendship. She was a very pleasant individual and an excellent conversationalist. In reality, it was Lady Blessington who courted Byron's company using her friendship with him to publish a couple of books of gossip and tittle-tattle which sold better than did any of her other literary efforts. Her husband also used a loan from Byron to mortgage his land in Ireland. Lord Blessington himself was a profligate spender and between his own wild spending habits and his wife's extravagant nature, it wasn't long before his estate was heavy in debt.

The nature of Lord Blessington's relationship with D'Orsay can be gauged from what took place on the death of Blessington's son - by his first wife - the only one of his children who was born with the appearance of "legitimacy." Blessington appointed D'Orsay as principal legatee and made him chief guardian of another child as born illegitimately to him. He also offered D'Orsay one of his two daughters in marriage, this despite the fact that D'Orsay had never actually met either of them. The daughters in question were aged just eleven and twelve then and only one of them, a girl named Harriet, was legitimate.

It was during one of his extended visits to Naples that Madden got to know the Blessingtons. He met them first in the palace of Prince Belvidere while working as a doctor and became a close friend of theirs shortly afterward, travelling with them through the various regions in and around Naples. Lord Blessington was an enthusiastic yachtsman and Madden spent a lot of time with him sailing across the bay beneath Vesuvius - although Madden admitted that he never felt completely comfortable about their chosen location!

Madden did not remain working in Naples too long, however. He had a longing to travel and to visit Turkey and the countries of the Middle East, in particular. Blessington wrote some letters of introduction on Madden's behalf for this purpose, describing him as a "Medical man and Gentleman of Literary talent desirous of seeing the interior Turkish modes of life." Madden reached Turkey where he decided to study for a doctorate while working part-time as a special correspondent for the *Morning Herald*. He didn't delay in Constantinople[29] deeming it a "half-barbarous" city, whose inhabitants were difficult and "the customary routine and surroundings of medical practice disgusting." Each doctor was assigned a particular quarter in which to work and it was up to either the medical practitioner himself or (as in the case of Madden, his Greek dragoman (interpreter) to source their own patients. Madden and his interpreter used to visit the cafés because it was here that one heard about anybody who was sick. Madden's dragoman always stood at triple-point while he was working and refused to allow Madden treat any patient unless the patient had paid his fee in advance.

Madden wasn't allowed to ask the patients any questions even as relating to their medical histories and was prohibited from providing any information concerning the patient's medical condition to anyone else – i.e. friends or family – who might be in attendance. Madden's dragoman also advised him to check a patient's pulse by checking the veins in the arm only, and to say "With the help of God" in cases where the patient's prognosis was uncertain. In those cases where death was almost inevitable, he advised Madden to use the formula: "God is good" - when advising his patients. Madden did as he was told and set himself up in a café where he could have a drink and smoke his pipe while the dragoman regaled the local Turks with stories of the incredible cures performed by his master on Effendi, a patient whom Madden had allegedly saved, just as man was at death's door. The dragoman[30] always went into detail on the manner whereby Madden had allegedly removed the man's kidneys, removed the disease from them and subsequently replaced them within the patient's body again. The patient in question had allegedly made a complete recovery and rewarded the doctor with five purses full of money. Needless to say, Madden himself couldn't recall performing any such miracle. The only thing he had removed from anyone's body was an infected boil that he had removed from a patient's back.

This boasting was a constant source of irritation to Madden, a fact which the dragoman conveniently ignored. It proved a very effective form of marketing, however. One day, for instance, a man sitting close by suddenly announced that a couple of his wives were sick and enquired what price Madden would accept to treat a woman whose illness was deemed incurable. Even with a medical "history" or diagnosis as limited as this, there were people who thought Madden could cure someone, even people who were terminally ill. In this particular case however, Madden couldn't bring himself to accept the man's money and told his dragoman to tell the man whose wives were sick as much. Madden disappeared into the back of the café and in an effort to smooth things over with the man who had made the enquiry, the dragoman pretended that Madden was angry about something or other. Meanwhile, the dragoman asked for one hundred *piastre* as payment - swearing on the head of his father and the soul of his mother - that he never accepted anything less than this. Madden saw fifty *piastre* change hands and the promise of another hundred if the patient made a full recovery - later observing that: "No man makes larger promises than a Turk in sickness, and no man is so regardless of them in convalescence." Madden did indeed visit the woman patient but was prohibited from seeing her in order to perform a proper physical examination. The unfortunate woman pleaded with Madden that he try and diagnose her disease from behind a wooden door. The door was slightly ajar but the only view. Madden got of his patient was a fleeting glimpse of his patient's head – which was covered with a sheet. He did manage to gather some information about the woman's medical condition from the servants, however, information which indicated that the woman was probably suffering from cancer. Madden did what he could for her and prescribed her a sedative. Madden seems to have been more successful in making some sort of a diagnosis with the second woman, whom he described as a young beauty. This younger woman had no hesitation about removing her veil to reveal her shining eyes and her radiant lips. She showed no obvious traces of sickness. It is likely that this woman wasn't sick at all but was simply interested in getting to see a handsome young stranger who was visiting their country. Madden provided her with a prescription for some medicine which he was certain that she had no need of, a medicine that she most likely never took anyway.

Shortly after this, another patient called to Madden, a man who claimed to be suffering from fever. When Madden enquired what exactly was troubling the man and where the pain was most acute, the man's friends gave the blunt reply: "That's what we want you to tell us. Check his pulse so that you can make a diagnosis." Based on what he could observe, Madden decided it was best to do a blood test first. As he tightened a cord around one of the man's arms so as to locate a vein and take the blood however, Madden discovered to his horror that the man's other arm had been blown off the previous week in a shooting incident and the stump was hidden beneath his robes. The man paid the ultimate price for letting his arm go untreated. He died quite soon after this from tetanus.

While Madden spent less than five months in Constantinople, he made sure to visit as many cultural and historic sites as he could, including a range of harems as run by men, both rich and poor. One man he got to know was a humble pipe-maker by trade, a man whose entire stock couldn't have been worth more than fifty dollars in total. This man still managed to feed and clothe a large harem of women as a side-business, a harem so big that an English tradesman of similar social status would have been driven to the poorhouse within a matter of weeks. When Madden asked the man how he managed to support so many people he replied: "God is good." In the slave bazaars Madden saw poorer women from Greece trussed together in groups and being scrutinised and manhandled by unruly soldiers who pretended to be slave merchants. He saw one girl of about fifteen years of age who was ushered out to display herself before an elderly Turk:

...he twisted her elbows, he pulled her ankles, he felt her ears, examined her mouth, and then her neck; and all this while the slave merchant was extolling her shape and features, protesting that she was only turned thirteen, that she neither snored nor started in her sleep, and that, in every respect, she was warranted.[31]

The women of Turkey were the most beautiful women Madden had ever seen. This, albeit that he was well-aware the harem women he saw as part of his medical rounds had already been carefully vetted before they were allowed to see him. The women were normally veiled on their first visit to the doctor and he could check their pulse only "through the medium of a piece of gauze." On subsequent visits, they allowed him to examine them as he saw fit and when their husbands were absent the women even laughed and joked with him. Some of the women were suspicious of him because he was a Westerner and verbally abused him in the beginning but as they got to know this "infidel" better, they became friendlier and gave him presents such as handkerchiefs and ornate purses. They also asked him what life was like for women from his country? Were they allowed outside without a chaperone? Were they allowed to fall in love with men who wore hats? Were the women ever drowned as a punishment? Did they have to bathe every week and did they wash their elbows? And the most inevitable question - was he (Madden) married himself and did he have many wives? Madden garnered a great deal of information at this juncture about Turkish women's use of cosmetics and the wide range of charms and prayers that they used to ensure a woman became pregnant, or gained or lost weight. He learned that a woman wasn't respected in their culture until she had given birth to a child and that they were held in high esteem when the baby was considered "beautifully fat."

Madden left Constantinople and journeyed on to Candia in Crete where the Greek War of Independence was underway. Crete was then under the control of the Egyptian Prince, Mohammed Ali. His Scottish (mercenary) soldiers were mercilessly annihilating the people of this region until there were so few people left that there were not enough people available to cultivate the fields in the vicinity of the Crete's largest city. Terrible atrocities were regularly committed in Crete at this juncture, atrocities that were committed indiscriminately. Making his way to the Turkish camp Madden saw the body of a murdered farmer lying on the side of the road, his head still bleeding and his panniered donkey still standing patiently next to the body of his master.

The Austrian Consul in Canea introduced Madden to Ibrahim Pasha who had come ashore in Suda just few days before when parts of his navy had been decimated by the Greeks in battle that took place just offshore. The troops were set ashore and the only marsh in the vicinity chosen as their camp. Ibrahim took no precautions against fever, however, with the result that he had lost a fifth of his army to disease by the time he left the island behind again. Madden gave some medical treatment to the General of this army, a man who sat dour and disappointed at the stern of his frigate cursing his unlucky troops and striking terror into everyone about him:

One day he flogs a sailor for some awkward manoeuvre; another day, shoots a soldier for some slight insubordination; now bastinadoes a captain in his navy, or strikes him in his rage, and foams like a madman. I saw him take an old captain by the beard, who had been out in a heavy gale and could not make his harbour; he held him for some minutes with his left hand at arm's length, as if he was going to use his sword, but he only shook the old man, and said if it had not been for his grey beard his head should be at his feet. The other...cringed at his feet and attempted to kiss his garment, but the haughty Ibrahim spurned him from his presence.[32]

Unsurprisingly given the levels of violence in that region, Madden found plenty of work as a doctor. Almost everywhere he went people enquired after his services and looked for him to get treatment. Madden wasn't too impressed with what he observed of the medical abilities of the Turks at this juncture either:

The medical officers of Ibrahim's army were the refuse of all nations and I am proud to say that there wasn't one Englishman amongst them. Most of them were Italian, some of them had been servants to doctors in Egypt, some apothecaries' assistants, and one confessed to me that he had been a watchmaker. I need not say how the unfortunate Arabs sank under their treatment. Never was privileged murder carried to such an extent. I ceased to wonder that the faculty were twice expelled from ancient Rome. The Egyptian officers refused to be attended by their own medical men so that they insisted on my remaining with them.[33]

Madden found himself fired on twice and decided to leave the island as soon as the next ship came along. A few days before he got this opportunity, he witnessed an incident that horrified him and amazed him in equal measure. The Turks hauled a captured Greek long ship - the San Nicolo - into the bay and the officers went aboard the ship and had a celebration in honour of the occasion. The noise and revelry could still be heard at midnight that night from the house where Madden was staying, a house situated at a height overlooking the bay. An enormous explosion was heard at two o'clock in the morning, however, and every window in the house was broken. The doors were destroyed, and the ground shook so that at first Madden thought an earthquake was taking place. The screaming of the people on the shore told the real story however. The San Nicolo had exploded into the air and with its entire crew, including the ship's captain and all his officers.

When Madden reached the shore, there were still a couple of badly-injured crew-members who had survived the blast floating out from shore. Madden arranged for a boat to go into the waves in order to save these few survivors. The explosion had taken place when everybody was drunk, the captain challenging the officers to test their courage by entering the gunpowder store and lighting their pipes while sitting on the very containers where the gunpowder was kept. Three foolhardy officers had taken up the dare and entered the gunpowder store. Two minutes later the ship exploded. This incident was a good example of the strange mixture of courage and madness that defined the Turkish temperament in those days, according to Madden.

The Pasha[34] Canea also called on Madden's medical services while the Irishman was still on the island. The Pasha was a dour, selfish individual who killed every Greek woman in his harem with the "death bag" as revenge for the fact that one woman had been unfaithful to him when he was absent for a period of time. When Madden attended him, he asked him to recommend medical treatment for one particular woman who was sick. Madden replied that he couldn't prescribe any medical treatment until he could examine the woman in question. The Pasha laughed heartily and told Madden that he was far too young to be allowed examine a woman who was "in a certain way." Madden replied that he had already been in many harems prior to this where they had expressed no concern about his age and he wasn't going to take a chance on murdering a patient of his by prescribing drugs without making a proper diagnosis. Madden went to go on his way again but the Pasha informed him with a smirk that he wouldn't be allowed leave again until he had prepared a medicine. Then the Pasha left the room. The dragoman implored Madden to prepare a pill made of bread, a few grains of magnesium, or anything at all so that both of them could get out of there as quickly as possible. The dragoman warned Madden that he didn't fully understand how serious their situation was. He was certain that the Pasha would have them both killed if they didn't do as he requested. Madden was very frightened, but he hid his fear. He was so angry, in fact, that he settled himself down on the sofa and waited to see what would happen next. It was nearly dark that evening by the time Madden had calmed down fully and decided to supply an innocent medical draught to the next person who stepped through the door. Eventually, the door opened again and in walked the Pasha, the same peculiar smile on his face. "What's this?" he said at the top of his voice. "Are the two of you not gone yet?" "The door was shut too tightly" replied Madden and he also assured the Pasha that the local British consul would hear about this incident - into the bargain. Not only would the consul hear about the abuse which they had received in the Pasha's residence, but so too would the ambassador and the Ibrahim Pasha himself. Madden's comments made the Pasha think twice. Perhaps he had gone a little too far, he suggested. He had only been fooling around he assured them.

Whether Madden decided to prescribe the medicine for the sick woman or not, there was no reason why he shouldn't stay and join them for a meal, the Pasha suggested. Madden refused this offer, however, and he and the dragoman left the house safely much to the delight of the latter. Madden spent a couple of years in Egypt subsequent to this, his arrival in that country coinciding with the outbreak of the Eastern plague:

> *Every house was shut tight. The servants were not allowed out and pieces of money were placed in vinegar before anybody touched them. Letters were burnt and people hounded the doctors to find out how many of their neighbours had died during the night.*[35]

Madden lost two servants to the plague before deciding to give up the blood-letting that was practiced by the doctors of Alexandria as a counter to the effects of the plague. Instead he decided to concentrate on:

> ...strong stimulating drinks...frequent small measures of brandy and Cyprian wine, the sponging of the body with vinegar and water, cold presses on the forehead and warm poultices on the bubonic infection.

Seventy-five per cent of the patients Madden treated survived the ravages of the plague. Madden also managed to survive the threat himself of plague - by the grace of God - as he himself acknowledged, and by his habit of throwing open the windows of the bedroom in the house of each patient he called upon. Other precautions against plague infection that Madden took included making sure he had a good meal and a glass of wine in his stomach before attending any patient, smoking a pipe or a cigarette while in the presence of a patient, and wearing "an ingenious oilskin garment" on his back while attending infected patients. His heavy workload left him completely worn out after a while however and he became very sick at one stage after contracting a bout of dysentery. An Italian doctor attended Madden when he contracted the dysentery, a man who recommended that Madden regularly place ice on his stomach. This doctor also advised Madden not to drink any alcohol but to use plenty of ice "to keep the aftertaste of the sickness down." Madden thought this advice strange but the Italian, who was a renowned doctor, assured him that, having treated dysentery for fifteen years previous to this, he was certain that ice was the only cure. Madden was in no condition to argue with him and decided to follow the doctor's instructions. His condition deteriorated very quickly however and when he realised that he was in danger of death, Madden ordered that this doctor be kept away from him from then on. Madden decided to dose himself with small amounts of camomile for three days running and the sickness gradually eased and eventually disappeared.

> I couldn't understand what sort of thinking lay behind the Italian's medical recommendation although it did cross my mind that it might have suited the medical fraternity of

Alexandria to have me out of the way. Of course it isn't something new in this country for the stranger to be got rid of.[36]

Madden's medical practice expanded a good deal during the two years he spent in Alexandria and his fame as a physician spread far and wide. Once, while waiting in the vice-regent's ante-chamber in Cairo, the officers had gathered around him to explain their various health complaints to him. In fact, Madden received so many requests for medical help that he was obliged to offer the entire Alexandrian court a medical prescription to be administered the next day. When he visited Philoe he was inundated with requests for his medical skills, the Nubian women - in particular – calling on him in large numbers. Many of these women believed that his healing abilities were supernatural in origin. On one occasion he was brought to a harem where a beautiful virgin admitted to him that she was suffering from a love-sickness. She asked Madden for a special charm with which to attract a particular young man that she was interested in. Madden denied that he was a wizard or a healer of this type but six other people who were in the company contradicted him on this. "We know that you are a wizard", they said to him bluntly.

We know that you helped a tiny-sized woman see a close-up of the moon by allowing her to look into a special glass and that you helped a man in Beir woo a woman who was initially not in love with him.[37]

Madden hadn't the heart to refuse these different requests, and he therefore wrote a Waranga for this young woman decorating it with a love heart that was pierced with an arrow. He accompanied this drawing with instructions that had the ring of truth about them. Any time she met the object of her affections, the woman was to cross his path three times, smile three times and place her ring-finger on the written charm.

Having written down the instructions for this charm, Madden found himself forced to write another half-dozen charms or so for the married women of the town. It seemed to him that:

Lear's curse was on the country and nature had drained away every source of fertility that existed there.[38]

When he was finished working here, Madden travelled onwards to Damietta. He intended spending just three days there but remained there for a full three months instead. His fame as a *hakkim* (wise man, seer) among the merchants of the Levant delayed his sojourn there.

I had previously performed a shoulder operation on a patient who had preceded me to Damietta and this meant that I was welcomed in that place as if I was another Hippocrates.[39]

Not all of Madden's contacts with the locals here was this pleasant, however. One day he found himself in the narrow passageway of one of the pyramids when he was confronted by group of Bedouins demanding *baksheesh*. When he refused to give them anything they tried to shut him inside the pyramid with large rocks, warning him that they would ensure he slept forever in the stone-coffin of the Pharaoh. Madden didn't panic, however. He remained calm, unaware that his guide was in cahoots with the Bedouin. The guide deliberately dropped his torch ensuring that darkness engulfed them. Madden gave in then and handed the Bedouin a dollar before appearing back into the light of day again - like a corpse risen from its grave. The Bedouin then swore by the Prophet - the Prophet's beard and his camel - that it was all a bit of fun. Although he got a scare that day, that incident didn't turn Madden against the Bedouin. Over time, the opposite happened, and Madden grew very fond of the Bedouin people. He admired the simplicity of their lives, their love of God and, above all, their independence. While travelling along the river Nile from Siout to Thebes one day a Turkish soldier fired at him with a pistol from a distance of only twenty feet. Luckily for Madden he missed. "What a bad aim the Turks have!" was Madden's comment. This soldier tried to shoot him because Madden refused to let him aboard the boat. A servant handed Madden a hunting rifle that was nearby and encouraged him to return fire as the Turkish soldier made a rush towards the boat. Madden's only response however was to lodge a complaint with the Cosheff when they reached the next town. Of course he might as well have been talking to himself for all the difference this made.

Among his patients in Damietta was the Governor of Turkey, a man who whose generosity was known far and wide. At one dinner, Madden attended in the company of the Governor he counted seventy guests all of whom were party to the finest meal Madden ever witnessed throughout his travels in the Middle East. There were so many people that the soldiers and servants were served in another room and each guest received a present in recognition of the fact that they had shared in the Governor's generosity. Following the meal there was Arab music, dancing and buffoonery although Madden didn't have much interest in either of these entertainments. The young doctor could be pompous enough at times and Madden was on record as saying that he didn't appreciate that which he referred to as "Turkish insolence and pusillanimity."

A Turkish officer standing near me when we were crowding around the jesters took occasion to pull off my turban without being perceived. I replaced it thinking it had not been properly secured. A second time it was pulled off in the same way, but on the repetition of the joke a third time I managed to secure the fellow's hand which he endeavoured to release, whilst with the other he attempted to draw his pistol, but ere he could do so I persuaded him to measure his length on the floor with a commotion which shook the room. There was a general uproar; but the other Turkish officers, instead of resenting the blow inflicted on their fellow comrade, slunk away from him, and the fellow himself as soon as he was raised up, took hold of my hand in the most abject way, entreating me to overlook what had passed and make no complaint of him to the Governor. If I had passed over this insult with impunity, its repetition would have been certain, but for having resented it he ever after respected me and would go out of his way to salaam to the ground before me on every possible occasion as long as I remained in Damietta. In short, the argumentation ad hominem is the only logic a Turk can be convinced by.[40]

From Damietta, Madden journeyed onwards by boat to Beirut and from there he went to D'Joun, where he spent a few days visiting Lady Hester Stanhope[41] who was the niece of his personal *"bete noire"*, the British statesman William Pitt. Stanhope was an unusual and courageous woman for her day. An inveterate traveller and adventurer, she lived alone in a villa she had had built for herself in an isolated and mountainous area near D'Joun. The local Bedouin considered her to be something of a queen by all accounts. They also considered her to be neither male nor female but a strange human creature that was a mixture of both genders. Madden spent only two hours in her company when:

...she was able to tell me the most secret of my thoughts. Whether she did this through reading my features or through the reading of the stars I am not clear.[42]

Madden felt certain that Stanhope's skill at divination was something out of the ordinary and yet he also felt sorry that "it was an unhealthy talent that she spent her time perfecting." Lady Hester dressed in the sweeping rich robes that were commonly worn by Syrian men and conversed in a lively fashion until three in the morning on matters of the world and state. She considered the Irish to be too hot-tempered a race in politics but excellent soldiers provided there was somebody to organise them. They were a wise and intelligent people, but their sense of judgement wasn't worth much in her view. In her opinion, there had been no statesman as well-disposed towards the Irish as Castlereagh had been, albeit that he wasn't a man of the highest intellect. Castlereagh and Canning had constantly obstructed one another and the Senate had been too small an arena for the both of them. As regards her own uncle, William Pitt, for whom she had worked as a secretary for a period when he was not in office, she had found him to be a loyal and cheerful individual.

> He was always exact and gentlemanly in relation to both me and all other women. But he was obsessed with matters of state to such an extent that death was the only thing that would separate him from such affairs.[43]

Madden impressed Lady Hester by all accounts. He knew how to "butter her up", it seems. He expressed his amazement at her astrological knowledge so often that she guaranteed him a position as her first student in a new astrological college she intended setting up. Madden asked her to put her supernatural knowledge into a "visible form" for him. "How do you mean exactly?" she said. "Is it that you wish to see a spirit?" According to Madden his reply was as follows:

> If you conjure up a good spirit I will go to Jericho tonight to view it. If it is a bad one it can't harm me in any way and therefore I am willing to have a look at it.[44]

Lady Hester then gave him a fright by describing a spirit dressed in black that had appeared to an Italian doctor. Despite this Madden left D'Joun without seeing witnessing any supernatural occurrence, his admiration for this strange and courageous woman apparently undiminished. He went to the Holy Land but found no welcome for him at the Latin-rite Monastery in Nazareth. Not for the first time, Madden would express criticisms of the work of some Catholic missionaries then based in the Middle East.

I was very poorly dressed in the fashion of the country Arab (as the country was quite unstable at this juncture, every English traveller was in danger of being killed) - and the monks considered him an unlikely candidate for the donation of alms. They informed me brusquely that they couldn't allow a man like me into the monastery, having taken into account the towns through which he had passed and the possibility that he might be a carrier of plague. If I didn't have the disease myself I might be carrying it on my person or in my bag. They decided that they could only let me into an empty shop on the ground floor, a room where a carpenter had once had his workshop.[45]

Madden thanked them for their kind offer but went to the house of the Greek Orthodox priest instead where he said that he was an Englishman looking for shelter. "Come in", he was told. "You are a Christian and that's enough isn't it? You'll get food and drink here and you can stay as long as you wish." Having washed himself and now wearing a flamboyant Turkish robe Madden walked back to the Latin-rite monastery. The servant who had given him dog's abuse earlier didn't recognise him on this occasion and fell down before him calling him every *Milorda* and *Vostra Excellenza.* The monks gathered around - "the same lazy dogs who had turned their backs...they were now trotting behind the *Effendi* to show him the holy places." As soon as he got the opportunity, Madden was quick to tell them what he really thought of them and their monastery. They were shocked later to see him entering the house of the Greek priest and his daughters. When those noblewomen observed Madden's changed state their "contemptuous looks" became "pleasant glances of approval" instead. The peaceful valley of Nazareth made a deep impression on Madden. He walked its quiet lanes each morning and overlooking the small town from a height, he marvelled at the incredible event which had taken place there so many years earlier, that miracle which had turned the world upside-down. His philosophical musings at this juncture resulted in a number of religious verses, none of which were particularly outstanding:

Jesus of Nazareth: on high all hail!
Jess of Nazareth: on earth all praise!
Weak through my voice, let mercy still prevail;
Hear me, Redeemer, and direct my ways

If ever folly urged my tongue in vain
To take they sacred name, thy wrath forego;
If ever madness worked upon my brain,
To doubt thy holy word, thy pity show

Here, gracious Lord, where thou didst humbly wear
The garb of poor humanity, and pass'd
The dawn of mortal life, vouchsafe to hear
The homage turns to thee at last.[46]

Madden's full adoption of a deeper form of Christianity would come later in life. His wholehearted embrace of Jesus of Nazareth's teachings was still of the vague and ambiguous variety at this point in his life but something clearly happened to Madden while he was living in Nazareth, which influenced that change in his religious outlook when he was older. He travelled by donkey from Nazareth onwards and journeyed through Cana, Tiberia and Samaria until he reached Jerusalem. Here he lodged at the local Latin-rite monastery where the devout monks extended him every courtesy unlike their counterparts in Nazareth had done. His journey through these various towns was tiring and not without incident. He was found held up by bandits five times in three days. He wasn't too put out about this on three of the five occasions as they were simply attempting to extract a "road tax" from him and he could fob off the bandits by paying them a couple of *piastre*. The fourth extortion attempt proved much more dangerous, however, as both he and his guide were ambushed in a mountain pass. Madden initially ran away from the bandits before returning to find the robbers dividing up the baggage which they had taken from his servant. He then spoke to the bandits in Arabic, a fact which shocked them greatly, explaining to them that he had returned to them not as a prisoner but as a guest - and it was not customary to raise a hand against a guest. He admonished them by saying that anyone who ignored the time-honoured customs of hospitality was not a real Arab but was clearly a Turk or a Kaffir instead. He then sat down on the ground and proceeded to light his pipe with the aid of a glass lens. The bandits were fascinated by this device, which produced fire by the rays of the sun and decided to tread warily around this stranger.

> *I was never surrounded by such a group of ferocious faces and while speaking I was sure that I would have my head beaten in at any moment. My words seemed to mollify them somewhat however and I produced a bag of (King) James' powder that I had secreted in the folds of my turban. I divided the powder into eight equal measures and passed it around to each of them advising them to keep it in reserve for that day when they might be sick. I reminded them of the hakkim who had lit his pipe with a fire emitted from Heaven and divided a few pounds of coffee and tobacco amongst them at the same time. Then I began to tie our baggage back onto the mule again. While I was doing this I pretended not to notice as one man stole my carpet and another swiped the coffee pot. I let my servant hurry ahead of me while I continued salaaming to the bandits until we had moved out of sight.*[47]

Madden's feet were sore by the time they reached Jerusalem, and he was happy to stay in bed for a while on arrival at the monastery. While resting there he found himself meditating on the "many memories I now had of those places which were inextricably linked with the life and death of Christianity's founder." He began to read the New Testament and prayed to God, imploring Him to help him find the truth. On finishing the New Testament, however, he was still unsure what he truly believed in. It would be a few more years before he came to a serious resolution regarding the true nature of his religious beliefs and his philosophy in relation to this life. Madden did everything that one would expect of a Christian then visiting Palestine. He visited all the holy sites and even helped the Catholics of that area gain full rights to the altar on the Hill of Calvary by helping out the Governor of Jerusalem with a medical complaint of some sort.

As another war was then about to begin in the Middle East Madden hurried back to Tyre and went from there to Damietta on an English boat. He was still congratulating himself on getting that far without a hitch when a Greek pirate ship came upon their vessel near Beirut and escorted them to Napoli de Romania. He went to speak to the captain of the pirate ship, a man who was so convinced by Madden's grasp of the local language and customs that he said he could have sworn Madden was a Turk or one of the followers of Mohammed Ali, who had spent a period of time in England. Surely, an Englishman couldn't have had such a long beard and skin as swarthy as Madden's was? Madden showed his passport to the captain, but he just flung it across the deck in anger. Then Madden took some pearl crosses from his pocket that he had bought in Bethlehem and asked the captain whether it was the custom for the Turks to carry Christian emblems on their person. The captain was taken aback at this move on Madden's part, and it wasn't long before he and the Irishman were on good terms. Madden received an invitation to dinner on the Greek ship later that day where he found the captain already slightly inebriated. While they were eating dinner, an Arab schooner came into view and the pirates decided to up and pursue it. They chased the schooner across the water for a while before boarding the vessel and ransacking it. The three youngest members of the crew as well as an Arab woman and a small girl were taken as slaves.

The child was torn from the arms of its mother who was hysterical with grief. The mother implored the pirates to take her in addition to her child but they ignored her. As they pulled the child on board their own vessel I saw the woman tear a fistful of hair from her head. She then made an attempt to jump overboard but she was caught as she was half-way over the side of the ship and she was violently dragged back below deck.[48]

Madden decided to help the captives if he could, his resolve strengthened by the discovery that the captives included two British citizens from Bombay who were returning from a pilgrimage to Mecca. The next day Madden found the pirate captain half-drunk again and proposed a large number of toasts in honour of the many Greek heroes throughout history. He then reminded the captain of the way that Britain had helped Greece in the past and informed him that the English people would be very disappointed if they knew that there were two British citizens being held prisoner on board a Greek ship. Madden kept pleading his case when they sat down to supper later on and it got to the stage where the captain couldn't refuse him. The pirate gave Madden the young girl as a present and also set free the young Arab woman.

The next day Madden sent a present to the captain, some more small pearl crosses and some shells - also from Bethlehem - a number of which had were inscribed with carvings of the Crucifixion. The captain loved these various presents. Although it seemed strange at first glance the captain was devout in his own way and despite his many faults he never broke the Ramadan fast - this despite his constant drunkenness. He also claimed to have never pillaged a ship without first saying his prayers. When discussing some atrocity or another, barely five minutes passed that the captain didn't make the Sign of the Cross. The happy end-result of all of this was that the mother and her child were re-united with one another and Madden happily continued on his journey.

CHAPTER 3
THE PUBLICATION OF MADDEN'S FIRST BOOK

Madden had a stroke of luck on his initial arrival in Alexandria when he was introduced to a man named Moses Montefiore[49] and his family. Montefiore who was an extremely wealthy Jewish businessman and who was known as Croesus[50] brought Madden with them on their yacht when they travelled to Malta and a friendship was cemented between themselves and Madden, which was to last for the rest of their lives. They were very fond of Madden and enjoyed his good humour, his storytelling ability and his fondness for card-playing. While in Malta, Madden could travel across to Naples quite easily and after staying there for a short time, he travelled up to Rome where he was welcomed by the Blessingtons in the Palazzo Negroni. It was here that he met Harriet Gardner, the Earl's legitimate daughter and the woman whom D'Orsay had just married in order not to lose out on his inheritance. The bride, who couldn't have been more than sixteen years of age was brought to Italy and introduced to the man to whom she had been promised, this despite the fact that the marriage seems to have been just "a marriage of convenience."[51] Madden, it appears, was completely unaware of all these behind-the-scenes familial intrigues although he did notice that the young and innocent bride appeared very unhappy. She was pale and withdrawn and appeared completely uninterested in what was going on around her.

Madden dined with the Blessingtons most nights during his stay in Rome when he also met many of the most well-known amongst Rome's émigré community in addition to many of the city's most prominent artists. Rooms in the Palazzo were then so highly sought-after and richly-furnished that to rent a room there cost the enormous sum of 130 pounds a month. The Palazzo's guests were treated so royally that Madden would later comment that he had witnessed the seeds of the *Irish Encumbered Estates Act*[52] (firsthand) as planted on the Continent of Europe.

An election to appoint a new pope was underway while Madden was in Rome as Pius the Eighth had recently died. Madden saw the crowds making their way to Monte Cavallo to see how the election was progressing. He also watched the black smoke rise from the chimney of the conclave as the members of the College of Cardinals burned the ballot papers indicating that they had yet to come to a decision. Eventually, this black smoke changed to white when the Cardinals were in agreement on their choice. A short while later, Madden listened to the first public sermon of the newly-enthroned Pope, who took the name of Pope Gregory XVI. Madden later travelled from Rome through Switzerland and, accompanied by a friend, he undertook a midnight visit to the grave of the most renowned tragic actor of this era., John Philip Kemble[53], an actor whom Madden had admired greatly from his youth when he had seen him perform Shakespeare's dramas in the old theatre on Crow Street, Dublin. To view Kemble's grave, Madden and a friend had to climb one of the cemetery's walls but as it was a bright night the two men had little trouble locating the grave and reading its inscription.

Madden was a big fan of theatre at this period of his life and had seen the likes of Edmund Keane when he was at the top of his form. He had also seen the famous Talmé from the *Comédie Francaise* performing on stage, an actor who – in his day - was considered to be without peer. Madden's interest in the arts increased even more at this juncture when he got to know the actor James Charles Mathew. Mathew was also a qualified architect and it was in this capacity that he first got to know the Blessingtons accompanying the Earl of Blessington on a trip to Ireland when the latter decided to build an apartment on his estate in County Tyrone. Mathew was a little over twenty years of age when Madden first got to know him at the Blessington's house in Naples but he was already a very competent draughtsman. An expert mimic, he too was then living with the Blessingtons as part of their extended family. According to Mathews, the beau Count D'Orsay was the ideal of male beauty in his generation, a man who combined grace, dignity and good looks, all of which made him a favourite with women. Mathews took to Madden also and sketched a picture of "little Dr. Madden...with his spare face, peaked nose, and semi-startled air like that of an ill-fed clerk on a stool in the city."[54]

While Mathews may have been complimentary of d'Orsay this didn't preclude an occasional falling-out between them. Lord Blessington used to become taciturn and difficult after drinking and one day, without any apparent reason, he mentioned to Mathews that D'Orsay had called him a lazy lout who carried his sketching book everywhere with him but drew very little. Mathews assumed that D'Orsay had been joking, and the next time he met him, he teased him about this alleged comment only to receive a mouthful of abuse in return. As there were women and servants in their company when this incident took place, a duel of honour between the two men was now unavoidable. Mathews chose Madden as his "second" for the intended duel but the duel never took place in the end. After a series of discrete letters had passed between Madden and D'Orsay, the two protagonists met up and apologised to one another.[55] Lord Blessington died suddenly of apoplexy[56] in March, 1829 and "There was no limit to poor Countess Blessington's grief."[57]

It wasn't too long however, before the gossip brigade were

saying that the Countess' grief was all an act and that D'Orsay was now separated from his young wife and living with the Countess in *Gore House*. On the death of her husband, the Countess' income was severely reduced to a sum of 2000 pounds per annum but in spite of this fact, both she and D'Orsay were more profligate in their spending than ever. To make matters more difficult, they also had to provide for at least seven or eight members of their extended family in addition to their own expenses. D'Orsay was in a particularly awkward situation since he had no money of his own and his wife's dowry had already been spent by him.

Madden got married in 1828, in Cheltenham, quite soon after his return to England. He was thirty years of age but we have very little information concerning his wife other than that she was then twenty-seven years of age and named Harriet Elmslie. She was the youngest daughter of a Scotsman named John Elmslie from Berners Street, London and another Scot - Jane Wallace, a woman who had a reputation for beauty. Jane Wallace had married John Elmslie when she was only sixteen and Harriet was the last of her twenty-one children. Jane Wallace died when she was just forty-one years of age. Madden and Harriet's first child was born within a year of their marriage, and was baptised William Forde Madden, the Forde in honour of Madden's mother who died around the same time as the birth. After his marriage, Madden began to practice again as a surgeon. He spent some time in Maidstone and transferred from there to St. Leonard's where he went into practice with another doctor, an arrangement from which he split at a later date when he felt that it wasn't working out.

Among Madden's patients was the Scottish poet Thomas Campbell, a man who was twenty years his senior and who had recently suffered the bereavement of his wife. His wife's death devastated Campbell, a man whose lifestyle was chaotic and disorganised in the extreme and the poet never really recovered from the tragedy of his spouse's death. Madden and Campbell became close friends with Campbell describing Madden to his circle as - "a very sensible and friendly person who is one of the few excellent conversationalists in the place." The two men met regularly for literary and political conversations in Madden's rooms, on the promenade and in other local hotels and pubs. *The Power of Russia* was the theme of one of the poems which Campbell wrote at this juncture and although he acknowledged it as a strange theme for a poem he viewed poetry as a medium for a more logical form of reasoning than prose. Campbell acknowledged Madden's influence on his thinking as follows:

I have been for weeks, (he wrote) *trying to hammer into the head of my friend Dr. Madden my views as to the danger of the world from Russia - all to no purpose. But when, in reading the poem to him, I came to the line:*

The stripling giant, strengthening year by year.

He said, "Now you have convinced me more than all the talk you ever said in prose." Here, then, a metaphor convinced a man.[58]

Depressed after her death, Campbell constantly spoke of his dead wife and the void which her death had left in his life. He was overly-generous by nature and Madden often saw him ransacking his pockets to give alms to beggars. When Campbell ran out of money himself, he would comb his own house for any food that he might give to the poor. Although the poet felt intimidated by his scolding housekeeper he was willing to put up with her reproaches for the sake of the poor to whom he gave food as an act of charity. He believed the stories of every beggar that crossed his path – partly for fear that he did might ignore the truly unfortunate cases. "Zounds, man, you never can believe too much when you listen to the unfortunate," was a frequent utterance of his. On one occasion, Campbell criticized Madden when the latter described a letter from a Polish refugee as "unduly exigent." "Exigent," he said, "why the devil, man, can't you speak English even when you do talk of things you know nothing about?"

Campbell was very fond of children and nothing pleased him more than to teach children about the literature and art and the finer things in life. One day when he and Madden were out for a walk they passed a nurse carrying a child in her arms. The child was sick and was vomiting violently but Campbell pulled a handkerchief from his pocket and ran back to the nurse. He began to wipe the child's face clean and even tried to sing a lullaby at the same time. He didn't have a great voice, however, and rather than calming the child down, the youngster began to scream and kick. The nurse wasn't sure what to do and Madden kept himself at a discreet distance from proceedings.

Campbell held strong views on the question of political freedom, views which came in part from his having attended the trials for treason held in Edinburgh before 1800. As a consequence of this he had a profound empathy with the tragic struggles for freedom of countries such as Ireland and Poland. He was very upset on hearing about the fall of Warsaw, for instance, and he became so emotional on hearing this news that Madden had to help him home and put him up in his own house.

Harriet looked after Campbell for the next couple of weeks until he came to himself again. On more than one occasion, Campbell said that he regretted not having been in Ireland for the 1798 rising when he could have died gloriously for the Irish cause. He had been on good terms with many members of the United Irishmen whom he met as a student in Glasgow between the years 1793 and 1797, and from whom he had learned some verses of their rebel songs. Campbell was an Irish sympathizer before he ever became friendly with Madden although it may have been Madden who inspired him to set up an organization in support of the Irish cause which went by the name of "The Monks of St. Leonard." This group had strong echoes of the Monks of the Screw[59] as initiated by John Philpot Curran but it didn't have the same staying power. After just five or six meetings of the Monks, it the organization transformed itself into a whist-playing group. Madden was in St. Leonard's when he got an urgent message to return to Dublin where his mother was very sick. Sadly he was delayed when he was caught up in an accident and his mother had already passed away by the time he reached Dublin. Her death upset him greatly so that he returned to St. Leonard's only for a brief period after the funeral. His friends advised him that a change of scene might help him come to terms with his grief, and he moved to London where he took a house in Curzon Street, in Mayfair. He set up a new medical practice there and with the help of the Blessingtons and some of his former patients who were now resident in Naples, it soon became a thriving business. In addition to work he kept himself busy with his other interests, including writing and the campaign to outlaw the Slave Trade that was then underway. A short time later he decided to give up medicine altogether. Afterwards, he never again officially practiced as a doctor although his medical knowledge did not go amiss from time to time.

Madden's first publication entitled *Travels in Turkey, Egypt, Nubia and Palestine in 1824, 1825, 1826 and 1827* was published in 1829. It was an account of his travels in Turkey and neighbouring countries in the Middle East, a travel journal that he compiled based on a series of letters as sent home to friends and family. His book was a success in so far as it went into a second print and he was paid three hundred guineas in royalties. The following year he published a novel in three volumes - a book entitled *The Mussulman* (1830). While he earned another three hundred guineas for this book, which was also translated to German, the reading public ignored it as did the literary magazines and newspapers of the day. As with his first book, this was based on his travels in the Middle East. The advertisements for this latest book compared it to *Anastasius*, a much-lauded book of the day (The Times, 3 May 1830).[60]

Although he would spend the next thirty years writing, Madden would never again attempt another novel. Instead, he put much of his energies into the anti-Slavery campaign as appropriate for somebody who hated injustice and was a human rights' advocate. He understood the tragedy of slavery for the millions of blacks then kept in bondage and what he had seen of slavery in the Middle East and oppression in his native Ireland only strengthened his resolve to combat slavery and repression wherever he found it.

On first arriving in London, he had joined the Anti-Slavery Association, a group which had a strong membership from the Clapham Sect. The Claphamites, otherwise known as the "Saints", were a scripture-based Protestant group who were so staunchly Abolitionist that they were willing to form alliances not only with other Scripture-based groups but also with Wesleylites, Non-Conformists, free-thinkers such as the Unitarians and even Catholics such as Madden to further their aims. The Claphamites were quite an significant group in the upper echelons of British society then, including in Downing Street, in the Civil Service and indeed in the Colonial administrative offices, a fact which would later prove to Madden's advantage. Madden befriended the Abolitionist movement's most influential figures, including the likes of Thomas Clarkson and Thomas Fowell Buxton. He also got to know James "Over-Secretary" Stephen, the Under-Secretary in the Colonial Office, a friendship which would also stand him in good stead later. Stephen, of whom it was said that he was the real administrator of the British colonies at this juncture, would later help promote Madden to the position of Special Justice of Jamaica in 1833 as part of a Bill which sought to rescind the laws promoting Slavery. Normally it would have been the Whigs (who were in office on a virtually unbroken run between September, 1830 and April, 1835), that decided on this appointment but it was during a brief interlude under their rule - when the Tories secured office - that the post became available. As a consequence Madden had to lobby some Tory figures for help in securing his appointment and he was obliged to go to a controversial individual, Sir Francis Burdett,[61] for help. Burdett, who sided with the Tories at this juncture, had spent much of life advocating causes as varied as freedom of speech and

Catholic emancipation, and he recommended Madden to Lord Stanley for this post in Jamaica.

Despite this move on Madden's part, his political sympathies almost certainly lay more with the Whigs than with the Tories since a number of Whig politicians were personal friends of his. Many people in the upper echelons of British society had more in common with the Whigs then than they did with the Tories and were attracted to their more liberal policies and approaches. The Duke of Wellington's support for Catholic emancipation was an indicator of this more tolerant atmosphere, the Duke's approach causing surprise and consternation amongst many of his supporters. Wellington's replacement in Office, Lord Grey, continued with these liberal reforms, bringing in the Reform Bill and campaigning for the abolition of "negro slavery." An 1833 Bill commanded that all slavery be "utterly and forever abolished and declared unlawful throughout the British Colonies" from the first day of August, 1834.

This Bill included a wide-ranging scheme whereby slaves would be freed from their bondage through various degrees of "apprenticeship." Two million pounds would be given to the slave owners in compensation and the scheme would be administered by justices specially appointed by the Colonial Office, justices paid by the Finance Office. In fact, this latter measure was how Madden first became involved in the Abolitionist question on a practical level.

This apprenticeship scheme proved a failure, however - (it was suspended in 1838) - primarily because the scheme was never correctly administered. The scheme was entrusted to the care of a group of specially appointed justices but there weren't enough of them to administer the scheme effectively. Neither was these justices paid on equal terms with the judges back in Britain. No training was issued to them with regard to their new roles and among the justices appointed there were a fair share of drunkards, brutes and political opportunists. In fairness to them, the majority of the justices did the difficult work to which they had been appointed with common sense and a certain degree of humanity. Many of them died at their postings as a result of over-work and the difficult climates they found themselves working in. Madden himself witnessed the worst aspects of the scheme in operation in the most difficult posting he ever worked in - on the island Jamaica. The white settlers in Jamaica were well-organised and they agitated forcefully against the freeing of the 302,000 "apprentices" on this island.

Although Jamaica proved a very difficult posting it's likely that Madden chose this job himself as his wife had relatives among the plantation owners there. As it will become evident later, however, Madden didn't let his family connection to the planter class and the monetary advantages that this connection entailed influence his administration of justice on the island. He was just about to leave England when the High-Church Tory publication *Quarterly Review* included a very hostile review of the second edition of Madden's book about Turkey and his newly-published book entitled *The Infirmities of Genius* (1833).

Madden found himself in good company. That same year the *Quarterly* had also attacked the poet Alfred Lord Tennyson so fiercely that it proved a topic of conversation for many years afterwards. The *Quarterly*'s editor John Gibson Lockhart had enjoyed the notoriety which his scathing review of Tennyson's work had provoked - so much so, that he had instructed his reviewer John Wilson Croker to keep a close eye out for any future publications by Tennyson.

The literary "slaughter" continued. Maria Edgeworth's book was torn apart so badly that the poet Byron made a complaint. Another of the *Quarterly*'s reviewers, John Wilson Croker, was described as "a stark rigid Tory, a churchman of the intensely-Protestant type common to his native land, and a most painstaking scholar who wielded his pen like a scalping knife"[62] and he attacked Madden any chance that he got. A good deal of "literary" drivel was being published at this juncture and nothing gave Lockhart and Croker more satisfaction than to expose these publications to the public. Madden's book about Turkey was described as being overly-familiar in tone, replete with anecdote, error-ridden and exaggerated. This description was kind however when compared with the twenty-two page review Croker gave of The Infirmities of Genius[63] (1833) The subject of the book was a good one but Madden who, according to Croker - was unfitted to such an enquiry by a peculiar degree of personal incapacity – had a made a mess of it. He was singularly ignorant of the class of men and facts he had undertaken to describe and his general learning, he was below what was called a "smatterer." Neither the turn of his mind nor the accuracy of his observations was very good. Neither was he precise in distinction, sagacious in analysis, or comprehensive in synthesis. He was little-versed in medical, and still less moral philosophy; and though his pages were illustrated with great names and copious quotations, he gave the impression of knowing men and books that he alluded to just by name within the text. Worse was to come. Croker belittled Madden's knowledge of the classics as follows:

> He had plundered old Burton profusely, though not quite so aptly, as did Squire Shandy and his friend Doctor Slop. In short there had never been so flagrant a case of plagiarism, presumption and ignorance. A man might be a very amusing traveller, a tolerable surgeon, and even a good reasoner, without being a profound classical scholar; but he who could indulge in the poor vanity of dressing himself in borrowed feathers was not the fittest examiner of the delicate sensibilities of genius...The main body of the work proceeded in a style of vague, inconsistent and often contradictory trivialities...All Madden's examples ridiculously contradicted the assertion by which he introduced them. The book was little else than a repetition of the very small and dirty gossip which Madden did but misquote and misapply. Indeed these alterations and distortions were almost the only exertion o his own mind which could be discovered in the whole

work. Madden in a word, was a bungler.[64]

Madden's memoirs make no mention of such poor reviews and focussed instead on another review which was more complimentary to the author.

CHAPTER 4
JAMAICA AND THE ANTI-SLAVERY MOVEMENT

On the fifth of October, 1833, Madden and his wife left Falmouth along with five other special Justices on board the *Eclipse*. They were a happy group on departure, although Madden's mind was elsewhere. His thoughts were with his son William Forde whom they had said goodbye on the previous day, leaving him in the care of a relative. "I had enough on the Jamaica die", he wrote, "without staking my little fellow's life. So we packed him off to Cheltenham." On the eighth day of their journey they caught sight of Madeira in Spain. As it was a nice morning, and the ship's captain was in fine form, it was decided to tie up one of the deckhands who had got drunk in Falmouth and struck one of gunners in the process. The man was tied by the hands and the feet and scourged with all the formality that went with such a punishment. Of this very public punishment, Madden noted that they could have done without the ensuing ceremony and "with all the awful adjuncts of swords, swabs and cocked hats."

This spectacle did nothing to improve the general atmosphere aboard the ship either. The passengers went ashore in Bridgetown, the principal city of Barbados, on the twenty-fourth day of the voyage, an island which Madden considered of little beauty. A black man greeted them as they went on the shore, and wished them "a peaceful journey", adding that when "the fuss of Angus" arrived - and it couldn't come soon enough - he himself would no longer be a "black damn teef never anymore." The travellers visited St. Vincent's and Grenada and on the thirty-third day of their journey, they arrived in Kingston, the capital city of Jamaica.

Madden's initial impressions of the island were that it was undoubtedly as beautiful as he had heard. One look at the capital's narrow twisted streets, its filth and its buildings with their lack of architecture were enough to change his mind on this, however. The only thing he could say in favour of Kingston's public buildings was that they were reasonably spacious-looking. In reality, the whole island was so rundown and ruined-looking that it looked like a place that had recently been abandoned. Madden was officially "sworn in" in the city's mayoral office by the Governor of Saint Andrew's, Lord Mulgrave. He was then given responsibility for Kingston, the most important part of the island.

The morning immediately following the arrival of the justices, the island experienced a minor earthquake, an occurrence which many of the islanders took as an ominous sign for the arrival of these new administrators. The local papers were derisory in their attitude to the island's latest arrivals claiming Stanley had recently sent out a group of cunning and opportunist Irish priests whose sole intention was to live off the backs of the poor, people who had already suffered the ignominy of colonisation. Madden let it be known that this newspaper's description of them bore no resemblance to the truth but far from retracting what had been said, the newspaper's editor weighed in with an another attack of his own. He called the new arrivals every name under the sun - referring to them as blow-ins, looters and political locusts. These insinuations were irritating enough for the newly-arrived justices but they soon had an even more serious issue to worry about - the expensive cost of living there. Madden's weekly lodgings and meals came to the princely sum of twelve pounds a week while he also had additional minor expenses of three pounds a week.

When he informed his employers that two-thirds of his salary was being spent on covering his everyday living expenses he was told to stop complaining. How many others who tried to make a life for themselves in the West Indies had an income as good as his, he was asked? The contrast between Madden's circumstances, the other "gentry" generally (the planter class) and the bulk of the Jamaican population could not have been starker. The upper-class of the island had the "life of Riley" and weren't shy in issuing party invitations to their friends so as to keep "the honour and glory of their home country alive." Jamaica was a great place for the *"bon viveur"* who had an unlimited supply of money and whose only worry was keeping his stomach full. Madden travelled throughout the island collecting information for another book and focusing in particular on the political, social and economic history of Jamaica's population, that of its black population in particular.

As was his habit, he visited the graveyards and took note of whatever genealogical history was available. He researched the death statistics of the island and studied how the climate of the West Indies affected the human physiognomy. Four of the previous Special Justices had died within the first nine months of their arrival there from inflammatory diseases and from yellow fever. Neither of them lasted any more than four or five days having become infected.

Harriet also kept a daily diary for their first six weeks spent on the island, one of her first observations being that there was a "distinct absence of female company on the island." One man told her that she was the first white woman he had seen on the island in ten months and the few planter women who lived there seemed to socialize with one another only rarely. Madden and Harriet took lodgings in a fine spacious house but Harriet didn't like the food that was the main diet on the island. She didn't like any of the seven different types of fruit with which they were presented at meal-times. The Harris family - who were relatives of hers - were very hospitable to Harriet, particularly when Richard was out of town on business, something that was a frequent occurrence. They brought her with them to the church, to the races and to the local barracks to listen to the military band. They also brought her to various parties and dances where she found herself much in demand.

> *A group of six young officers arrived from the naval fleet and we danced quadrilles and waltzes until one o'clock in the morning.*[65]

It wasn't all fun and games on the island, however. Changes were in the air and old Mr. Harris told Harriet that he foresaw troubled times ahead. Harris noticed that the island's Governor, Lord Musgrave, didn't appear particularly healthy, and he was normally a handsome man with a regal bearing. That the Governor's health was poor was unsurprising given the difficulties he faced in terms of the island's social conditions and the hostility to the colonial project in many quarters. From the beginning, Harriet was worried about the difficult climate on the island and the effects that it had on the young, in particular. She noticed that the Governor's children looked very unhealthy, despite having spent just five months on the island. An Irishman named McGann living there told her that five of his children had died although he didn't think that the climate there affected youngsters of European origin any worse than it did the locals.

Harriet didn't agree with him however and she was glad that she had left her own boy, Forde, back in London. In fact, it wasn't long before the climate began to take its toll on her personally. She found that she tired very easily.

She kept a diary while she was on the island in which she related a range of observations as typical of a member of her class at this juncture. She described the island's climate, its beautiful scenery, the swarms of midges which tormented them, and the joy she felt on receiving any news from home. Clearly she found her time on the island a very lonely one. As the first of August,

1834 drew close, the Jamaican population became more agitated and the atmosphere in the streets was increasingly tense.

Would the Anti-Slavery Act be passed? Everything depended on the viewpoint of the island's colonial class. The black population considered the British term "apprenticeship" too limited but, needless to say, they weren't in a strong position to argue their case against the military strength of the island's rulers. On the other side of the equation, the island's landowners were also in an aggressive mood and wanted some form of recompense for the loss of profit and power that the abolition of slavery would entail. In addition to these losses, the landowners would see many of their privileges under the law cut back and the local justices were far from happy with these "strangers" who had recently arrived on the island and overruled them.

Madden himself wasn't particularly happy with the way in which the preparations for change were being implemented. In his opinion, the landowners should have been compensated for the "injustice" they would suffer by purchasing machines, which could replace the manual labour that their slaves had undertaken prior to this. Such an approach was the only way to ensure that the land's productivity was kept up to normal levels. The black men would have to be trained to use the new machinery and it was vital therefore that the landowners remained in the country rather than becoming absentee landlords – i.e. simply appointing administrators to manage twenty estates or more simultaneously or officials who were lazy good-for-nothings. Madden was hopeful that the Act would be passed but believed that it would take some time before the two classes in Jamaica would come to accept one another as fellow citizens. The British had little understanding of the real situation on the island, Madden felt. It was the mulatto man against the black man, and the British colonial administration had little time for either group.

Madden took Governor Mulgrave's advice on board and did his best to overcome whatever barriers of race and skin colour he came across in his daily work. He invited both black men and mulattoes to his table, neither of whom would ever normally receive an invitation to sit at the table of a planter or a steward. No one else followed Madden's example, unfortunately. One of the plantations which Madden visited regularly was Marley, a plantation that had once been owned by his grand-uncle, Doctor Lehane at one time. He had a journey of seventeen miles on one burning hot summer's day to get to the hillside plantation where some of his grand-uncle's black workers were still living. The fairest-skinned of the men amongst this company was an elderly African who had been his grand-uncle's "man-servant" for a long time. Madden had prepared himself for this visit imagining that the elderly African would be excited to see a relative of his former master. But that wasn't what happened at all.

> *The negro was brought before me; he was a hale honest-looking, grey-headed old man, about eighty. Did he remember the old doctor? He remembered him well. Where did he himself come from? Massa brought him out of a Guinea ship when a piccanini boy: him wait on massa - serve massa very well; him serve massa when young and 'trong; but what use talk of such things now? Did he know what had become of master? Yes, him hear massa die in England. Was he sorry to hear of master's death? No, massa had plenty of people in England to be sorry for him; him no want poor nigger to be sorry for him. Would he like to see one of the master's family? No, him want to see nobody. Did he see no resemblance between me and the old doctor? No, him want to see nutten at all of nobody.*[66]

The elderly man became impatient with the conversation and Madden tried to impress on him the unique circumstances of their encounter. He reminded the man that he must be the first relative of his former master whom the elderly man had seen for over forty years. This approach didn't elicit the expected response either however:

For true, (said the old man), you belong old massa; well, what you want here? You come to carry away old stones from Marley - plenty of old stones on grounds at Marley - you come carry away more old massa's money - where you find it? - no more poor niggers to sell at Marley.[67]

The elderly man then moved away slowly towards the garden, singing an old song under his breath:

Hi, massa buckra, sorry for your loss,
Better go to Lunnon town and buy another oss.[68]

Madden made some enquiries and discovered that this Jamaican estate, like hundreds of others, had been allowed to drift into a state of rack and ruin over the years. The elderly black man had good reason to be sulky and churlish. Madden was likely the first person in decades who had implied that this elderly man was somehow lucky to be working on this ruined estate. Doctor Leehane, Madden's grand-uncle was a brother of the attorney Robert Lehane. This grand-uncle made a lot of money in Jamaica at one point before returning to Ireland where he later died. On his death, his inheritance, including this Jamaican estate, had been passed onto his brother Theodosius Lyons and when he died only a few years later the estates were bequeathed to a cousin of Madden's, a young man less than 21 years of age. A long and protracted law case had then ensued about the guardianship of the inheritance. An uncle of the boy who was a Catholic claimed that he was really the guardian of this inheritance because the young man's father had appointed him to the role. This was challenged by another uncle however, a Protestant who claimed the guardianship of the inheritance on the grounds that the law in Ireland at this juncture gave priority to Protestants. It was the Chancellor of Ireland who decided the case in the end.

A few flippant words from an Irish lawyer settled the matter that had been at issue between man and man from the earliest ages of the world. With the seals and mace before him, the emblem of legal and theological inspiration, he decided that the minor's true creed should be that connected with the State.[69]

A few years later the case came to court again and both parties spent such vast sums on their legal arguments that they were wiped out financially and an estate that had originally cost in the region of 25,000 pounds was let go to ruin. All Madden inherited in the heel of the hunt was a house that was falling apart and a large tract of land that had remained uncultivated for years. On entering the house he discovered two white women who were dressed in a fairly respectable fashion. These were the illegitimate daughters of the man who had purchased the property from the Chancellor's Court.

There were three other women living in the house also, one of whom was an elderly mulatto woman. These were his uncle Theodosius Lyons' daughters and the elderly woman was their mother. The eldest of the daughters was about forty years of age and the other woman was just a year or two younger than this. One of them was so similar in appearance to Madden's own family that there was no denying her the moment he heard her name. While the women were happy to see that a relative of theirs had visited them, they were also quite concerned that this visitor had come to take over the place. They had been through some very hard times since the natural inheritor of the property had died, their only good luck being that they weren't "sold off" along with the rest of the property as a brother of theirs had been years earlier. Madden presented the women with a small present before heading off to explore the plantation where a brother who had been his mother's favourite, a man named Garrett Forde, was buried in a field of sugar cane. By July, 1834, Madden had come to the following conclusion as regards the nature of the Jamaican newspapers. The Jamaican press were nothing but "a thing that crawls in the mire of party politics…a nondescript reptile, partaking of the nature of the bull-frog and the galley-wasp." The Jamaican press had attacked Lord Mulgrave on a regular basis for the twenty months that he had spent on the island. He had come to the island initially to put down a rebellion which had turned the island upside-down, a rebellion which was endeavouring to wrest power from the administrative body that was the Imperial Assembly. In Madden's view, Mulgrave had handled the rebellious faction who set themselves against the parliamentary Imperial Act regarding slavery in a prudent and measured fashion but, in spite of this, the opposition had managed to get an act of their own passed through the local parliament, an act that was unworkable according to Madden.

While the Imperial Act was quite complex, the Jamaican Act Madden deemed worse still. It created severe difficulties for the island's special justices whose needs the British parliament had effectively ignored. The Jamaican house of parliament was insisting that the apprentices refuse to undertake work, whether of a paid or unpaid nature. Despite this campaign on the part of the local Jamaican parliament the principal tenets of the Imperial Act were enforced. When the bill came before Lord Mulgrave to be signed, he was able to claim with a certain degree of pride that he had managed to administer a deathblow to the most inhumane aspect of the island's social history - i.e. slavery. The British government felt that an "interim stage" between the promulgation of the new Act and its enforcement would ease tensions on the island and would have been delighted if they could have found an appropriate substitute for the word "apprentice" as defined in the Act. One way or the other, Madden was in the gallery along with the Countess Mulgrave and the other noblewomen of the island on the day that the "Great Liberation" was announced. He thanked God privately that he had lived to see the day when slavery would be outlawed on the island. The first of August came and went but there were no protests or violence. The House of Assembly had instigated a day's holiday for that day and the black population filled all of the churches except for those which were Protestant and which remained closed that day. The island was eerily silent for a holiday, however. The only indication which Madden saw of the momentous change that had taken place involved the sight of a number of small black children who ran up the street pursued by a sailor who was blind drunk. The children stopped at a safe distance from the sailor and threw stones in his direction before Madden heard them say – "Why are we running away from him? Sure, aren't we all free now? Hurrah for the fuss of Augus!"[70]

Mulgrave left the island soon after this to take up the position of Viceroy in Ireland. It was just as well that he made this move as Madden thought the severity of Jamaica's climate would have killed him fairly quickly otherwise, its severity having impacted so heavily on him. His replacement was Lord Sligo who noticed on his arrival that the new apprentice system was already falling apart because of the difficulty in filling vacancies for Special Justices in Jamaica.

A significant number of the original Special Justices had died very quickly on arrival in Jamaica while others had resigned from their positions because of the high cost of living and the fact that the government had not provided them with houses as they had originally promised. Some of the justices who were already *in situ* were simply unsuitable for the job, so much so that Lord Sligo petitioned Spring Rice in the Colonial Office to fill many of the jobs on a temporary basis with military men who were financially self-sufficient and who were already living on the island. Lord Sligo preferred to appoint people already living in Jamaica himself as opposed to being at the mercy of employers who were at a remove from the reality of island life and therefore ignorant of the local conditions. It was as a consequence of all of this that Madden was initially appointed to one of these positions although it has to be said that he subsequently acquitted himself very well and was more than suitable for the appointment as indicated by a private governmental internal memo:

...an eminently suitable person to appoint to the most difficult position on the island. This job is one where every possible slip-up on the part of the incumbent is highlighted by the local media and those who have nothing better to do. Madden is a very suitable appointment for this position.[71]

It is not clear but the above comments may have been written by Mulgrave who was very fond of Madden and a man whose work it was Madden's habit to praise highly. Both Madden and Mulgrave could be defined as "Doctrinaire Abolitionists", a position which wouldn't have suited Madden so well under the new administration of Lord Sligo. Madden did not spend too much longer on the island as it happens. Both he and a fellow Justice named Captain Dillon were physically attacked one day when they were going about their work and the administration of law on the island seemed to go from bad to worse from this point onwards.

The catalyst for some of the subsequent chaos was triggered by a local Justice named Hart who brought an apprentice before Madden and Dillon one day, alleging that the black man had stolen five shillings from another apprentice. When Madden investigated the incident he found no evidence against the accused to sustain the charges and this situation was exacerbated by the fact that Hart had actually brought the apprentice before the court without an arrest warrant.

One of the primary aims of the new Anti-Slavery law was to prevent situations where the masters could inflict physical violence against their black workers, a practice which had occurred frequently prior to this. One way in which the masters were circumventing this legal prohibition was by hauling their apprentices before the justice instead. Madden explained the provisions of the new law to Hart who apologised and left the court, apparently appeased. Hart returned two hours later with the same apprentice, the newspaper editor of the *Dispatch*, a Mr. Bruce, and a large group of mulatto men in tow. A long argument ensued before Madden ordered Hart and his men to leave the court. Hart refused to leave, however, and turned his back to the railings of the court instead before placing his hat on his head. He challenged the court in a loud voice with the words "Let's see now who will put me out then." Madden ordered the police to remove Hart but no one made any move to do so. He then called on the special constables present to uphold the law that was being contravened. A Mr. Mitchell, a reporter with the *Dispatch* came forward and identified himself as a Special Constable. He told Hart that he was behaving shamefully, and that he had better clear off. Mitchell placed his hand on Hart's shoulder but Hart grabbed him by the collar and pulled him out onto the street where a fight ensued for the next quarter of an hour. The Mayor was absent and the Police Commissioner was nowhere to be found and by the time Madden got back from the Mayor's office, Hart had ensured that the same police who had refused to raise a hand against him earlier had now taken Mitchell into custody!

Mitchell subsequently lost his job as a result of the whole incident. The day after this incident another of the Special Constables also lost his job, a man who had tried to help Mitchell and who had attempted to put a stop to the fight outside the court. Madden sent a report on the incident to Lord Sligo stating that this entire episode was part of a coordinated plan to undermine the recent anti-slavery change, a plan in which certain members of the City Corporation played a strong role. Madden also informed Lord Sligo that he could not continue his work as a Justice if he didn't have the full backing of the police. If the Corporation couldn't ensure this minimum level of support, then it would not be right for him to sit in session again as a Justice. He also recommended that Hart be charged for his criminal behaviour. Lord Sligo gave a letter to Madden which he asked him to bring to the Mayor to be signed.

At first it appeared as if the mayor was in favour of a proper resolution to the issue, but when it came to the crunch, he took Hart's side. He claimed to have heard about Madden's awkward temperament and said that he did not want his position undermined in any way. Madden went back to Lord Sligo again and explained his position on the issue in no uncertain terms. The reality was of course that Hart's trick in the form of this "trial" measure had been planned in full a good three weeks prior to this. The entire corporation had set themselves against Madden, the police were untrustworthy, and if the island's newspapers had seemed biased previous to this they were seven times more biased now. Madden now found himself in a difficult position:

> ...because of the strong stance that I took to protect the apprentices and my zeal in fulfilling my duties that brought with them very heavy responsibilities.[72]

The corporation's threatening language including their talk of an inquiry frightened Madden very little, however. The Corporation had no authority to instigate such an inquiry and the person appointed to lead such an investigation could not be shown to be a neutral party on the issue. Since the members of the corporation were all united against Madden because he would not give in to their demands however, he knew that he might be placing Lord Sligo in a very difficult position if he remained in his job. Madden weighed up his options. He wondered whether he might be better off to resign while all of this was going on. A provisional date of the following Monday was laid down for the court case. It was unclear however who would preside over this court and what police force would protect it. It seems that the entire controversy was then put on the long finger until the middle of October when Lord Sligo raised the issue before the authorities in London. He had already instructed Madden and Dillon not to organize any session in Jamaica until they were certain that their royal commission would not be slighted or undermined in any way. However they were left with no choice other than to instigate the sessions as Lord Sligo discovered that it was a legal requirement under the abolition act that these sessions could be held on any day of the week.

On his first day back at work Madden found himself sharing the bench with a Jewish merchant by the name of Pacifico. This man was the mayor's representative and a local landlord and during the recent disturbances he had threatened Madden with tar and feathers. Madden inquired of him what he was doing inside the court chambers but the only reply he received was along the lines of: "I am here and I intend to stay here." Madden ordered that the merchant be evicted from the court. About ten days later, however, Madden was physically attacked on the street. Somebody grabbed him from behind by the arms and knocked him to the ground. Madden managed to grab a hold of his attacker's arm but received a heavy blow to his side. Madden did not fight back then in case he would later be accused of instigating the fight. Luckily his friend and fellow justice Dr. Chamberlaine arrived on the scene and grabbed the attacker. However Chamberlaine was then himself quite viciously attacked. Between them, he and Madden overcame their attacker and kept him pinned to the ground. Unfortunately, they were unable to find a policeman to arrest him. Apparently, the local mayor had ensured that none of the island police were on duty that day. The corporation also ensured that no such policemen would find themselves brought before court for the dereliction of duties.

> The consequence of this exemption - said Lord Sligo to Spring Rice - and the non-compliance of the mayor with any request to punish the city constables who refused to protect these gentlemen (Madden and Dillon) is that in point of fact my authority and that of the special justices is completely set at defiance and I do not see any method by which I can obviate the difficulty.[73]

Sligo was hopeful that Spring Rice would send him clear instructions on what to do if similar incidents occurred again:

> Dr Madden, (he said), is a very awkward individual he has submitted his name to the office of the circuitry as is customary for someone who is planning to leave the island I realised that

there was no point in me trying to persuade him to stay here on top of this review is my duty to inform you that the mere has resigned from the corporation board I trust that you will take due consideration of the injustice that I have suffered personally and consider the specific case which I have outlined to you.[74]

It was the thirtieth of December before Spring Rice decided on an appropriate response to Sligo's letter. Six weeks prior to this Madden left his post, having secured an excellent recommendation from the Governor. Madden had been thinking ahead and it was just as well that he had secured a good recommendation from the Governor because he soon found out that the Colonial office had no intention of supporting him in any way. Spring Rice insisted on investigating the matter for himself. He wasn't happy to rely entirely on Lord Sligo's view of the matter – and wanted to make some enquiries himself in order to confirm whether the whole blame for this controversy could be laid at the door of the corporation and the planters as Lord Sligo had intimated. Spring Rice would examine the matter in detail referring to the entire controversy as a "transaction" rather than as an "outrage" -the word that both Madden and Lord Sligo had used to describe it. In the end Spring Rice claimed not to be able to decide between:

The contradictions between Dr Madden and the Mayor of Kingston...or to ascertain, with reasonable certainty, while actually took place.[75]

It was also Spring Rice's opinion that nobody else could resolve the ambiguity surrounding this entire controversy either – at least without having to instigate an official inquiry, an enquiry which Spring Rice claimed - would have been unwise for the Governor to instigate:

It would have kept alive a dispute of which the tendency was injurious to the effective administration of the Law and the advantage which could have been anticipated from it was slight and problematical.[76]

On the day that Madden had arrived to the island an earthquake had taken place. Bizarrely, another earthquake took place on the day that he left the island. At approximately two o'clock in the morning he heard a noise like *"vast brazen bodies coming into furious collision in the caverns of the earth."* He was sleeping on the ground-floor of the house. He immediately ran towards the front door of the house but stopped to run upstairs where his wife Harriet was lying prone on a bed, suffering from fever. On reaching the upstairs of the house, a second, massive quake shook the ground and threw him against the stairs. The rafters overhead shook with such violence that he was sure that the roof would fall in at any moment. A third quake shook the ground as he entered the bedroom and carried his wife back down the stairs. He put her lying down on the lawn in front of the house and folded a blanket over her. Then he went back upstairs to warn the elderly black nurse who shared a room with his wife that it might be safer to leave the house. She was snoring away peacefully, but he gave her a good shake to wake her up:

> *"Why Massa wake me up so early?"*
> *"Get up, woman,"* said Madden at the top of his voice, *"an earthquake has occurred. She looked at him unconcerned. "Thankee, Massa,"* she said yawning. *"That's all? An earthquake - hi! hi! That's all, is it?"*[77]

And she turned back onto her side and began snoring again. On the fifteenth of November 1834, an American ship named Orbit brought Madden and his wife from Kingston to New York. Madden was so delighted to be free of Jamaica that he said his last sight of the island was his best. While he may not have enjoyed his sojourn on the island, he always remained very fond of the Jamaican people and would do his best on their behalf in any of his future political and social dealings. In 1840, for example, he brought the case of a black Jamaican man named Aban Bakr to the attention of the External Affairs Committee of the British Anti-Slavery Society, a Society which had been founded only a year previously. Madden helped free Bakr, an intellectual, from his position as a slave and ensured that he was allowed to travel freely back to Africa in the company of the well-known traveller and adventurer Davison. Davison was murdered on the return journey, however, and Bakr was forced into slavery again. Madden informed the Anti-Slavery Society that he had the means to send a group of men to Gambia and Accra in an attempt to free Bakr once more, and he requested that the Society translate posters announcing a reward for the safe release of Bakr into Spanish and Portuguese - so that the posters could be passed around among the Spanish and Portuguese traders who travelled along these trade routes into Africa. Madden himself supplied similar posters in Arabic.[78]

The trip to New York was Madden's first visit to America, although he would visit that country again twice later in his career. They reached New York on the eighth of December and found a fairly decent lodging-house for a fee of thirty shillings a day. The first thing which made a big impression on Madden upon arrival was the "race question." He noticed that the blacks and mulattoes of New York were prohibited from entering all churches except those which were Catholic.

One Sunday he attended a service in the black church on Saint Anthony's Street where the only two whites in attendance were himself and the minister conducting the service. He wasn't long in realising that he had committed a cardinal sin by attending the service in the first place – of course! He had gone in the company of a very devout man to whom he had given a letter of introduction from Jamaica. As they walked along the road together he noticed the passers-by staring at them and muttering under their breath. Madden ignored them and went into the "nigger-church" as the building was insultingly referred to by many of the whites. Inside he heard a sermon that was as anti-Catholic as anything that would be heard then at a similar-type Protestant church in Ireland, and that was saying something! - as Madden himself noted. When the service was over, and the well-dressed congregation was leaving the building Madden heard the shouts of the passersby: "No amalgamation!" "No abolition!" and "Down with the friends of the niggers."[79] Madden laughed and feigned indifference to the shouts, although he was actually worried for the safety of his companion and stayed by his side until the crowd had scattered and gone home.

Madden visited Philadelphia, Baltimore and Washington while in America. He found the sound of cutlery on plates almost deafening when he visited a restaurant in Washington and commented that there was no class of people in Europe who ate as much food as the Americans did. If the Americans had grey complexions it was their over-indulgence in food and their propensity for smoking tobacco that was responsible, in his view.

He visited George Washington's tomb - Washington was a hero of his - in spite of the fact that Washington had done nothing to eliminate slavery in the United States. A black man, "Mr. George's waiting boy," directed him to the grave and told him - "that Washington had conferred freedom on him and the rest of his household's slaves while lying on his deathbed, a gesture that was completely meaningless."[80]

Madden saw no guards or servants dressed in livery anywhere when he called on the President, General Andrew Jackson, with his letters of introduction. All he saw was a thin and hunched elderly man, dressed in a modest manner who was smoking a small pipe made from meerschaum. This elderly man turned out to be General Jackson himself! The President said that he was delighted he was to meet someone from Ireland, the *ould country* of his forefathers. Madden liked the President and found him kind, courteous and funny, and completely unlike any of the previous descriptions he had heard of Jackson. He was invited to dinner the following day, an event where the renewed conflict between America and France was one of the principal topics of conversation. "I thought that I was finished with the sword," Jackson commented to the assembled company - "but if the situation worsens and we are forced into war I will be prepared for battle again."

Madden was brave enough to bring up the question of abolishing slavery and said to Jackson that if he was to abolish this practice in the United States it would make his presidency go down in history forever. The President burst-out laughing and called his private secretary over.

"Come here Donaldson. Put that piece of wood on the fire and bring a keg of gunpowder in as well. When I'm sitting up on, top of the keg, hand the reddened piece of wood to the doctor and in the wink of an eye he'll make me famous forever after."[81] A woman who was listening to the conversation suggested that Donaldson ought to be blown up first as he was considering putting a limit on the amount of slaves he kept. Donaldson retorted by saying that he had little choice in the matter as he was only a subordinate officer who could not afford to keep more than a few dozen slaves!

Madden got to meet many leading Irish-Americans while on this visit to the United States, including members of the Emmet, Sampson and MacNeven families, three groups who had intimate ties with the United Irishmen campaign almost thirty years prior to this. These meetings would have a big influence on Madden's thinking as these families advised him to re-direct his energies away from the problems of foreign countries and to focus his attention on the injustice that his home country of Ireland was suffering. His encounters with these families awoke in him a strong sense of national pride, the sense of Irishness that lay buried within him. He had often been considered an Englishman before this and he himself had been happy enough to speak of himself as English prior to this visit to America. His sense of Irishness was awakened particularly on meeting the Countess Pamela Fitzgerald who had recently married for the second time – her husband was an M. Pitcairn, the American

Consul to Holland. His Nationalist sensibilities were truly awakened, however, on meeting Thomas Emmet, son of Thomas Addis of the United Irishmen, and a nephew of Robert Emmet, "the darling of Erin" who was hung and then beheaded for his role in the rebellion of 1803. Thomas Emmet invited Madden to his house in Harlem where he introduced him to the entire extended family including his brother Robert. These émigré families were all very close to one another, their bonds of friendship solidified by marriages between families. In memory of this visit Madden wrote a ballad which was sung to the tune of *The Wearing of the Green*:

> *Arrah, sure, it was in Baltimore*
> *Our Emmet's son I met,*
> *And he axed me: How ould Ireland bore*
> *Her griefs since Ninety-Eight?*
> *Och: bad enough, says I, avick,*
> *The sights that she has seen*
> *Has made her heart with sorrow sick*
> *Lamenting for the Green;*
> *For the poor ill-fated Green,*
> *For the long-insulted Green,*
> *Och, it drives me mad to sing the sad*
> *Ill-usage of the Green...*
> *Och! Pat, Mavoureen, tell me how*
> *My Father's brother died,*
> *Did Erin weep to see the blow?*
> *That reached him in his pride?*
> *He bravely died, agra; he bent*
> *On death a fearless brow,*
> *And many a heart that dare not vent*
> *Its guilt that day -doth now.*[82]

Doctor William Macneven[83] was the only one of the rebellion's original Irish leaders still living by then although he was already in poor health. Madden generated an enthusiasm in Doctor

MacNeven for the Anti-Slavery cause and MacNeven immediately began to work for the cause by alerting the American public to the way in which the American flag was being used as a banner for the protection of slave trade. Despite his involvement in these various campaigns Madden never lost interest in the profession for which he had originally trained. While in the U.S. he visited the New York College's of Medicine and Surgery where the College's President introduced him to a Doctor Watson from Spa Fields who had been instrumental in the Cato Street conspiracy that attempted to remove Lord Castlereagh from office years earlier. Doctor Watson had left behind his rebellious days and was now living a quiet and unobtrusive life in America. The fact that Doctor Watson had left his more radical days behind was proof - according to one person who spoke to Dooley - "that it was better not to execute people who broke the law but rather give them a chance to reform themselves into good and responsible citizens instead." Madden, who was against the death penalty was quick to remind the speaker that sparing Watson from the hangman had done no harm to Britain's imperial interests or the American public's for that matter. He also reminded him that Castlereagh was now dead and that nobody in Ireland mourned his loss while Watson, who was still alive, had nobody with a strong incentive to kill him.

Madden visited at least one prison while he was New York. In one cell he found an Englishman who had been given a four-year sentence for fraud and who still had another year of his sentence left to run. Madden enquired as to whether the prisoners were allowed to read or write while in custody and was told that they were not. "Not even the Bible?" Madden enquired. The man showing him around the prison explained that allowing the prisoners to read the Bible while alone in their cells would be considered a past-time and any form of hobby or past-time was prohibited in the prison. Madden also discovered that the Irish prisoners there were denied access to a chaplain. Each Sunday the Irish were pressurized to attending Protestant services despite the fact that the vast majority of them were Catholics. Madden was a man of wide interests, and he didn't limit his tour of America to a focus on humanitarian issues only. He visited the theatre on a number of occasions in New York but wasn't particularly impressed by the fare on offer. He also met a number of journalists on his travels and was surprised to discover how open and ruthless they were about attacking their competitors in other newspapers. For instance the editor of the *Hartford Review* referred to his counterpart in the *North River Times* as a "scoundrel" and a "liar." The Hartford Review editor was then informed that he was little more than a "frog" in both intellect and appearance and - (in another newspaper article) - that he was "a lazy, lounging, lousy, lying loafer who had neither brains to conceive, nor heart to feel." Madden managed to spend just under six weeks in Canada for less than sixty pounds. During the Canadian leg of his trip, he was unfortunate to have the company of a "saint" for one part of the journey, a man whose devotion and religiosity was completely over-the-top:

He hardly gave us a moment's peace but was constantly bawling out hymns at the top of his voice - as if prompted by a slew of demons. As a medical man I tried to advise him that he would do considerable damage to his vocal cords in the long-run if he continued to keep up such a racket. My advice went unheeded however. Instead, he made some ridiculous statement about the necessity to celebrate the New Year with a raft of joyful and spiritual songs. I have never heard anything as bad in my life as that monotonous wailing.[84]

On the third of February 1835, Madden and Harriet sailed from New York to Liverpool on a ship carrying stores of cotton. They were eight days at sea when a "melancholy catastrophe" took place. A crew-member escaped the clutches of the ship's first mate and climbed the rigging until he was at the cross-bar. He then shouted out "catch me if you can" before jumping into the sea where he immediately drowned. Nobody made any attempt to save the man, who had joined the crew in New York as Madden remembered. Worse than this, not a word was said to the blackguard of a first mate who had tormented this highly-strung man in the first place. Madden remembered the young man's first arrival on the ship when he had appeared agitated beyond the norm, like a man who was suffering from some type of *delirium tremens*. In spite of this, the new arrival was able to perform his duties on ship in a satisfactory manner. Madden was shocked therefore to discover that the young man had been tied up a few days later, a gag shoved in his mouth to muffle his shouts. The gag was tied so tightly that the man was actually bleeding from the mouth. Madden went straight to the captain and warned him that it wouldn't be in his interests if the authorities found out about this incident and the young man was immediately set free. Nothing untoward occurred after this until the young man jumped to his death a few days later. Madden's diaries don't tell us what the consequences of this whole affair were for the captain and the first mate. The rest of his descriptions concerning the voyage relate to the way in which sailors found new jobs in the shipping business back then:

> *When a ship comes to port and the crew receive their pay they usually head to certain pubs which are run by publicans from amongst the rougher elements of the lower-classes. The sailors usually spend their days ashore in these pubs until they have drunk their entire pay. Usually a contract has already been drawn up between the owners of these hostelries and the masters of the ships that are next getting ready to sail. Usually, too, these same publicans and hostel-owners have robbed their unlucky customers into the bargain. They then keep filling them with beer until the sailors are legless with drink. It is in this helpless condition that poor old Jack finds himself carried aboard for his next voyage. Sometimes Jack has been fleeced so completely that he is barely wearing any*

clothes or if he has clothes they certainly aren't warm enough to survive the brutal weather of a trans-Atlantic winter voyage. The bulk of the crew on our trip were brought aboard in this drunken state. Some of them were so drunk that they were unconscious while others were still fighting and the mates shoving them down the steps of the sailors' quarters.[85]

Madden had a solution to this disastrous state of affairs, however. "An Institute needs to be set up both in Liverpool and New York which would look after the welfare of those sailors who are temporarily without employment. This Institute would not be a charity shop, it would be an organisation that would pay its own way." Such a development would benefit not only the sailors but also the ship owners and the port masters. It would also be a relief to the passengers on these ships. That Madden was thinking along these lines comes as no surprise, given that he must have been fairly anxious about safety matters generally when he first laid eyes on the tiny, rickety-looking sailing vessel – barely over five hundred tons – on which he and his family were about to set sail across the Atlantic ocean.

It was nearly the end of March by the time they arrived in London. Madden, his wife Harriet, and their young son – (who was almost six years of age by then) went to live in the residence of a woman named Miss Cope, a house which was situated at 7 Panton Square. Madden was familiar with this house since his student days and had used it as his pied-á-terre in London on many occasions since then. In fact, it was this address which he used on most of his postal correspondence with various governmental departments and with the Anti-Slavery Society. Once they were settled in, he began to put the finishing touches to his book *Travels in the West Indies*. Harriet role in the production of this book was a seminal one given that she re-transcribed every page of the original manuscript so that it was submitted to the printers just two months after their return to England. As with Madden's first travel book, the chapters of this book took the form of "imagined" letters as sent to various renowned people with whom Madden was acquainted. The publication came out at an opportune moment, given that its' first chapters and its appendix dealt with the issues of the apprentice-system as it then operated in the West Indies and the manner whereby Madden had found himself forced to resign from his special judicial position there. There was a big demand for this book when it hit the shelves and it was even reprinted in America. Despite its popularity, an unfortunate turn of events ensured that the American publisher of the book found himself in serious financial difficulty and actually went bankrupt. Madden was never paid his copyright dues and – worse than this – he found himself having to pay off the debts incurred on the American end during the printing of his book. Now that he was back in London and wasn't too far away distance-wise – Madden paid a visit to his married sister Lizzie, who lived in Dublin. It was in the back of his mind also, no doubt, that Lord Mulgrave, under whom he had previously worked in the West Indies, might be able to help him secure a suitable job, preferably in Western Europe somewhere.

Having returned from Jamaica, Mulgrave turned down the position of Postmaster General in Lord Grey's government. He was appointed to the position of Lord Privy Seal instead, and was given a seat in the Cabinet of the government formed by Lord Melbourne. Mulgrave[86] was made the King's representative in Ireland in 1835 and Madden made certain to call on him quite soon after his arrival in Dublin. In fact, the poet Tom Moore accompanied Madden to a "high-society" dinner one night in Dublin, an occasion subsequent to which they would also come across Mulgrave. The poet was his usual eloquent and witty self on this particular night and he was the life and soul of the party until an innocent comment by one of the quietest men in the company caused a row. The person who took offence at the party was never actually named but was said to have been very similar in appearance to Sir Lucius O'Trigger.[87] The anecdote to which this individual took offence allegedly concerned a

Protestant prelate and the party broke up abruptly. Determined not to waste a good night out, Moore brought Madden to the theatre with him where a production commissioned by the King's representative was then showing. Lord Mulgrave himself was in the audience that night, accompanied by his wife. Recognising Moore - as he and Madden entered the theatre - the audience began to call out the poet's name in welcome. Moore was invited to sit in the Royal Box and returned later to Madden with an invitation for two to a supper at the Viceroy's Residence. It was Madden's first time ever inside the residence of the Viceroy and he would say afterwards that he never enjoyed an occasion as much as he did that one. Also in their company at the meal were Lord Cloncurry,[88] a man who had been imprisoned for some time in the Tower of London for his part in the 1798 rebellion and his wife Lady Pamela Fitzgerald, the eldest daughter of Lord Edward Fitzgerald,[89] whose biography Moore was then in the process of writing. No wonder then that Madden - who was himself already in the initial stages of his research into the history of the United Irishmen - remarked that the ghosts of the old Orangemen must have been turning in their graves at the company that the King's Representative in Ireland had gathered together that evening!

The self-same Orange ghosts would certainly not have appreciated the sound of Tom Moore's own songs as he sang them to the assembled company. Some of his songs made reference to various individuals who had fought in the rebellion of 1798 and were so moving that Lady Pamela Fitzgerald wept openly. Strange as it may seem, this gathering in the Viceroy's residence was not as unusual an event as it might appear at first glance. From the very first day of his appointment, Mulgrave consulted closely with Thomas Drummond, the Chief Secretary and a man who worked hard to alleviate the unhealthy social conditions that so many Irish people lived in as a consequence of centuries of British misrule in Ireland. While Drummond wasn't a Catholic himself, he was considered sympathetic to the plight of the Catholic majority in Ireland and brought in a number of measures in order to secure better rights for Irish Catholics generally. He supported the appointment of a number of Catholic prelates and politicians and emptied the prisons of many "political prisoners." He "embraced the masses" to such an extent that Daniel O'Connell would refer to him as the best Englishman that had ever ruled in Ireland,[90] while Jemmy Hope[91] – one of the most eminent of the United Irishmen still living at this juncture - would refer to him as "our illustrious viceroy."[92] Madden would later dedicate another work of his to Mulgrave and would also turn to him for help when he had an official administrative difficulty. Mulgrave would also subsequently inform Madden that his policy in relation to Ireland was one of:

> ...treating Ireland as I would an English country, i.e. implement the law without fear or favour – improve public support for the judiciary, improve the transparency of the selection procedures for minor administrative posts in Dublin Castle as much as possible. This would do away with the previous system of appointments based on prejudice as relating to an individual's religion and would ensure that jobs would not always be filled by military people.[93]

Madden believed that Mulgrave was a very suitable person for the job of implementing British colonial policy in Ireland, a view which wasn't shared by many other members of the British administration however. Mulgrave was subjected to vicious attacks from his enemies on a regular basis and the king, himself, was suspicious of Mulgrave. "Tyrconnell O'Mulgrave" was the nickname which one branch of the Orange press had for Mulgrave. Jamaica, as opposed to Ireland, was the primary focus of Madden's attention at this juncture. By the time Madden reached England - having resigned his commission in disgust - the situation "on the ground" in Jamaica had become much worse. Conditions there had deteriorated to such an extent, in fact, that the country's colonial administration had abandoned any plans to implement a new constitution as had been proposed for the island. The attempts to stymie constitutional progress in Jamaica were not successful in the long run however. While the Conservative party favoured using strong-arm tactics on the island, there were many other people in British politics who favoured increased attempts at reform through constitutional means in Jamaica and these politicians and public servants were not shy about indicating their views to the then British government. Madden was amongst this latter camp and he indicated his anger with the British government's handling of the Jamaican situation through both official and non-official spheres. He outlined his feelings on the issue through his official report as prepared for the Colonial Office and through the medium of the Anti-Slavery Association which continued to highlight the continual mistreatment of the black population in Jamaica, as a consequence of decades of British misrule.

Controversies concerning various aspects of British rule on the island were a major theme in many of the parliamentary debates of this era as evident in the parliamentary speeches of politicians such as Sir George Grey,[94] the then Secretary of State for the Colonies and William E. Gladstone, who spoke on behalf of the then opposition – i.e. the Tories. Grey argued that the *Repeal of Slavery Act* was being implemented well and that the special justices were no longer simply the pawns of big landowners as before. It was untrue to say that use of the whip hadn't also declined on the island, he claimed. Equally false was the claim that women were continually subject to physical abuse there. It was the British government's intention to fulfil its promises with regard to the improvement of the Jamaican people's daily living conditions and they would ensure that the island's local authorities undertook their obligations in respect of social change, he added.

Gladstone criticised Buxton's followers as being too naïve, however, and once both the government and opposition deputies had agreed to it, a Special Committee of Investigation was set up to ascertain what the situation was really like "on the ground" in Jamaica. Buxton, Grey, O'Connell and Gladstone were all appointed members of this Committee, a Committee before which Madden gave evidence for two days running. As compared with the evidence he gave before this Committee, Madden was less immoderate in his opinions than when stating his views on the situation to the Anti-Slavery Association. Whether overly-naïve or no, Madden told the Association that he thought the apprentice system could be implemented correctly if it was given a chance to work. If the law was enforced correctly, he opined it would not be necessary for justices such as himself to resign in the future.

At the same time as he was expressing these views, Madden was also doing whatever he could behind the scenes to improve the situation for the black population of Jamaica. For example, it was from Madden that George Stephen, the Association's attorney received most of his information so as to formulate his concerns over the treatment of the Jamaican black population, concerns which he subsequently presented to the British government. The Parliamentary enquiry undertaken by the Special Committee of Investigation completely ignored the views of both Madden and the Anti-Slavery Association when it came to its final conclusions, however. It dismissed each and every one of the recommendations put forward by the Association. It was the Committee's conclusion that the apprentice scheme was working reasonably well in Jamaica but that the change from slavery from freedom required a huge cultural shift and would therefore take many years to oversee in its fullness.

CHAPTER 5
CUBA, ABOLITIONISM AND THE CASE OF THE "AMISTAD"

Madden was home in Ireland for more than a year before he began his next bout of advocacy on the Abolitionist front. He spent that first year searching for a job as a medical supervisor in a mental institution. He had a particular interest in institutions where people were incarcerated and when he found the time to do so he published a series of essays on the question of institutions and institutionalisation in 1846. His quest for a job in Ireland was unsuccessful however and in the end he was happy enough to take another job abroad.

His next job was based in the colony then known as Spanish Cuba, a place which was then one of the world centres for slave trafficking, some of which was organised through formal contracts as agreed between England and Spain. Slave trafficking had been officially declared illegal in this region from the year 1817 onwards as a consequence of an agreement signed by both England and Spain in that same year. In 1835, the two governments agreed some further "official" measures to put an end to this barbaric practice through the implementation of another, stricter agreement. According to this new law the vast majority of the slaves in Cuba – there were over a quarter of a million slaves in

Cuba then – would be entitled to their freedom provided that they could prove to the Anglo-Spanish Integration Commission in Havana that they had been trafficked to Cuba after 1820. The Spanish government dragged their heels over the legal implementation of this new agreement, however, and Palmerston and the British Foreign Office had to keep the Spanish under constant and insistent pressure so as to force them to fulfil their side of the bargain.

It is worth noting that the threat of force - in the shape of the Navy - was always there to "buttress" the diplomatic efforts of Britain's then representatives in Cuba. The whole issue would ultimately prove both long drawn-out and costly for the British government. It proved expensive because of the necessity of keeping roving squadrons of navy officers all along the African coast, especially near those coastal regions where slave trafficking had originated and where the trade was a long-established and well-developed one.

The upkeep of the mixed-race commissions based at Sierra Leone, Loando, Kingston, Rio de Janeiro, St. Helena and Havana had to be taken into consideration also. It was the job of these mixed-race officials to examine those vessels which were taken in for searching. These commissions also had responsibility for the provision of housing and other facilities for those slaves who were freed at each of the aforementioned locations. The 1830s had seen slave-trafficking reach epidemic proportions with nearly 135,000 slaves being trafficked from Africa annually, this despite the fact that slavery had (officially, at least) - been abolished in the British West Indies - as had the trafficking of slaves into the United States. Brazil and Cuba were the two biggest markets for this hugely-profitable trade at this point. In the case of Cuba, this was as a consequence of the expansion of the sugar trade in this era of Free Trade.

It was estimated that between 10,500 and 60,000 slaves were sent to Cuba in 1838 alone, and even that number wasn't enough to satisfy the demand for labourers in that country's cane fields. Given the fact that many slaves worked 20 out of every 24 hours during the sugar harvest, it is unsurprising to find that many of the slaves died young and the slave-traders were always sourcing more slaves to work in the fields.

The terrible conditions endured by those slaves unfortunate enough to find themselves trafficked from Africa to the slave markets on the other side of the world, don't bear thinking about. Sometimes there were upwards of a thousand slaves herded together aboard a small clipper. These unfortunate people were all squeezed tightly together in rows along the flanks of the ship, their heads bent between the legs. They were so closely packed together that when one person shifted position, everybody else had to move also. The slaves were forced to relieve themselves in these same cramped conditions, and it wasn't unusual for fights to break out between groups of slaves from different ethnic groups or tribes, this despite the fact that they were all trapped in this hellish situation together. Many of them had already been sold to a particular slave merchant even before they had docked on dry land but it wasn't unusual for one of these merchants to find that his "product" had died a long time before arrival. On at least one occasion a ship docked in Cuba on which more than two hundred slaves had already perished at sea, usually as a consequence of hunger, dehydration, sickness or violence as sometimes occurred between tribes such as the Akan and the Ebo.[95]

Madden had two jobs while in Havana. He was appointed warden of all the freed African slaves there and it was his duty to ensure that they really had been freed from bondage and that the Cuban landlords were no longer abusing them. This task was not an easy one given that many of Cuba's landowning class refused to accept that slavery was now illegal and used every form of trickery and corruption to circumvent the new laws which prohibited the keeping of slaves. It was the Secretary of State to the Colonies, Lord Glenelg who offered this job to Madden, explaining that it was to the public's benefit that a capable person be appointed to the job. Madden was to receive a salary of £800 pounds a year in this post. He was also appointed to a temporary vacancy on the Anglo-Spanish Commission of Integration.

As this post was under the auspices of the Foreign Office, it was Lord Palmerston who appointed Madden to it. This post provided him with an extra £400 pounds a year and a rental allowance of £250 pounds – a figure indicative of the very high cost of living in Cuba at this time. "My situation is arduous but honorable and not ill-paid,"[96] Madden would say to his friends. In truth, this annual salary was the highest that Madden had ever earned. The journey to New York, which took thirty days in total, was a stormy one but Madden made some useful contacts on the voyage. Amongst the other passengers was a Captain Masson who was had been a friend and fellow-officer of Captain Sturgeon, the man who had married Sarah Curran,[97] the one-time girlfriend of Robert Emmet. Masson would write an account of his reminiscences of Emmet and Sarah Curran for Madden at a later date. Madden didn't have much time for research on this journey, however. As one of the few medical doctors aboard, he volunteered to care for the immigrants in his spare time.

The ship's poorest passengers were all travelling to America to escape poverty, and many of them were already extremely sick. Madden's skills as a doctor were required day and night but he was happy to minister to the sick and the dying. "Physic," he said, "is a glorious profession to practice for your pleasure, not for profit." If he had twenty sons, he would ensure that each of them became a doctor, he said. He would not be unhappy either, if they were to choose another profession, he admitted – the job of medical doctor was not an easy vocation in those days. What was most necessary to succeed in life in those times was neither an acute intelligence nor a liberal education. Most necessary of all was the stubbornness and the will to succeed, or what Doctor Paris had once described as "a pachydermatous sensibility."

Madden spent six months in the U.S. where he visited many of his Irish friends who were now living there. His political and advocacy activities meant that he was more well-known now than he had been on the last occasion that he had visited the U.S. The Irish-Americans there were proud of his books and MacNeven, whose health was now in decline, was particularly happy to have Madden, Harriet and their son Forde (now seven years of age) as his visitors. MacNeven used their visit to pass on further archival material as relating to the history of the United Irishmen to Madden. MacNeven had asked as many people as he could in the Irish-American community to provide any historical information they had in relation to the United Irishmen. The response from the Irish community there had not been great, however. Naturally enough, most of the Irish emigrants to the U.S. were too busy trying to make ends meet in their adopted homeland to have any time for historical research.

The Emmet family in the U.S. were preparing some historical material for Madden at this juncture as were a Mrs. Sampson and a Mr. Tone, the latter being Theobald Tone's grandson. MacNeven died in July, 1841 but his family continued to correspond with Madden in the following years. Between themselves and a number of other prominent Irish Nationalist families in America, Madden would eventually garner quite a substantial amount of archival research material from the U.S. No matter what corner of the world Madden found himself in, he continued researching and collating material for his eventual book about the United Irishmen. He worked on it even while he was in Cuba as indicated by a letter he sent from "this outlandish place" in January, 1837 to one of his relatives, the Catholic publisher, William Powell, whose office was on Parliament Street in Dublin.

> *Have you been able to procure any further intelligence for me? I would wish to have your copy of the Press newspaper, or if you could purchase a set for me and another of the Northern Star - a copy of Redhead York's letters. William will trace this out on some catalogue. A copy of the trials for high treason*

for 1798; and pray ask Mr. Clinch in what work of Barrington's he saw a letter of John Sheares lithographed, and beg of him to get a copy of the letter...Any volumes or magazines for the year 1798 I would be also glad to get, or anything else on that time. There is a bookseller of the name of Geraghty in Anglesea Street who knows me, and on mentioning my name would show you what he has: the works of Tone, Emmet, & Co., McNevin, Sampson, Cloney, Teeling, Hay, Gordon. Arthur O'Connor's letter I have...I would be glad to have a copy of Barrington's Rise and Fall of Ireland and above all anything that relates in any way to the Sheares. The amount, whatever it may be, Mrs. Cogan will settle for me with you...There is a little volume of poems, chiefly songs, which Battersby lent me. The author's name I forget, but I know amongst the songs was "Mary le Moore" which I also would be glad to get. The books I would have sent packed in a box to John O'Donnell, Merchant, Dale Street, Liverpool...and he would ship it for me to Havana. Would you beg of my old friend and school-fellow, R. Blake, whom I met in your house before I left Dublin, to do me a service, namely, to find me out (as I know he is a book worm) if the transactions of the Dublin Historical Society are published, and if so pray get them for me. If they are not, I want him to consult the archives of the Courts and see what part either of the Sheares took in the business of the Society...and to get any speeches of theirs copied for me. I am afraid to ask William to do this on account of his business, otherwise I would inflict the task on him. There is one more trouble more I have to give you and I am done. Will you beg of your Clinch to ascertain for me at the Inns of Court when both the Sheares were called to the bar; and one more last request, and I am done; can you do anything with Murphy's widow about the manuscript of her husband.[98]

Madden made another interesting contact for his United Irishmen research on the trip from Havana to New York. This was Robert Fulton,[99] the American radical and engineer who had once offered the use of his submarine to Robert Emmet. When they had originally left England, Madden and Harriet had been quite worried about their son Forde's lung problems. Ironically, the journey by sea to Cuba helped bring about a huge improvement in Forde's condition. Now, however, they felt it safer and more appropriate to send him back to England again. It must have been quite traumatic for the Maddens to have to separate from their son for such a long period and Richard Madden captured his broken heart at this parting in the following verse:

> *Then parting came, sad words that thrilled the core,*
> *My own Papa! my dear Papa! Goodbye!*
> *Words uttered o'er and o'er, and on the breeze*
> *They died away at last, long ere the eye*
> *Lost sight of thee; but women's thoughts are these,*
> *And on a mother's heart alone, such thoughts should seize.*[100]

In addition to being the capital of Cuba, Havana was one of Spain's principal colonies and a focal point for the slave trade in the West Indies. He was no sooner *in situ* when Madden was taking on the slave-traders and Miguel Tacón, the island's Captain-General, in particular. The reality was that the effective administration of the Commission of Integration was dependent on the attitude of the Captain-General towards it. Complicating matters further was the fact that the governmental administration in Havana was a huge beneficiary of the slave-trade as a result of the money it received in the form of Customs revenues. This meant that the administration there tried every trick in the book to "unofficially" bypass any international agreements relating to the slave trade.

Tacón was a hard-hearted dictator. When he first arrived in Cuba, the island was in uproar. Robbery, murder, gambling and lawlessness were rife, and the island was functioning according to a system whereby favours could be bought or sold to the highest bidder. Public works were in private hands, the police were corrupt and every public service was in disarray. Tacón hated the very sight of the "mob" and the disorder which was the consequence of inept political rule. He applied himself with vigour to sorting out this state of affairs and displayed an unusual zeal in this regard – a zeal which even his enemies were obliged to acknowledge. He was in the lucky position that his word was law and he had full authority to implement whatever new rules and regulations he wished to apply, irrespective of how draconian they were. He used his power to expel many people from Cuba and he sent many people into exile without trial. He had soon packed the prisons and removed all beggars and other "undesirables" from the streets. He ordered that all the wild dogs wandering the streets be slaughtered and that all roads be clean and usable. He set up various public services including the fire brigade and initiated the construction of a range of new public buildings. As Madden admitted, Tacón did leave after him a legacy of sorts in terms of bricks and mortar.

Tacón's legacy was a two-edged sword however. He stamped out every form of democracy and independence that the Cuban people had enjoyed prior to his rise to power. The truth was that Tacón loved power and tyranny for its own sake. He was always suspicious of intellectuals and never slow to show his contempt for the Cuban people themselves. He decided to give the Cuban populace what he thought it was lacking, whether the people liked it or not. Military courts became the principal mode of trial for criminal cases and Tacón also used his authority to remove all Creoles from important jobs and replace them with Spaniards. He generated great hostility amongst the Cuban people and it wasn't long before the Cuban nobility were refusing his invitation to visit the Palace. His actions also caused a resurgence of tension between Creoles and Spaniards, old enmities that had remained dormant for many years. These older and long-standing tensions exploded once again, particularly after 1837, when the only Constitutional rights the Cuban people still held were finally removed, rights which included the right to representation in the Cortes or Spanish Parliament. Rebellion was seen as the only answer to this and it wasn't long before Cuban exiles were organising in the bars of New York and Madrid in an effort to try and overthrow Spanish rule. Despite these various draconian measures on Tacón's part, Madden didn't see much evidence of any improvement in relation to civic or societal morality. He noticed that religion was let fall into a decline and that scandals were commonplace in the Church. Madden's papers from this time record some of his impressions of Cuban life, in particular as relating to what he witnessed on his visits to prisons and urban ghettoes.

When Madden visited an Englishman incarcerated in the prison known as *Gallera* (an inferno de *inmoralidad*)[101] he was warned by one inmate as follows: "nobody goes in here for fun or if you do you better keep your wits about you and a knife by your side and a pistol too." From time to time the prisoners would murder one another; "enraged wild beasts" is how Madden referred to them. It was Tacón who had built this prison along with the other public buildings that were funded by illegal profits from the sale of "freed" negroes. He had provided a church there and a chaplain who would say Mass each Sunday although one prisoner told Madden that he never saw any chaplain or heard of any religious service either.

Upon his arrival in 1835, Tacón had publicly criticised the slave trade but by the time he left the island he had himself made 28,000 doubloons from the sale of illegal slaves. In fact there were five or six slave markets or barrios located within a stone's throw of Tacón's country house near Havana. Various businesses in this city were making a fortune from the slave-trade and some individuals became exceptionally rich on the back of it. One document found aboard a ship that was raided in Havana around this time stated that the ship was carrying 484 slaves and had made a profit of $93,000 dollars (slightly over 18,600 pounds) from this one business transaction alone. It was common for vessels like this to make two journeys in search of slaves each year. Men were regularly whipped to death, he said, and women were separated from their children upon arrival in Havana and often never saw their families again. There were many estates on the island where no elderly black men could be seen at all (they all died young from the harsh treatment they received) and where less than a third of the workers were black women. These slaves usually worked in the sugar trade and from dawn to dusk as the slave owners considered four hour's sleep to be enough for their slaves.

Despite these dreadful violations of human rights, the Spanish authorities had their defenders, even within British political ranks. Their consul in Havana, a man by the name of Tolmé, informed Palmerston that Tacón's draconian legislative and punitive measures to restore public order would count for nought if he also decided to cut back on the slave-trade in that region. (According to Tolmé) - if Tacón began to interfere with the various vested interests that were then becoming wealthy from the slave trade, people would lose their respect for him throughout Cuba. Unsurprisingly – in the light of his views on the slavery question –Tolmé was later suspected of being on very friendly terms with some of Cuba's biggest slave traders. James Kennedy, who took over Madden's post on the Integration Commission on the 28th of September, 1839, made a formal complaint to Palmerston about Tolmé's links to the slave trade and informed Palmerston that Madden had even more serious or incriminating information to this effect.

One of the more serious allegations against Tolmé was that he had passed on private parliamentary documents to the accountant of Joaquin Gomez - one of the biggest slave traders then operating in Cuba – and that these sensitive documents were "doing the rounds" amongst the slave-trading fraternity. Palmerston became very nervous at these developments and decided to remove Tolmé from his post. At the same time as this was happening Tacón was striking another blow for the slave-trader lobby. He began a "behind-the-scenes" campaign to ensure that Madden was removed from his post, claiming that the Irishman was a sympathiser with the African slaves, a misguided individual whose reputation for making false and unfounded allegations of corruption against other officials was well-known to senior officials in the British government. Madden was a man notorious for his insinuations and "strange demands," according to Tacón. It wasn't long before D'Aguilar, the Spanish Ambassador in London – acting "on the instructions" of Tacón – began to spread false rumours about Madden and to push for him to be fired from his job. When Madden heard about this smear campaign against him, he decided to lobby some of his own supporters in London to make them aware of what was really going on in Cuba. He contacted Lady Blessington, who subsequently made representations on his behalf with both Mr. Fox Strangeways in the Foreign Office and Mr. Byng. Once these representations were complete, Lady Blessington was able to give Madden a private assurance that his job was safe. Rather than give in to Spanish pressure, Palmerston also decided to stand by Madden and staunchly defended the Irishman's record in Cuba. Palmerston went public, and announced that Madden's dedication to duty, a dedication that was well-recognised by the British government and, one which ought also be given due acknowledgement by the Cuban government.

> *There is absolutely no reason for the King's government to give the slightest consideration to these false allegations as referring to Doctor Madden's ability to carry out his duties as both a (temporary) officer of the Integration Commission and as a Warden for those slaves who have secured their freedom or the terrible insinuation that Doctor Madden should be forced to resign from his post. On the contrary, Doctor Madden has provided clear evidence of the incredible dedication and ability that he has brought to the often-difficult and unpleasant duties to which he was assigned in Cuba, proving, in the process, that he was by far the most suitable candidate for this particular mission.*[102]

Having defended Madden in the staunchest possible manner,

Palmerston went on to criticise what was then happening "on the ground" in Cuba.

> As General Tacón positively declares that he in no degree or manner encourages or protects the...importation of slaves into Cuba, His Majesty's Government is bound to believe that he is ignorant of the gross and continued misconduct of all the subordinate authorities under his command...But that an extensive continual trade in slaves does take place in and from Cuba, that slave ships are notoriously fitted out in the Havana and sent to the Coast of Africa for slaves, that many of these ships return to Cuba and there illegally land their cargoes, that the names of ships going to and returning from the Coast of Africa are no longer published in the official gazette, that such ships are no longer required to hoist the distinguishing red flag at the masthead...all these and many other facts of a similar tendency are well known to His Majesty's Government and it is of great importance for the honour of the Spanish Government which suffers by the continuance of such practices that these facts should without delay be made known also to General Tacón in order that he may for his own sake and out of regard for the character of Spain take those prompt and energetic measures which will doubtless occur to him for putting an immediate stop to these scandalous proceedings which are at variance with all the professions of the Spanish Government, and incompatible with the solemn engagements of the Spanish Crown.[103]

A new constitution inaugurated by Spain in 1833 left the Cuban colonial class without any representation in the imperial Parliament there. It engendered a hatred for the "old country" amongst many of the Cuban colonial elite and was the catalyst for a move towards independence in Cuba. Increased taxation levies as imposed upon them by Spain also encouraged many Cubans to the creation of enhanced trading links with the United States, instead of Spain, a development which Madden took a good deal of interest in.

> Cuba ever since I knew it, (he says), has been slowly but steadily becoming Americanized. I pestered my superiors with my opinion on this subject in 1836-9. Liberavi animam meam might be fairly said by me if the star-spangled banner were flying tomorrow on the Mora Castle…In the course of years a feeling of fervour for independence has been changed into a desire for connection with the United States.[104]

If the British had been willing to assure the Cubans that they would protect their island from the interference of other foreign powers in 1837, there is a strong likelihood that the white settlers on the island might have thrown off their Spanish shackles and made a *bone fide* attempt to prohibit the slave trade as practiced there. From the 1840s onwards, it was in the direction of America that the white population of Cuba increasingly focused their attention and not towards Britain, however. On a personal level Madden found the state of religious practice on the island to be a source of much concern. The corrupt influence of the slave trade had spread everywhere and even tainted the functioning of the local Catholic Church. The slave-traders were such a powerful group in Cuba that, with the support of local government, they made certain to intimidate any priest who might have considered speaking out on the slavery issue.

> God help any priest who might counsel his flock not to buy those slaves at the slave markets on a Sunday…God help him if he warned the sinner in confession to desist from having any connection with the slave trade and to hand over the profits accumulated from this evil trade to the poor…I enquired of a number of priests whose consciences had not been completely silenced – as of yet – why they didn't do more to prevent the Church being tainted by the wiles of the slave trade. (With sorrow and shame in his voice) he answered by referring to

the levies that the state imposes based on the Church's administration of the Sacraments. "The system is so rotten here that the clergy are frequently forced to sell the very vessels which they use on the altar as part of the Sunday Mass.[105]

Madden personally believed that more damage had been done to the institution of the Catholic Church in Cuba by the corrupt influence of the Spanish nobility and their courts than had ever been done by Henry VIII when he organised the dissolution and destruction of the British monasteries. As an example of this Madden, alluded to a newspaper announcement he had read in a Cuban newspaper where the Archbishop of Havana had ceded to the corrupt influence of the Spanish colonial authorities by signing his name – thereby acquiescing – to "scenes of riot and debauchery that mark the orgies of a public masquerade ball in the theatre of Havana on a Sunday night." Worse again was a Lenten advertisement which announced the sale of slaves on a Sunday, "even during Mass, and at the door of the local church."

On his return to England, Madden described all of these corrupt practices on the part of both Cuban church and state to the General Anti-Slavery Convention that was held in Exeter Hall, London in June, 1840. In his speech to the Convention, Madden contradicted the claims of Alexis de Tocqueville - who had stated in the French Parliament, in July, 1839 - that the practice of slavery within the Spanish colonies was carried on in "a fashion that was both distinctive and benign." Madden's blood boiled when he heard comments such as de Tocqueville's, particularly given what Madden had seen with his own eyes of the slave-trade both in Cuba and Jamaica. Madden provided evidence of a number of cases where slaves had been tortured and beaten to death, and the only punishment their murderers had received comprised either a short prison term or a monetary fine.

While General Tacón was in charge of the Cuban administration - in 1837 to be precise – a slave-master ordered the murder of one of his slaves, a killing which was carried out in a small district known as Guanabacoa, just three miles from Havana. Macado is the name of this murderer and he is an esteemed member of "high society" in Havana. Apparently, he suspected that the slave in question was guilty of stealing a number of ornaments…a charge which the man denied. This slave was tied up and then beaten to death. The beating started at three o'clock and came to end three hours later when it was clear the man was dead. Shortly before he died, the slave had just about enough strength to shout out that he would confess to the crime. The slave-master then called the local police sergeant to take note of this "confession" but by the time the policeman bent down to take this evidence from the slave, the man was already unconscious. The police officer said that the man was now unconscious but the slave-owner disagreed with him. The slave-master then kicked the man who was already dead at this stage. "That dog isn't unconscious; he's only pretending that he is!.". The police official examined the man once more and said: "This man is dead." The slave-owner then sent for two doctors who signed a death certificate to the effect that the slave had died from a brain haemorrhage, and that this was an illness that had had occurred suddenly and by natural causes.[106]

The Captain-General had subsequently ordered an investigation into the circumstances of this man's death but the investigation had recommended that the murderer be absolved of all blame. Tacón had been unhappy with the outcome of this particular investigation and had instructed the military officer for the district of Guanabacoa to re-examine the case. A second investigation confirmed that the man had died from the effects of the beating he had received. The military officer had requested that Tacón ignore the outcome of this second investigation however, because the officer in question had taken evidence from a number of black witnesses when their master wasn't present. The end result of this terrible affair was that Macado was subsequently cleared of all blame for the death and it was the military official that lost his job instead! At the time, Madden had made some unofficial investigations of his own into the circumstances of this case and discovered that Macado had bribed his way out of trouble through payments of 4000 dollars in solicitor's fees and bribes.

The second murder which Madden reported to the Commission in London concerned a beautiful-looking American woman whose lover had presented her with one of his female slaves as a gift. For reasons of jealousy, this slave was physically beaten every evening by her new owners and it was some time before her cries for help alerted the local authorities to what was going on. The police came to the American's house and discovered the female slave chained inside the barn next to the house, chains which were bound so tightly that the metal had actually rotted its way into the woman's flesh. The woman was brought to the hospital in agony but subsequently died of her injuries.

Judging by anecdotes such as these, as recorded by Madden, Cuba seems to have been a particularly violent and lawless place at this time. In later years Madden and his wife Harriet would also recount some of the dangerous and violent incidents that had taken place near where they were living in Havana and how lucky they were to escape with their lives on a number of occasions. One particularly frightening incident occurred to them when Madden was inspecting the conditions in which various slaves were being kept by their slave-owners. Harriet and he had arrived late one night to a *posada*[107] that was situated in quite an isolated and mountainous area. Madden had already climbed out of his coach when Harriet noticed something alarming in the behaviour of the owner of the lodging house. Harriet refused to come out of the coach and insisted that they move on until they found somewhere else where to stay, this despite the fact that the other nearest lodging house involved a long journey through other equally dark and isolated forest areas. The Maddens would later discover that the first dwelling they had stopped at was actually a well-known meeting-point for various bandit groups and that many travellers who had passed that way had never been seen again!

Madden had found himself at loggerheads with the other British representative on the Commission of Integration, Edward Windham Harrington Schenley[108] from the very first day of his arrival in Cuba. Madden considered Schenley inefficient and negligent in equal measure and said as much to Palmerston. Schenley, in turn, was irritated by Madden's refusal to sign a joint protest that was due to be sent to Tacón and which Madden had originally written – afterwards, Madden considered it to be worded "in language so likely to exasperate the local authorities." Private notes written by Schenley at this juncture find him describing Madden in terms such as the following – "Of all the downright wrongheaded ones this M.D. beats them all and I now find Lord Sligo's words correct - that he would not agree with an angel in heaven" and "the Office was almost out of paper and a great deal too much had already been expended upon Dr. Madden's nonsensical and groundless complaints."

At one point Schenley discovered that Madden's complaints about him were both confused and (actually) at variance with an Agreement as signed between Britain and Spain in 1835 – an Agreement that they, as Commissioners, were obliged to work in accordance with. Their squabbles became worse and both men complained about one other to Palmerston on a continual basis. Their disagreements frequently centred around official documentation that they were obliged to co-sign, but which both men would not sign on different occasions. At first Palmerston assumed that the difficulties between both men were as a consequence of some sort of misunderstanding or breakdown in communication and ignored the seriousness of the matter. He ignored the crux of their arguments and focused on more minor or peripheral issues in his responses to both men. At one stage he asked another official to pass on the following and somewhat-bizarre request to Madden - whose hand-writing was as good as anybody else's at this juncture – "Request Dr. Madden to write a larger hand." The official who received this instruction already considered himself "tormented" by the various long-winded missives which Madden passed onto him on a regular basis - and he went somewhat further in the note which he sent to Madden saying: "Will you allow me to suggest to you privately the propriety when addressing his Lordship, of writing in a larger hand, and of condensing, if possible in a less number of words the substance of what you wish to communicate."[109] Palmerston received an assurance from Madden that he would do as requested in relation to the disagreement with Schenley. The reports kept coming to the Foreign Office however, this time with the signature of Schenley alone. When Palmerston sought an explanation in the case of one of these reports and Madden explained to him what had happened, he gave Schenley a real tongue-lashing. Schenley responded to verbal attack but his explanation wasn't sufficient to satisfy Palmerston. Schenley's comments reveal much about the adversarial atmosphere that prevailed at this juncture. His comments did little to satisfy Palmerston however.

> I understand it to mean that the despatches which he sent with his single signatures were communicated to Dr. Madden in proper time before the mail was despatched, that Schenley afforded Madden full opportunity of discussing the despatches with him in personal conference, and that Dr. Madden upon discussion refused either to sign the despatches, and give up his objections, or to state those objections in writing in order that they should be transmitted to this office, together with the despatches themselves. If that be so it was Schenley's duty to have reported it at the time, and not by sending despatches with his single signature, and without any explanation appear to set aside by his own authority the colleague with whom he was by the authority of the Government appointed.[110]

Schenley admitted that he frequently avoided consulting with Madden in person for fear that they would end up insulting one another. "I have absolutely no intention of letting him accuse me of cantankerousness!"[111] At the same time as these accusations and counter-accusations were flying, Palmerston presented Schenley with a letter from Madden which intimated that Schenley was deliberately delaying dispatches until after the mail-boat to England had already left port. Schenley was livid when he learned this and he called on both a "special envoy" and Jackson, a clerk in the Commission of Integration for their support. Trist, the then American Consul, referred to this man Jackson as "a humble jackal", but he (Trist) too was so afraid of getting dragged into this argument - particularly when he wasn't at all sure that Schenley would win the dispute in the end - that he sent a confidential letter to James Bandinel, Under-Secretary in the Foreign Office to explain his position in the ongoing disputes. He explained that he wanted to have absolutely no hand or part in the argument between the two gentlemen. He also gave the same message to both parties in the dispute - and on more than one occasion, making it clear he didn't want to hear any complaints from either of them.

He was very put out therefore when Schenley pestered him about writing a letter and indicated that he felt forced to take up his pen against his will - not (necessarily) to satisfy Schenley, but rather to prevent him "who has endeavoured to make me expunge a part thereof" from getting the better of him. Jackson refused to forward the letter however and Schenley took it upon himself to forward a number of extracts from the letter only.[112]

> *It is unnecessary for me to enter into the particulars of these disagreements, and I have only to remark that the letters in question afford proofs, that if public officers are determined to differ they never can be at a loss for subjects of difference but that such a determination to waste in groundless disputes that time which ought to be employed in the public service, indicates an imperfect understanding of the nature of official duties.*[113]

Palmerston said it was a pity that a copy of Jackson's letter hadn't been forwarded to him although subsequent comments on the entire controversy indicated that the special envoy had already won the battle on Schenley's behalf anyway. Madden received a letter in the same post indicating Palmerston's decision. Palmerston then informed Madden that he saw no basis for Madden's doubts concerning Schenley's integrity. Furthermore, he added the following:

It was unnecessary for me to enter into the particulars of these disagreements, and I have only to remark that the letters in question afford proofs, that if public officers are determined to differ they never can be at a loss for subjects of difference but that such a determination to waste in groundless disputes that time which ought to be employed in the public service, indicates an imperfect understanding of the nature of official duties.[114]

A man named James Kennedy reached Cuba at about the same time as this dispute was still rumbling. Kennedy arrived to take up a senior post on the Integration Commission. His arrival meant that Madden lost whatever status he had held on the Integration Commission - including the good financial remuneration which went with his position. Losing his position in this manner was a public slap in the face for Madden. Of course, Madden was aware that he was likely to lose this latest job of his at some stage. What hurt him most however was that he had really believed Palmerston would show the door to Schenley rather than him; he had even been hopeful that this would have happened before he was forced to resign from the job himself.

No man who was conscious of the reality of his intentions, (he wrote to Palmerston), could feel more profound regret than I do under your censure, and that censure, my Lord, I could have escaped had I chosen to expose Mr. Jackson...by calling on that gentleman to declare to your Lordship what circumstance had come to his knowledge respecting the attestation of the person who is a footman of Mr. Schenley and has been described to your lordship as his special messenger. It, however, only remains for me to bow to your Lordship's decision in respectful silence and I do so, my Lord, with a trust in a higher influence than any other I can hope in - that time and circumstances will bring the real merits of those subjects of complaint to your Lordship's knowledge - understated as they were by me throughout, tho' too often I confess at a length inexcusable and too plausibly replied to by a gentleman so experienced as Mr. Schenley in these defensive exercises to leave me much hope by any simple means to uphold the singleness of my views...I am fully assured my conduct will meet with justice at your Lordship's hands.[115]

That was the end of the argument for the time being. A few years later, however, Palmerston may well have asked himself if he had made the right decision on that occasion. By then, Schenley was himself under suspicion of being involved in the slave-trade. The evidence against Schenley was very strong and the matter so grave that Palmerston was obliged to set up an enquiry into Schenley's business dealings, in particular as relating to the fate of six black men who had been working for him and whom Schenley claimed to have secured their freedom for them. Kennedy, who conducted the investigation found the truth of the matter to be very different, however. He concluded that Schenley had ignored the advice of people such as Maclean, Madden and others, and had instead followed the example of other colonial figures such as British Consul Tolmé, who bought and sold slaves instead of hiring servants as was permitted by law. "My investigation leads me to the conclusion that the blacks who worked for Schenley were kept as slaves by him and were unfortunately kept in this harsh and enslaved condition from the very first day of their arrival on the island." The loss of his position on the International Commission meant that Madden's annual income was now reduced by the enormous sum of 650 pounds a year. Although his salary was now halved, he still had enough money coming in from his main job as Warden to the freed African slaves - to get by, and he continued to remain on very friendly terms with the Colonial Office. In fact, Madden was only in this post a short while when he received much praise from Lord Glenelg regarding a plan he (Madden) had drawn up to look after the welfare of slaves that had been confiscated by the International Commission. Glenelg also praised Madden's actions in caring for an abandoned blind boy who had been left in Madden's care and instructed Madden to continue caring for the boy, the costs of which would be paid for by the British government. April, 1838 saw Glenelg sending Madden another congratulatory note regarding how efficiently the Irishman had handled a controversy concerning a large amount of African people that had been discovered aboard a schooner engaged in slave-trading. Glenelg's replacement as Secretary of State to the Colonies, Lord John Russell, continued in this vein, ignoring the complaints of one Doctor MacLean in relation to Madden and heaping high praise on the Irishman and his:

> ...diligent and unstinting efforts to oversee the primary tasks of his mission in Havana and the improvement of the island's social conditions generally.

Madden was still living on the island when Tacon lost his job and was replaced as Captain-General by a man named Espeleta. This new official turned out to be a champion of the slave-traders and as stubborn and unyielding as anyone who had preceded him. While it was a hopeless case really, Madden still did his best to bring Espeleta around to his way of thinking. He alerted him to the six major slave-markets then operating in the vicinity of Havana. The one located on the *Paseo Milita* was the primary focal point for slave-trading. A special stand was set up here for any white slave traders who wished to view the entire slave-market. It was always in early-evening by the time that the traders finished their supper and the majority of the visitors came to view the slaves. And it was a rare evening that some type of exhibition or public spectacle wasn't organised – whether this involved the male slaves in their loincloths or the female slaves being paraded back and forth in their tattered and multi-coloured cotton clothes.[116] Madden made certain to inform Espeleta of just how easy it was for the slave-ships to unload their cargoes in the port of Havana. The Captain-General considered Madden's comments as the mad ramblings of a British conscience, however and the good doctor fared little better in his dealings with Nicholas P. Trist, the American Consul to Cuba, a man who favoured the take-over of both Texas and Cuba with a view to expanding the slave-trading territory under U.S. control. He was normally inhospitable to Madden's entreaties and would respond to Madden's complaints by simply denying that that his government had any involvement with the slave-trade at all. "We know that the bozos are arriving here every single day", (Madden would inform him) "but the Integration Commission do not have the power to do anything about this immoral trade in human cargo. The Spaniards continually circumvent the law and if the British vessels don't discover the slaves while they are still on the open sea they have no authority whatsoever."

The only response Madden ever received from Trist was an admonishment which went something along the lines of "Is that so? Well, you shall have to make sure that the British vessels are more vigilant then, won't you?" The truth of the matter was that Trist himself was a strong supporter of the slave-trade and actually did everything that he could to sustain the trade and put as many barriers as he could in the way of the Anti-Slavery Commission. The likes of Madden disgusted Trist. He considered lobbyists such as Madden to be individuals who were more interested in promoting their own personal and political interests and ensuring that they had a group of followers – then anything else. To the American Secretary of

State, Trist described Madden in the following derogatory terms:

> A low-class mongrel of a person – a bigot and a fanatic who has some of the traits of a "man of the world" mixed up in his character somewhere; this combination has, over time, allowed him to secure a position of minor importance, one where he has been able to influence some people with relative ease. He invents travel books and other odd types of books, all of which presumably find a following amongst the Irish of New York, a crowd he infiltrated some years ago. There is no doubt that he hates me with a passion. For him to hate me; all he needs to do is categorise me as a "trader in human meat" from Virginia...[117]

Madden was never one to back off too easily, however, and he took the battle to Trist nonetheless. The next time he visited the U.S. he published an open letter criticising Trist and sent it to William Ellery Canning, the leader of the Unitarians in Boston, and a man who had made the abolition of slavery a part of his life's work. In that letter which was a full thirty-two pages long - he exposed the arrogant way that Trist had behaved in his job, his negligence with regard to what he was employed to do and the scandalous way he was actually contributing to the institution of slavery in Cuba. He concluded this open letter by saying:

> ...whatever the exact truth is concerning the company he keeps or the integrity of his moral principles, one thing is for sure - that Mr. N.F. Trist's role as American representative to the island of Cuba is of little benefit either to the American people or to the human race generally.[118]

Shortly after Madden wrote this letter, Trist was actually removed from his post because of his political leanings (Democrat) and the doubts raised concerning his integrity. Outside of Ireland Madden's name would become most widely-known in relation to one particular slave-ship, however – the

Amistad. In actual fact, Madden acted as the chief witness in this, the well-known of all American legal cases ever taken in relation to the Slavery issue. The case of the *Amistad* received widespread coverage in the world press, in August, 1839. It involved a revolt aboard a schooner where the majority of the ship's white passengers and crew were also murdered. American war-ships were ordered in pursuit of this vessel and soon caught up with the schooner. J.R. Gedney, the captain of the *Washington* which pursued the schooner then sent one of his officers aboard where he found a big crowd of black men and two Spaniards named Pedro Montes and Joe Ruiz. One of the Spaniards claimed that he was the owner of the black men and requested protection. Gedney took possession of the schooner and sailed it into the port of New London. The local District Court judge and the Marshall of Connecticut then conducted an in-depth investigation of exactly what had happened aboard the Washington. They questioned the two Spaniards and a Creole cabin-boy named Antonio - under oath - about the matter and their investigations uncovered the following information.

The schooner was named the *Amistad*[119] and she had been journeying from Havana to Principe, a journey of about three hundred miles in total. The Spaniards claimed to have been at sea for just four days when the black slaves had revolted one night, killing the captain and the mulatto cook in the process. Two sailors, including the man in charge of steering the ship, left on a smaller boat and headed ashore. This left just two white men on board the *Amistad*, the Spaniards Montes and Ruiz, who were imprisoned in the ship's hold overnight. The next day Montes was instructed to steer the ship in the direction of Africa. Montes did as instructed during the day and steered the ship in the direction of the African coast. At night, however - when the absence of the sun made their general direction unclear - Montes guided the ship in the opposite direction so that they were actually going back the way that they had come again. They were going forward and back like this for a few days in the Bahamas Channel, on occasion passing close to the islands themselves. The black men would not allow the ship to dock anywhere however and once, when they were very close to Long Island, they forced the ship away from shore again. The Spaniards, meantime, were just hoping that they would be spotted by a warship that would pull alongside and set them free. On their initial arrival in the U.S., no-one came forward to speak on behalf of the Africans and there was no no-one amongst their group who could speak English. The District Justice made no effort to interview the Africans and this group of thirty-eight people was sent forward for trial at the Circuit Court in Hartford, Connecticut. They were all charged with murder at sea and the cabin-boy Antonio and four small children were called as witnesses. The blacks, who stated that they were all members of the Medi tribe from Sierra Leone, were all sent to Newhaven prison, Connecticut. Originally abducted by the slave-traders in Sierra Leone, the Africans had endured a torturous sea-journey before being transported to Havana in a Portuguese vessel. It was in Havana that all of the slaves were fitted with fetters, sold to Montes and Ruiz, and then transferred to the *Amistad*, where they were shackled again to the lower deck. It was while they were below deck that they managed to free themselves and from that point on, the story had progressed as related by Montes and Ruiz.

Madden was physically exhausted after the three-and-a-half years spent in Cuba. He asked for six months holidays and his request was granted. He was just on the point of leaving Cuba, in fact, when he heard about the *Amistad* controversy. Instead of returning to England as he had originally planned and - acting against the advice of his superiors - Madden immediately set out for the United States. On departure, he sent a farewell letter to Espeleta rather than being forced to say goodbye to him in person and having to reveal any of his future plans. Madden's initial view of the *Amistad* case was that the courts would have to rule whether those accused of piracy and murder were to classified as Latinos or as Bozals - i.e. blacks who had already been classified as legally-held slaves in Cuba. The central issue that need resolving was whether the accused had been taken from Africa and sold at the slave-markets of the outskirts of Havana only recently or whether they had really been held captive outside of Africa for a long period prior to the events on the *Amistad*. If the latter scenario were true and Montes had bought three of the slaves - and Ruiz the other fifty (a small girl amongst them) - then Madden felt that he would legally be able to prove that the blacks ought be considered as Bozals. Madden was also willing to make the legal case that the blacks had been held captive illegally anyway, because their detention was in breach of Spanish law under which they should have been considered as free citizens. In addition to this, the type of passports used by the traders were fraudulent - or "trespasso." Under Spanish law the blacks had exactly the same right to object to their abduction as English or American citizens would have had, had they been abducted by a group of pirates. Madden also believed that the blacks had a good case based on the fact that the majority of them were under twenty years of age and could not therefore be legally kept as slaves according to Spanish law. Neither could they suffer any punishment for resisting attempts to force them into slavery according to the same law.

Madden travelled from Havana to Boston on an American ship transporting molasses. He was the only passenger aboard and the journey was an unpleasant one. He believed from an early stage in the journey that the ship's captain also worked as a slave-trader and the captain and crew responded to this by refusing to speak to Madden whenever they passed him on deck. On arrival in New York Madden visited the Lewis Tappan store on Hanover Square. En route to this store he purchased a Bowie knife with the inscription "Death to Abolition" written across its handle. He had in his possession a letter of introduction from the famous abolitionist William Lloyd Garrison in which Harrison had described Madden's mission in America as one of "unmasking" Consul Trist - (amongst others) - for the person he really was. Tappan welcomed Madden with open arms and the Irishman was overjoyed to finally have the opportunity of meeting this middle-aged merchant who, in addition to being a religious man, was then considered the embodiment of abolitionism by many of the U.S. public. The various newspaper reports about the *Amistad* case had only recently appeared in the American press and had re-invigorated the struggle for the abolitionist cause in Tappan's heart. He had already set up a fund-raising and publicity campaign on behalf of the blacks involved in the *Amistad* case and had also hired a team of lawyers to argue their case. Tappan had no confidence in the then American President, Martin Van Buren, however. He thought it very unlikely that Van Buren - who had the reputation of being the cleverest and most conniving politician in America - would grant the blacks their freedom, particularly if such a move affected his vote in the upcoming election. This was the same politician of whom Davy Crockett had said:

> ...that he'd chew a piece of meat in one side of his mouth, a piece of bread in the other and a piece of cabbage in between; he'd chew the different foods and then swallow the lot without mixing any of them together.[120]

Undaunted, Madden decided that he would pay Van Buren a visit at some stage, anyway. Madden and Tappan must have made strange bed-fellows in New York city. The American businessman with the Puritan upbringing who was then a deacon of the Broadway Tabernacle and the Catholic Irishman with his multiple interests in medicine, travel and administration. The two men would spend a number of days together, walking through the streets of New York and discussing the Abolitionist issue in some depth. Tappan, for his part, did not consider Madden an overly-religious man. The way he saw it, Madden was a reasonably open-minded man who liked his glass of wine and was not averse to teasing him regarding his own abstemiousness.

What Madden thought of Tappan is not clear as he left no account of this in his papers but the two men clearly enjoyed one another's company and admired one another's sense of humanity and idealism. Madden presented Tappan with a copy of the spiritual book *Breaths of Prayer* – which had then been recently published - and Tappan would later claim that he would never have associated the man he knew with the author of this same book! His visit to New York at an end, Madden travelled onto Newhaven after this stop-over so as to speak with the African prisoners there. He was unable to remain in the U.S. for the trial of the *Amistad* crew but he did what he could to help their cause by organising a mock trial where he himself gave his view of the case as based on the evidence then in the public domain, evidence that was frequently sympathetic to the plight of the imprisoned men.

His mock-trial took place in the City Court of Newhaven before Judge Andrew T. Judson and attracted a large crowd of interested spectators, some of whom were violently opposed to the Abolitionist cause. Madden clearly impressed his audience during this trial event however as the newspapers of this time refer to him as a "high representative of a high culture…" He gave his testimony "…with the skill of a man long experienced in giving and taking testimony" and his arguments that were presented in a manner that was both gentle yet persuasive, served to bring many members of the public over to his point of view. The mock-trial concluded Madden returned to New York again in the company of Tappan. On their return journey by ferry to the Big Apple, Tappan and he planned various strategies to ensure that the slaves might have a reasonable chance of success in the forthcoming trial.

Madden still felt it might be worthwhile calling on Van Buren although he was inclined to agree with Tappan that efforts at lobbying this Machiavellian operator were likely to be a complete waste of time. He also decided to lobby Henry Stephen Fox, the British representative in Washington on behalf of the *Amistad's* crew. One unnamed source, cited in William A. Owens *Slave Mutiny* (1953), ascribes the following statement to Madden, as issued by him at this juncture:

And when I return to England I will write a report about these events for the Queen. I have no doubt that she will order a strong message to be sent to Van Buren. When England and Spain are vying with one another in the near future, Van Buren will soon find out which is the stronger of the two.[121]

Madden would fulfil every promise that he made at this juncture in relation to preparations for the upcoming trial. While in Washington, he passed on whatever information he had to Fox and he, in turn, passed this same information onto the American government in a letter where he enquired what the likely fate of the *Amistad* Africans would be. Madden then called on Van Buren himself and warned him that if the African slaves were sent back to Cuba, they would all be put to death. The President wasn't happy at all that Madden had decided to involved himself as a witness in the *Amistad* case and he left Madden under no illusions about how angry he was that such a contentious issue was being raised at election time. "I believed him", Madden said, "when he said that this was very awkward for him and so I did whatever little I could to make the issue even more awkward for him - as long as he handed over the black men." Madden had planned for a "battle" in this case and he advised his friends and supporters to drag the issue out as long as possible. As soon as they heard any word – (i.e. the most likely scenario was that the Africans would be sent back to Havana) - Madden's supporters were to inform the British Admiralty and the latter would ensure that one or two coasters intercepted the *Amistad* as it left New York. Madden's pessimism proved unfounded however. After two trials, the prisoners were set free and various Abolitionist supporters raised the necessary monies so that they could return to their home countries.

Subsequent to the trial, Madden was congratulated on all sides as his evidence had proved vital in securing the release of the prisoners, particularly in the first trial where the trail judge had based many of his arguments on Madden's contribution to the evidence. Lord John Russell praised Madden's dedication and energy in this case and when Madden subsequently visited the Foreign Office in London, he was thrilled to hear that an order had been (originally) been sent to Fox in Washington - to act as he saw fit in relation to this contentious case. An official communiqué had also been sent to Spain requesting that the Africans be repatriated. "The plight of these Africans had had a big effect on the then queen of England and the English populace generally."

It was Christmas, 1839, before Madden and Harriet were back in London and when they could see their son Forde again. Their other son, Thomas More, named after the renowned English Catholic Chancellor who had been martyred for his Catholic beliefs, accompanied them on the long sea voyage from Cuba. As frequently happened on long sea journeys of this era, the Maddens witnessed a few hair-raising incidents on the voyage back to Europe including a daring "rescue" in the middle of a very stormy Atlantic Sea. Just ten days out of New York, their mail-boat, the *Roscius* also came upon a commercial vessel – the *Scotia* – emitting distress signals. The crew of the mail boat made contact with the *Scotia*, which replied to them as follows: "We are half-drowned – we've shipped seventeen feet of water below deck." The captain of the *Roscius* sent a swift response where he told the *Scotia's* crew to hold steady until the gale had blown over and he would take the crew aboard his ship. He also instructed them to take to their life-rafts as soon as they felt able to do so.

> *A cheer from the people of the sinking vessel followed - such a thrilling cry as men in the extremest peril suddenly restored to hope alone could utter. An effort was made to near us, but the water-logged vessel was utterly unmanageable; she pitched heavily, as if she would have gone down headlong; the sea swept over her, and as she rose, it poured through her broken parts. Her mizen mast and the main-top-gallant masts had been cut away to ease her, and the prop deck, where the crew were congregated, seemed the only place of safety left them.*

In attempting to approach, she came staggering down on us, and we were compelled to escape out of her way. The sea was very heavy. We again lay to about a mile from the Scotia. Night came on, and the disabled vessel was lost sight of. [122]

The *Roscius* remained where it was throughout the night its' 86 passengers flung this way and that, with the power of the ferocious gale. About seven o'clock the following morning they heard shouts from the direction of the *Scotia* and two life-rafts – containing the ship's captain and crew – made their way through the huge waves. The crew of the sinking vessel were exhausted and in a state of shock by the time they were dragged aboard the mail-boat. The *Roscius* then continued on her onward journey although it was sometime before the gales receded. Madden would spend the couple of days immediately after this incident composing an epic poem in recollection of it.

CHAPTER 6
MADDEN'S RELIGIOUS "CONVERSION"

As outlined in the previous chapter, Madden had a very poor opinion of Cuba's social and political structures and the country's administration generally. His impression of the Christian Churches in Cuba, whether Catholic or Protestant, was little better, particularly as relating to these Churches acquiescence in activities that were both immoral and extremely unjust. In spite of this, however, it was actually during their sojourn in Cuba that both Madden and his wife underwent a religious conversion that would have a profound influence on the rest of their lives. In June, 1838 Madden sent a letter to his sister Lizzie, in Dublin, informing her that – within the space of just a few days – he would lose his £650 pounds a year job on the Integration Commission. This was the bad news, he told her. He had some other news, however, which would make her very happy, he added. On the occasion that he had last written to her, he had been unsure as to whether he subscribed to any particular religious belief. Indeed, for sixteen years previous to this, he had never been sure as to whether he felt any real religious or spiritual sentiment at all. Now however, he could confirm that he had discovered a new-found sense of faith, a faith in the absence of which there was no real peace to be found – either in the this world, or the next. Lizzie Cogan must have been in a bit of daze as she read this "bolt-out-of-the-blue" of a letter which included Madden's in-depth descriptions of "the mysteries and great miracles" which now consoled him. Prior to this, it had been his habit to dismiss any phenomenon for which he could find no rational and obvious explanation. He understood now, however, that this attitude of his had been an unreasonable one:

> *I live, move, and have a being,* (he said), *but what do I know of life or the mystery of the first movement of its breath in the breast of man, or the marvel of the last flutter of it at the end of that existence? This mystery of life and death is even beyond my comprehension. Life and death are facts which cannot be doubted and denied; reason is compelled to assent to them and yet cannot solve the mysteries of their origin, their power and their universal law.*[123]

He outlined to Lizzie how it was now his firm belief that the sooner one sacrificed oneself in true humility, the sooner God revealed Himself to us. Humanity possessed an intellect that was superior to that of the mere brute and it was in human nature to search for that which was permanent and eternal in nature. The sooner one came to a realisation and an acceptance of this reality, the sooner the human being in search of truth moved in the direction of Christ. Christ was the teacher whose message was always the most clear. The clarity of his teachings spoke for themselves. Madden went on to list the errors which he perceived as identifiable in natural religion and the theism then very prevalent in society. While he himself may have had a stronger inclination towards a similarly theistic worldview at one point – as opposed to the Catholicism which he had inherited from the cradle – his rational nature had now demonstrated to him the superiority of Christianity over other belief systems.

> *...to it turned those who are sickened with the legends of the*

Talmud, the fables of the Koran; unsatisfied with all the ethics of pagan philosophy...and weary of all the hashings up of old philosophy, of the new-fangled systems of infidelity of Germany, France and England.[124]

The person whose spiritual search was genuine would nearly always come to Christ – whether sooner or later - in Madden's view:

I say eventually, for these arguments occurred to me years ago: nay I even wrote them down and tried to force myself to believe them, and I could not for reason, faith and grace is not the order but grace first that faith may follow, and reason last, that the power of God may be shown and the weakness of man may find mercy made manifest to it.[125]

Madden's travels in the Holy Land years earlier had done little to aid his search for a deeper spirituality and he now understood more clearly why this had then been the case:

I was about to engage in a spiritual business, I prayed to be enabled to ascertain the truth as if the mind was all that needed help and the heart none; I did not humble my heart before God and look upon my reason except as a medium through which the light of the Great Father of Spirits might manifest itself to me. I read my Bible more as a critic than a Christian enquirer searching after the divine truth.[126]

Whatever it's exact nature or circumstance, the religious conversion that Madden described in this letter occurred sometime during 1837, and would ensure that his Catholicism remained a strong source of spiritual strength to him for the remainder of his life. One immediate consequence of his new-found spirituality was a tendency to be overly-scrupulous. One of the first manifestations of this very scrupulous nature occurred when Madden asked a black man who worked as a cook in their household to help him destroy the (original) copy of his (Madden's) own work – the travel book entitled – *Travels in Turkey!*

> *This work which occupied me two years in writing, I found this day (22nd March, 1839), (he says, in a note which I found amongst his papers). It did not occupy me much above ten minutes in burning...And yet I liked the book better than any I ever wrote...The love of literature and not the glory of God's name, or the real good of the members of his Christ...induced me to write this book. The love of Christ and His Cross led me to burn it.*[127]

While this book was no literary masterpiece it certainly wasn't deserving of this type of treatment! It may well have been the case that Madden paid too much attention to a review of the book which had accused him of providing exaggerated descriptions of the various sights and incidents he had witnessed while on his Turkish journey and that he now felt guilty about certain aspects of the book - his criticisms of the Latinate community in Nazareth for instance.

Unsurprisingly, Madden would find it difficult to sustain this early burst of religious fervour during certain latter periods of his life. Six years later (1845), and living in Lisbon, he would write that his religious sentiments of old had weakened again and "that the sentiments of six years earlier had lost their practical influence." "Oh, my God," (he would add) "what miserable, inconstant, fickle creatures are men!" While his enthusiasm for spiritual matters may have waned from time to time in later decades, he would never lose faith in Catholicism or in its promulgation of the path to true happiness. While Madden's religious "conversion" was notable in itself, his wife Harriet's was even more so, especially as she had originally been baptised a Protestant. She became a practicing Catholic around the same time as her husband did, a decision she took despite her Protestant upbringing and the fact that she had expressed no very overt interest in Catholicism previous to this. Married to a Catholic as she was, Harriet would have had a good knowledge of Catholicism and would have been very aware of the differences between the two main Christian denominations as expressed by the majority of people in both Ireland and England. She would also have been very sensitive to the substantial barriers to interdenominational dialogue that had yet to be overcome.

Such barriers were reflected in an incident where Doctor Miley, the priest in charge of Dublin's Catholic Pro-Cathedral, had advised her young son Forde that it was not appropriate for him to pray with his mother – given that his mother was a Protestant! For her son to have done this would have been enough to have had Harriet excommunicated her from her own Church (Harriet knew), especially given that Dr. Miley had made the following comment on the then question of inter-denominational prayer: "I never tasted the gall of error till then." Madden was diplomatic enough to invent some new versions of various well-known prayers so that his entire household, whether Protestant or Catholic, could pray together - and this put an end to the worst of any such difficulties. Harriet's (apparently) sudden conversion to Catholicism did coincide with a critical event that occurred in her own life however, an illness which Madden details in a number of letters that he sent to Harriet's sister Sophie, letters written at approximately the same time that he was writing to his own sister Lizzie Cogan and describing his own religious conversion. Harriet had been extremely sick for some time, an illness which Madden had diagnosed as a chronic inflammation of the spine.

While this ailment undoubtedly caused Harriet a good deal of physical suffering there was no way that this illness affected Harriet's mental capacities in any way - although Madden suspected that people would say as much when they heard that she had converted to Catholicism. Whether her physical sufferings were an aggravating factor or not, Harriet certainly seems to have suffered some type of depression or mental breakdown at this period as indicated by her tendency to:

> ...still labour under the impression of a phantasm of the mind in its disordered state, or the spectral illusion of vision temporarily impaired in the gloom of the sick chamber, being a reality and no delusion, long after all the causes that might have transpired to decide the senses ceased to be in operation.[128]

Madden's personal papers for this period indicate that Harriet witnessed (or thought she witnessed) some sort of a vision at this juncture. Unfortunately, Madden never left us any detailed description of what this vision might have consisted of other than to say that it involved "extraordinary things." His papers also indicate that both he and Harriet believed these events to have been supernatural in nature and, as a consequence, they both felt obliged to keep the details of what had they had witnessed private. Madden didn't even tell his sister about Harriet's "vision", this despite the fact that both she and Harriet were very close friends. He only (ever) told one other person about this strange event and (although it is never made clear) – this person is assumed to have been the Franciscan Dom Pedro, who welcomed Harriet into the Catholic Church and baptised her. Madden referred to this "event" as witnessed by Harriet as "a signal manifestation of the divine mercy miraculously wrought," although Harriet never actually mentioned it to him until a few months after it had occurred. It was at this point that Harriet said to him that she had had a strong feeling while sick and after this "supernatural" event that it ought to be a Catholic priest who should anoint her with the holy oils that were part of the Last Rites and provide her with spiritual guidance from then on. She wanted someone to teach her more about the meaning of Catholicism and the teachings of the Catholic Church. It was only then, "when she had already become a member of the Catholic Church of her own accord, that, I myself provided her with whatever useful material that I had relating to Catholicism and put her in touch with whoever might spiritually advise her as appropriate. I hardly need to tell anyone that I would never seek to impose my own religious beliefs on Harriet. We were married for a full nine years before we ever even discussed religious questions in any great seriousness."

This "event" was such a defining moment in the Maddens' lives that they decided to prepare two testimonies or "manuscripts" both to express their gratitude to God, and to leave as a permanent reminder for their families. The priest blessed these manuscripts or books of thank-you prayers and Madden sent copies of them onto Sophie. They were also folded into miniature form and were placed in a small silk pouch which Harriet wore as a necklace from then on – as a memento of the All-Merciful. Madden wrote to Sophie then and said to her that he knew she would read these manuscripts very carefully – he also asked her the following:

What is your impression of the manuscript? Do you find them of interest? Possibly not. Or do you think I am too innocent and gullible a person? No. I don't believe so. I hope you wouldn't consider me too gullible a person given my temperament, my professional experience and my experience of life generally.[129]

He sent a copy of the third manuscript to Sophie also. This consisted of a series of written questions which he had put to Harriet so that any false rumours concerning her conversion could be quashed at a future date. He waited a full year-and-a-half before he handed these questions to Harriet so that she was in the full of her health again and so that she had more time to reflect on her decision.

Here you go with the questions that I posed to Harriet and her responses. Her responses are provided verbatim - in her own word i.e. without input from any priest or layman – and no hint that either of us (i.e. Harriet or myself) were "brainwashed" in any way.[130]

Sophie was both surprised and somewhat put out that Harriet had become a Catholic without informing her beforehand. She wrote a letter to her and, as she was still sick, she asked Harriet's husband to read out this letter to her and to note down her answers. As was usual for him, Madden wrote a long and somewhat repetitive letter where he outlined the various issues and stages in relation to Harriet's conversion as he saw them. Sophie knew him well enough to know that he would be scrupulously honest in his recollection of such matters.

Your letter was read by me with deep attention and a strong sense of its sober interest. I fully appreciate the propriety of your observations, their plain sound sense, the tolerant spirit evinced in them, the anxiety naturally shown for the eternal welfare of a sister, and the danger of arriving at a wrong result in a matter of such awful moment as a change in one's religion, and not least worthy of notice the indulgence with which the motives for that change are treated notwithstanding the firmness of your attachment to the religion you profess, in which you were brought up, in whose communion your father and your mother lived and died. To leave a Church possessed of great worldly advantages, for one neither popular nor powerful, is a step that needs indulgence. Your religion is that of the State, strong in power, powerful in wealth, popular in public opinion, high and palmy in its prosperity, plumed up in the trappings taken from the hearse of the establishment that preceded it...[131]

Why did Harriet take this particular step? Was it because of her own unusual experience, an experience which had also raised doubts in some peoples minds regarding her husband – i.e. that he was an overly-naive or incredulous person or that he was capable of taking advantage of other people's naivety or incredulity. One thing was certain and this was acknowledged by anybody who knew Harriet - she was incapable of telling a lie. While, in theory, it could be argued that her sickness had impaired her judgement in some way or other, or that she was unduly influenced by Madden in relation to religious matters, the reality was quite different. Harriet was gentle and modest in manner but she also possessed:

> ...a strong perception of moral truth and a tolerable share of that firmness of character which is generally the concomitant of a clear view of what is right and good and plain commonsense.[132]

Madden finished his letter by stating that he had related the events which had taken place with absolute accuracy and with a truthfulness that would allow him to meet his Maker at that very instant if such a thing occurred. Madden also kept amongst his papers a copy of another letter which he had sent to Sophie Elmslie concerning her sister's conversion. While Sophie was satisfied that Harriet had converted with the best intentions, she seems to have had her doubts about the fundamentals of her sister's decision, particularly given the fact that Sophie considered the Catholic Church mistaken regarding the meaning of Transubstantiation and the belief concerning Christ's True Presence in the Sacrament of the Eucharist. Madden was well aware of where this debate by written correspondence was leading. "If we are mistaken," he said, "the power which converted Harriet to Catholicism could not have from the Heavens." In other words, if Harriet's conversion was an error of faith, it was a much more serious issue than that of simply changing from one Christian faith to another. It would, in effect, involve a move away from the certainty of truth to darkness and superstition.

Madden brought up this discussion by intimating that Sophie herself might not be as certain of her life's mission as she may have thought. Did she remember the statement of Dr.

Marsh, one of Protestantism's greatest defenders who argued that "though we believe that we are right, we admit that we may possibly be wrong. Though we believe others are wrong, we admit that we are ourselves possibly wrong." Did Sophie believe that the Scriptures went against the Catholic worldview? If that was so, Madden asked Sophie whether she could provide him with even one paragraph from Scripture that would affirm the Protestant teaching on the meaning of the Eucharist – as opposed to the eighteen proofs – "in the fullest plainest and most obvious sense establishing ours." He, for his part, was unable to find any reference in the Scriptures to the "substance" of Christ's body or the "form of Our Lord's blood." The words cited in Scripture were very clear and left no room for ambiguity: - "This is my body - This is my blood." Christ himself had spoken these words. The Gospel writers had put them on paper and the Church had interpreted these words according to their original and literal meaning, a meaning that he considered both enlightened and very clear.

Madden continued his letters in this vein, outlining the strong basis for the Catholic interpretation of Christian belief. As far as we know, his arguments had very little influence in the theological sense on Sophie's beliefs, albeit that she was certainly convinced of the sincerity and seriousness of his convictions. Madden was a staunch defender of the truths of Catholicism as he interpreted them, a fact reiterated by an anecdote which Madden related to Sophie in one of his letters - where he described a dispute he had had in the West Indies with a Protestant minister by the name of Norman. Madden noted a profound ignorance on the part of many Protestant publications at this juncture with regard to what Catholics actually believed. Consequently, he urged this Mr. Norman to read either Bossuet, Milner, Wiseman or the Catechism of the Council of Trent. By studying such writings, Norman could no longer base his opinions of Catholicism on "the pages of Methodist magazines, Calvinistic discourses, the polemical politics of religious newspapers and all the trash of the diatribes therein against the Roman

Catholic Religion." Norman had no intention of following Madden's advice however, having already confirmed for himself - based on his reading of many the previously-mentioned "religious newspapers" – that it was he who was saved and not Madden who was a member of the "Fallen Church." No amount of cajoling would persuade him otherwise and in one of his letters to Sophie, Madden described Norman's character as follows:

> ...vain of his virtues, conceited of the odour of sanctity in which he was held, and proud of his position in the evangelical world. It was lamentable to find out some much error being held in the belief that it was the truth, so much religiousness and blindness blended in the same individual. The blindness was not the result of gazing too boldly or too intently on the light of Christian knowledge, or of contemplating too incautiously the high truths of Christianity.[133]

In Madden's opinion, Mr. Norman was to be pitied because he was:

> ...simply in a state of mental darkness such as persons of limited intellect are very likely to fall into exposure to the contagion of speculative error and inability or indisposition to resist its influence.[134]

We don't know what Sophie made of this debate, as her responses haven't survived. All the indications are that Madden got the upper hand in his debate with Mr. Norman, however. Norman responded to Madden's request that he ought to read some of Catholicism's most influential writers by sending him a book entitled *True Religion*[135] in the post. Madden's response was to post the book back again with an accompanying acknowledgement that had a hint of sarcasm in its tone. He had read the book from start to finish, Madden said, and noted the numerous false statements made by its author in relation to the

Catholic religion. He hoped Mr. Norman felt as sorry for the book's poor author as he himself did, given the confused mish-mash of ridiculous claims that the author had posited. Madden also said that he was grateful to Mr. Norman for holding the sincerity of his (Madden's) personal beliefs in such high regard. The very fact that he had lent this book to him clearly indicated that Norman considered there to be nothing sarcastic or insulting within its covers. Clearly, Norman perceived there to be no offence inherent in such statements as "atheists, infidels, Jews, and Roman Catholics have the foundations of their belief and their error in the lusts of a depraved heart."

> *So you were right, (said, Madden) - in supposing I would be amused with this ludicrously trashy work...Had you thought otherwise, it is quite clear to me, in your charity, in the courtesy of a Christian gentleman, you never would have sent it to me. Therefore, accept my thanks for your good intentions towards me.*[136]

This theological skirmish strengthened Madden in his resolve to defend Catholicism, and he would never let any opportunity to do as much escape him in later years. This dispute with Mr. Norman was a good example of this defensive and combative trait in Madden, but it was not the only one. Prior to his departure from Cuba, Madden was again "manning the barricades" against another anti-Catholic assault. He had just translated *Poems Written in Slavery* (1840) and helped their author, Juan Francesco Manzano to get them published. Manzano was a Cuban black man on whose behalf Havana's literati had collected eight hundred dollars in order to secure his freedom from slavery. This writer, who bore the same name as another slave executed in 1844 for his part in the slave uprising of that year,[137] had, by a strange coincidence, actually died in the same year as the uprising also. Madden had been surprised come across Manzano reading Voltaire and downplaying any "negative influences" this writer might have in terms of an individual's religious belief. Reading Voltaire relaxed the mind, Manzano maintained, and he told Madden not to worry himself - that his (Manzano's) reading of Voltaire might not have any lasting influence on him. A worried Madden warned Manzano that the chameleon could blend in with the colour of its surroundings, and that such an animal analogy was very appropriate to the literary sphere also. In Madden's view, the reading of certain types of literature left the reader vulnerable to being influenced by certain ideologies and, worse still, entirely unaware that such ideologies had been absorbed into the mind-set or sensibility. Another reason that Madden was concerned as regards Manzano's reading habits was because he knew Manzano's education had been very rudimentary. He advised the Cuban of the importance of educating himself thoroughly on all aspects of the Church and its philosophy before reading those authors that were very hostile to it. It was necessary to read the Scriptures with humility and devotion, Madden said to him. Only by reading Christianity's sources could an individual come to a clear understanding of the reasons for Christianity's development. In Madden's view, it was much better to read authors such as Bercastel[138] than it was to read the philosophical musings of Voltaire. It was also important, Madden considered, that Manzano did not judge the nature of Catholicism according to the standards of its clergy, whether these clergy were Cuban or of any other nationality. Madden considered his advice to be sensible in nature - since spirituality was ultimately the most important aspect of any human being's life.

Madden kept himself busy during the holidays with his work on the Anti-Slavery front. He was under no illusion about the enormous task that faced him in trying to interest the public in Britain and Ireland regarding the realities of the slave trade in Cuba. A letter he wrote to Joseph Sturge[139] at this time – a letter which is, in essence, a *cri-de-coeur* – shows how aware Madden was of the difficulties the Anti-Slavery campaign then faced with regard to getting the issue publicised:

> I don't know that anything has been published of the horrors of slavery that comes up to anything like the hardships of that system in Cuba. In God's name, now that the apprenticeship has broken down in our Colonies, do turn your attention to that subject. I look upon you as the man destined to lead our cause. Most assuredly never was there one that needed so much all the efforts that can be made for it...You have seen nothing that can give you an adequate idea of the amount of murder arising in Cuba...and yet our Consuls, our merchants, our officers who eat and drink with these planters and pay them holiday visits to those hells upon earth, the sugar estates, come away enamoured of Spanish slavery and of Spanish law in slave colonies, think that because the law is good, it is carried into execution and because Negro children are found in Spanish families in towns and cities, the negro labourers on the estates are worked with moderation and kindly treated...I am heartsick of what I have seen and I would be hopeless if my reliance was not in God, for I see nothing in the present means of meeting the evil...[140]

Madden's determination to highlight the Slavery issue was also in evidence when he presented Daniel O'Connell with a set of chains that had been used to shackle a group of slaves on a ship near the Gold Coast. He included a letter with the chains, part of which went as follows:

> To bring chains to Ireland (he says) is like carrying coals to Newcastle, and to offer them to you, whose employment for the last thirty years has been the breaking of them, is perhaps a Cuban compliment. I don't ask you to wear them on account of the love I bear to Cuba or you to slaves - but I do pray you to shake them in the ears of the English people, and to stir their hearts if it be possible and move them to put a stop to the work of rapine that goes on in Africa and Cuba in the face of agents of the British government and in the teeth of treaties entered into for the suppression of this most prosperous and daily improving trade.[141]

O'Connell was a great man in Aubrey de Vere's[142] opinion, a man whose largesse and humanity was so great that it was difficult to believe that he only had one heart, the same as every other man. The problems of the world were always of concern to him and there was no aspect of human suffering that he would turn away from or ignore. De Vere's assessment of O'Connell was one which Madden would have agreed with, to a large extent. Madden held O'Connell in very high regard as an anti-Slavery advocate, considering him to be in the same category as Thomas Clarkson[143], Thomas Fowell Buxton[144] and Sturge. Madden, O'Connell and Richard D. Webb[145] were chosen as the Irish delegation to the World Anti-Slavery Convention[146] that was organised in London in June, 1840. Their delegation was also elected to represent the Iberian Anti-Slavery Association at an international meeting in Paris in 1842.

This same Association was disheartened to learn that some of the Irish diaspora based in Pottsville, Pennsylvania were refusing to give any backing to their cause and was even casting aspersions on the Abolitionist petition that had been sent to them from Ireland. Sixty thousand people signed this Anti-Slavery petition, O'Connell, Madden and Father Theobald Matthew[147] amongst them. That these various states-people actually signed the petition was officially confirmed at the time so that any rumours to the effect that O'Connell had become lukewarm on the Anti-Slavery issue could be quashed. Madden was to exact a sweet revenge on those Irish-Americans who opposed the petition at a later date when he would refer to the "trumpery resolutions" that had been issued from Pottsville and would refer to the people who had issued them as "recreants to the cause of liberty and unworthy of being descendants of the Emerald Isle." This was also Tom Moore's view, an artist whose sister helped Madden gather together a range of sources for his history of the United Irishmen. She wrote to Tom on Madden's behalf and he replied saying that Madden's anger upon his return from Cuba came as no surprise to him:

...more especially against those fellow-countrymen of ours, and fellow Catholics, who by their advocacy of slavery bring so much disgrace on their country and their creed.[148]

A few years prior to this correspondence Madden had written to the Irish bishops asking them to promulgate a recent pronouncement criticising the Slave-trafficking that had been issued by the Pope.[149] The Anti-Slavery Association also advised Madden to write to all of the parish priests in Ireland in addition to the bishops, a tactic aimed at pressurising the stubborn Irish in America, in particular. In America, the then epicentre of the slave trade, some bishops and priests still taught that slavery was permissible and slave traders were allowed to frequent the Sacraments without censure. Some of the Catholic aristocracy in the U.S. were even involved in the purchase and imprisonment of slaves at this juncture.

The necessity to abolish slavery and - in the process - remove this stain on the character of Catholicism was crucial in Madden's opinion. The answer he received in relation to his various entreaties was not a good one, however. The attitude of the then bishops as regards the slavery issue was similar to the stand taken by Lucas, the editor of the *Tablet*, a man who had no time for Madden or his views. Lucas believed that Madden had misinterpreted the Church's teaching and blamed him for naively giving grist to the prejudiced view of Catholicism then prevalent amongst many Protestants. According to Lucas, Madden had misinterpreted the Catholic position because he hadn't understood the distinction between slave trafficking and the keeping of slaves! Lucas' view was that the Church did not have any inherent objection to the keeping of slaves *per se*, but that it prohibited the deliberate stealing/abduction of people in the same way that it prohibited the stealing of goods. It did not permit the mental or physical abuse of slaves either of course but did not see fit to publicly criticise every manifestation of slavery, an institution that was then still very widespread in many Western European countries. Lucas continued as follows:

> *What the Church did was different, and was far more effectual for the purposes of charity, than all this modern fanaticism of which we hear so much. It first, indeed, taught slaves the duty of obedience...And then, also, as the masters became Christians, the Church taught them the duty of their state, taught them to be placable and merciful to their slaves...And in this way the Roman slavery was first mitigated, and finally abolished by the Church...*[150]

As regards *Rescript 1839*, he explained that it did not include any condemnation of slavery. In fact, it didn't include any reference to the legality of slavery or otherwise at all - or any reference to the idea then current in certain racist circles that slavery was a consequence of the societal status into which certain human beings were born. Given these types of reviews, it is unlikely that Madden's writings on the question of slavery would have been read by many upper-class Irishmen at this juncture or that they would have had a great influence on their thinking in relation to the Slavery issue. Many parts of Ireland were still quite rural and insular and awareness of world affairs such as the Slavery issue would only have been prevalent amongst that small societal elite with access to newspapers and foreign travel. In addition to this, the vast majority of the Irish people suffered huge social problems of their own, including widespread and extreme poverty and regular bouts of starvation. Madden would have first-hand experience of this reality himself.

One day, on one of his return visits to Dublin, Madden came across a man dying of starvation on one of the city's streets – an incident that prompted him to write a letter of protest to the Irish newspapers – a letter in which he criticised the paucity of services available for poor relief. He never let up on the Abolitionist front either as indicated by the following excerpt from his personal correspondence with a relative of his named William Powell:

You argued with me once in favour of slavery for which I hope God will forgive you, but I cannot. On what principle an honest Irishman, a slave himself, outlawed of his natural rights, oppressed and familiar with persecution, can advocate the bondage...of another race, made in God's image like himself...and differing from him only in the colour of his skin, I am wholly at a loss to conceive. And you told me some priests, I forget whom, sanctioned the opinion. I tell you, whoever they were, they were not fit to preach the gospel.[151]

The year 1854 found Madden chastising his good friend John Mitchell[152] because of the latter's indifference and hostility (even) towards the Abolitionist cause. Madden's personal papers reveal that he told Mitchell that he had always been able to address him as "My dear" previous to this – but that Mitchell's negative attitudes as expressed towards the Abolitionist cause – and Harriet Beecher-Stowe[153], in particular – were a source of shock and sorrow to him. Mitchell had also exhibited a dislike towards another member of the Abolitionist movement, the then well-known Irish Unitarian, James Haughton[154], referring to him as "an amiable monomaniac." It was unfortunate, Mitchell had uncharitably added, that someone hadn't snatched Haughton from his cradle when he was still a baby "thus saving a generation from a depressing and tiresome creature." Madden rebutted Mitchell in no uncertain terms for these comments, admonishing him – that if he (Mitchell) didn't think that slavery was incompatible with Christianity – then he really didn't know what he was talking about! Mitchell's problem was that he had no first-hand knowledge of the horrors the slave trade involved and the huge and immoral profits that unscrupulous criminals made from the misery and hard work of others:

I am, (Madden said), one of those abolitionists you so much disparage. Nevertheless, you never would have written one of these articles...had I been within reach of you...You would rather have suffered your right hand to be cut off than to have penned one of those articles which have pained your friends,

> brought disgrace on your country and given satisfaction only to its enemies and your own...An Irishman who has supported the cause he believes to be of his country, who has suffered for it, and is ready to endure more on its behalf, surely places himself in a false position when he assails the stout supporters of a cause which has for its chief object to win and secure the liberty of a vast portion of his fellow-creatures. Surely if Irishmen have been as "strangers in their own land" they should feel for those who are oppressed in any other and sympathise with the advocates of the weak and the wronged.[155]

Having said this, Madden admitted that Harriet Beecher-Stowe was not without her faults. While she may have been opposed to slavery, she was not averse to expressing anti-Catholic prejudice. Beecher-Stowe seemed to accept as "gospel" the words of one Liverpool-based Orange preacher who regularly launched into violent invectives against that city's Irish-Catholic population, Daniel O'Connell and against Catholic religious traditions such as the devotions to particular saints. Madden rebuked Beecher-Stowe saying that her support for this type of sectarian bigotry would undermine any attempt that she might make to bring American Catholics around to her Abolitionist viewpoint. Putting up with attacks from members of other religious denominations was bad enough. Having to endure attacks from newspapers with regard to your own religion was worse again. In March, 1852, *The Tablet*[156] published an indifferent review of Madden's *The Shrines and Sepulchres of the Old and New World* (1851) describing the book as:

> ...a kind of conglomerate, made up of extracts from a great variety of books on the subject of funeral rites and ceremonies interspersed with many scraps of original observation, picked up in the course of Mr. Madden's pilgrimages to diverse lands.[157]

The review implied that Madden had not brought any great analysis or expertise to bear on his subject area or brought much information that was new into the public sphere either. Although he was a faithful Catholic, the review stated, Madden had analysed his subject by displaying more of an interest in the literary aspect of things than in the religious. His writing on the subject of Kemble's[158] tomb was more eloquent than that concerning the sacred shrine of Loreto.[159] The review also alleged that Madden was careful to disguise his own Catholicity while attempting to provide "justifications" for certain traditional Catholic rituals which non-Catholics might have considered strange. "In one place at least" – (the anonymous reviewer, who may easily have been Lucas himself, said) – "we have noticed that this has betrayed him even into language absolutely heretical." This was a reference to the point in the book where Madden referred to "the most holy element *in which after a spiritual manner* as the Church teaches, the Body and Blood of the Lord are contained and co-existent." Another allegation the review made against Madden was that he was overly-sympathetic to the worldview of the Jansenists. That a newspaper such as *The Tablet* was virtually accusing Madden of heresy was bad enough. Worse was to follow in this same review, however:

> *We are quite aware, (said the critic), of the refuge a man of letters is apt to take in his ignorance of theology...He would probably declare with truth that he meant to be a Catholic, and that ex professo he only looked on these matters on the surface. All we say is, that in the case that a writer had better not talk of what his pursuits do not enable him to understand, or on questions of which he has not the means of appreciating the immeasureable importance, and where, without that rare gift of Catholic insight by which, in the case of the Saints, piety has sometimes compensated for lack of learning, such a writer can hardly open his lips without uttering heresy or giving occasion for scandal...*[160]

These last comments amounted to a slanderous and vicious attack on Madden's integrity in the opinion of one Doctor of Divinity from Castlerea, County Roscommon, and a priest named

Father Dermot O'Donovan, who sometimes corresponded with Madden. Cognisant of Madden's pugnacious nature, however, O'Donovan advised Madden to say as little as possible and refuse to "rise to the bait" by responding in anger. Another Church scholar also contacted Madden at this juncture to express his disgust at Lucas and the *Tablet's* attack on him. The whole thing was disgusting but the best thing that Madden could do was ignore the attacks completely.

Madden didn't listen to the advice of his friends, however. Instead, he wrote a letter to the *Tablet* defending himself, a letter that included a long memorandum from Dr. O'Donovan where he defended Madden from the allegations made against him. The *Tablet's* response to this letter was a "low" one. As a "cheap shot" it placed the letter and the memo in the section of the newspaper that discussed miscellanea, claiming the valuable pages could not be taken up with every controversial issue that happened to be "flavour of the month." The newspaper did admit that Dr. O'Donovan was a "high authority" in religious matters but also claimed that it had not implied that Madden was guilty of any heretical sentiments. The newspaper was willing to admit that perhaps it had misconstrued some of Madden's sentiments as elucidated in his writing but refused to apologise or withdraw any of its comments. Although he was quite upset by the whole affair, Madden did not pursue the matter any further.

CHAPTER 7
THE ANTI-SLAVERY CAMPAIGN ON THE GOLD COAST

Madden spent most of the year 1840 in Europe. His living expenses were paid during this period as his first holiday period from the Cuba post was extended while his suitability in relation to a specialised governmental post for which a vacancy was being considered. He spent as much of this free period in Dublin as he possibly could. He spent the Christmas of 1839 in the city staying in a house in 8 Rathmines Terrace, a house that was only a short distance from his sister Lizzy Cogan's house, where he normally lodged. He also spent a couple of nights with his friends, the Franciscans, at their monastery in Meelick - near Eyrecourt - on the Shannon, and praised them afterwards for their prowess in singing hymns - the *Salve Regina* - in particular. This particular Franciscan community were quite poor but the head-friar - or Friar-Guardian - exhibited great generosity to Madden.

The only small request the Friar-Guardian had of Madden was that he might be permitted to introduce him to the local people in the area. The Friar-Guardian got this opportunity one day when Madden was in the monastery's graveyard where he was noting down the names of his ancestors from the tombstones there. A funeral procession entered the graveyard, a number of keening women amongst the mourners. After the burial a group of elderly men went on their knees close to a particular tomb where they prayed in Irish for Madden's dead antecedents who had played a significant role in the original foundation of the monastery. The Friar-Guardian went over to this group and introduced them to Madden. The crowd attending the funeral then gathered around the doctor, shaking his hand and giving him a great welcome. They wished him a long and happy life. When Madden was leaving again on the following Sunday, many of the local country people who had attended the early-morning Mass were waiting at the door of the monastery to say goodbye to him. The elderly Friar-Guardian also wished Madden a fond farewell, praying that Madden, his children, and his children's children would always remain faithful to their ancestral beliefs - and that they would never lose the love of their country - a country for which many of their ancestors had sacrificed their lives and their property.

That summer, having obtained a certificate in the study of Latin from Dr. Murray, the Archbishop of Dublin, Madden travelled to the Middle East with his friend Sir Moses Montefiore where the two men intended to help refute the allegations concerning ritual murder as regularly directed at the Jews there. The controversy concerning alleged ritual murder had allegedly begun in Damascus when a Capuchin brother and his attendant had disappeared without trace one day - as if the very ground had opened and swallowed them up. The Jewish community in that city were blamed for their disappearance, the allegation being that the clerics had been ritually killed so that their blood could be mixed into the Easter cakes. The mob then took it upon itself to attack the city's Jewish quarter with rocks.

As the French Consul wished to court favour with the local Moslem population, he hired three of the meanest thugs in Damascus - or so it was claimed - to spread false allegations against the Jews and to initiate a pogrom against them. This mob captured many of the Jewish community, tortured them and destroyed their homes. The disorder then spread from

Damascus to Rhodes where the Jews were alleged to have killed a young boy - again for ritual purposes. This allegation incited further pogroms against the Jews in some of the other major cities in that region including in Tyre.[161]

Madden's good friend Moses Montefiore was a leading member of the Jewish community in Britain and he had set up a campaign to protect his co-religionists in the Middle East. A meeting was organised in relation to this issue for the residence of London's Lord Mayor, a meeting attended by (Daniel) O'Connell, John Blake Dillon[162] the poet Thomas Campbell[163] and a large number of other public figures. The meeting agreed to organise a mission that would travel to the Middle East and negotiate with Mohammed Ali, the then Moslem leader in Damascus. Madden was chosen as a member of the Mission, a selection that highlighted the esteem in which he - a Catholic activist - was held at this juncture – particularly with regard to the protection of the downtrodden in no matter what corner of the world. The important factor in Madden's selection was his acknowledged expertise in relation to the politics and the social conditions in the Middle East. By the time the Mission reached their destination, the ethnic tension had calmed again, an improved situation for which Madden gave Lord Palmerston most of the credit. Palmerston had ensured that a British naval squadron was situated close to the Egyptian coast, forcing the nefarious Governor Ali to order the Governor of Damascus to ensure that the persecution of the Jews was brought to an end and any prisoners that had been taken were released.

Madden himself had very little to do on this Mission by all accounts. He did pay the Pasha a visit, accompanied by the Consul-General, where he presented him with a testament from the Anti-Slavery Assembly praising him on the fact that he refused to allow his army officers pay their foot-soldiers in the form of slaves as opposed to money. The Pasha was delighted to hear that he was held in such high esteem in London and vowed - with God's help - to promote the Anti-Slavery cause as much as possible in the years ahead. Madden's attitude to Mohammed

Ali was quite different to his view of the Pasha. He considered him to be a corrupt individual. Bayonets could be seen everywhere on Alexandria's streets with the unfortunate Arabs being dragged out of their houses to join the army. Neither had the slave market seen any significant change since his previous visit to the region twelve years earlier. It was still packed with female slaves, the majority of whom were young girls under the age of fourteen. These girl-slaves could be purchased for sixty-five dollars each, just a third more than the cost of a child boy-slave. A grown-up woman sold as a slave for a price of eighty dollars. There were no white slaves on view but the rumour was that they too could be purchased if one knew where to ask for them.

These various observations were included in a series of essays that Madden sent home to the *Morning Herald*[164] and from which he later compiled the book *Egypt and Mohammed Ali* (1841), a book he dedicated to Beattie[165] and in which he included a reference to the "kind care of the magnanimous Victoria who had cast her compassionate regards upon those distant regions..." On the journey out to Egypt, Montefiore's Mission passed through Avignon where Madden went to see the Palace of the Avignon Popes in the company of Alderman David Wire who would later become Lord-Mayor of London. What Madden saw there horrified him - the dungeons, the judgement hall, the torture chamber - all of which set him considering the treacherous deeds to committed in that place under the auspices of the Inquisition.

The services of religion had given place to that of a military department. Is it any wonder that great judgements have been visited on our Church? Is it greatly to be wondered at, however greatly it is to be deplored, that heresies have sprung up on every hand around us? Is it not our bounden duty to acknowledge the scandals our own ministers have brought upon our Church, and to see rather with pity than with anger the separation of our brethren occasioned by these scandals...?[166]

Walking away from the place afterwards, Madden was speechless with shame. Wire, who was a Baptist, was the first of them to break the silence - "Yes, Madden", he said, "so what's your opinion of your religion now?" Madden's response was one which has often been cited before and since - and it was one which could not have been more timely - "I am absolutely certain, Wire", he said, "that it is a true religion, because, without enduring principles it could never have survived the many crimes committed in its name." Madden visited Cairo where he went to see the Pyramids for a second time. He was accompanied on this visit by Andrew Doyle the editor of *The Morning Chronicle*[167], the two of them were like schoolboys, stretching themselves lengthways across a number of stone coffins of the former Egyptian royalty. They got a great kick out of finding the spot on one gravestone where Madden had inscribed his name with coal almost fourteen years earlier, having initially engraved his initials using a penknife.

This pleasant tour of the Middle East came to an end more quickly than Madden would have wished and he returned to London and what was probably one of the most difficult periods in his life. A squadron of British cruisers had been keeping a close watch on the West African coast for some time prior to this, preventing those Spanish and Portuguese vessels who attempted to deliver materials to the slave camps or slave factories on the coast - items such as guns, gunpowder, maritime weapons wild tobacco, jewelry, beer and cheap clothes. Various groups in London decided to act as the exclusive suppliers of these materials instead - or so rumour had it. The factories which they supplied were actually bolstering the slave-trade since they allowed the slave-ships to drop anchor under the protection of their ports and fortifications, thus permitting the slave-ships to register as legal trading vessels. This process completely neutralized the effectiveness of the naval ships attempting to monitor the situation. A notice was issued to this effect, and it was as a consequence of this notice that a general enquiry was instigated by the Marquis of Normanby[168], the then

Secretary of State for the Colonies. A Spanish slave-ship, named the *Dos Amigos* was captured illegally trading on the Gold Coast, a ship that had as its supplier an English trader. When Lord Normanby's assistant, Lord John Russell[169] discovered that such a situation was not unusual, he issued his department with an instruction that all such activities be outlawed. He also announced that it would be better in his opinion for the Crown to take possession of these trading posts, locations that had previously been under the jurisdiction of groups of traders, officially referred to as Justices' Councils Russell also ordered that a Commissioner be sent to Gold Coast, to Sierra Leone and to the various Stations along the Gambia River to - to enquire into all of these matters.

In fact, Russell had already made up his mind that it was the Council President of the Justices, Captain George Maclean, - based in Cape Coast Castle - who was responsible for most of the corrupt practices in that region. Russell's officials advised him to appoint a man named Dr. Lushington to head this investigation given his excellent record on humanitarian issues as pertaining to the different African tribal groups. Russell preferred Madden for this position however, and informed the Irishman of his intentions. Madden agreed to the job and gave up his post in Cuba in July, 1840. Russell himself drafted the specifications for the new job and he left Madden in no doubt that his acceptance of his African position meant exchanging a permanent post (Cuba) for a temporary one, for which there was no guarantee of future governmental employment upon completion of the contract. Madden was unconcerned about this lack of permanency and was very excited about this new post, given the likelihood that it would be the most prestigious position he would ever be offered. Therefore he was very honoured to accept this new post. Prior to this he had been just one official among many, a functionary whose role was simply to implement the decisions of others. Now, for the first time, however, he was being specially appointed to a position of great responsibility, one where his actions in relation to this proposed independent investigation would be subject to the scrutiny of others. It was also a job that might also entail the opportunity for him to influence Government policy at a fundamental level.

Strangely, Madden's salary wasn't decided upon until after he had been formally appointed. He agreed to leave Britain on the first of December along with the group who had been appointed to help him in investigating conditions in those countries that bordered that incredibly long and vast river - the Niger. He was still in London by the twelfth of December, however, and still involved in negotiations concerning his salary. He was initially offered a deal which he refused point-blank to accept - i.e. a salary of 1500 pounds, 900 pounds of which would be spent on travel and other expenses. Such a salary would leave him with just 600 pounds as his annual income. Madden informed Russell that he was "very averse from making objections to any pecuniary arrangements" made for him, but that he had to be blunt about such matters nevertheless. There was no way that his post would be a success if he had to worry consistently about the financial aspects of the African project or go without some of the most basic necessities in terms of day-to-day living and health. A clear 1000 pounds would be necessary for expenses, at the very least. Stephen[170] met Madden in the Colonial Office on the nineteenth of December where Madden explained to him that he would reject the posting if he didn't receive a promise to the effect that his wife would be paid the money anyway should he not return from Africa.

Given that fever was very widespread in that part of Africa the chances that he might never return were very high indeed. "He employed most circuitous and cautious terms to express his meanings", Stephen informed the Government minister with responsibility in that area, "but I think I cannot be mistaken in understanding these as his final terms." It isn't actually clear what arrangement was reached in the final analysis. Having reviewed the situation, Russell considered that the project could be completed within six months and that the necessary salary and expenses could thereby be reduced. That Stephen recommended an offer better than this again is clear by the fact that Madden received a letter prior to his embarkation at Liverpool acknowledging Madden's acceptance of the (final) terms on offer - and indicating that there would be no attempt at further negotiation of these terms. In the final analysis Madden spent a full six months on his African mission which lasted from the beginning of January to the middle of the following July when he was back in England again.

It seems clear that Madden found himself overly-rushed in the job. The pressures of this tight time-frame and his valiant attempts to finish all the work within such a short space of time likely contributed to many of the problems he would experience later. The target-area for the investigation was ridiculously large and included about three thousand miles of the West African coastline. Taking into account the length of time he spent travelling both to and from the region and the days he was bedridden with fever, it was obvious that he could spend just short time in each important port that he wished to visit. Madden did manage to meet a large number of people despite this lack of time, however - although his enemies would later allege that he had only met people who were of a similar view in relation to the slavery issue as himself. Indeed, they would also accuse him of investigating issues that were outside the remit of his position.

Madden instructed the Royal Navy to board a number of vessels and search them while they were at sea although he interpreted the law incorrectly in issuing some of these orders - as he would find out later. While the vessels in question were not transporting slaves, Madden considered the fact that they were transporting provisions for those involved in slave-trading grounds enough for their apprehension. Russell left Madden under no illusion about what he considered to be the major problems on the Gold Coast and the recommendations that Madden ought to be making in relation to them. His official departmental letter included guidelines for what he expected Madden to do in the job – a type of "terms-of-reference" if you will. Captain Maclean had already admitted that the slave traders in this region had "free rein" to purchase whatever food and other supplies they needed to supplement and maintain their slave trading activities.

To that subject, (Russell said to Madden), you will ascertain whether there are any means of procuring evidence to convict the parties who may have been engaged in such illegal proceedings, and whether there is, in point of fact, any difficulty in distinguishing the slave traders who ask for supplies of goods and provisions, from traders employed in lawful commerce. You will not, however, confine your enquiries to those points; you will have to consider whether the present constitution of government in those establishments is one which has a tendency to favour connivance with the slave trade, and to withdraw the persons exercising authority there from the superintendence and control of Her Majesty's Government.[171]

On returning to Dublin in mid-July, Madden immediately started compiling his report for the Colonial Office, a report which he divided into three sections. It was an extremely long document and one on which much midnight oil must have been expended. His report was replete with long-winded appendices and statistics and even included instructions and health advice for Europeans wishing to travel in Africa. He sent the first part of his report as relating to the Gold Coast forward in July of that year and the second section regarding Sierra Leone in August. The third section about Gambia, he forwarded in September. The report discussed the various issues which Sir. John Russell had asked him to investigate and his conclusions and recommendations broadly agreed with Russell's. Madden didn't confine himself too strictly to the central issues however. He also included a good deal of material about his travels in this part of Africa generally and the different sights and incidents he had witnessed there. He criticised the infrequency with which the Governor and the council of the Gold Coast invoked the legal powers that officially governed the region. Of the ninety-nine Africans whom he had seen imprisoned in the dungeons of the Gold Coast Castle, there was only one individual on whom a criminal sentence had been imposed.

The absence of a correct legal process and the lack of judges to implement a fair and correct system of justice in this region was all too apparent. Madden succeeded in securing the release of some of the prisoners held in Cape Coast Castle. He was also informed, however, that British law did not have any authority in the region, this despite the fact that certain assurances to the contrary had been given when the Bill had initially been put before Parliament in Westminster. When Madden requested further information from the authorities on the Gold Coast regarding this supposed exemption, he was informed that they had indeed received a written exemption from the Colonial Office. They refused to show him a copy of this alleged exemption, however. As regards slave-trading, Madden provided two examples which proved that slave traders in that region were still being provided with supplies and other support, both moral and practical.

One example which Madden referred to was that of the *Dos Amigos* while the other example he cited was a ship originating in London and which was actually owned by Forster and Smith. This ship sailed under the British flag, was captained by a British citizen, but was trading for years under a Portuguese trader's name – a man by the name of De Souza. Madden had actually discussed the case of this ship with Maclean who was very angry that Madden would make an accusation of slave-trading against De Souza, who was actually a friend of his. Madden refused to retract his allegation however.

I came upon British citizens who were kept as either unpaid servants or slaves, Madden wrote. *These people were purchased at slave markets in neighbouring African countries where slavery is still permitted or were accepted as credit for the unpaid debts of others, or for debts which the prisoners themselves owed. Then when the debt was unable to be re-paid, these poor people were kept in permanent bondage.*[172]

As with various matters, Madden and Maclean argued over the system of credit employed there - whereby slaves were used for barter and payment. Maclean claimed that there was a difference between buying the person and buying their work but Madden countered by saying that no honest distinction could be ever be made between a person and their work. Instead of letting the issue lie, or (solely) highlighting it in his written report, Madden challenged Maclean about the slave-trade there, instructing him to do whatever was necessary to put an end to all forms of slavery. Previous to this, Maclean had sent around a notice amongst the British community there, informing them that it was no longer permitted to buy or to keep slaves.

Madden now asked Maclean to send out a circular reminding the British citizens there of their obligations in this regard, a request which Maclean refused. The way the colony was organised meant that the keeping of slaves was a normal, everyday aspect of the colonial community's lives and to disturb this equilibrium would be dangerous, Maclean argued. He also claimed to have previously written a letter to the Colonial Secretary in London advising him that slavery was a normal and regular aspect of life in that region and requesting that the Colonial Secretary issue him with instructions on how to deal with this "sensitive" issue, a letter which received no reply. In the absence of any response to this letter, Maclean said that he saw no reason to take any action on the slavery issue as it related to the Gold Coast colony. Maclean's attitude naturally angered Madden a great deal as he felt that the Colonial Secretary would certainly not have been in favour of the way Maclean was treating the slavery "issue" in that region:

I could do nothing to change Maclean's mind, Madden wrote. Seeing as I was more au-fait with current developments as relating to the Slavery question, I tried my best – without success – to convince him of my point of view. I reminded him that the indifference to slavery that had been common in the British colonies previous to this was no longer acceptable and that it was now expected that all slaves should be freed. I also tried to impress upon him the reality that any involvement in this trade, no matter how small, could result in the colonial authorities either being threatened with the law or being punished.[173]

Three or four weeks went by but Maclean did not give in or act on any of Madden's recommendations. Madden then sought advice from Sir John Jeremie, the then Governor of Sierra Leone, a man who was also a committed Abolitionist before taking any further action. Jeremie appointed Madden a Justice of the Peace and operating under the auspices of Jeremie's office Madden was able to issue posters announcing the necessity to end the slave trade in that colony. The posters which Madden attached to the Castle gates, to the doors of churches, and to the trees in the marketplace, reminded the British citizens of this colony that it was their duty to free all enslaved black people who were British citizens. Some of the expatriate community there did as requested and immediately released their slaves. Many also refused, however - in particular among the upper echelons of the colonial community there.

The local justices, the council members, and the merchants then organized a protest against Madden's announcement. A deputation informed the Irishman in the bluntest of terms that any attempt to implement his recommendations would result in a revolt amongst the colonial class there. Madden attended the meeting and gave his side of the story, but after he had left the meeting again a formal motion was passed rejecting everything he had suggested. From that day until the day that he finished working on the Gold Coast, none of the white colonial settlers there followed any of Madden's recommendations or statements with respect to the slave-trade. In Madden's view, Maclean was a rough and unscrupulous character – "a colonial sybarite with an impaired liver" who did nothing to disguise the disdain for his writer-wife and her poetry.

On her arrival in the Gold Coast Madden had found a room prepared for him in the castle that was Maclean's home. Maclean himself was not at home when Madden arrived and Madden found himself assigned to the same bedroom in which Maclean's wife had only recently died! When Maclean returned to the Castle a day or two later, one of the first comments he made to the Irishman was that he hoped Madden had been sent to the Gold Coast to investigate the circumstances of his wife - Landon's - death. This was important Maclean stated, particularly given that so many scandalous rumours were circulating concerning the circumstances of her death. Madden informed Maclean that his wife's death had nothing to do with his mission to the Gold Coast and the conversation between the two men ended abruptly. Later, when they spoke to one another again, Maclean asked Madden whether he would oblige him by investigating (his wife) Landon's death, a request to which Madden acquiesced.

Madden was unable to unearth any new information concerning the cause and circumstances of her death and had to be satisfied with the same bare facts that LEL's[174] friends back in London already had access to. Madden also managed to overcome his initial hesitancy to mention that Lady Blessington wished to have a tombstone erected in memory of her friend Landon. A few days later, a tombstone was taken from the store where it had already lain for some time and erected at the head of Landon's grave to the accompaniment of a military salute. Soon after this, Madden experienced a horrible feeling while lying prone in the dead woman's room. At the time he was suffering the torments of the African fever that had killed so many Europeans in that region. One night between waking and sleep, he imagined that he saw Mrs. Maclean lying prone on the floor in the exact spot where her servant had found her dead.

Madden became very ill with fever and felt sure that he would have died if it hadn't been for the dutiful care provided by his

English man-servant. To expect any concern on the part of any of the others in the Maclean household would have been futile in the extreme. On a number of occasions when Madden was close to death, Maclean showed no concern whatsoever about his visitor. All he did was to enquire at the door of Madden's room as to his condition - "after which he would turn on his heel and walk away, as if it was a matter of the smallest possible importance whether I lived or died." Madden feared that an attempt was being made to poison him and asked that he be moved to a more friendly lodging where the people could be trusted.

It is no wonder that Madden would later portray Maclean in a negative light in his Report. It was while engrossed in the writing of his Report that Madden got the first hint of the trouble that lay in store for him upon its completion. Forster and Smith and their company sent a letter to the Lords of the Admiralty in which they complained about Madden's investigation. Their letter expressed their extreme shock that a Captain Tucker from the Royal Navy had boarded their vessel, the *Robert Heddle* and examined the ship's papers, all on Madden's orders. They complained bitterly to the Lords about Madden's behaviour but asked that Captain Tucker be excused from blame given that he had mistakenly responded on the orders of an idiot. The fact that he had made a serious error was difficult enough for Tucker, they said, but what was worse than this was the fact that he had put himself at such risk by following the orders of someone who was without any legal standing, a person who was as unfit to hold any serious public responsibility as Madden clearly was. This letter of complaint was quickly followed by another, a letter which was addressed this time to Madden himself. This letter written by Matthew Forster, a senior member of the trading company, included the following:

Now that your health is restored, and you are free from the irritability and infection which African fever never fails to produce on the soberest and strongest of minds, I am sure you will be one of the first to admit the injustice done.[175]

Madden replied to this letter and informed the company that he was sending a copy of their correspondence on to the Colonial Office. He then resumed work on his Report. He followed the same procedure in drafting a follow-up letter from the company, informing Forster that he did not agree with his interpretation of the law. Around the same time that this correspondence was going on, the Colonial Office were openly maintaining a façade of respect vis-à-vis Madden. This facade hid a changing attitude towards Madden as expressed behind closed doors, however. Privately, the Colonial Office asked that Madden give his opinion regarding the suitability of a Captain Huntley, the Governor of Gambia, for a job that he had recently applied for.

Madden didn't think very highly of Huntley and indicated as much. He also said that he would discuss the question of this appointment in more detail when he met Lord Edward Howard, the Parliamentary Under-Secretary. Referring to this later, Stephen said that he wasn't certain that he could attribute the same faults to Huntley that Madden did and he would have to wait for the findings contained in Madden's Report. When the findings of this Report were finally issued Stephen was in agreement with Madden that the English merchants in that region of Africa and traders such as Forster and Smith in particular, were promoting and supporting the maintenance of the slave-trade. Stephen forwarded the first two sections of Madden's Report to Russell, using Howard as an intermediary, but before doing so he also included an addendum to the effect that:

...they were not only of great importance, but of peculiar urgency. I refer especially to the question of prosecuting Messrs. Forster and Smith and Company and the other persons whom Doctor Madden so distinctly charges with slave trading.[176]

Howard also added his comments to the file and indicated that the findings of Madden's Report corresponded with his own preconceptions regarding the situation on the Gold Coast; Madden's findings confirmed what had long been suspected - i.e. that the slave trade was being organised and controlled indirectly by the British traders. Russell read all of these various reports and on the twenty-sixth of August he wrote as follows:

> Dr. Madden is a very able individual and his intellectual rigour is very apparent in this Report. Having said this, the traders living in this region claim that Madden only spent a few days or sometimes just a few hours at some of the trading stations that he describes, and they also allege that there are many errors in his Report. I would prefer to ask the traders in question for their general comments in relation to this Report before taking any action based on its recommendations. I am afraid that the commercial spirit has superseded the spirit of humanity in the way our trading concerns are being organised on the Gold Coast.[177]

Although he was wary of taking any concrete action based on the Report's recommendations, Russell did order that a certain number of Madden's recommendations be implemented. Amongst these recommendations were the following:

> That the governance of the Gold Coast be taken over by the Colonial Office; that the Treasury's attorney make contact with Madden so that the evidence of financial impropriety as relating to the Forster and Smith Company be collated - the group whom Madden had accused of being involved in the slave trade. If Forster and Smith were prosecuted and a new and more severe legal ruling was instituted; then such measures ought to act as a warning to British traders in the region as to necessity of conducting their trading interests in an honest fashion.[178]

While all of this was going on, the political situation in Britain was in a state of confusion. The then Government was teetering on the edge of collapse and would have fallen apart completely if it hadn't been for the efforts that the (by-then) elderly Lord Melbourne[179] had made to keep everybody united. The Government suffered a mortal blow, however, when the Budget was rejected and shortly after this the government was defeated again when it lost a vote of confidence by just a single vote. Parliament was dissolved and the Whigs took a hammering in the August General Election. This defeat must have worried Madden since he had given up his permanent post in Cuba, on the assumption that his friends, the Whigs, would be in government for a long time afterwards. What would happen to him now employment-wise in this altered political landscape?

The first thing Madden decided to do was to go and see Russell and Normanby. Unfortunately, he didn't get to meet either of them and only managed to speak to Robert Vernon Smith, the then Parliamentary Under-Secretary in the Colonial Office. Smith informed him that there were only two jobs available and he could have his choice of either of them if he so wished. One was the Governorship of Sierra Leone, and the other was the Vice-Governor position in Gambia. Madden didn't want either of these jobs, however. He had only just returned from a stint in Africa and was in no hurry to go back there again.

Mr. Smith imagines - (Madden wrote) - that a man can just pitch his tent anywhere in the world but I'm beginning to think that it is better for a man to die at home than anywhere else.[180]

What Madden was really saying of course was that he felt that he had the right to a position somewhere where the climate was more congenial than in Africa. Smith replied only to say that there were no other vacancies available but that the Office would be certain to do whatever they could on his behalf, whether they were in Government or not. In the end

Madden had to be satisfied with a memo that Russell left after him in the Downing Street files which said: "I commend and recommend Dr. Madden to my successor." Lord Stanley[181] succeeded Russell in this post; he was the Tory who was infamously referred to as "Scorpion Stanley" in Ireland. Madden couldn't have expected too many favours from him and as if to compound his misfortune Mr. Forster was elected as a member of parliament on behalf of the Whigs. This was the same Forster - from the company Forster and Smith that Russell was intending to bring a legal case against - as backed by Madden's testimony. Stanley was only a short period in office when he was forced to deal with the ramifications of Madden's report on the slave trade on the Gold Coast. Stephen gave it to him to read on the third of September and included with it the following note:

The Report wasn't finished before Lord John Russell left office and as a consequence no action based on the Report's findings have been taken as of yet. It is clear that the Report is a very important one and raises some urgent issues. I myself have studied the Report carefully but it would be fruitless to take any practical steps based on its recommendations until it has been read by Lord Stanley and his Parliamentary Under-Secretary.[182]

The Report was still a confidential one and needed to be edited before being put before Parliament.

Madden accuses a number of British traders of playing a regular and coordinated role in the trading of slaves. One of the accused traders is Mr. Forster, who is, as I understand it, a member of Parliament.[183]

Having read the Report, Stanley agreed with Stephen that there was no way that the findings of the Report could be presented to parliament as they currently stood and in the style in which these recommendations were phrased. It would be necessary to summarise the Report's findings and Stanley explained the type of summary that he had in mind. Stanley had no objection to Madden compiling this summary if he was available to do so. He did recommend however that copies of the Report be sent privately to Captain Huntley in Gambia and Colonel Doherty in Sierra Leone so as to get their opinions regarding the Report's findings. Both of Stanley's instructions were complied with and Madden received a hundred pounds as a fee for writing the summary. The replies from the two British representatives were almost exactly the same.

This was now their opportunity to get their own back on Madden. Until recently - Madden had been in discussions with the Whig government regarding Captain Huntley's suitability for an important job vacancy. Now the Captain had his chance to tell the powers-that-be what *his* opinion of Madden was. Huntley tore apart those pages in the Report that concerned his area of operation in Gambia section by section, thereby demonstrating - according to himself - the "unfair reportage and unjust accusations" that had been laid against him in Madden's report as follows: "When a witness makes statements that are without foundation, in a court of law, the remainder of his statement is accepted only after intensive scrutiny." Unsurprisingly, Huntley attributed the "false" accusations to a sloppiness on Madden's part and a lack of adequate time in which to correctly research the Report. At the end of the day, Madden had only spent one week in Bathurst![184]

Colonel Doherty claimed that Madden's findings were so far from the truth that the only possible explanation for them was the following: Madden had spent far too short a time in the colony and as a consequence, he was heavily reliant on second-hand information and rumour-mongers for his whatever information he had collated. If he had had the opportunity to spend a longer time in that part of Africa he would have learnt a great deal more about the reality of the region's social organisation. Madden's report would have come to some very different conclusions as a consequence, according to Doherty.

The faults which Doherty identified in Madden's Report referred to those sections of the Report which he could correctly understand. Other sections of the Report were replete with incorrect assumptions and vague generalisations, most of which were mistaken. In later years both Doherty and Huntley were rewarded with knighthoods and transferred to better jobs as a reward for their deliberate sabotage of Madden and his Report - (as Madden himself would later claim). Meanwhile, Stephen summarised the Report and its contents, a summary that Madden was probably fortunate never to have been seen. We can only assume that his disgust at the mis-interpretation of his Report would have been profound. Stephen claimed that the reviews of the Report provided by both Governor Huntley and Governor Doherty had confirmed him in his opinion that Madden was an inaccurate observer of the trading patterns on the Gold Coast, an official whose report was replete with generalisations and a lack of in-depth research.

> *A number of Madden's character traits need to be taken into account when judging this Report, including Madden's pugnacious nature, his unashamed sympathy for the Negro race, his propensity for travel-writing and the production of books full of exotic and interesting oddities. We must also take into consideration how little time Madden spent on the Gold Coast, the poor state of his health, the various controversies in which he became embroiled over there, the lack of any in-depth interviews with appropriate witnesses and the rushed nature of the Report's compilation upon Madden's return from Africa. When all of these factors are taken into consideration it is clear that this Report is of very little value, other than for its references to the slave trade, many of which had to be confirmed later from other sources anyway.*[185]

The reality of the situation was that Madden's compilation of the Report's summary was just an academic exercise and was a complete waste of time. According to Stephen, Madden was the type of person who wasn't fully assured about an issue's veracity until he saw the requisite evidence with his own eyes. This did not mean, of course, that the Irishman hadn't written the truth as he perceived it. The Parliamentary Under-Secretary, G.W. Hope, was the first to receive Stephen's memo. He added a short note to the memo where he stated that the report's contents were valuable and had been the source of much detailed work. He also cautioned that the memo's contents be handed with great sensitivity, however. This is what Stephen decided to do as a consequence. He put the questions the Report had raised before a Select Committee of the House of Representatives and he advised Madden that he would have to give evidence before this Select Committee. Russell didn't oppose this move; he was friendly with Stanley and the likelihood is that he unofficially informed Russell concerning Stephen's opinion of the report. The civil servants in the Colonial Office considered the details of the report inadequate in terms of proving that the then laws concerning slave-trading were being breached. Having put out his "feelers", it wasn't long before Russell realised that all of the parties represented in the British Parliament were united against implementing any of the recommendations of the report, as compiled by Madden.

Madden visited Dublin at the end of 1841 and stayed there over the Christmas period. While he was at home, he spoke at a public meeting of the Iberian Anti-Slavery society held in Dublin's Concert Hall. At the meeting Madden gave a summary of the state of the slave-trade as he had witnessed its machinations. Most of the slave-trading "on-the-ground" was carried out by Spanish and Portuguese traders, Madden said, but the profits from this trade were going into the pockets of three or four wealthy English merchants then controlling the trade "behind the scenes." Such public allegations were dangerous and somewhat indiscreet for someone like Madden to be making, particularly given that he was also asking Stanley for a new job at this same juncture. Unsurprisingly, Madden received the usual polite yet diplomatic response to his enquiry regarding further employment - i.e. – he was informed that the Colonial Secretary would be happy to employ him but was uncertain as to when and where such employment would next be available.

Madden wrote another letter seeking employment in February, 1842. This time he complained that people suspected the Government held a grudge against him. If this suspicion was unfounded, then how was it that the Government had left him jobless? In addition, the fact that Madden's report on the slave trade continued to remain unpublished meant that the Irishman was powerless to defend himself against many of the rumours and false stories then publicly circulating.

Stanley didn't understand what Madden was "playing at" and indicated as much in the notes as recorded in the Colonial Office files. No doubt the continued to refusal to publish his report was a deep source of frustration and concern to Madden at this time. He tried to pressurise Robert Vernon Smith the former Whig Undersecretary to propose a motion requesting the publication of the Report or a summary of the Report at the very least. Vernon Smith[186] was very reluctant to do this however and was waiting to see whether the Report was completely ignored or (even) shelved for good. Vernon Smith replied to Madden's entreaties informing him that he had great sympathy for the difficult position the Irishman found himself in. What Madden had done to oppose slavery deserved much greater credit than either the British Government or the public had given him, Vernon Smith added. When Stanley announced to the House of Representatives shortly after this that a Select Committee was being set up to discuss the slavery issue, he made no reference at all to Madden's work. It was left to Vernon Smith to do this and even then he didn't mention any of the troubling questions which Madden's report had highlighted. The House was undoubtedly aware, Vernon Smith stated, that a very valuable report had recently been compiled regarding the British colony in West Africa. This report had been written by

Dr. Madden, a gentleman whose name was linked to the cause of Anti-Slavery and who had been posted to this part of Africa to investigate the situation in this region. While he was aware that this report was a very confidential one and that it might not be possible to publish the report in its entirety, was there any possibility that certain sections of the report be made available to the Select Committee without generating any controversy? This is what actually happened in due course when the Committee based its deliberations on these select sections from the report.

The large number of people appointed to this Committee and their prominence in terms of British politics and the colonial policy of this era illustrate the importance of the issues then under discussion. There were twenty-one people on the Committee including Stanley, the then Colonial Secretary and the man who had held this office prior to Lord John Russell. On the surface of things, this appeared to be a reasonably fair beginning to the proceedings, although Madden had strong suspicions that the Committee was hostile not only to his work but also to that of the government minister who had appointed him to the West African posting. Madden's personal papers note, for example, how inappropriate it was that one of the Committee members was the public representative for Liverpool, a city then accumulating massive wealth as a direct consequence of the slave trade. Even more ridiculous than this was the fact that Stanley appointed Forster to the Committee – the same individual whose corrupt practices and involvement with the slave trade - Madden had attempted to highlight in his report. From the very earliest stages of the Committee's work, Madden was made to feel like a prisoner in the dock, a prisoner without any attorney to defend him. Russell only attended three meetings of the Committee and did not make the slightest effort to defend either Madden or his work, this despite the fact that it was he who had initiated the enquiry into the West African colony, laid out the plan of action for Madden, and commended the Irishman on the diligence with which he had undertaken the work. Stanley, on the other hand, attended every meeting of the Committee and was not shy about getting his point of view across. His comments were very hostile to Madden and he lost no opportunity to attack the Irishman and his report. For example, Madden, had advised Governor Maclean to seize the ship known as the *Robert Heddle* but he had never instructed Captain Tucker to impound the ship.

"I only informed this naval officer of the circumstances relating to this ship. What actions he took were entirely at his own discretion," Madden said in relation to this incident. "Do you mean to suggest that everybody who is not in agreement with your view of slavery is an advocate for the slave trade?" Forster asked him. Madden responded to this question in a circuitous manner. It was his view that anybody who was predisposed towards aiding and abetting the slave trade could hardly be considered as opposed to this same trade. Not only did Forster attend every single meeting of the Committee but he also had a seat right next to the Committee chairman and it was he who took it upon himself to direct most of the Committee's activities and to question the various witnesses. No limits were imposed as to how much time Forster spent cross-examining the various witnesses and the Committee never called the two witnesses whom Madden had named to speak on his behalf. The excuse for this omission was that the Committee had run out of time. The same excuse was provided as an explanation for why Forester was never questioned about the various written statements/submissions he had given to the Committee on his own behalf.

Bizarrely, the Committee accepted Forster's submissions as fact, this despite the strange anomaly that Forster was himself a member of the Committee then investigating the matter. "I", said Madden, "was less fortunate, for I underwent an examination and a cross-examination at the hands of this highly favoured gentleman, which must have given any stranger the impression, that the man charged with crime was the witness, and the examinant was his accuser and his judge." Forster denied Madden's evidence concerning the *Robert Heddle* and another vessel, known as the *Sea Witch*. It was true that that the Robert Heddle was carrying 2000 feet's worth of timber at the time but this was not intended for the use of a number of slave traders living there but was to be delivered to some missionaries instead. Forster also defended Captain Maclean and denied that Maclean had failed in his public duty by writing a number of letters giving preference to Forster's company in the setting-up of a number of large trading initiatives. In effect, Forster was denying that Maclean was actually a representative in the employ of his company, another allegation which Madden had made based on the goings-on he had witnessed at Maclean's home in Cape Coast Castle. Forster found it difficult to put into words - or so he claimed - the disgust that he felt at Madden's implication of Maclean, particularly given the fact that Madden had been a guest at the time in Maclean's residence. While it was true that a good deal of correspondence had gone to and fro between Forster and Maclean, none of it concerned Forster or his business affairs. Instead, it concerned entirely different allegations against Maclean, allegations that were refuted to the complete satisfaction of another Parliamentary Committee.

The letters concerned this issue and the death of Maclean's unfortunate wife, Letitia Elizabeth Landon. A horrible rumour had circulated in the newspapers and in English high society generally which laid the blame for Landon's death firmly at Maclean's door. This was the reason for the large volume of correspondence that had passed between the two men at this period. Forster wasn't sure who was so dead-set against Maclean but he had his suspicions that it was somebody who worked in the Colonial Office.

Perhaps - (Forster said) - it was somebody in that office who was jealous of Maclean since he was able to run the colony on a tenth of the cost that the Colonial Office found necessary to expend on the management of the colony in Sierra Leone. Speaking in a general sense concerning Madden's Report,

Forster argued that it was just another example of how difficult it was to gather accurate information on matters relating to the African coast. The local African people could not be trusted when seeking information about their personal or social conditions, he claimed. From what Forster could make out, Madden had - for the purposes of his Report - taken on board the views of random individuals whom he had come across his travels or people who were already in agreement with his preconceived notions of what life was like in that part of Africa. Madden had also been sick for a time during his stay on the Gold Coast and had admitted that this sickness had affected his mental state at the time. This would explain the inaccuracies and sloppy observations which were evident in the Report. It was only a supposition on his part to imagine that the trading initiatives on the Gold Coast formed one big and interconnected monopoly. Forster claimed never to have come across a more open and mutually-beneficial network of independent traders in his thirty years involved in business than that which operated on the Gold Coast!

But it seems as if there is nothing, however ridiculous that Dr. Madden wouldn't use as ammunition with which to tarnish the Gold Coast and the traders who operate there. It looks as if he had the same unreasonable motivations when visiting Gambia, except that his claims regarding the trading culture there were even more improbable if such were possible.[187]

Given these various statements, Madden must have been expecting a very unfavourable conclusion to the Special Committee's deliberations. The one thing that he didn't expect however was that Committee's entire membership would put their names to whatever form of concluding statement would be issued. He was particularly upset therefore with those members of the African Civilisation Society who were also on the Special Committee. They proclaimed to have strong religious and Abolitionist principles but when it came to the test they didn't abide by them. It was true, of course, that the Committee made a small attempt to tone down the personal nature of the criticisms as directed at Madden. For instance, the Committee congratulated him on the large volume of valuable information he had collated so diligently and it claimed to agree (in principle at least) with many of the recommendations that he had made.

All of this was academic however when compared with all of the issues raised by Madden and which the Committee claimed to be dubious about; the accuracy of Madden's judgements and the impartiality of the evidence on the most controversial issue of all that Madden had highlighted i.e. the network that connected the British merchants and those traders specialising in the slave-trade. In relation to this, the Committee expressed big doubts as to the truth of Madden's allegations. The Committee claimed that it could find no evidence to suggest that ships owned by British merchants had any connection whatsoever with the slave trade, or that they were benefiting financially from such a connection.

The Committee did however acknowledge that British traders and traders from other countries frequently sold legally-produced good onto the slave traders and that these goods were sometimes then bartered for slaves. Senior legal authorities were of the opinion that such forms of barter were illegal and ought to be a punishable offence. A close examination of the Act[188] indicated that there was no way that - the Act as it then stood - could be interpreted as providing for any prohibition or penalty in this regard, however. This was also the Attorney-General's view. A majority on the Special Committee indicated that they were not in favour of the legal enshrinement of such prohibitions either. While it would have been relatively straightforward to officially ban trading in any station where slave trade was a proven fact, the actual implementation of such a ruling on the ground would have proved very difficult.

We can't propose – (said the Committee) *- that a ruling be instituted in relation to an issue which would be as* *complicated and as impossible to implement as this. We are relieved to note however that this major work is progressing. Recent steps taken with regard to illegal trading have borne much fruit. It is our information, as verified by all naval captains, that the slave trade is in its death-throes, north of the Equator, and along that coastal region that stretches for many thousands of miles.*[189]

The Committee expressed its gratitude to Madden claiming that his Report had already influenced many people. His efforts to destroy the ugly business that was the slave-trade were to be commended. All of this was just "talk" and "hot air" however. Forster had won the battle and it was not a victory that he was content to leave between the covers of one of the blue books which resided in the House of Representatives. He wanted to exact as much retribution as he possibly could and wrote letters to various newspapers in an effort to humiliate Madden. He referred to Madden as "a hungry Whig Radical" - a man for whose personal benefit the mission to the West African coast had been organised in the first place. The mission had really been so as to distract the public from the misdemeanours of the Whigs who were in government at the time, and also to compensate for the failure of the Niger Expedition[190] Madden wrote to the newspapers denying these allegations and pointing out that he had never played any public role in English political life. He had enjoyed the support of Lord Stanley and Sir Francis Burdett[191] from his earliest years in the public service and both were loyal Tories. As regards the Niger Expedition, this expedition had yet to be organised when Madden's mission was already up-and-running. Other false allegations relating to Madden's mission were also circulated. It was claimed that the Irishman had received 1800 pounds as payment for his mission in addition to the promise of a pension for his wife in the event of his death overseas. An individual named Mr. Bunter, who was a good friend of Forster's, declared that Madden had acted in such an imprudent and stubborn manner during his stint in the

West Indies that he had been physically beaten up on two occasions. Madden proved that there was no foundation to such allegations and he and a number of Anti-Slavery Movement members and journalist friends responded to such accusations in the broadsheet pages. All Madden got for his efforts was another torrent of abuse from his detractors, however. Forster continued with his denunciation of Madden's Report.

The Committee had been unanimous in its view that Madden's Report was error-ridden in relation to all of the major issues. The truth was that the Report had been rejected outright albeit that those members of the Special Committee sympathetic to the Irishmen argued for leniency as regards the censuring of Madden. They cited the short time that he had spent on the Gold Coast and the illness which had affected him for a part of the mission as mitigating factors that ought to be taken into consideration. Forster also now claimed that Madden had never been sick but had spent a full seven weeks relaxing in his room. He had been so afraid of the African climate that he was like a frightened child, he alleged. He accused Madden of removing sections of his evidence before presenting it to the Committee, an accusation which Madden later refuted in a memo to Normanby, a memo which was never made public. The selective culling of his Report was in fact a nasty trick as perpetrated by Forster himself. In fact, it was the first draft of the Special Committee report on the whole controversy that had to be withdrawn and reprinted the day after it had been presented to Parliament, the reason being that Forster had secretly inserted private information of his own into this Report that the Special Committee had already agreed was not to be included. Forster's accusations and allegations went completely over the top during the course of the controversy. At one stage he cast doubt on whether Madden had actually ever qualified as a doctor and he also made the ridiculous assertion that Madden was no better than a slave-trader himself, given that he too was making a living on the back of the slave-trade. When, at one point, the *Morning Chronicle*[192] wrote something about him that he didn't like Forster challenged the newspaper's owner, Sir John Easthope[193] to a fight. Madden intervened to sort out that particular issue and saved Easthope from a potentially awkward and embarrassing situation. In spite of this good turn on Madden's part, however, Easthope refused to pass him on the letters which had been sent to the newspaper referring to Madden as a born liar, a slanderer, a contemptible individual and a crook. Easthope's refusal was undoubtedly based on the probability of litigation and the fact that Madden would possibly sue the letter-writer for defamation of character.

Madden had to be satisfied with responding to Forster's letters one by one as they appeared in the various newspapers, a correspondence which he later collated and published as a small book – *The Slave Trade and Slavery* (1843). In this short monograph Madden was to make particular mention of the degree to which his original Report on the Gold Coast was culled by various unscrupulous individuals and without any consultation with him. While completing this latter book Madden became so indignant at his treatment at the hands of Forster and his friends that his various arguments and grievances became overly-convoluted, and it was increasingly difficult for the reading public to follow the intricacies of all the arguments. As the controversy drew to a close, Madden was reduced to defending his reputation as doctor of medicine in response to various ridiculous allegations regarding his medical qualifications. Madden sought the support of an eminent physician - one Dr. James Johnson - who publicly outlined the exact nature of Madden's medical qualifications. Madden even got Dr. Johnson to supply him with a certificate of proof as regards his various qualifications so as to appease any member of the public who might have been influenced by the false rumours spread by Forster and his friends - "I have known Dr. Madden both on a personal level and as a doctor for the past twenty years and in my opinion there is nobody alive today who is more direct or honourable in manner than this man." Johnson had been personal physician to the King of England at one stage and was the highly-respected editor of a number of prestigious medical journals - facts which Madden was never slow to highlight whenever he got the opportunity. Understandably, Madden neglected to mention that the real connection between Johnson and himself was the fact that Johnson had been one of the United Irishmen involved in the rebellion of 1798. Madden was sidelined from the public service as the Gold Coast controversy faded and the Tories consolidated their political power. He had more time on his hands and could reflect in more detail on his run of bad luck as a consequence - "Discountenanced by my superiors, I was left defenceless and at the mercy of those whose interests I had offended in my endeavours to carry into effect the instructions of Lord John Russell." Madden would never forget his shoddy treatment at Russell's hands and his antipathy to Russell would seep into some of his later writings. Russell took Madden's criticisms personally and mentioned his irritation at Madden's bitterness towards him to Lady Blessington. She saw herself as a patron-protectress of the Irishman and wrote to Madden, advising him to make peace with Russell. She advised Madden to write a letter to Russell explaining the sense of hurt he felt and the reasoning behind the various political stances he had taken.

> *You don't have to go into the rights of your case in too much detail or the various slanderous statements your enemies have made either. Lord John Russell is well aware of all of these. Just outline what your intentions were when you issued that statement in your own defence. Outline briefly all of the injustices you have suffered prior to the issuance of your statement. I would prefer to see a man as decent as he (i.e. Russell) on your side...*[194]

It is not clear whether Madden ever followed up on Lady Blessington's advice. If he did, it could only have been very grudgingly because his antipathy to Russell and everything he stood for seemed to increase as time went on. Unsurprisingly, the same was true of the relationship between Madden and Stanley. Madden had never liked Stanley but an incident occurred just before Madden left for his next post in Lisbon in 1843 which really sickened him. One day Madden was walking in the vicinity of Downing Street when he felt he should call into the Colonial Office and request an interview with the Secretary of State, if possible. He must have felt that by adopting a new and overly-humble stance, he might be able to make a claim for a new job other than the "insignificant" post he had already agreed to accept in Portugal. Having entered the building, he was left waiting for a very long time, all the while ruminating on "the sweetest and the bitterest fancies, alternately." Finally, an easygoing and elderly manservant who worked there named Dodsworth emerged to tell Madden that Stanley was unable to meet him. It may actually have been true that Stanley didn't have the time to meet with him that day but whether true or no, Madden didn't believe it. He felt so hurt by the way that he was treated that he sent Stephen one of the longest and most bitter letters that he ever wrote. Stanley was a man with no heart, he maintained. The man had an annual inheritance of 70,000 pounds a year; he was surrounded by the pomp and trappings of public office and held in high esteem amongst the country's nobility; and yet he had no consideration for or understanding of anyone people lower than him in the social hierarchy. Here is a sample of what Madden wrote:

> *I won't bother Lord Stanley any further with regard to my rights to a job or with regard to the manner in which he has treated me. He must know in his heart that he has not treated me fairly. If he granted me an interview I would explain to him that it makes no difference as to whom an injustice is perpetrated against; an Irishman; an Englishman; someone of a different religion, colour or creed; or a Briton with the royal blood of the Hanovers running through his veins. I would inform his Lordship that he wronged me in the worst way that a man can wrong his fellow-man. He left me defenceless*

against the unscrupulous enemies of the State, those who perverted the course of justice and whom I had the misfortune to draw on me while fulfilling my responsibilities in an honest fashion. I would remind his Lordship that I sought his protection while enduring the most venomous assault on my character that I ever experienced, whereupon he informed me that my case was entitled to no social protection whatsoever. I now leave the matter in the hands of that small voice that speaks quietly to both the noble and the common-man - the voice of conscience. Lord Russell's decisions culminated in my spending a good deal of time in foreign lands where I endured many difficulties while cut off from family and friends. I held a permanent post with the Royal Commission with an annual salary of 800 pounds a year. In addition to this I was busy as an active Commissioner of Mediation for the legal system earning 400 pounds a year. Having previously earned a total of 1200 pounds a year I am now reduced to just 200 pounds. I spent a full eight years in the government department that Lord Stanley currently has responsibility for… eight years without a blemish in terms of work of character… but little thanks I received when I found myself in difficulty.[195]

It is not clear whether Stephen ever showed the letter to Stanley. Madden no doubt hoped that he would but ultimately his letter changed nothing. Madden was forced to take up the job in Portugal and make the best of a bad situation. He would never be able to forget that long wait in the Colonial Office and told Stephen that it was his *dies irae*. He would have been completely depressed that day if it hadn't been for the peculiar antics of another angry man who had also been forced to wait for ages before being told whether he would get an appointment or not. This man had spent his time taking long loping strides up and down the space that separated the waiting room from the hall outside. The man had chewed the official pen and issued a stream of "imprecatory and deprecatory ejaculations" while waiting. Madden had observed that day the tragi-comedy that was the queue of "poor devils" who entered the building "submissively, solicitously and dejectedly" in search of employment.

Some of the men were middle-aged, with an astute look about them, as if they were well-versed in the ways of the world; these men were dressed in a dignified black. Then there were the respectable-looking country youths, fashionable rings on their fingers and a country look about them. Young men in the prime of their health and still full of hope in the face of life's vicissitudes. A clerical post in Sierra Leone may lie ahead of them; or a position as a tax official in Gambia; a secretarial position with Captain Maclean on the Gold Coast even. The old stagers in the Colonial Office here look upon them with pity. But when these young men have left again they say coldly and indifferently - "Give it six months and some of those strapping fellows will be six foot under."[196]

Afterwards Madden wrote a poem about the fateful and hopeless day he had spent in that waiting room:

> *Patience, good stranger, here you'll surely find,*
> *Most ample space and time to exercise*
> *That public virtue - Prithee be resigned,*
> *Humble thy heart, and learn how you must rise.*
>
> *Nay, sit thee down and wait for thou shouldst know*
> *This is a waiting room indeed, where men*
> *Full many a time have kicked their heels as thou*
> *Dost thine my friend, and still may do again.*
>
> *Job had his trials and temptations sore*
> *But one there was he did not undergo;*
> *He never danced attendance at the door*
> *Of a Colonial Minister I trow.*
>
> *Hour after hour counted as time past*
> *By the slow minutes the porter's clock*

*He never spent in Downing Street, nor cast
His wistful glances around at every knock.
Be more than Job, nay do not curse the day
'Twill not appease thy appetite to swear
These hungry walls to people seem to say
Eat they own heart whilst thou art waiting here.*[197]

CHAPTER 8
THE LIVES OF THE UNITED IRISHMEN

Between 1840 and the end of 1843, Madden lived in Dublin. This was the longest stretch he had spent in his native city since childhood. For a while Dublin was ranked the second largest city in the British Empire. While this was no longer the case by the mid-1840s, Dublin was still a very imposing capital, a more compact city then than it is today. It was as city with a relatively small population then, comprising just one quarter of a million people. The large increase in the Irish population, an increase which took place within the space of a few short decades, was one of the most pressing problems facing Ireland's urban economy and infrastructure at this time. Within the space of just sixty years the Irish population had tripled or quadrupled and the non-stop subdivision of land holdings in the countryside couldn't keep pace with these demographic changes. Poverty was driving more and more rural people into cities like Dublin, a mass migration that resulted in very difficult social and living conditions. Living conditions in the quarter of Dublin where Madden had grown up were extremely poor by then, for example. Large sections of the population had no employment at all or only found employment very occasionally. Thousands were hungry and without adequate clothing. The houses were overcrowded and the streets teemed with beggars. Dirt and disease were widespread.

Madden saw all of this deprivation and knew how fortunate he was that he didn't have to try and eke out a living in such conditions. His own family had left the inner-city area where they had originally lived a long time before this and Madden himself now set up home in Rathmines, a more well-to-do area where the air was less polluted. Like anyone else who didn't have a job he did not enjoy being idle and it was this period of unemployment - while the Tories were in power - which was the catalyst for his "Irish" period, a period of his life when he found himself more involved with Nationalistic issues than ever. Ireland was a hive of political activity at this juncture. The Repeal Movement was in full swing and the Repeal Association was thriving in most corners of Ireland.

At first it was only the Catholic Archbishop MacHale[198] who had had the courage to stand with Daniel O'Connell on the Repeal question but he was later joined by a group of young lawyers who regularly attended the meetings O'Connell organised in Dublin's Corn Exchange. Two of the most prominent people in this latter group were Thomas Davis and John Blake Dillon. Davis was a Protestant and the son of an army surgeon while Dillon was a Catholic who had spent a couple of years in Maynooth[199] studying for the priesthood. In autumn 1841, both men got to know a young journalist from Belfast named Charles Gavin Duffy and a year later the three men founded a weekly newspaper they titled *The Nation*. The foundation of this newspaper gave a new and powerful impetus to the Repeal Movement, an impetus that surprised O'Connell amongst others. The talent and intelligence that these Young Irelanders[200] brought to their writing was to reinvigorate Irish Nationalist aspirations in a country that had never previously had a propaganda tool as effective as *The Nation* was.

The work of this coterie of Young Irelanders, when combined with O'Connell's mass appeal generated such an explosive growth in Nationalist sentiment that the British Government in

Ireland began to seriously consider repressing the movement. The Government got its opportunity when a rumour circulated that O'Connell was to speak at a Monster meeting[201] in Clontarf, Dublin, on the same site that the Vikings were defeated in the eleventh century. The Government announced a ban on this meeting the night before it was due to take place, a meeting where an estimated one million people were due to gather. The Government also sent soldiers and military supplies to the proposed venue and fearing a massacre O'Connell decided to cancel the meeting. O'Connell was arrested and imprisoned, however, a prison term that would do irreparable harm to his political power.[202] Madden found himself caught up in these revolutionary rumblings when he gave a speech at a public dinner in Dublin shortly after his return from West Africa. Any Irishman who was familiar with oppression in his own country had a duty to do whatever he could to do away with tyranny in foreign lands also, he said. This statement reflected his personal philosophy on life, where there was no distinction made between love of country and love of humanity. The Irish and Black Africans were two races that found themselves in a similarly downtrodden position, in Madden view. Around this time, Madden got to know the group of intellectuals associated with *The Nation* and Thomas Davis, in particular. He had huge respect for this group and their work. Davis believed that Ireland's traditions and heritage needed to be revived so that they could become potent symbols for the Irish people again.

With this in mind, he encouraged Madden in the research for his latest project i.e. the history of the United Irishmen, this despite of the fact that O'Connell spoke so contemptuously of the 1798 rebels. O'Connell could quote - "She is far from the land of the O'Moore" and Emmet's Speech[203] perfectly from memory but he considered the United Irishmen a "pack of miscreants," a term which he used when referring to them publicly on a number of occasions. Madden had a very different opinion of the United Irishmen, needless to say. While he wasn't a bone fide republican and while he wasn't averse to publishing material that was critical of some of the United Irishmen and the actions they had taken, the bulk of what he wrote about this revolutionary group was sympathetic to one degree or another. The truth was that Madden had been gathering material for this research project on the United Irishmen for many years before he had Davis or any of the other members of that circle. He had gathered a range of material on the history of the United Irishmen while in America and even – via correspondence – while he was stationed in the West Indies.

Now that he was back in Ireland, he could actually meet or correspond with the few 1798 rebels who were still alive or with their relatives. With the benefit of hindsight, we can now see that Madden sometimes misinterpreted the information he collated. Nevertheless, he still deserves great credit for the huge efforts he made to preserve material that would otherwise have been neglected or destroyed. Despite Madden's best intentions, not all of the archival materials he collated survived the passage of time. For example, one of Madden's bibliographies that survived to the present day and is held in the Royal Irish Academy (RIA) in Dublin, lists 72 volumes of pamphlets which Madden collected during his researches – the majority of which related to the period 1798-1803. These pamphlets have never come to light however and where they ended up or whether they still exist somewhere today is not clear. What this RIA bibliography does indicate is that Madden was just as diligent about collating printed archival material as he was at recording the oral history relating to 1798 *ipsissima verba* from the rebels themselves. Like every historian, Madden's trawl of the research sources was not always successful.

While his account of the Sheares family was a very complete one, it would have been even more detailed if he had managed to locate the papers John Sheares had left in the safe keeping of "the worthy Charles Coughlan" in Cork. Fearing that the British army might find these papers, Coughlan had hidden these documents in the ceiling of his old house but when he went to search for them again, he found that they had (unfortunately) been eaten to powder by mice! This must have been quite a blow to Madden as nothing upset him more than the discovery that irreplaceable historical material had been permanently destroyed. Madden made an arrangement with a London-based publisher whereby the first four volumes Madden wrote could be published consecutively. This London-based publisher, also named Madden, (no relation) – produced all of the volumes on time, one pair in 1842 and the other pair in 1843. The first series of the *Lives* was dedicated to W.H. Curran as a mark of respect for a man who was the son of John Philpot Curran[204] and his father's biographer.

In addition to his own introduction, Madden also included a long historical essay by William Cooke Taylor introducing the first series of the *Lives*, although Cooke Taylor's name was not listed in the text - presumably because he preferred to remain anonymous. The first volume comprised a general account of the United Irishmen's Rising and its suppression. A particular subject of discussion was the fighting in Wicklow and Wexford and the roles of the various spies and informants who were working "behind the scenes" during these battles. One spy whose role was discussed in some detail was Thomas Reynolds who informed on Oliver Bond, Felix Byrne and John McCann.[205] The second volume of the *Lives* outlined the story of the two brothers Henry and John Sheares who were hanged for their part in the 1798 Rebellion and the various appendices to this text included thirty pages outlining the payments made by the British secret service to informants on the Irish rebel side. Madden dedicated the second series of the *Lives* to Dr. James Johnson who had himself been a member of the United Irishmen. This man had provided a good deal of archival information for Madden as relating to the events of 1798 and had also defended Madden when his qualifications as a medical doctor were questioned by those individuals who disliked Madden and his political views.

This series included some very long introductory essays by

Madden where he provided a good deal of valuable biographical information on the roles and lives of many well-known United Irishmen including Samuel Neilson, Thomas Addis Emmet, William James Macneven, Arthur O'Connor, William Sampson and Henry Joy McCracken – in addition to a number of appendices and addenda chronicling the spy system then operated by the British authorities in Ireland

Madden was lucky to have his wife Harriet as a willing assistant in this research relating to 1798. In addition to re-writing much of his material in a more succinct form Harriet provided much-needed assistance as regards tracking down research materials and archival sources. She was as much of an expert on 1798 as Richard Madden ever was, and was able to respond to the large range of correspondence and enquiries as forwarded by other 1798 scholars when Madden was working away from home. The vital role played by Harriet in her husband's research is evident in a letter she wrote to "dearest Richard" from 52 Rathmines Road, Dublin on the fifteenth of February, 1842, in which she described a postal correspondence she had with Robert Brampston Smith, the son of Maria Steele, a woman who had once been engaged to John Sheares and who had died only a few months prior to this correspondence. Lizzie Cogan had collected some songs on Madden's behalf also at this time and Harriet was eager to forward copies of these songs to Madden at this time also.

> *Mister Smith called here this morning with a number of letters and other papers. These included the last ever letter written by John Sheares to his sister Julia and two other letters he wrote to Miss Maria Steele which include some verses of a poem...Smith said that the Sheares papers were of no personal value to him; he didn't have a high regard for the Sheares', particular John, who he said never practiced any religion. Smith is happy that you should have all of these papers...Miss Steele informed me that she can find no copy of that final letter which John wrote to her prior to his hanging.*

She thinks that Smith may have burnt that letter. Smith seems like a very pleasant and well-informed individual. He would love to meet you some time.[206]

One of Madden's best biographical notes, as produced in the *Lives*, was based on these papers as provided by Smith. Madden's biographical essay on the two Sheares brothers has a romantic air about it but it also provides a very clear and concise portrait of the revolutionary atmosphere that swept Europe as a whole during the 1790s. The Sheares brothers lived in France during 1792 and 1793 and it was here that they came under the influence of the philosophy of revolution. With some excitement they had witnessed the ransacking of the Bastille and the execution of Louis the Sixteenth. Of the two brothers, John was the more extreme in his views. He was a member of a radical political club while living in Paris and it was he who brought his brother Henry into the Young Ireland movement when they returned to live in Ireland. The brothers soon came to prominence and they would assume control of the movement when the government incarcerated its entire Ruling Committee.

The Sheares brothers began to prepare the ground for rebellion and John published a number of public proclamations inciting the Irish people to revolt, proclamations which the British authorities were extremely unhappy about. In one of these proclamations Sheares referred to the then Lord Chancellor of Ireland, Lord Clare, as "the prime miscreant, the Robespierre of Ireland, the nefarious author and apologist of atrocities without name and number." The colonial government soon discovered that the Sheares brothers were now in charge of the United Irishmen and – according to Madden – they tried to get John Warenford Armstrong, a Militia officer to infiltrate the movement in order to betray the Sheares and destroy the United Irishmen. Captain Armstrong did his job well. He got to know John Sheares in a bookshop on Grafton Street, Dublin, one day by pretending to be a Republican. John Sheares was so "taken in" by the militia man that he even invited him to his house on Baggot Street where he introduced him to Henry. Unfortunately for him, John was indiscreet in his talk and before long he had told Armstrong all of their plans for the rebellion. Naively, he even asked Armstrong to help him influence those members of the army garrison in Loughanstown who were sympathetic to the rebel cause in order to bring them into the United Irishmen organisation. Already, a good number of the men in this garrison were already secret members of the United Irishmen. While John Sheares was indiscreet, Henry appears to have been a shrewder individual and a better judge of human nature. He was suspicious of Armstrong from the very beginning and avoided his company as much as possible whereas John Sheares was too forthright in his conversations and found it very difficult to keep classified information to himself. He let Armstrong in on the workings of the organisation and had him acting as a look-out on more than one occasion. He also introduced him to other leading members of the movement including the well-known Dublin surgeon Dr. Lawless, a man who was actually related to Lord Cloncurry. Armstrong ingratiated himself with John Sheares and other members of the United Irishmen so well that the last time he spent in the Sheares company before betraying them was at a dinner in their house on Baggot Street, a dinner where most of the Sheares family were in attendance.

> *He sat down in the company of the Sheares' mother and her daughter and enjoyed the witty repartee of one of the wives of the Sheares' brothers. He even played with their children on his knee. One of the Sheares' brother's wives even accompanied Armstrong on the harp as he sang, little realising that within a couple of days, his treachery would leave her children without a father.*[207]

Such was Madden's account of an occasion that was "too ugly to bear thinking about." A few days subsequent to this dinner, Sheares brothers were arrested and imprisoned in

Kilmainham Jail. While in custody, Armstrong paid John a visit. Amazingly, John Sheares still had no inkling of who had betrayed them and he provided Armstrong with even more damning evidence that would be used later against him and other leading members of the United Irishmen. Sheares even told Armstrong about a document that was hidden in his house the contents of which would implicate him even further in the rebellious plot if the colonial authorities were to get their hands on it. Armstrong vowed to go their home and move the document to a safer hiding place but instead of doing this, he informed the authorities who immediately raided the house and seized the document.

The Sheares brothers were charged with treason and a date was set for their trial. In the meantime the chief attorneys for the prosecution were changed, a fact which didn't bode well for the fate of the two brothers, in Madden's view. The trial judge appointed to hear the case was (Kind) Arthur Wolfe – later titled Lord Kilwarden – as a reward for his:

> ...securing the services of a Chief-Attorney of the correct calibre – (The Very-Honourable John Toler – later Lord Norbury) – a man who was ruthless and speedy in his application of the law.[208]

What Madden was suggesting here was that the Lord Chancellor, Lord Clare, was about to exact revenge for personal "issues" and rivalries and that he was doing this with the help of the Chief-Attorney. As a young attorney, Clare was in love with Alicia Swete from Cork, a woman who had rejected him and who had eloped with Henry Sheares shortly afterwards. Maria Steele, who had been John Sheares fiancé at one point in time, was the person who told Madden of these personal "aspects" to the trial. As she told Madden the Lord Chancellor had never forgiven this slight to his ego. Consequently:

> As Attorney-General, Toler did everything that his patrons and employers asked him to do. It is doubtful too whether a

closing speech – (as relating to the Henry Sheares case) as unjust as Toler's was ever given either. The manipulation of the real facts and the dismissal of that evidence that was favourable to the accused. He made various statements that were in direct contradiction with the evidence, even the evidence as provided by the prosecution.[209]

The two prisoners were found guilty and were sentenced to (immediate) death by hanging. The severity of this judgement came as a great shock to Henry. It also came as a big surprise to his brother John who was sure that Henry would be released irrespective of what happened to himself. All along, Henry had been completely unaware of how much danger they were in, and he broke down when the judgement was announced. He was so shocked that he was barely able to speak in order to issue his final request – i.e. that he, his wife and six children be allowed say goodbye to one another prior to the execution. As it turned out, neither of the Sheares brothers were given the opportunity to say goodbye to their family. Both men were hanged the following day despite an official last-minute attempt to stall Henry's execution, a request which - Madden stated - was refused by Lord Clare.

Madden's biography of the Sheares brothers provoked a letter from one corrupt individual - none other than Captain Armstrong himself. He was an elderly man by the time the biographies appeared in print but he was still alert and in good health. He informed Madden that his history of the United Irishmen was "well-written, entertaining and interesting" but that the text contained some misunderstandings. He recommended that he and Madden meet one another to discuss the various issues raised in Madden's book. Madden accepted this offer and the writer and the elderly informer came face-to-face for two hours in Madden's house in Rathmines, Dublin when they discussed the events of 1798 in the presence of legal representative, Thomas O'Hagan[210], who would later become Lord Chancellor, the first Catholic to hold this position since the reign of James II.

Madden and Armstrong prepared a report highlighting the main issues that they debated that day in Rathmines. The following day Madden also wrote a private memo for his own benefit, however, in which he gave a more concise account of his discussions with Armstrong and the manner in which the latter had denied all of the allegations Madden made against him. For example, Armstrong claimed that the original contact between himself and the Sheares was at the instigation of Browne the bookseller in Grafton Street and not on the promptings of the British Government. Armstrong also claimed that Browne had advised him to get to know the Sheares as they had similar political leanings to himself! It was not true that he had played with Henry Sheares children the night before the Sheares brothers were taken into custody or that he had encouraged Mrs. Sheares to accompany him on the harp. He had only been to dinner once ever in the Sheares house, Armstrong claimed, and this had been at the instigation of Lord Castlereagh who had encouraged him to try and find out as much as he could about the Sheares and their plans for rebellion. He had done this once only but had regretted it immediately afterwards. This was the one and only link that he had had with the Sheares or their demise – or so he claimed. Castlereagh[211] had regarded it as vital to capture the Sheares given the acts of high treason that they were engaged in:

> It is clear to me, he said to Madden, that you are a man of a certain political persuasion and that your views in this area are clearly already long-established and biased in nature.[212]

Madden's history of the United Irishmen was a very exact and valuable treatise, Armstrong maintained, but only somebody who was partisan in their political views could have done so much work on such a subject. Madden refuted Armstrong's various claims as regards inaccuracy and bias. With hindsight it can be said that the only sliver of truth in the captain's arguments was the assertion that Madden was biased against him prior to hearing Armstrong's account of events. He had indeed accepted word-for-word every minor fact proffered by Henry Sheares' wife as relating to events which had taken place more than forty years previously. Madden would never have admitted to holding any pre-conceived positions or prejudices as regards his historical researches of course. His second edition of the memoir - i.e. the Sheares biography – would be prove even more damning of Armstrong's involvement in the executions of some of the principal rebels in the 1798 rebellion. When Armstrong died, Madden wrote the following epitaph for him:

He lived a long time and died as he had lived, inhuman till the end. He showed not a hint of shame as regards his grave dishonour. No pity nor remorse did he ever express.[213]

Madden had even had the temerity to ask Armstrong just how much blood-money he had received for his services to the State. Armstrong had never given a reply to him on this but Madden had already worked out that Armstrong had been paid over 20,000 pounds during the course of his career. He had received the guts of 500 pounds per annum for a total of 58 years. This recompense made him worse than Judas Iscariot himself, the latter a wretch who had received only 30 pieces of silver for his trouble, money that he had thrown away almost as soon as he had accepted it. The Irish had always had a hatred for spies and informers. An anecdote illustrating this long-entrenched hatred described how a woman was once accused of referring to her husband as "Carey." This was only few days after someone with that same name had really betrayed the insurrectionist group known as the Invincibles.[214] Rejecting the accusation, the woman had stated that she would call her husband the Anti-Christ before she would even think of referring to him by such an insulting name. One hundred years prior to this it was Leonard McNally, the lawyer, who composed "The Lass of Richmond Hill" who betrayed a large number of the United Irishmen. Incredibly, the same McNally had the neck to act as defence attorney for Robert Emmet after the rebellion of 1803, where he actually passed on his client's private instructions to the then colonial Government. When Madden was a young man he passed McNally a number of times in the street and his description of him gives another insight regarding the loathing that the general Irish public felt towards spies or those who betrayed others.

> *MacNally's complexion, (he wrote), did not contribute much to improve his peculiar cast of countenance; it was extremely sallow; it was the complexion of a man who had no red globules in his blood, but a great deal of bile commingled with it - that mouldy complexion of a dirty brown hue, unctuous and unwholesome withal, which gives an appearance to the face of being always soiled, and an idea that its owner is either sickly in the flesh, uncomfortable in the spirit, or labours under that complicated form of hydrophobia manifested in a horror of soap as well as water...The predominant expression of his cold, unimpressioned countenance and dead-setting look, was that of quiet laying in wait tendencies, indicative of adroitness, sharpness, an instinctive weariness and habitual watchfulness; one was reminded by it of the hawk's beak, and the cold, grey twinkling of another bird of prey, of an ominous and evil-looking character.*[215]

Madden researched long and hard to prove Leonard McNally's betrayal but he worked even more feverishly to expose whoever had betrayed Lord Edward Fitzgerald, the most senior leader in the United Irishmen of 1798. He carefully sifted through the archival evidence ruling out each individual on whom suspicion had fallen as he went along - for instance - Samuel Neilson,[216] about whom Madden had corresponded with the composer Tom Moore when he was writing his life of Lord Edward. Others who had been "in the frame" as potential informers on Lord Edward Fitzgerald included Nicholas Murphy and his servant girl - in whose house Lord Edward had been captured;

two government functionaries named Thomas Reynolds and John Hughes, and Peter Finnerty, Lawrence Tighe, the "notorious" Walter Cox[217] and Felix Rourke. The list detailing the various monies paid by the British Secret Services which Madden appended to the *Lives* (first series), called attention to a payment of 1000 pounds as paid to "FH for the discovery of L.E.F." Madden surmised that the letters F.H. referred to some type of educational qualification. Madden's hunch was that the letters were a coded reference to someone who might have had some type of association with the legal profession. Madden's guess proved wrong however as revealed when the correspondence of Lord Cornwallis[218] the head of the English army in 1798 was released into the public domain in the form of a publication. The letters F.H. actually stood for Francis Higgins[219], the then editor of the government newspaper *The Freeman's Journal*. It was Higgins who - according to Cornwallis, was:

> ...the person who procured for me all the intelligence respecting Lord Edward Fitzgerald and got - to set him.[220]

Another question which remained to be answered was - who had "set up" Lord Edward Fitzgerald for Francis Higgins? Unknown to him, Madden as good as answered this mystery. Someone named Francis Magan appeared on the secret services list and unsurprisingly, Madden's suspicions were aroused. Accompanied by his nephew Willy Cogan, Madden visited a number of different places where he thought he might find an example of Magan's signature. James Lynam was an officer in the Common Pleas Office of the Four Courts and was very helpful to Madden when he went there seeking any information he could find on Francis Magan in 1847. Madden discovered that Magan had been:

> ...a lawyer who had no work, a Roman Catholic, an individual who was both shy and anxious by nature. He was a man of few words, a man who put on a front in an effort to disguise his own inadequacies.[221]

Magan had lived at 20 Usher's Island near Watling Street in Dublin. On the day that he had been captured and unaware that he was being followed, Lord Fitzgerald had made his way from this address on to the house of a family named Murphy on Thomas Street. As soon as he arrived at this house he was set upon by a group of men. Fitzgerald was a tough individual and put up a good fight. In the struggle that followed, a policeman was killed and Fitzgerald himself was injured before being captured and taken into custody. Fitzgerald's capture on that fateful day had been set in motion by a message that the Government Under-Secretary, Edward Cooke, had passed on to the City's Provost, Major Sirr. Madden found this out when he consulted Sirr's papers in Trinity College, Dublin, after they were released for public consumption. He noticed Magan's name again in the correspondence pertaining to Cornwallis which included a list of government pension recipients. Madden had - to all intents and purposes - identified the informer at this stage and would add Magan's name to the list of people paid "for services rendered" that he had first published in the 1842 edition of the *Lives*.

The three hundred pounds payment to Magan was referenced as "Magan per Mr. Higgins." Madden had identified one of the most surreptitious traitors in Irish history, although he didn't get much credit for his discovery - the result of a good deal of pain-staking research. Another historian of this period, W.J. Fitzpatrick, whose book, *Secret Service under Pitt: Shame Squire* was published in 1892, went carefully through Higgins' letters when Dublin Castle's archive was opened to the public and discovered more about the intricacies of the plot to trap Lord Edward Fitzgerald. He discovered that Magan was friendly with Higgins, and was possibly even his godson. It turns out that both men were in close contact throughout the period when Magan was associating with many of the United Irishmen's most important leaders. Magan had insinuated himself so well into the United Irishmen's structures that he was elected to the United Irishmen's Central Council. In fact his degree of influence on the organisation had been such that he had even persuaded Lord Edward Fitzgerald to delay the Rebellion somewhat. This delay was designed to give the Government more time to organise the round-up of those leading United Irishmen who made up the Ruling Council. It wasn't just his friendship with Higgins that had steered Magan into an informer's role however. His father's business had gone into liquidation in 1797, having been in financial difficulty for a number of years prior to this. His father had also borrowed heavily to the tune of 4000 pounds with Higgins as benefactor. The younger Magan was well aware of these loans and had himself acted as guarantor for the mortgages on a number of houses owned by his father.

The story of how Magan "set up" Lord Edward Fitzgerald is somewhat bizarre. A neighbour of Magan's, a Miss Moore, mentioned to him that Fitzgerald was looking for lodgings. Magan offered to put up Fitzgerald in his own home on Usher's Island, a house that had a reputation for grandiosity stretching back to the days when the Archbishop of Dublin had lived there. Miss Moore was delighted by Magan's kind offer and relayed the news to Fitzgerald. Magan sent a message to Dublin Castle in the meantime and the government placed a cordon of troops around Usher's Island that evening. Miss Moore and Lord Fitzgerald made their way towards Usher's Island the same evening but turned back as soon as they saw the large military force in the area. They then managed to make it back to Thomas Street in safety where they found lodgings for the night in the house of the Murphy family. The following day the unsuspecting Miss Moore told Magan what had happened the previous evening and the Castle were sent another message detailing where Fitzgerald could be captured. The ambush was set up and Fitzgerald was carried from the house injured and in a wheelchair. Incredible as it may seem, Magan was elected to a more senior position again within the United Irishmen that very night! Later that year, a Bar meeting was organised to discuss the Unification project then being mooted between Ireland and England. Magan was in attendance and still invoking his

Nationalist credentials by siding with individuals such as Charles Kendal Bushe, Jonah Barrington, Peter Burrowes, John Philpot Curran, W. Conygham Plunkett and Leonard MacNally - all of whom were against unification and in favour of more independence for Ireland. In 1812, Mangan, Daniel O'Connell and others were involved in the organisation of a monster meeting in favour of Catholic Emancipation. By then Magan had a reputation as a generous supporter and benefactor of various Catholic causes, monies, some of which (ironically) were coming straight from the coffers of the British Secret Services. He received a government pension of 200 pounds a year until he died in 1834 and this was probably bolstered by other gratuities as provided by a number of other government sources. Whatever his various sources of income, he went from an (apparently) penniless position before the 1798 Rebellion to being a very wealthy man by the time he died thirty-six years later. His wealth was inherited by his sister and it is some consolation to know that when she died most of his money went to various charitable causes.

Magan and his sister spent the bulk of their lives living in the splendour of their residence on Usher's Quay, the house that George Saintsbury referred to as the *domus portentosa* - a residence that was modified year-by-year so as to heighten its grandeur. While he lived in very genteel surroundings Magan spent the last twenty years of his life terrified that his dark secret might be uncovered. Amateur historian Joseph Hamilton was the first to come close to lifting the veil on his murky past. Hamilton almost stumbled on the truth about Magan by accident as investigated the betrayals of 1798 with a view to clearing the name of Samuel Neilson of any suspicion in this regard. Tom Moore had had his suspicions about Neilson and he was pursuing a number of different angles of enquiry when somebody suggested to Hamilton the possibility that Magan had "fed" Moore the rumours about Neilson so as to get himself "off the hook." While Hamilton eventually proved that Neilson was not guilty of any treachery he also mistakenly managed to shift suspicion onto other people who were innocent. Nevertheless, when Hamilton published the results of his researches he came much closer to the truth than he realised, so close as to make Magan very worried. Magan had reason to be worried again in 1842 when that inquisitive doctor named Madden began to ask questions around his neighbourhood, particularly when he went to interview Miss Moore (now known as Mrs. Maccready's, her lips remained sealed; she didn't as much as mention Magan's name during her conversations with Madden. Shortly before her death however she shared her suspicions with her son as follows:

The government received information that Fitzgerald and I were going to Ushers Island that evening. This was information that only two people could have been aware of i.e. Magan or I; even Lord Fitzgerald didn't know where we were headed until we set off that evening. Then Mrs. MacCready said something that was full of meaning. If Magan is innocent, then I am the betrayer.[222]

Magan was buried in the crypts of Saint Michael and John[223] which were on the same site on which the Smock Alley theatre once stood. His resting place was clearly situated at a distance from the crypts of the other people buried there, an indication of the hated many people felt towards him - even after his death. The terms of his will stated that the parish priest say an annual Mass for the repose of his soul. While the crypts are long-forgotten now it was once the custom for visitors to the graveyard to kick Magan's tombstone or spit on it as an expression of their hatred for the informer. Ironically, Madden himself was years later to find himself buried quite close to Leonard MacNally, who was probably the most notorious of all the informers during this period of Irish history. The survival of Nicholas Murphy's[224] - (it was in his house that Fitzgerald was taken) -account of the events of that era proved a very useful source for Madden's memoir of Lord Edward Fitzgerald.

Madden procured a copy of this manuscript from his own relative, William Powell, and he was particularly taken by the manner in which Murphy had suffered both poverty and derision at the hands of his own people and yet remained loyal to the cause of Irish freedom.

> *If he had played the villain with his friend, a monument might have been erected to his memory; as it is there is not even a common headstone over his grave.*[225]

Madden visited the Murphy family where they still lived in Thomas Street, Dublin, accompanied by Tom Moore's sister, a woman whom he knew well and who also had a deep interest in the exploits of the 1798 rebels. The two of them followed up this visit with another where they examined Herbert's[226] painting of Lord Edward Fitzgerald's capture. Madden expressed his dismay at the fact that no public body had as yet shown an interest in purchasing this painting on behalf of the State:

> *...this painting which depicts that most deadly attack after which the most noble Irish person ever lay fatally wounded.*[227]

In Christmas 1857, Madden visited the room in Newgate Prison, England, where Lord Edward Fitzgerald had died. He was accompanied on this visit - where he made copious notes about the prison, the surrounding area, the prison's scaffold – by Sir John Lentaigne who was one of the directors of Irish prisons and a member of the Loan Fund Board. When Madden first began to put his history of the United Irishmen together, a few prominent members of the United Irishmen were still alive. These included Macneven who was living in the United States and Arthur O'Connor who was based in France. Madden had a close friendship with Macneven and as a consequence was able to source some valuable material from him at an early stage of the project. His correspondence with O'Connor began a good deal later into the project - in the year 1842. He received a letter from O'Connor in September of that year where O'Connor denounced Daniel O'Connell for the back-biting and criticisms he had made in regard to the United Irishmen. Without the efforts of the United Irishmen, O'Connor said, O'Connell would never have achieved Catholic Emancipation for the Irish people. O'Connor responded to Madden's list of questions about 1798 and it was on these responses that Madden based his account of O'Connor's involvement in the 1798 rebellion.

There were certain "gaps" in this essay as printed in the first edition of the *Lives* however. This was because Madden didn't want to generate controversy by involving himself in "personality clashes" as relating to O'Connor's memory of events. When O'Connor himself published a memoir entitled: *Monopoly the Cause of All Evil* (1848), Madden felt compelled to make public the material he had omitted previously in relation to O'Connor for this, the second edition of the *Lives*. This new account as relating to O'Connor's role in the 1798 rebellion included information which did not reflect well on O'Connor who had a deep-seated dislike of the Catholic committee's view of the 1803 rebellion. Napoleon Bonaparte allegedly told O'Connor that he had no respect whatsoever for the leaders of the 1803 rebellion. O'Connor agreed with him on this saying that he thought the attempted rebellion of that year was a crazy idea. O'Connor's book had also been scathing of the two Emmet brothers. In O'Connor's view, one of them was a coward and the other was impetuous and crazy. Madden was upset at this attack on the Emmet brothers, an attack which he felt was so exaggerated and malicious that it couldn't be taken seriously.

Madden would later write a memoir of Robert Emmet where he would explain that the deeply-held animosity which O'Connor had for the Emmets had its roots in a personal "grievance" - an argument that had once occurred between O'Connor and Robert Emmet. Madden held in deep respect the memory of all of the United Irishmen. The only one issue that "bothered" him with respect to the rebel's memory was the fact that some of the rebels had not been particularly religious.

Madden took note of the anti-clericalism that underlay the prejudices of a few members of the United Irishmen and outlined O'Connor's views with regards to institutional religion as an example of same. The central thesis of that book had been O'Connor's attempt to prove that the ranks of the Christian clergy consisted solely of "corporate priests", i.e. philistines and pagans who were in reality the enemies of Christianity. The "poor old gentleman" had published what Madden viewed as this "farrago of polemical twaddle" when he was all of ninety years of age. There was little doubt that he was "of sound mind" and honestly believed in these views, however, given that Madden had visited him in person the year before the book was published (1847), when he was still very mentally alert.

O'Connor's views on religious matters and his irrational hatred of all clergy irrespective of denomination were excessive and eccentric however. He believed that there was a body of "corporate priests" within Catholicism who were conspiring with the help of the Jesuits to prevent democracy from taking a full hold in every European country. Volney and Voltaire were the intellectuals whom O'Connor admired above all others and Madden cited brief passages from O'Connor's book to highlight "the rabid malevolence of a fanatical infidel and a reckless calumniator." Despite the fact that both men held philosophical positions that were diametrically opposed to one another, Madden was quick to acknowledge the fact that O'Connor had been a loyal Irish patriot, a man who had suffered much for Ireland and whose presence brought with it a very real sense of authority to the cause of Irish freedom. Arthur O'Connor was not the only person with whom he disagreed at this particular juncture. He also criticised O'Connor's brother Roger, hinting that he, along with some other members of the family were all a bit odd. The first thing that Madden questioned was whether the O'Connors were actually entitled to refer to themselves as O'Connor at all. The family had been known as the Conners from Connerville, County Cork going back three generations and Madden wrote a satirical excerpt in relation to Roger as if to confirm this.

> *Yet Roger well an O can claim*
> *Tho' not of old connection:*
> *The O that suits this hero's name*
> *Is O! the interjection*[228]

Roger, like Arthur O'Connor, had spent time in prison because of his involvement in the 1798 Rebellion and upon his release he had bought a house which he allegedly later burnt down in order to claim the insurance money. He was later tried for his alleged role in an attempt to rob a mail train, but the charges did not stick and he was released. It was later rumoured that the same train had been "held up", not in order to steal money but in order to "intercept" a batch of love letters that were passing between Sir Francis Burdett and the woman he was in love with – i.e. Lady Oxford. Roger's own "domestic life" was complex. Two of his wives having predeceased him, he eloped with a married woman whose servant girl Roger was also particularly close to. Later again, he fell in love with a young Kerry girl who was decades younger than him but whom he believed was a descendant of the ancient high-kings of Ireland and it was this girl who cared for him in his dotage. As one wit quipped - "It was not without reason," "that Roger was as attentive to females as he was to mails."[229] As with Arthur, Roger was a disciple of Voltaire and his writings. The Old Testament was nothing more than a historical story in his view and the New Testament was the same - the story of a good man who, convinced of his own uniqueness, had deceived himself. This sort of talk offended Madden and precluded him from praising Roger O'Connor's other virtues - e.g. his nationalistic fervour which he had a good deal of respect for.

If the United Irishmen had succeeded in their rebellion, Madden stated, Roger O'Connor - a man who had no scruples about publishing a collection of inaccuracies and lies while simultaneously claiming their veracity - would now be a major figure in the government of a Christian country, a country whose population believed strongly in Christ's divinity and the inspiration of the Scriptures. When Madden later heard that Roger had returned to Catholicism prior to his death, he investigated the rumour with some optimism. The results of his enquiries are a good example however of Madden's tendency to note unverified and randomly-acquired facts as if they were one hundred per cent accurate. A man named David Crowley died and his papers which were given to Madden by Crowley's wife including a description of Roger O'Connor's death. Crowley had been a Catholic priest at one stage but had fallen foul of the Church authorities by publishing a number of articles which were critical of the Catholic Church. He had then married a Presbyterian woman in a wedding ceremony that was officiated over by his brother Matias, a man who was already a Protestant having previously worked as a Catholic priest and a professor of theology at one time.

Twenty years after becoming a Presbyterian, Crowley changed his religious affiliation again when he joined the Unitarian community based at Strand Road in Dublin. He made this change because he believed that the Unitarians had interpreted the Christian message in the most rational way possible and had abandoned those elements of pomp, superstition and state-affiliation that still burdened other churches. Madden had this to say with reference to Crowley's religious explorations and scholarly abilities -"If the unfortunate Mr. David Crowley had lived in Tertullian's era, he would have been a well-renowned heretic. He outshone anybody whom I ever met in terms of intellectual ability with the exception of my poor friend the Abbé Lammenais."[230] Madden recalled the description of how Crowley - (then a priest in the parish where O'Connor was resident) - had been called to administer the Last Rites to Roger O'Connor as he lay on his deathbed. Satisfied that O'Connor was contrite regarding the various sins committed by him during his life, Crowley gave him absolution and anointed him with the holy oils. Crowley's description of that occasion had concluded with this verse:

O'Connor's dead, the foe of church and state -
A chieftain too in his own wild conceit;
He spurned all precepts - even kept a whore,
And lived life a thorough epicure.
But in death's hour the priest stood by his side,
And prayed. O'Connor said Amen, and died.[231]

The first number of the *Nation*, "Young Ireland's" weekly, newspaper was published shortly after the first series of the (United Irishmen's) *Lives* appeared in print, and Madden began to write poetry for the new newspaper under the pen-name "Ierne." His poetry wasn't of the same quality as that of poets as accomplished as James Clarence Mangan[232], Samuel Ferguson[233] or Thomas Davis who also wrote for the *Nation* but this didn't concern Madden unduly as he enjoyed the social and intellectual milieu that went with the newspaper. It was a similar intellectual milieu to that in which he had moved a number of years before when his work was published alongside that of writers like Campbell, Moore and Beranger[234] - a group who believed that Madden possessed "a sort of instinctive knowledge of the genuine pathos, or that which is true in poetry." Madden once said to Aubrey de Vere[235] that he had never written a dozen lines of true poetry in his life and this was an assessment with which most of the literary critics of his day concurred. Only one of the many hundreds of poems which Madden wrote was ever anthologised apart from the poem entitled "The Bishop of Ross" that appeared in the anthological series "The Spirit of the Nation"[236], a poem that began as follows:

The tramp of the trooper is heard at Macroom;
The soldiers of Cromwell are spared from Clonmel,
And Broghill - the merciless Broghill - is come
On a mission of murder which pleases him well.

Some of Madden's poetry did have an influence on the reading public however, as evident after Madden's death when examples of his poetry were published in the compilation

Literary Remains of the United Irishmen, which appeared in 1887. In actual fact, James Connolly[237], one of the leaders of the 1916 Rebellion liked to cite a few verses of Madden's poem - "Who killed Cock Robin?" from time to time and Pádraig Pearse learned this poem from Connolly and was known to hum verses such as the following while working:

> *What did the Volunteers?*
> *They mustered and paraded,*
> *Until their laurels faded,*
> *This did the Volunteers!*
> *How died the Volunteers?*
> *The death that's fit for slaves,*
> *They slunk into their graves,*
> *Thus died the Volunteers!*[238]

It is likely that verses such as this would have strengthened Pearse's determination that the rebels of his era would go down fighting.[239] Charles Gavan Duffy's assessment of Madden's potential contribution to the Nationalist cause was a perceptive one from the very beginning, however. Duffy,[240] one of the original founders of the *Nation* was regarded as one of the most able and astute of all the Young Irelanders. In a letter he wrote to Smith O'Brien[241] he mentioned that Madden had come to live in Dublin for a while and that the Young Irelanders could rely on him for support if they so wished. "He is more of an information-gatherer, however, as opposed to a planner or a man of action. Nevertheless, I will make it my business to speak to him and there are ways in which he would be useful to our aims…" In the second volume of his *My Life in Two Hemispheres* (1898), Charles Gavan Duffy says that it was during a chance meeting one day in Piccadilly, London that Madden and he realised they had identified the same individual, a person whom they had both independently suspected of operating as a spy and as an agent provocateur. They were referring here to a man named Mark O'Callaghan who had called to Madden's home a short time prior to this and claimed to be interested in setting-up a political movement which would be far more militant than any group then agitating for the rights of Irish Nationalists. Madden immediately became suspicious of O'Callaghan's motivations and asked his wife Harriet to take notes of his conversation with him. The latter hurriedly left again, however, a fact which only added to Madden's suspicions.

This O'Callaghan was actually a brother of John Cornelius O'Callaghan, an historian of the Irish Brigade and a man who would become a close friend of Madden's in later life. Mark was later to die in exile in Tasmania in a house he shared with another former spy – his body wasn't discovered for a full two days after his death - a J.D. Balfe. This story concerning the dangers of informers was only one of many which Madden came across at this juncture. The necessity for constant vigilance as relating to possible betrayal was also made clear to Madden in some postal correspondence he had with Thomas Davis after Madden had moved back to England:

> It would be safer for both yourself and myself if you destroy my letter as soon as you have read it. Some investigators on behalf of the security services here have recently issued us with threats and accusations of sedition and it could be that the same thing would happen if this letter was followed up by these same people and traced to England. A few stray sentences could be interpreted as evidence of a possible plot and presented to Parliament as such. And there is no question of an impending plot on the part of ourselves. We are far too astute to make any such attempt at plotting.[242]

Based on the then newspaper reports, Madden, who was recently returned to England, might have been under the impression that a bloody rebellion was imminent in Ireland.

Davis quickly set him right on this score however:

The threat of war isn't half as likely as you people based in England may think. The people here realise that the long haul is the strongest card that they can play. Unless the government here initiate a conflict with either its own troops or through the use of the Orange rabble, then there won't be any battle here in the near future. We are making great progress politically in bringing the upper classes around to our point of view. They won't join with the [Repeal] Association yet but they many of them will sign up to a Coalition Party or some type of Federal party which is on the point of being formed. If the leaders of this party are brave and clear-sighted they should be able to dictate their terms to England within two years. It is up to us them, the people in favour of Repeal,[243] as to when there will be war or peace. O'Connell could be in control of Ireland within three months but his wisdom and humanity dictates that a violent struggle be avoided for as long as it is possible to do so. He gained victory in '29 because of his potential for violence and not by the actual use of force. Who's to say that such an approach wouldn't work again? It won't work, you may say, because England is completely opposed to us. But where is the proof of this? I don't see any evidence for this, I have to say. On the contrary, my interpretation of the situation is that the English people may help us in our struggle if the situation remains peaceful here. Do you get an opportunity to read the provincial papers in England and Scotland? Most of them are on our side. It may be that the Whigs are actually helping us unknown to themselves. And the Assembly and its publications are actually writing and operating in such an indecisive fashion, reckless even, that we should surely get the better of them, provided we don't make the same mistakes that they make. If we have to take the hard road we know that they will come for a fight, however weakened by their recent actions - we, on the other hand, will see our responsibilities through and fight to the bitter end. Maybe it is unfortunate but we are not without hope if it comes to the crunch, a fact that I could prove to you if you were over here.[244]

As indicated in the previous excerpts, a strong bond of friendship existed between Madden and Davis, so much so that Madden even shared with him various details as relating to his own personal background. In fact, some of Madden's comments suggest that he may well have been attempting to counteract false rumours as regards his own loyalty to the Nationalist cause:

My father was a citizen of Dublin, a man who was respected both for his honesty and his religiosity. For sixty years he lived in the same house and on the same street. He was a well-travelled trader and was a wealthy man by the time I was born in the famous year of 1798. Years later, when he passed away, he left after him just two simple things, his good name and his children's pride in this legacy. My mother came from a long-established County Leitrim family. Her qualities and those of my father are summed up in a few words as inscribed on a tombstone which I had erected in their memory in Donnybrook cemetery - "They lived and died in the love and fear of God"[245]

Davis also heard about Madden's childhood and the early year's of his adulthood - how he was the youngest of twenty-one children and how his health had been poor as he approached his twenty-first birthday with the consequence that he (Madden) had proved an additional burden on his family. This burden had also been a financial one with the consequence that Madden had initially been unable to complete his studies.

Madden enjoyed Davis' company and in 1843 the two men made a pilgrimage to Wolfe Tone's grave in Bodenstown cemetery, from whose grave they took some flowers home as a memento. The two friends decided on this visit that a memorial stone ought to be erected over Tone's grave, as it had been run-down for some time, a job which Davis ensured was completed the following summer. During this "pilgrimage" of theirs, the men also spoke of poetry and Davis asked Madden to try and persuade Beranger to write a poem for the *Nation* similar to his well-known ode "Fontenoy" on the next occasion he was in Paris. While Madden knew Beranger, he was on even friendlier terms with the erudite French priest Abbé De Lammenais. The fact that the Abbé had rejected certain tenets of Catholic teaching and was also challenging the then Pope did not upset Madden unduly as he found the priest a very pleasant individual and excellent company. Madden would visit him in Le Chesnil any time that he was in Paris where he would encourage De Lammenais to research his genealogy, including his mother's heritage which was Irish. One day de Lammenais brought Madden to meet Beranger at his house in Rue Vineuse, Plassey in the suburbs of Paris. Beranger, the poet of revolutionary politics and the man whose songs roused the French populace to overthrow Charles the 10th and the Bourbon Dynasty, was, by then, an old man. In fact, he was living in a one-room flat and in very impoverished conditions and he would have died of hunger if not for the kindness of Lafayette.[246]

Madden was particularly impressed by the old man's kindness, erudition and good humour despite the very difficult circumstances he found himself in, while Beranger commended Madden on his campaigning for the abolition of slavery. Subsequent to his initial meeting with Beranger, Madden regularly invited various guests to accompany him on his visits to the elderly composer of political songs. On one occasion the guest was an American congressman from one of the states where slavery was permitted. Beranger was very polite to his American visitor and only raised the slavery issue when the Congressman was on his way home, remarking how strange it was that a country where everybody was supposed to be equal permitted slavery, thereby making a mockery of all Republican ideals. Gavan Duffy, like Madden, was an admirer of Beranger and was also a biographer of Thomas Davis.[247] While Duffy didn't cite Madden as a source in the index to this biography of his, there are three references to Madden within the text itself. Duffy refers twice to the practical help which Davis gave Madden in relation to the publication of the first series of the United Irishmen's *Lives*. When the initial publisher he was working with failed to produce the first two series of the *Lives*, it was Davis who put Madden in touch with another publisher with whom he was able to arrange a suitable contract for the publication of the various *Lives* series. This publisher named James Duffy would become the official publisher of the Young Irelanders and was a man whom Madden trusted completely as indicated by the following note referring to the publication of the *Lives*:

> In one word…I am very happy to agree to whatever deal you propose, and there is no need to send me any further particulars in relation to the contract.[248]

Another reference to the Young Irelanders respect for Duffy as a publisher occurs in a letter (undated) from Davis to Madden where Davis says: "I received your manuscript and passed it onto J. Duffy. Of course you can correspond directly with the man himself if you wish, and if you don't mind he will send proofs to you directly, as this would be the most efficient way of doing things…J.D. will send you on the fifty pounds whenever it is convenient for you." Some of the same sources indicate that Davis was also hoping to use some of Madden's writings as a resource for a "History of Ireland" which he was then planning, while Madden himself credited Davis in the introduction to his book *Historical notice of penal laws against Roman Catholics*(1865)for inspiring him to write this (latter) book. Madden also submitted another manuscript of his - *The Connexion between the Kingdom of Ireland and the Crown of England*, a manuscript which was officially published in 1847, for an essay competition organised by the *Nation* newspaper. The competition, with the valuable prize of 200 pounds for the winner, had 47 entries. Amongst them was an essay by an unemployed public servant named Michael Barry, the composer of the well-known marching song *Step Together*, which took first prize. The judges for the competition included Thomas Davis, Smith O'Brien, and John O'Connell all acknowledged the quality of Madden's entry as outlined by Davis:

> *The judges were united in their praise of your excellent writing style. We also felt that the appendix to your work also deserved publication and that the work as a whole would be of great interest to Irish people in general, if published. The General Committee asked me to write to you (the author) to enquire as to whether you intended publishing your work. You might let me know what your intentions are in this regard. If your book was published the Committee would recommend that the Repeal Association buy a good many copies.*[249]

As it happens three hundred copies of Madden's book were divided out amongst the Repeal Association's various reading rooms. The appendix to the book was a very effective propaganda tool for the Young Irelanders including as it does the minutes of the Privy Council Correspondence between the years 1811 and 1817. It was possible to reproduce this correspondence word-for-word as it had been written up in Dublin Castle's minute books and published by the Young Irelanders. "There is no need to highlight how important these documents are given that they lay bare the Secret History of the English Government in Ireland subsequent to the Act of Union." Davis finished his letter to Madden as follows:

> *As regards other matters, you have enough information without me informing you further. There is a big growth in education here - the literary conservatives becoming more nationalistic by the week. The bigotry that appeared with the Bequests Bill has died away and there is now a greater sense of unity and*

purpose between our councils and representatives than at any other time within the past two years. Of course there are difficulties and dangers as relating even to our legal attempts to set up local structures ... but still...[250]

When eventually published, Madden's book included two dedications. The first was "to the people of England who love justice and to the people of Ireland who are longing for it." There was little difference between the descendants of the Saxon and the descendants of the Celts in Madden's view. Neither did he subscribe to the view that one race of people were more politically-able than the other. The second dedication read "to a dear friend and schoolmate" and was dedicated to his old friend Barney McCabe.

CHAPTER 9
THE *LIVES* OF THE UNITED IRISHMEN: THE REVIEWS

The Lives of the United Irishmen caused quite a stir when they were first published. While they were "meat and drink" to vast sections of the Irish populace, the colonial authorities in Dublin hated the books, cognisant of their potential to incite unrest and resistance to the colonial project in Ireland. It is likely that the authorities in Dublin Castle reported their concerns regarding Madden's writings to London. If so, their report had no immediate impact on Madden professionally as there was a world of difference then between Dublin and London as regards the toleration of a historian's writings. Madden's friends and admirers in England could justify Madden's writings on the pretext that his treatises on Ireland's oppression were simply an extension of his advocacy work on the Anti-Slavery issue. That was the situation in London. In Dublin, the authorities had little sympathy with such a viewpoint. Their primary concern was the effect which Madden's writings would have had on the ordinary people of Ireland. In Ireland the events of 1798 were far too close for comfort, especially when discussed in print now - just four decades later, in 1840. In the view of the authorities it was bad enough that Madden had outlined the United Irishmens' aims and influence in language that was clear and concise. Madden had gone a good deal further than this, however. He had researched the 1798 period in depth, praised the actions of the United Irishmen and explained that the United Irishmens' actions were a form of self-sacrifice on behalf of their fellow Irish countrymen. Madden reiterated the point that Daniel O'Connell had previously highlighted i.e. that it was in 1798 or the years subsequent to this that the Act of Union of 1800 had been decided upon. This development had made the idea of a closer amalgamation between Ireland and Britain more likely and had precipitated the United Irishmens' decision to rebel. Madden's book reminded its readers that Wolfe Tone had been a loyal citizen at the same juncture that Lord Castlereagh (or Colonel Robert Stewart as he was referred to then) had spoken of the necessity for Ireland to learn the lessons of democracy and freedom as garnered from America. Madden made no attempt to disguise his sympathy for the aims of the United Irishmen. In 1798, the concept of loyalty and honour had found itself in conflict with servility and sordidness. Pitt[251] had overseen a policy of barbarity by propping up a political regime that included Beresford[252] and his friends, all of whom were solely serving their own material and political ends. Pitt had preferred "skilful dealers and accomplished shufflers" as opposed to pleasant and honest individuals such as Grattan.

While these comments were cutting, they did not come anywhere near the real level of hatred which Madden felt for Pitt and the effects of his policies. Madden's book created a "rogue's gallery" amongst whom he mentioned just two people he considered to be equal with Pitt in terms of crookedness and dishonour. Who the two politicians Madden had in mind isn't clear, but we can surmise that he may have had Castlereagh and Clare in mind. His opinion of Castlereagh was certainly a very poor one as indicated by the epitaph he composed for him and which can still be read in the *Literary Remains of the United Irishmen* published in 1887:

> Under this flagstone lies whatever part of the Robert, the Right-Honourable Stewart, the volunteer, the United Irishman, the noble one who turned his back on his own race; who

betrayed every cause he had once been associated with except the cause of dishonesty and its high-priest, Wiliam Pitt. His entire life was a tragedy for the Irish people and in the end the shame of it became too great a burden for even him to bear.[253]

In relation to Lord Clare he wrote the following: "'Twould seem that nature formed that man to show, how many voices in one heart might grow," and "The grave itself entombs not half his crimes. For guilt like his outlives the worst of times." The London newspapers, the more liberal-minded papers included, were very critical of Madden's *Lives*. The *Spectator's* review[254] began like this: "So far as a chaos can be reduced to form, this publication can be considered to consist of three parts," with the reviewer describing the second part as "one of the most crude, wordy and purposeless productions" he had ever read:

> We can make neither head nor tail of this jumble of material. He starts with a history of the Irish Volunteers and it is short on facts and the book's layout is poor. The writing includes a raft of verbose statements on the part of the author himself and other members of the Repeal Association. He then attempts to write an account of the United Irishmen in a similarly jumbled fashion to his account of the Irish Volunteers except that this account is even more confused than the first. Following these two accounts, and interspersed with them, are a series of biographical notes on the leading members of the United Irishmen but these are so poor that it is impossible to refer to them as either character sketches or biographies. These biographies aren't comprehensive enough to do justice either to the importance of these individuals or the major incidents in their lives, including whatever villainy they committed. The information included is all dependent on whatever slivers of information Madden could pick up during his enquiries. You couldn't recommend this book to anybody. And anybody who does bother to read it has to admit that it is a pity that a more competent hand hadn't written this history of the United Irishmen.[255]

The reviewer of the *Dublin University Magazine* was equally dismissive and claimed to have counted nearly a hundred serious errors in Madden's text.

> Not only do these errors undermine much of the information provided in Madden's book, it also calls into question the work's integrity and is a major embarrassment to the publisher. The publication of this book could do serious damage to the publishing trade in Ireland.[256]

Madden did look to correct some of these errors in a later edition of the book but he wasn't very successful. There is no doubt that, despite its importance, the information provided in the *Lives* ought to be treated with caution. W. J. Fitzpatrick, author of the *Secret Service under Pitt: Sham Squire* (1892) claimed that Madden had mistakenly and unfairly accused a number of people of betrayal, and that he could identify thirteen errors in the various letters which Madden had cited in the book. Ironically, Fitzpatrick's own work wasn't free of errors either. Irish reviews of the *Lives* varied according to the "politics" or ideology of the reviewer. The Unionist newspapers claimed Madden's books were without any value while the Nationalist broadsheets made extravagant claims for the *Lives*. The reviews which appeared in the *Dublin University Magazine* are worth noting as this was the premier literary publication of the period and had held an international reputation since Charles Lever[257] became its editor. The *Magazine's* views would therefore have been a fair reflection of upper-class opinion and the views of the Dublin Castle "set" at this time. It was customary then for book reviews to be very long and detailed with the reviewer frequently as well-acquainted with the material under review as the author himself. Any glaring errors were easily spotted as a consequence. What made matters more difficult again for Madden was the fact that Lever had left his post as editor of the *Magazine* by the time that the first volume of the *Lives* came to be reviewed. His departure saw the return of the old atmosphere of vilification that had been prevalent prior to his tenure and Madden saw the first two volumes of his *Lives* subjected to a torrent of criticism. It is not clear which critic reviewed Madden's volumes but there is a strong chance that he was the Honourable Sorley O'Sullivan; he was the person whom Madden suspected anyway.

O'Sullivan and his brother Mortimer were Protestants who were connected to a group that had instigated what they termed the "New Reformation"[258] ,a movement led by the Reverend Caesar Otway, a cleric who was extremely bigoted against Catholics. While Mortimer was acknowledged to be a talented intellectual; the same wasn't true of Sorley who was frequently referred to as "Sham" O'Sullivan so as to distinguish him from his brother. Whether the O'Sullivans had written the review as a joint effort or not is irrelevant. Whoever reviewed the book had no interest in debating the book's merits or deficiencies in any constructive manner.

The reviewer dismissed the *Lives* as a completely useless piece of work. Not only was the book's basic premise a despicable one and the end-product was no better. By basing his account of events solely on the direct testimony of those few United Irishmen who had survived the Rebellion, Madden had committed an unpardonable sin. Of course, the reviewer was himself equally biased in his approach and his ill-will towards Madden was particularly pronounced in his comments regarding the third volume of the *Lives*:

> It is our duty to outline the nature of the various moral judgements which the Doctor scatters like faggots to an inflammatory crowd. We feel that Madden is nothing more than a bigot who has been blinded by his own political biases. These biases render him unable to interpret history correctly or to escape the ravings and fantasies that drove the outlaws of '98.[259]

The reviewer's comments on *The Life and Times of Robert*

Emmet (1847) included the following:

> He left no stone unturned in his search for reliable material as relating to that young man. He was a martyr for the Irish cause according to Madden who has a deep respect for Emmet's principles; if there is anything noteworthy in this heap of printed poison, it will take a discerning reader to discover it... It is our opinion that this book is more of the same inflammatory material that is being circulated amongst the masses. It is nothing more than an attempt to pave the way for a seismic social change which could turn the kingdom completely upside-down.[260]

The *Evening Packet* was the most virulent of all the Dublin newspapers in its criticism of Madden's *Lives*. The *Lives* were the work of a biased individual who viewed everything through the prism of his own political leanings, according to this newspaper. He had done his best to adjust his opinions in accordance with the truth but exaggeration was a very clear fault in every single chapter of Madden's book. Thomas Moore had once written that:

> Some few flowers of Eden...
> Ye may still inherit
> But the trail of the serpent
> Is over them all.[261]

...and the truth was that "the trail of the serpent" could be seen in all of Madden's work. Undisguised bigotry, a sense of group bitterness and exaggeration without limit; these traits were evident in almost every page Madden wrote. Madden must have expected this abuse from the likes of the *Dublin University Magazine* and the *Evening Packet*. If so, their reviews of his work probably didn't affect him unduly. It would have been a lot worse if Lockhart, the editor of the *Quarterly Review*, had incited his normal reviewer and Madden's "tormentor" John

Wilson Croker to go on the warpath against Croker's "old victim, the Puffy Dr. Madden...He has perpetuated two volumes, (Lockhart said), "which it might amuse you to make mince meat of." The various attacks on Madden galvanised the Nationalist newspapers to come to Madden's defence, however. The *Nation*, in it's first ever issue, took on the *Dublin University Magazine* referring to its "silly and malignant notice" regarding Madden's book. The *Nation*'s second issue included a long essay from its editor Thomas Davis titled "An Irish Vampire" which initially directed attention at "that fearful record, the items of expenditure of Secret Service Money in '98" that Madden's book had exposed. While admitting that the organisation of Madden's book wasn't perfect by any means, Davis' essay praised it for its detailed exposé of the range of fees the British Secret Service had paid informers to infiltrate and stymie various Irish attempts at insurrection. Wolfe Tone's *Memoirs* aside, Madden's book was the best written account of what had been the Irish people's most daring attempt ever to unite and to attempt an overthrow of English rule in Ireland. Such praise of his work from an intellectual as capable as Davis was praise indeed, and Madden can't but have been very pleased with this review of his book as published in 1842.

Of course, the inclusion of Wolfe Tone's name in such a review essay only confirmed the Unionist commentators in their denunciation of Madden's work as "a blind and bigoted earnestness in the cause of sedition." Madden's private papers, his personal correspondence in particular, indicates that his friends weren't in agreement with every aspect of his analysis of the 1798 rebellion as outlined in the *Lives*. For instance, James Stephens, the Undersecretary in the Colonial Office told Madden that he had been too hard on Castlereagh, Clare, Cooke and their contemporaries. Madden's reply to Stephen acknowledged the latter's views and said that he had taken them into account. He didn't accept Stephen's viewpoint however and made no attempt to soften his attacks on Castlereagh and his associates in subsequent editions of the *Lives*. A son of MacNeven also wrote to Madden from America praising him on the way he had salvaged these first-hand accounts of 1798 for posterity. He disagreed with Madden's assessment of the rebel's planning for the rebellion however. Madden's opinion was that the Rebellion had been an ill-conceived and foolhardy attempt with a minimal chance of success but the younger MacNeven took issue with this aspect of Madden's analysis.

Madden also received other letters which were full of praise for his work, and the long hours of research he had put in during his compilation of the *Lives*. Sir William Napier, a historian of the Iberian Peninsular War and the Governor of Guernsey wrote to Madden, for example, and congratulated him on the publication of the *Lives*. Napier and Madden had much in common of course - as they were both Irishmen who believed in the democratic model of Government and were they were equally fond of political debate. They also shared a mutual friend in Tom Moore. Napier's letter began by highlighting a minor error he had spotted in Madden's text and went on to say that:

> *They have just handed me a copy of the* Dublin Evening Packet *where I see an ugly article disparaging your work. You have to expect this, of course. The review writer accuses you of exaggeration. Given my extensive reading as relating to the social and historical conditions in 1798, a more reasonable argument could be made that you were too soft on the then governing elite in my opinion. You could, in fact, have been even harsher in your descriptions of the terrible cruelties inflicted by government (the Tories) then in power. It's no wonder the newspaper men are politically affiliated to such a party are now hopping mad at your exposé of the naked truth of that era of Irish history. The crimes committed then should be highlighted for all to see and in order that such events never happen again. It is my hope that your book will not only act as a reminder of what happened in Ireland but will influence people internationally also.*[262]

Comments such as Napier's made Madden very happy. He couldn't think of better praise for his book than that it acted to promote justice and human rights generally. He hadn't been at all sure that his motivations in writing the *Lives* would be understood so well. Neither had he worked so diligently on his essays in memory of the United Irishmen so as to gain either personally or financially in any way:

I chose this subject fully aware that it would make unpleasant reading for the English public. This fact, in itself, highlights where my political sympathies lie. If my aim was to ingratiate myself with the Public Service for whom I have worked for the past nine years; then my modus operandi would be a particularly strange one. The historical events which I have thrown some light on won't make me any more popular with the people in Downing Street than I was a year ago.[263]

Madden referred to the way the *Lives* had been belittled in the newspapers, particularly the Liberal ones and said that it was a contempt for the Irish race that really underlay all of these attacks. His critics had no love for Orangeism and neither had they any particular affection for the likes of Sirr, Sandys, Swan, Beresford, Castlereagh and Reynolds; what united them was a deeply-engrained hostility towards the Irish people as a whole. Every possible evil motivation had been attributed to him personally for his decision to write about that dark and violent period of Irish history. The main motivation for his writings on a personal level however was the necessity to expose injustice and oppression wherever it existed. Napier agreed with all of Madden's sentiments as expressed in their postal correspondence. He gave Madden this final word of advice as a conclusion to their correspondence concerning the *Lives* advice that had an almost military "ring" to it:

Dear Sir, no honest man who reads your book could be in any doubt the motivations which inspire your work. I would just forget any worries that you may have regarding the criticisms of your work. Your critics are just liars who twist language to suit their own purposes. They are the people who praise liberty in public yet oppose it in the quietness of their own hearts. The attack which Mr. Reynolds made on you is the most underhand of the lot, particularly as it has no logical reasoning to support it... [264]

The attack which Napier mentions here was a reference to a letter sent to the newspapers by the son of Reynolds[265] the spy, criticising Madden's work. The younger Reynolds was angry because the *Freeman's Journal*[266] had published an article about his father's treachery, some of which was based on material from Madden's *Lives*. The *Freeman's Journal* described it as an absolute disgrace that the people of Ireland, many of whom were starving to death, still had to pay the huge sum of one thousand pounds a year in their taxes so as to support the family of a retrograde such as Reynolds, a disloyal individual who had sold out his own country. The *Journal* also wondered whether there was anyone in the British House of Representatives who would recommend that payment of this "blood money" be brought to an end.

The younger Reynolds contradicted Madden's allegations regarding his father and claimed that the extracts Madden had printed from the Secret Service files were just lies that were without foundation. Madden answered Reynolds in the second edition of the *Lives*.

> *Mr. Reynolds is angry, the son of the Reynolds who betrayed Bond, O'Brien and McCann. He is angry because he has been caught out attempting to twist the facts and the figures; he is angry because he has been exposed while attempting to mask treachery with the appearance of patriotism, while disguising greed for money with an apparent love for the king.*[267]

Madden also had these withering comments to make about the letter Reynolds, who had worked as a spy:

Having betrayed all his friends and forsaken his country he abandoned his religion and in the decline of life assumed a sanctimonious demeanour and was said to have "put off the old man." He had retained, however, to the last his pension, and this produce of perfidy enabled him to pamper his appetites and live and die in luxury in a foreign land.[268]

As outlined earlier, Thomas Davis' review of the *Lives* had drawn a parallel between the work of Tone and that of Madden. It must have hurt Madden then to receive a letter of complaint from Tone's widow. She was living in retirement in America and critical of the manner in which Madden had collated his reminiscences of Tone and his lack of any consultation with her before publishing the *Lives*. Madden told Davis what had happened and the one-time editor of the *Nation* advised him to forward a copy of the volume which related specifically to Tone. He also advised him to enclose a letter of explanation with the volume, something which went along these lines:

It is with the trepidation of an acolyte approaching the altar that I bestow this small present on you. This volume includes a short biography of your husband who is no longer with us. It describes your husband who is no longer with us. It describes your husband's calibre as a man, his unique character traits, his tactical ingenuity, his patriotism and his noble death as an Irish martyr. When I recall the unconditional love that was between you both, your role as guardian angel to him and your actions as counsellor and protector to him in times of danger. When I remember that it was your combination of Roman steadfastness and Gaelic truth that gave him sustenance in his sacrifices for Ireland, sacrifices which you yourself also made; when I call to mind all of these things I realise that you alone are worthy to act as guardian of this small token of remembrance, a token which commemorates the great man who today rests in Bodenstown.[269]

The above letter was never posted, it seems, and neither was the book. If Mrs. Mathilda Tone Wilson[270] had received either of them she would surely have mentioned them in the letter she sent to *Truth Teller*, in New York on the 19th of October, 1842 from her home in Georgetown, D.C. Hers was "a rambling and diffuse letter" as she admitted, excusing her inability to write a more coherent missive "being under the weight of 73 years and a broken heart." She complained that Madden had been careless in his selection of extracts from her husband's memoirs. In addition to this she was also annoyed that Madden hadn't visited her when he was in New York in search of sources and archival material for the book:

> *I had never heard of him,* (she said), *till I saw his book advertised - perhaps he was ignorant of my existence, for I live in complete retirement, and to use Carolan's words "lonely and desolate I mourn the day."*[271]

Her letter of complaint was reproduced in the *Nation* on the seventeenth of December, 1842, enabling Madden to compose a rejoinder for the same newspaper. This letter of response was one the most eloquent letters Madden had ever written. The letter outlined how he had been involved in literary endeavours for the best part of sixteen years by then and like many other authors, he had suffered his share of attacks on the part of the critics. On occasion, he felt that the same critics had wronged him by treating him unfairly. Sometime his work had been misunderstood or what he had written had been misinterpreted in a dishonest way. Despite of all these attacks, this was the first time that he had put pen to paper to defend his literary work through the medium of the press. He wouldn't have bothered writing such a letter to the newspaper except that he recognized that Mrs. Tone, as the guardian of her husband's memory, deserved a response to her earlier letter outlining her concerns. While visiting America on his researches, he had actually tried to find out whether Mrs. Tone was still alive or where she lived, a fact that MacNeven could have verified if he was still alive. He had also made enquiries with the newspaper owned by her son-in-law, a Mr. Sampson, where he had heard that Mrs. Tone was alive and living in a rural backwater somewhere. This fact had not inhibited Madden from visiting her. Instead, it was the fact that he sincerely felt that he, as a stranger, ought not to impose on somebody like herself who had suffered so much in during the course of her life including the recent death of that bravest and most intelligent of men, her only son.

Therefore, dearest gentlewoman - (Madden wrote) – I have made my effort to defend my actions as relating to the issues which you raised. Maybe my attempt at explanation has fallen short or appeared inadequate. In any event, believe me when I say that if there is even one sentence in my book which is a source of hurt to you or has dishonoured the memory of your spouse in some way, then it is entirely by mistake that and unknownst to me that such a sentence was ever written.[272]

Another "1798 widow" praised Madden for his work and expressed no reservations about its reliability. Henry Sheares' wife wrote to Madden to express her appreciation for the copy of the *Lives* that he had forwarded to her, and included the following comments:

You depicted the traits of both of my beloved relatives (i.e. the Sheares brothers) in the most accurate of fashions and your descriptions were a balm to the grief that I felt when I called to mind once again the memories of the distressing events which we endured during this period of our lives. Your biographical sketches of both men were honest and true with no hint of either exaggeration or fabrication. If you had been less praiseworthy of both men, it would not have done sufficient justice to their noble characters. This life wasn't deserving of them... What you said regarding at the time of your researches is also true. I would not have been able to add any further information to what you have provided. All I had in my possession were a number of letters which my beloved Henry wrote to me while he was in Kilmainham (Jail) –a correspondence which was for my eyes only.[273]

Mrs. Sheares, a woman who in her day was considered an exceptional beauty and a devout person, had emigrated to England after the deaths of the two brothers and had only returned to live in Ireland sometime after 1840. Living in Dublin again, she had a specific annual ritual which she performed in memory of the two brothers on the anniversary of their deaths. She would lock the bedroom door, close the shutters on the windows and surround herself with pictures of her dead husband and his brother, locks of their hair, their letters and various other artifacts – "On those days she fasted and prayed and lived, as it were, in communion with those whose ideal presence she had called into existence." If Mrs. Sheares had lived to see the revised version of Madden's *Lives* published in 1860, there is no doubt that she would have been saddened at the way circumstances in her own family had developed in the generation which succeeded her.

Both Henry and John Sheares fathered children prior to their deaths. "Little Louisa," John's beautiful and level-headed daughter, had married a man with a drink problem named John but had later left him to join the theatre. Her career in the theatre did not prove successful however and she died young. Henry's daughter fared even more poorly and Madden traced her to a poorhouse in Cork city in 1858. It was there that he found this daughter who was over seventy years of age by then and living in great poverty. While Wolfe Tone's widow was critical of the *Lives* there were far more Nationalists who sent Madden their congratulations and praise on the book's publication than there were detractors. Madden was particularly pleased that the Emmet family in the United States had expressed their delight on the book's publication. Madden confirmed this in a letter to Robert, the son of Thomas Addis Emmet[274] which he wrote on the twelfth of February, 1844:

Nothing pleases me more greatly than the fact that you are happy with my efforts to honour your father's name... Your papers reached me just in time for me to include them as addenda in the last series volumes in the Lives series which I am currently preparing for print. My health has not been very good recently and I can only hope that I have enough strength in me to continue the task until it is finished. My gut feeling is that the purpose of my life now is the publication of the fruits of this research. Attempts have been made to stifle me in my efforts to finish this historical research. I have been condemned not on the grounds of literary error but because the facts which I have unearthed, have pointed to the criminal behaviour of some of the people mentioned in my historical writings.[275]

The third series of the *Lives* was initially supposed to come out in October, 1843, but it was three years later in the summer of 1846 before it actually appeared. It comprised three volumes. The first volume included a new and enhanced introduction to the *Lives* in addition to essays concerning William Corbet, James Napper Tandy, James. B. Blackwell, Theobald Wolfe Tone, Matthew Tone, the Reverend James Porter, Henry Munroe and B.P. Binns.

This volume also included previously cited material; extracts from the autobiography of James Hope for example; a chapter on William Putnam McCabe[276] submitted by Madden's friend Barney McCabe; and a short biography of Bartholomew Teeling[277] as written by Teeling's niece. In the second volume, Madden included short biographies of James Coigley, John Tennant, Hugh Wilson, Felix Rourke, Bernard Duggan, Thomas Russell and others. He also provided detailed appendices on Major Sirr and his band of thugs, as well as information concerning collaborators and spies such as Reynolds, Jemmy O'Brien and Captain Armstrong.

The third volume of this series was given over entirely to the story of Robert Emmet. The fact that an entire volume was dedicated solely to Robert Emmet helped to enhance Emmet's reputation further among the Irish reading public of this era. Sales problems as relating to the second series of Madden's *Lives* caused a delay in the publishing of the third series. To ensure the third series was published Madden had to promise his London publisher that he would pay for any losses in terms of sales, presumably because the second series didn't sell very well. The monied class in Ireland weren't interested in the work of a perceived traitor to the Empire such as Madden while the people who were keen to read it were generally poor and would have been entirely reliant on accessing the copies of the *Lives* available in the in the Repeal Association's reading rooms. Madden actually paid a Dublin bookseller to look after the sales of the *Lives* (third series) in Ireland but the bookseller went broke and Madden had to pay off these debts. As was customary with Madden his sense of honesty would not allow him to sweep this embarrassing fact under the carpet, a fact which he admitted to in a prospectus he issued in 1860, along with the second edition of the *Lives*. He admitted that he had already lost 350 pounds on the *Lives* series, a figure which would increase to a frightening 2000 pounds a short time later.

This figure included all the expenses involved in the production of the series including printing expenses, travel expenses, pictures which were reproduced for the various volumes, the editing costs, and small amounts of money which Madden paid to some of the people he interviewed during his researches. While these costs were a heavy burden in themselves they were not the only price which he paid for his devotion to the *Lives* series:

> From 1842 to 1847 other disadvantages resulted to him from it which it is unnecessary to enter into. (Prospectus)[278]

Madden was recalling here the various jobs administrative or governmental-type jobs he could have applied for if it hadn't been for his devotion to the *Lives*. One benefit which did accrue from the delays which dogged the publication of the third series of the *Lives* was that he had more time to eliminate errors that may have appeared in the first two series. In the introduction to the *Lives* (third series) Madden admitted that the lay-out of the earlier volumes had been faulty and resolved to improve these in the future. He qualified this admission however by saying that a book's layout and the order in which its material was printed wasn't the primary arbiter when it came to assessing a book's worth. What was more important was the quality of the information that was available within the book's covers. Today it is generally acknowledged that a good deal of the information unearthed by Madden during his researches is invaluable. What is still open to debate are some of Madden's judgements and his selections from the research materials then available to him. It was these issues and the manner in which Madden had written up his material that prompted some literary critics of the day e.g. Litton Falkiner - to attack his work; Falkiner criticised Madden's work as replete with "perfervid eulogies of indiscriminate partisans." Falkiner also slammed Madden's argument that it was the then colonial government that had triggered Emmet's rebellion and it had also preyed on Emmet's youth and fiery nature to do incite him and others to action. A number of historians who have reviewed these questions since have accepted Madden's thesis[279] at face-value, however. Interestingly, not all twentieth-century Nationalist commentators have been entirely convinced of Madden's Nationalist credentials. Brian O'Higgins, for example, included Madden in the category of "the thoroughly anglicised and self-confessed loyal subjects of the crown."[280]

Madden had originally intended to publish a fourth series of the *Lives*, but the introduction to the third series indicates that he was finished with the bulk of his researches and the sourcing of material by that stage. As it later turned out, he wasn't finished with his writing and research pursuits by any means. He was simply tired and rundown after a couple of years of intensive research and non-stop work. His health was not the best and more than once he expressed regrets at having taken on this immense research project in the first place given the huge toll it had taken on both himself and his family. Whatever success he had achieved was entirely down to the help and support he received on a day-to-day basis from his family, his wife Harriet in particular. Harriet, who was an Englishwoman, had a deep love for her own country. The only value which Harriet held higher than this was her love of truth and justice however, and she had never given up hope that these virtues would ultimately prevail.

While Madden had nothing but praise for his wife the same could not be said in relation to the public figures of his day that were not supportive of his political views. Madden was heavily critical of Lord Henry Brougham,[281] a man who had once helped him source a public document in Paris, and who was now cosying up to a government which was hostile to Ireland and its people. Lord Eliot,[282] who had recently been appointed to the position of First-Secretary - was another whom Madden was particularly disappointed with. The end of the *Lives* (first series) saw Madden mark Eliot out as a very capable and just individual whose actions might prove to Ireland's benefit. Over the course of time the opposite had proven true however as Madden now indicated:

I feel bound to confess that I formed an erroneous opinion…it was not justice but tyranny which his measures were calculated to plant in Ireland…All that I have said of his Lordship's love of justice I retract.[283]

In spite of these disappointments, Madden still liked to recall the generosity of his friends who had helped him while he was working on the *Lives*. One of these friends was Dr. James McDonnell from Belfast who had made important contacts on Madden's behalf when he visited Belfast in the Autumn of 1840 as part of his researches. Among the many Northerners he had advised Madden to liase with were Robert Simms, Mary McCracken, Dr. Magee's widow, Mr. Hughes from Holywood, County Down who had appointed Napper Tandy as his agent in Dublin, Sir Edward Newenham, Israel Milliken and "an elderly man named Hope."[284] The elderly man referred to here was James Hope, a renowned weaver, who in his youth had been friendly with Robert Emmet, Henry Joy McCracken and Thomas Russell, three men who were hanged for their roles in the 1798 Rebellion. "One of nature's nobility," was how Madden described Hope and in this he was stating the truth. Not only had Hope sacrificed himself for the cause of Irish freedom, but he had also done his best on behalf of his fellow-Irishmen in terms of both social and political advancement. Madden met Pope who was thin and bent with age - he was over eighty by then - in Israel Milliken's house in Belfast in either 1842 or 1843. Hope was poor by then but his independent streak was still as strong as ever. In fact Hope had been so wary and stand-offish of him on their first encounter that Madden had come away with no worthwhile information for his researches at all. Hope's aloofness had disappeared completely by the second time that they met however, as he had read the volumes of the *Lives* which Madden had already written and sent onto him by then.

> *You couldn't have sent me anything more valuable than these volumes. They stir my memory and recall to mind the battles we fought against the unjust government of 1798. Your neutrality as a historian particularly impressed me. Justice, truth and impartiality are so important to me that my notes of these events are available to you if you consider them worth bequeathing to the country. After all, it was with this in mind, that I wrote them originally.*[285]

Hope was true to his word; he gave Madden "a mass of unconnected materials, piled on one another in reference to events, not in order of their succession but as passing circumstance or topics of conversation chanced to recall them." Madden edited them and prepared them for publication. Hope passed his personal papers over to Madden sometime in 1843. He wasn't sure whether he would live long enough to see them in print. In the meantime Madden was reading some of the "strangest" views from someone who had used his guns in the Battle of Aughrim[286] and later again in 1803.

The slightest physical assault causes me shortness of breath. When I'm relaxed my breathing is shorter than normal but it is at least free. I can only lie down on my left-hand side and I can't get myself into a standing position without placing my elbows on my knees, and I am getting weaker as time goes by. My mind and my memory are both still alert however. The growth of our movement is a source of great joy to me. Who would have thought that the failure of the potato famine would leave us without a government for a number of weeks? And the people remained quiet, a fact that demonstrates the power of the moral battle; thankfully this aspect of the struggle has developed greatly and that Daniel O'Connell is there to direct this aspect of things...I have reached page fifty-two of this manuscript. Maybe some readers will take an interest in it when I am in the grave. I have a box full of manuscripts here. I haven't the gumption to think that they will all ever be read. They were a hobby for me once, and some of them were an exercise in forbearance, because I have seen things come true...[287]

Only Joy McCracken's sister Mary and Israel Milliken came to visit Hope on a regular basis. Mary would read to Hope and both she and Milliken would also run occasional errands for him. For example, they trawled the pawnshops in search of one of Madden's volumes which went missing, "lost by a faithless acquaintance" in one of Belfast's Repeal reading rooms. On the forty-fifth anniversary of the Battle of Antrim - that is, the sixth of June, 1843, Hope wrote the following:

When you read the manuscript accompanying this scribbled note you will see my own thoughts regarding the Repeal

Association… I agree with the plan that O'Connell was laid out. Even if the entire leadership of the Association were traitors - which isn't possible - I am convinced that they would be unable to prevent the people's independence - or to make a distinction between of the Irish people and the well-being of the Crown, that is the titular link between each of the three individual kingdoms. Some people may yet regret interfering with that link. I have myself joined up with the Repeal Association, and am approaching this issue with the same intensity that I once took part in battle. All that is needed now is that we exhibit the Moral Force. Such an approach suits me best at this stage of my life and is actually better suited to my natural inclination. I would never have gone down the route of armed struggle except that it was a dire necessity at the time… a fact which will be evident when the history of this era comes to be written…[288]

Hope and Madden became so friendly that they even discussed religious issues with one another, a fact which was all the more incredible considering that, before then, such discussions between a Belfast Protestant and a Dublin Catholic would have been very rare indeed. Hope – (an unusual character, given his era, it must be said) - lived to a good age, and died in 1853. When he died, Mary McCracken and the elderly Israel Milliken organised for a headstone to be erected over the grave in the small cemetery in Mallusk, County Antrim, while Madden composed the inscription for it. Later, when Jemmy Hope's son Robert began drinking heavily, Mary McCracken[289] asked Madden to write to him and to impress upon him the virtues of teetotalism.[290]

CHAPTER 10
IN PORTUGAL FOR *THE MORNING CHRONICLE*

Sometime during autumn, 1843, Madden came to the conclusion that he could not remain living in Ireland any further. He had no future there in terms of employment opportunities unless he was to go into politics or to write books on a full-time basis and neither of these options were realistic in terms of making a living in Ireland. His wife Harriet's brother had helped the family out from time to time and Madden made some money by selling the furniture that they had left behind them in London. He began job-seeking in London again but only received one offer. A friend of his named Doyle who was the then editor of the English newspaper the *Morning Chronicle* asked Madden whether he was interested in the position of Portuguese correspondent for this newspaper, as based in Lisbon.

Madden reluctantly accepted this job. *The Morning Chronicle* had been one of the leading newspapers in London at one point in time; for a while, it was nearly as influential as *The Times*. The *Chronicle* once was home to such well-known columnists such as Sheridan, Coleridge, Lamb, Moore and Hazlitt. Its readership had declined greatly by the time Madden joined their staff, however. By then, it had become a relatively insignificant newspaper linked to the Whigs, a newspaper that wouldn't have survived without the donations it received from that political party. *The Times* of the day referred to the newspaper as "that squirt of dirty water" and claimed that its journalists were just:

...scuttlers out of the treadmill whose exposures give foreigners proof that there has crept into the press of this country scoundrels who are not only unfit for the society of gutter men but would not be a disgrace to the vilest coteries of Europe.[291]

Madden's new job was therefore nothing to boast about in terms of societal standing and the same was true was as regards as his salary. He received a probable initial down-payment and after that he was paid a set amount of money for each article of his that was published. Before leaving for Lisbon Madden appointed two "representatives" to look after his affairs back home - Willie Cogan in Dublin and Barney McCabe in London. In fact, Madden was so disconsolate at having to accept this Lisbon job that even his friend Lady Blessington had difficulty in enthusing him about it. "Anybody who thinks that this job in Portugal is a backwards step for you, is mistaken," she told him, "some of the most famous men ever have written for the newspapers." In away, he was lucky to be escaping Ireland considering that the country was then in such an agonizingly difficult situation both socially and politically. "But women," she said, have, in my opinion, no business with politics, and I, above all women, have a horror of mixing myself up with them. I must content myself in wishing well to my poor country, which no one more heartily loves." The sub-text of Lady Blessington's letters to Madden at this juncture indicate that she was happier because his new post would mean that he was separated from his rebellious friends in the Irish Nationalist community. No longer would he have the opportunity to spend his days searching the graveyards for the graves of previous Irish Nationalist martyrs, his own antecedents amongst them. Madden knew that Lady Blessington meant well for him when she made comments such as the aforementioned and that she was thinking of his own personal safety. He was loathe to accept her opinion in relation to the Nationalist cause however and told her as much. Indeed, Madden probably shocked her with the intensity of his Nationalist convictions. He pulled no punches in his responses to her and wrote in the tone of a crusader as was customary for him. The difference now, however, was that this crusade did not refer to a faraway region like the Caribbean or the African coast. This time Madden's crusade was directed to conditions in Lady Blessington's own backyard. If Ireland was ruled fairly, he told Lady Blessington:

> ...great happiness might be expected for its people who are naturally joyous, sprightly and easily contented. The middle classes at the time of the Union were generally tolerably educated. They enjoyed life and had no idea of slaving themselves to death for the purpose of leaving enormous wealth to their children...The Irish people only want to be dealt with fairly by their rulers irrespective of creed. The system of government in operation was devised, not to improve them morally or intellectually, but to weaken them, to separate them, to produce religious strife amongst them, and to give power to one faction, the small wealthy Orange faction. This body was fierce and fanatical, insatiably covetous and continued, after it ceased to be an element of Government, to be greedy of power, and unscrupulous as to the means of attaining its ends, whether by blood, intimidation, hypocrisy, cajolery, backdoor official influence, or corruption. The people of England were utterly in the dark about the evil of Orangeism or, as they pleased to call it, the Protestant Ascendancy and its effect on the Catholics of Ireland, especially the intellectual middle and upper classes among them. With exceptions in the days of Wellesley, Anglesey and Normnby, it was positively a calamity for an intellectual, high-minded Catholic, firmly believing in his religion and sensible of the wanton and outrageous insults

offered to it, to live in his own land without having his feelings exasperated. Why England should lend its countenance to Irish Orangeism was always inexplicable to me. If persisted in it would contribute towards the decline and fall of British influence abroad; in Ireland too it would fail, for the laws of justice are not violated for ever with impunity. Whether the day of retribution comes slow or fast, it would come surely. But in the meantime, of what avail was it to the Irish people to hear their brawling patriots praising the fertility of this soil, the loveliness of the country? Would to heaven she were less beautiful, less fertile, and more independent, better educated, had more food for her people, and more force and union to employ against her foes.[292]

Madden then had the temerity to find fault with Lady Blessington herself and to give her some advice for a change!

You have written against Roman Catholic demagogues and agitators, but you never wrote a line against Orangeism and Protestant Ascendancy; you never wrote a line against the persecutors of your religion, and of your own race. Do you, dear Lady Blessington, you to whom nature has given noble gifts, use them for a new account in literary labour, for a better one than fashion, for the advantage of the country that gave you birth, and against those pernicious interests that have been so long inimical to its peace. By the influence of your opinions, the distinguished people you have around you may be made serviceable to Ireland; and pardon me, Lady Blessington, if I remind you that Ireland has a claim on your pen and a controversy with it. Your country is now entitled to other services at your hands than the production of polished novels, pleasing to her enemies and painful to her friends to read. Employ some portion of your leisure in the reprobation of a system of Government which administers its powers against the great bulk of the people of a country on account of their religion, and with a special view to the promotion of selfish purposes, hypocritically pursued under the name and guise of Protestant zeal for the interests of true religion.[293]

Lady Blessington had her own concerns at this juncture, most of which had nothing to do with the issues then bothering Madden. Since the death of her husband the income from her estate in Ireland had fallen to 2000 pounds a year, but she was still managing to move in London high-society circles on the income she now made from her writings. Her book *Conversations of Lord Byron with the Countess of Blessington* (1834) was very successful and she followed this up with further books including a number of three-volume novels and a huge volume of essays for the fashionable papers of the day. The regular receptions that took place at her home Gore House were attended by the leading scientific, artistic and political personalities of the day and this gave her first-hand access to all the gossip and political intrigue of the day, much of which found its way into her books.

Her writing projects doubled her annual income but this still wasn't enough to cover all of her bills. She had to write at a constant and ferocious pace to prevent her expenses from getting completely out of control. She wrote her novel *The Repealer* within the space of five weeks for instance; after a full twenty years of working at this ferocious pace it comes as no surprise that she claimed to be utterly exhausted and ready for the quiet life. She encouraged Madden to take up novel-writing but when he sent her a story he had written for her perusal she was unable to read it due to her hectic schedule:

> When I tell you that I have five hundred pages to write and compose between this and the end of the month for a work which, unless completed by that period, I forfeit an engagement, you will understand why I cannot read over the story you sent me, and which I am persuaded is like all I have seen from your pen - graphic and full of talent.[294]

About the same time that he was forced to leave Ireland in

search of employment, Madden also informed the Anti-Slavery Association that he would have to sever his official links with them. For eighteen months, he had done his utmost for the Association, highlighting the slavery issue in West Africa, in particular. He had done his best to try and counter those powerful groups who were working against the human rights principles of the Anti-Slavery Association. Despite his best efforts however, he had suffered a great deal both personally and professionally. He and his family had been discriminated against to such an extent that in order to be true to both his family and himself, it was better for him to retire from the Association.

> I believe I have done my duty to your cause. I have sacrificed my official prospects to it. It now only remains for me in quitting this country with the view to permanent residence in another, to bid you farewell and to assure you of my heartfelt wishes for the success of your efforts in the most righteous cause to which the high purposes of good men were ever directed.[295]

Unsurprisingly, the Association sympathised with Madden and were sorry that he felt obliged to come to such a decision, and as consequence of the reasons he had outlined. As a former senior member of the organisation, the Association considered it appropriate to pass an official motion expressing their sorrow at his departure. Madden informed Buxton[296] and Clarkson[297] respectively of his decision. Believe me, Buxton said, it is a huge blow that your valuable help won't be available to us anymore. Both he and Clarkson knew the effect that the absence of Madden would have on the productivity of the Association. The elderly Clarkson, who was in poor health and almost blind by then, just about managed to write Madden a letter stating that the Anti-Slavery Association had never had a more diligent member and friend. He recalled the great work which Madden had done in both Egypt and his dangerous posting on the Gold Coast where he had courageously taken on a group of men who were completely without principle. Clarkson seems to have been under the impression that Madden had got the better of his old enemy Forster and "his vile and servile agents" and he expressed an optimism which Madden certainly didn't share regarding Stanley's promise of finding a job for him. "I have found,"he said, "that great men in general are not to be relied on for their professions and promises but I do think there is something like sincerity in this case."

There was no necessity for Stanley to make any promises to Madden, no matter how tentative, Clark added and the very fact that Stanley had made such a promise was due acknowledgement of Madden's merit as a public servant. Clarkson also recognised that the government ministers of the day were unanimously opposed to the aims of the Abolitionist Movement, however. Clarkson was so weak that he was unable to write anymore and finished up his letter by saying - "I must therefore bid farewell in the most extensive meaning of that beautiful word. I am sure that wherever you go my spirit will accompany you." This isn't the whole story however. In fact Madden hadn't been happy with the Anti-Slavery Association for some time prior his resignation from it. The first signs of tension had reared their ugly head in the previous October when Lewis Tappan[298] was upset at reading Madden's complaints about the Anti-Slavery Association and its journal, the *Anti-Slavery Reporter*.[299]

To read Madden's comments at the time one would almost have thought that he was about to set up a competitor journal to the *Reporter*. Disappointingly for Madden, his complaints did not initiate any further debate at the time however. Madden was suspicious of the journal's editors from then on, however. The basis for this mistrust was the fact that in 1845 he had questioned the journal's attitude towards the slave-traders in West Africa whose actions Madden had previously challenged. He felt that the journal was not critical enough of Forster and his supply of goods to the slave-traders. Madden tried to bring up this issue in the Irish branch of the Anti-Slavery Association so as to generate controversy and to initiate a campaign of protest. His efforts were to avail, however.

The editor of the *Reporter* was horrified at the challenging tone of Madden's essays for the journal and it was left to Richard D. Webb, a friend of Madden's, to try and explain Madden's behaviour. Webb explained Madden's essay away as an awkward attempt at irony and, an example perhaps, of his Irish conceit. Webb considered the English to be inexperienced in this type of writing although no-one could surpass them when it came to word-play or linguistic dexterity. Madden was far from happy with the manner in which the language employed in the journal's articles was so circumspect and the careful editing of its articles prior to publication. At one stage, he threatened to make public his correspondence with the journal's editorial team in order to show them up.

In the end, Madden did not actually resign his membership of the Anti-Slavery Association when he went to Portugal. Instead, the Association included him as a member-by-correspondence and kept him informed of any developments which they considered he would be interested in. It was through such channels that Madden heard talk of the possibility of a further parliamentary debate on the ramifications of his West African report. In February, 1844, Madden was unclear about what was happening "behind the scenes" in London at this point and wondered whether the government proposed to re-instate the old (investigative) Committee or appoint a new one.

> *In the former case the humbug would be too transparent, at least for any anti-slavery body to be taken in by it. What, another committee with the chief felon upon it sitting in judgement on his own misdeeds?*

In the end, Madden concluded that such speculation (in relation to another parliamentary debate on the West African slavery issue) was simply gamesmanship and bluffing on the part of the then British government. If the Committee of Investigation was re-established it would only be to disguise

Stanley's dishonesty even further, he conceded. No-one could trust any plan that this government might instigate. Indeed "the anti-slavery body must depend no more on political support than on the aid of guns and gunpowder", Madden wrote. When Madden travelled to Portugal in November, 1843, he only intended to work there for the winter. In the end, he would spend nearly a full three years living there, however. His health was poor during his first few months there and he found it difficult to write any more than the column and a half he was regularly required to do. His strength returned however and he began to prepare the second series of the *Lives of the United Irishmen.*

This Portuguese posting would actually provide him with plenty of spare time in which to work on a number of different research projects. Harriet and he found a place to live in a very scenic area not far from the port of Lisbon. They also spent some time living in the town of Cintra, not far from Lisbon. Their son Thomas More attended the Irish Dominican school in Corpo Santo which was close to their home but the Maddens sent their other son Forde, who was a good deal older than Thomas More to Paris, where he attended the Royal College of Versailles and later, the École Polytechnique, where he began to study engineering. A relative of Madden's, a fellow Irish Nationalist named Éamonn Byrne, was married in Paris, where he had a villa in Corneille, on the outskirts of the city. Coincidentally, this house was directly opposite the house where Thomas Addis Emmet had first heard the terrible news regarding the hanging of his brother, Robert, in 1803.

A friend of Byrne's was a priest, also named Byrne, in one of the Parisian parishes and between the priest and he, they made sure that Forde, "a very good boy, very religious, steady and extremely studious" - but whose health was delicate - integrated well into French life. Forde did very well in Mathematics, a subject he had a particular aptitude for, but he found French particularly difficult and only improved his French by taking extra, private lessons in the language. He was considered a shy and reserved individual rather than a child who was given to "rattling and prattling away like other children."

This was an era of social upheaval in Portugal. A representative government had been formed for a people who had no previous experience of the democratic process. The upper-classes had no respect for the Government ministers; the lower classes had little enough say or interest in matters of state, while the middle-classes were either too lazy or too caught up in their own financial concerns to pay any heed to the government. A situation as apathetic as this made it very easy for power-hungry despots such as the Cabral brothers to siphon off whatever they could from the country's coffers. Madden said what he thought of these brothers whom he considered corrupt and unscrupulous to the core in his weekly newspaper column and also in a special essay he wrote in July, 1846, in the *Foreign Quarterly Review*. Nowhere else in Western Europe could compare with the bribery and corruption that had occurred in Portugal during the previous four years, he stated.

This corruption was worse because it was endemic to the Portuguese administration as a whole and not simply confined to the Cabral[300] brothers themselves. Between stock market trading and the selling of contracts and patronage, the Cabrals had become extremely wealthy and, despite their notorious reputation, they had also managed to hold onto the monarchy's (Queen of Portugal's) support for their Government. As regards deception and connivance, Madden said that there was hardly a politician alive who could compete with the younger of the Cabral brothers, Antonio. He was arrogant and ignored those who tried to help him, and his politics was based on hostility and revenge. He cancelled the country's Constitution on three occasions and persuaded the Queen to give her approval to bills that were contrary to Portuguese law on at least thirteen occasions. The country's financial affairs were destroyed from the very first day that the Cabrals assumed control and went into a steep decline. More and more loans were taken out to support the buying of stocks and shares and the State's finances were thrown into disarray but for the duration of this financial anarchy, the Cabral brothers' bank balances soared. Madden also described some of the corrupt practices other members of the government were engaged in. The Council President of Portugal, the Duke Terceira was a "soldier of fortune, or rather a fortunate soldier." Since he was unable to make enough money to keep himself in the style to which he was accustomed, the President aligned himself with the Cabral brothers and, together, they worked "hand-in-hand" to fleece the country's coffers for what they could. It had been assumed that the Minister of the Marine was an honest individual prior to his appointment to this ministry, and yet, despite his modest salary, the man had been able to buy a large estate, an enormous palace and many horses and other valuable accoutrements, subsequent to his appointment.

While he was never convicted of anything, it appears that the Minister for Foreign Affairs was no saint either; he too seems to have used his appointment for corrupt dealings in relation to the government's finances. The Finance minister was much the same as described by Madden. While he, himself, was careful not to be caught with "his hand in the till", he appeared to turn a blind eye to others who did so in the certain knowledge that he would be rewarded in due course. Prior to his appointment this Governmental Minister was worth approximately 30,000 pounds. Four years later, when his tenure in this post came to an end, the same man was worth 300,000 pounds and he had sunk about the same amount of money again into various business enterprises of his. The politicians were also quite anti-clerical and repressed the religious orders as much as they could. They shut down the monasteries and stole whatever valuables they found in them. They even stole the gold and silver-engraved bindings from the holy books used for the Mass and other religious occasions. Many of the clergy were reduced to destitution and one day, Madden even composed a poem at this juncture about an elderly priest he had seen begging from door to door in Lisbon:

That aged man who bends beneath
The weight of woes as well as years,
Who begs his bread in bated breath,
With downcast eyes suffused with tears,
Whose arms are folded on his breast,
As if long habit fixed them there,
And those poor withered hands sought rest,
And found repose alone in its prayer.

Eventually, the Portuguese became sick of the corruption of the Cabral regime and the brothers were driven from office and forced to flee for their lives. The country was ruined economically and the Portuguese government was forced to borrow vast sums of money to pay off the many large debts that had been incurred. Madden's letters and newspaper articles from this juncture, describe the situation in Portuguese society as he witnessed it on a daily level.

This revolution differs from all previous revolts. There has been no buying of troops, and the people have simultaneously and spontaneously risen in the different provinces. It commenced with a large body of women assailing the authorities and the troops with desperate fierceness; and throughout the struggle women, young and old, have taken an active part in almost every contest with the troops.[301]

Madden's criticisms of the Portuguese administration in his letters home and his regular newspaper articles in the *Morning Chronicle* didn't go unnoticed among the higher echelons of Portuguese society who attempted to silence him in whatever way that they could. Firstly, they attempted to bribe him in an effort to silence him and, when that didn't work, they threatened to assassinate him. At one point, Madden informed Lord Howard de Walden that he felt his life was in danger and asked whether the British government could do anything to provide him with protection. His experiences in many different and far-flung regions of the globe had inured him to many dangers but now he found himself under surveillance and living in a state of fear as a consequence. His letters were being opened and sometimes, they never reached his address at all. Madden must have been relieved when his appointment in Portugal came to an end, a relief that is partly indicated in the following verse which he wrote while still living in that country.

> *A fertile soil - a genial clime is here!*
> *A land that God with goodly gifts has blessed;*
> *A glorious sky, serene and calm and clear,*
> *With gorgeous sunshine glowing on its breast.*
> *And this is nature's work! But all the rest*
> *Is man's - the gloom that shrouds intelligence*
> *That sinks the spirit saddened and oppressed,*
> *And grieves the heart and gives at once offence*
> *And pain to every feeling and to outward sense.*[302]

Madden made two trips abroad prior to his leaving Portugal permanently. He visited both London and Dublin on two separate occasions - in February, 1845 and in January, 1846. One of these trips turned out to be a bit longer than he had expected as he found himself attending to his niece Margaret, who was very ill with the measles. He also used his time at home to search for employment on behalf of his son Forde who had completed his engineering studies in Paris and to sell off whatever copies of *The United Irishmen* that he still had in his possession. His publisher, Duffy, paid Madden royalties of 85 pounds for this book and agreed to publish a third series of the book. Harriet wrote his weekly column for *The Morning Chronicle* while Madden was away from Portugal, although Madden's preference had been to simply cancel the column for those weeks given that Harriet was in poor health and he was afraid that the column writing might have sapped her energies even further. On Madden's second trip home, he spoke to his friend the newspaper editor Doyle, of his concerns regarding the job in

Portugal and the fact that he would prefer to be transferred to another city such as Paris or Madrid. Doyle refused to agree to a transfer however and told him that the newspaper preferred if he stayed in the Portuguese job until the end of his contract. Madden told Doyle that another newspaper had approached him with a job offer but that he didn't want to move job again so soon and that he would remain in the Lisbon post provided he was "estimated duly… and strongly supported…"

"That was promised, in the most emphatic terms. So I go back to Lisbon," Madden informed Harriet in a long letter, he sent to her from London. He planned to spend a fortnight in Dublin, returning to Paris via London, where he could visit his son Forde. He found his travel plans somewhat waylaid by poor weather conditions, however.

> *I may now tell you we had a most vile passage, and sufficient peril off the Isle of Wight to produce a very unpleasant state of excitement amongst the passengers…I have called on the Elmslies. Captain Gordon (one of the Elmslies was married to him, it appears) has been going about abusing my works, and telling people how dreadfully rebellious some of these works are. I feel no anger for the poor young man.*[303]

Some positive changes were afoot on the political front as relating to Ireland, Madden informed Harriet. August 1845 had seen the Tory government holding a position of total parliamentary dominance, one where they could do whatever they wished and where they did not pay the slightest heed to pressure groups whom they did not approve of. Six months later and the situation had changed significantly, however:

> *The Whigs will be in office, it is supposed in twelve months. I visited Lord Clarendon on Tuesday, and was very kindly received.*[304]

The sixth of January, 1846 saw Madden receive a letter from

Lord Clarendon, a letter which indicated that both he and Clarendon were among that small group of politicians, diplomats and public figures who hoped some positive change might be in the offing for Portugal in addition to Ireland. In Clarendon's view felt such positive change could only be affected if the British took a more serious interest in Portuguese affairs:

> *I shall of course be happy, (said Clarendon to him), to receive the communication you have been requested to make to me. The parties to whom you refer do me but justice in believing that I take a deep interest in the affairs of the Peninsula, and that I must lament the deplorable state of things now existing in Portugal as well as in Spain. At the same time, however, I do not see how any intervention of mine can be useful, for experience proves that Parliamentary discussion respecting the internal affairs of another country far more often aggravates than diminishes the evils complained of. A Minister here must always reply with great caution, but if he condemns or laments the policy of the country in question it is magnified there into an attack upon its national independence and the Government makes it a point of honour to persevere in their obnoxious course. If he defends or palliates it, it is taken as an encouragement and it is disheartening to those by whom the complaints are promoted. These reasons have made me keep silence of late with requests to Spain. I believe that they are equally applicable, if not more so, with respect to Portugal. It is not my intention to go to London before the meeting of Parliament, but if you are about to leave England and wish to see me immediately I will go up to London some morning or be happy to see you here if you thought it worth while to come down.*[305]

Not only was Madden interested in what potential positive changes the ascension of the Whigs to government might bring to Ireland and other countries but he was also angling for any future civil service job opportunities a change of administration might herald for people such as him. He had already written to Gladstone who was then still a member of the Tory party enquiring as to whether there might be any civil service openings available in the future - and was waiting for a response. The reply, when it came, did not indicate any immediate openings but it did hold out some hope for the future.

> *I am aware of your character as an honourable and able man and also of the public services which you have rendered; and it will give me pleasure if I should have the opportunity of acknowledging them by tendering to you my appointment.*[306]

Madden's letters to his wife Harriet at this juncture make reference to other parts of the world in which he still clearly took a strong interest, and in which both social and political strife were still widespread - including Cuba and West Africa.

> *The other day I met Schenley "bearded like a pard" airing his effeminate beauty in Regent Street. We had a mutual stare, neither of amity nor enmity. Shortly after I stumbled in the Strand on Maclean of Cape Coast Castle; another stare, more of sorrow than anger. He looks miserable and is down in the world - at war with Hutt, who is come home, and also with the Government. Your letter "Our Lisbon Correspondent" did admirably. I had the revision of it, and took a few liberties in leaving out a little. If I had anything to suggest it would merely be: do not enter too much into minute details on any point that does not concern English interests. Do not imagine I am finding fault. Your letter was excellent, and has gone round the family with great éclat. Take care of yourself, and let no notion of economy keep you from anything essential to your comfort. I long to be back with you. This, you will say, is a romantic conclusion to a very prosaic letter; nevertheless, it is most true.*[307]

Madden made full use of the free time he had available to him while living in Portugal to engage in various cultural and literary pursuits. He was appointed to the membership of a good number of medical, scientific and literary associations. He also undertook research in the National Library there where the libraries of the various religious houses that had been shut down and which had amalgamated in many cases. He examined these collections for any historical material relating to Ireland and his own areas of research interest. Madden had friends amongst the Irish Dominican community in Corpo Santo who were his neighbours in Lisbon, and whom he visited almost every day. They provided him with some of the information he included in his book, *The Shrines and Sepulchres of the Old and New World* (1851). He also received a warm welcome in the British Ambassador's residence, in the English College, and amongst the Irish diaspora then resident in Lisbon.

He got to know Liam O'Doherty, an elderly man from County Tipperary who had absconded from Ireland almost fifty years before, fearful that he might be charged in relation to the death of a Protestant landlord in his home parish. This landlord had attempted to force Doherty's father into selling him a valuable racehorse for five pounds; he attempted to pressurise him by calling on the excesses of the anti-Catholic legal strictures then in operation. Madden also gathered together the material for a book about Portugal and wrote up a good deal of it. A publisher in London - also named Madden - expressed an interest in publishing the book but advised Madden not to write the book too hurriedly. Clearly the publisher had heard previous complaints that Madden had a tendency to complete his books too quickly resulting in a propensity for textual errors. In this book Madden directed his attention to the question of the Inquisition and the campaign against the Jesuits. He was fortunate in that a number of British government ministers and the British Ambassador sought permission so that both Harriet and he were allowed to examine and copy documents relating to the Inquisition at their own convenience. Madden continued this research when he visited Madrid in 1845 but then gave it up for a while to undertake archival research on Francis Tregian,[308] the Elizabethan courtier who was imprisoned for a full twenty-eight years and stripped of all his worldly goods, having sheltered Blessed Cuthbert Mayne[309] while he was on the run. While in Madrid, Madden met with such "society" figures as Washington Irvine, a man whom some people considered both innocent and coarse in equal measure. Irvine was the then British Ambassador to the Spanish Court and one of the most renowned literary men in the "New World." Both Irvine and Madden shared a common interest in the United Irishmen with Irvine writing poignantly about the passionate yet doomed love that had once existed between Robert Emmet and Sarah Curran.[310]

On one occasion, when Madden and Irvine met one another the Ambassador called to mind the dreadful dinner they had attended in London a few years previously when the voice of the poet Thomas Campbell[311] was drowned out by shouting on the part of some of the other guests. Irvine himself was a particularly poor orator and Madden once witnessed him sitting down again after only a few words of a speech, his nerves having failed him. The fact that the author of a book as eloquent and as commercially successful as the *Sketch Book*[312] had been stuck for words surprised many in the audience on that particular occasion. Madden had been sitting next to Tom Moore on the night when Irvine had frozen and Moore had covered for Irvine, thereby saving his blushes somewhat. Moore, who was an outstanding after-dinner speaker, had surpassed himself that evening particularly in view of the fact that he had been going through a difficult and depressing period personally. His son had just given up a commission in the British army and returned suddenly to Ireland from India, without a penny to his name. In fact this son did not live long after returning from India and died young just like a brother of his had who had died previously from tuberculosis. When Madden informed Washington Irvine that he was researching various aspects of Irish history in Madrid, in the Escorial and in other archives as located in Lisbon, Mafra and Belem, Irvine advised him not to forget to search the archives that were in Shimaneas. There was no fear that Madden would forget to search anywhere that there might be manuscript material available, of course. When Madden was himself personally unable to visit an archive he generally sent someone along in his stead. He actually employed an agent on two separate occasions to research the documents in the Vatican archives which related to the Inquisition and to Galileo's case in particular.

Madden considered it vital to gain an understanding of the motives and attitudes of the governmental authorities during the period of the Inquisition. For example, the attacks on the aristocratic class and the Jesuits which took place in Portugal particularly pleased certain sections of the British public and various politicians on the Continent, including Senor Carvalho in Portugal had kept the structures of the Inquisition functioning for his own aims, long after the oppression associated with the Inquisition had ceased in other countries.

One high-profile example of the Inquisition's effects in Portugal was the case of Father Matagorda, a priest against whom so many accusations of heresy were directed that he had eventually gone mad while in prison. Madden kept in close touch with his friends and family back in Ireland for the three years he was in Portugal. He continued his close links with home through the voluminous correspondence that passed back and forth between his friends in the Abolitionist Movement and in the Young Irelanders. His advice to these friends was consistent - to stick to their objectives and never to abandon them. For example, he heard from British Abolitionist Joseph Sturge about an attempt on his part to heal a rift which developed among the members of the Irish Society of Friends (Quakers) who were campaigning on the Abolition issue. When Sturge informed Madden shortly into their correspondence that he intended to resign from public life now that his sister had died, the Irishman replied to him immediately urging him against such a move. Madden explained why he disagreed with Sturge by referring to his own circumstances. He too had considered opting out of public life only a short time previously but had come to the conclusion that there was an onus on people like themselves not to take the easy way out by retiring to a "quieter life." "So long as we are on our pilgrimage in this world, the obligations that lie upon us cannot be dispensed with." These obligations included the necessity to do good for as many other human beings as possible and to fight against the evil that was still widespread throughout the world. It was only by the fulfilment of such obligations that it was possible to truly serve He who had forged a humanity that took shape in the form of the poor, the oppressed and the vulnerable in society. They were even obliged to reach out to the malicious in their communities as they, more than most, were deserving of both sympathy and kindness. Madden also corresponded with Thomas Davis at this juncture, an extract of which included the following:

> *Things go on so marvellously queer in England in all that relates to Ireland that it is difficult for an absent gentleman...to imagine what are to be the results. I would not willingly judge of them by the hyperbolical effusions of gratitude I read of amongst you. We paid for the morbid kindness and monstrous incredulity of Mr. Grattan's disposition in 1782. We paid dearly for it. The force of circumstances, the necessary and inevitable force of a destined contingency I think pushes on your cause before it, and obviates many impediments and difficulties, by shuttle-cocking them across the channel and sending them spinning in the air at every impulse of gratitude...Was the struggle for which Ireland embarked the College of Maynooth? I thought and still think that the cause was not money, neither 17,000 pounds per annum nor 17,000,000 pounds but the rights of eight millions of men.*[313]

The above paragraph was a reference to the *Charitable Bequests Act*[314], a project that included the proviso that government funding for Maynooth be increased. Madden was concerned about the British government's motives here suspecting that it was an attempt on the colonial government's part to subjugate the Irish clergy and to diminish their influence on the general populace in Ireland. Madden wrote a long letter to the *Freeman's Journal* on this issue in January, 1845 outlining his concerns as regards the proposed Bill. By mooting an increase in its annual subvention to Maynooth the colonial government was really attempting to gain control over the Catholic hierarchy and the clergy with a view to breaking their moral and intellectual influence in Ireland. Madden saw this as part of a process whereby the Catholicism which had sustained the Irish through generations of oppression and violence would be gradually diluted with a view to its eventual elimination. Every Irish person had the right to resist such a process if they so wished.

Madden also wrote a private letter to his friend Dr. Miley on this issue impressing on him the necessity to support the opposition to this anti-Catholic agenda. What was needed in Ireland now was "bold champions" and not "sorrowful spectators" who would simply ignore the imposition of this new form of tyranny, as if it wasn't even happening. Miley referred to this insightful letter which Madden had sent him in his next editorial for this newspaper. Its writer, Dr. Madden had been living on the Continent for a short time Miley explained, but while he may have been in exile his heart would always be intertwined with that of the Irish people. The doctor had as much right to protect the rights of the Irish now as he had defended the reputations of the Irish whom a tyrannical government had put to death years before, men whom the same government had denigrated as outlaws and traitors. Madden visited Paris in September 1845, where his friend Willie Cogan informed him about the sudden death of Thomas Davis in Ireland. A short while later he received a copy of the *Nation* which included Gavan Duffy's elegy for Davis:

Davis, (said Duffy), was the finest man, the most faithful, the least selfish, the noblest-minded being I ever knew...He was capable of making any sacrifice (except of honour), even of life itself if an emergency called for such a trial of his integrity and intrepidity of spirit; nay, in the cause of his country's independence were it necessary to die for that object, Davis would have walked to the scaffold with as much composure as if he had been going to his bed. There was not in the range of Irish history a better example for the awakened intellect and patriotism of Ireland than that which was furnished by his short but notable career. The warriors of England have statues and triumphal pillars erected to their honour in our public places; but our heroes have no trophies, no monumental piles, no marble records of their worth. It would seem as if we had no valour, no genius, no patriotism to honour, or that we had too many wrongs to remember to be reminded of benefits to the nation by one of our own countrymen.[315]

Gavan Duffy praised the project which was already underway to commission a special plaque in Davis' memory. Now that Davis was dead and Dillon[316] had emigrated to Madeira (Spain) in search of some respite from his chest problems, only Duffy remained from the original group who had founded the *Nation*. He was still working to keep the Young Ireland movement going through the auspices of the paper; although Smith O'Brien was now - in a way - the person who was directing the movement. Prior to this O'Brien had kept a certain distance between himself and the movement and turned a blind eye to the ideological differences that separated O'Connell from some of the movement's younger members. O'Brien found himself unable to ignore these differences of opinion in the long run, however, primarily as a consequence of the apparently politically-indiscreet nature of O'Connell's son, John.[317]

The clearer it became that Peel's government was likely to be short-lived, the worse the disagreements within the Repeal Association were. The O'Connells - privately initially, but then more openly - made a deal with the Whigs which Smith O'Brien denounced. The O'Connells responded to Smith O'Brien's attack and Smith O'Brien spoke out again concerning the government's plans for the economic improvement of Ireland. When a new government came in under the stewardship of Lord John Russell, it was announced that a few governmental positions would be divided out amongst a small number of Irish constitutional Nationalists. Smith O'Brien strongly opposed this development and argued that no-one should be nominated as a potential candidate in the forthcoming by-election unless they openly vowed to continue the demand that Repeal be implemented in Ireland. John O'Connell had a different opinion on this issue, however; he wanted to force the Young Irelanders out of the Repeal Association and with a view to this, he recommended passing a series of motions that would outlaw any attempt to grant legitimacy to the use of violence for achieving political ends. With this suggestion, John O'Connell was really targeting the younger cohort of the Young Irelanders who would find it difficult if impossible to oppose these motions as put forward by him.

The irony of O'Connell's tactic was that these motions were, in reality, completely irrelevant, as none of the Young Irelanders had any intention of using violence to achieve their political aims at this juncture. As Daniel O'Connell became increasingly old and frail, his attendance at the meetings of the Repeal Association in Conciliation Hall became more infrequent. His son John who wished to assume his father's mantle became increasingly jealous when it became evident that the other members of the Repeal Association would not accept him as the natural successor to his father Daniel. This resentment on the part of the younger O'Connell was a source of annoyance to the other Young Irelanders who were already attempting to cope with the arrival of another lively young man named John Mitchell in their ranks. Mitchell was a "larger than life" character who seemed to stir up controversy every time he spoke publicly or put pen to paper.

The blight that struck the Irish potato harvest in the Great Famine of 1845 only fuelled the tensions between Smith O'Brien and Daniel O'Connell; as both men disagreed fundamentally on how best the Irish people should respond politically to the crisis. Smith O'Brien felt that Ireland would be forced into an even more perilous position than she was already in if the Corn Laws[318] were cancelled while O'Connell, on the other hand, believed that the promotion of the free market was the country's best option. His view was that there was no point in the Irish people asking the British government to provide them with the urgently-needed aid that was required to prevent starvation, if, at the same time, they were going to go against Britain's demand for cheaply-produced food. Smith O'Brien pre-empted later Nationalist groups such as Sinn Féin by refusing to take up his seat at Westminster and suffered a prison term as a punishment for this act of defiance. John O'Connell had vowed to follow suit with this tactic but when the opportunity came, he changed his mind. This exacerbated the tensions between the Young Irelanders and O'Connell further.

The Nation took Smith O'Brien's side in this controversy, a stance which O'Connell publicly criticised. He was particularly critical of the Nation for drawing the ire of the British government by publishing a detailed article by John Mitchell outlining how Nationalists could damage the country's railway infrastructure, thereby preventing British troop movements around Ireland. In the same article Mitchell also described how guerrilla warfare could be very successfully employed on Ireland's roads, if a military insurgency became a possibility at some future date. The newspaper's editor, Charles Gavan Duffy was immediately brought to book about the seditious tone of this article, however.

The clearer it became that Peel's government was unlikely to last much longer, the more the tension increased within the Repeal Association. O'Connell's supporters made a deal (secretly at first, and publicly, at a later date) with the Whigs, a move that prompted a strong protest from Smith O'Brien. The O'Connellites tried to counter Smith O'Brien's objections but he cited the initiatives which the then government had put in place in order to improve the poor economic state of Ireland as the reason for his opposition to this political deal on the part of the

O'Connnellites. When the new government under the stewardship of Lord John Russell was eventually established, a group of Irish Nationalists found themselves appointed to government positions. This development was one which Smith O'Brien also attacked, his view being that nobody should be nominated in the bye-election who didn't publicly declare that they supported the Repeal campaign. Smith O'Brien hated disunity in the Repeal Association and fought hard against it. But John O'Connell was of a different view. It was his aim to drive the Young Irelanders out of the Repeal Association and with this end in mind he proposed that a series of resolutions be passed which would prohibit the Repeal Association being involved in any agitation whatsoever that might instigate violence.

It was the younger activists in the Repeal Association whom O'Connell was really targeting here, since he knew that they would never support a blanket ban on the potential use of force to achieve their political aims. Smith O'Brien reminded these younger activists that these tactics on the part of O'Connell were completely meaningless, however, especially since the Repeal Association had no real interest in using force to achieve any of its stated aims. John O'Connell kept up his campaign against that group of Young Irelanders whom he considered the most radical until Smith O'Brien stormed out of one of the meetings in Conciliation Hall after some heated exchanges. He was followed by Thomas Francis Meagher,[319] Gavan Duffy, John Mitchell, P.J. Smyth and a number of others. This turn of events left John O'Connell in full control of the Repeal Movement. The younger O'Connell had a very strong hold over his father Daniel and persuaded him to write a number of public letters criticising the actions of the Smith O'Brien faction and bemoaning the damage that their actions were inflicting on constitutional efforts for reform. The Whigs gave sustenance to O'Connell's stance by appointing Lord Westborough, an old friend of Daniel O'Connell's to the position of Irish Viceroy[320] and another of his friends, D.R. Pigot as Lord Chief Baron. They went further again and appointed Thomas Redington[321] to the position of Under-

Secretary, the first Catholic to hold such a post in centuries. The rumour-mill had it that the approval of the O'Connell's had been sought on all of these appointments, and these rumours were given further sustenance when a number of justices who had been dismissed from their posts because of their support for Repeal found themselves suddenly re-instated.

Unsurprisingly, these justices did not include Smith O'Brien or any other supporters of the Young Irelanders. The membership of the Young Irelanders increased in spite of these political setbacks and an elderly and frail Daniel O'Connell could not but have been worried by these developments. The group who left the Repeal Association asked whether they could become members again and O'Connell enquired of his curate, Dr. Miley - who was also an old friend of Madden's - to see whether he could arrange a mediation process which would culminate in their return to the fold. Madden's sympathies remained with the Young Irelanders throughout this split amongst the Nationalists, a fact which was evident in the letters he sent home from Lisbon. In February, 1846 he introduced himself to Smith O'Brien and sent him a copy of *The Connexion between the kingdom of Ireland and the crown of England* (1845) "believing tho' it has been run down by a portion of the Anti-Repeal press that you will recognize in it honest intentions towards Irish intentions." Madden had a very high opinion of Smith O'Brien and he wasn't alone in this. Many Irish exiles at this juncture were quite proud of Smith O'Brien's efforts in relation to the Repeal Campaign and were anxiously following his battle against his more powerful foes - the majority of whom were intent on preventing him from making any political headway. Madden praised Smith O'Brien's political courage and encouraged him as follows:

> *I pray you do bear this in mind in all your difficulties and embarrassments interposed either by open or secret enemies - the thinking people of Ireland look up to you with confidence, with gratitude for your past conduct, with entire reliance on*

your wishes, integrity and intrepidity for the final accomplishment of the hope they have at heart, the restoration of their independent parliament.[322]

In an appendix to this letter he added - "I have taken the liberty of sending you a copy of a song I made today." The song Madden composed was an elegy for Robert Emmet.[323] Smith O'Brien sent a friendly reply to Madden but one which was couched in such general terms that it gave the impression he hadn't actually read the book which he had forwarded to him. Smith O'Brien expressed the hope that Madden would find health and happiness in Portugal and that he would live to see the day when he could return to an independent Ireland, a country that would be prosperous enough to allow all of its citizens to live in dignity and freedom. He also expressed his hope that Madden would one day publish his elegy – a promise which he fulfilled a number of years later in his biography of Emmet. While the elegy itself had little merit as literature, it was full of emotion and patriotic feeling. Madden sent Smith O'Brien another letter a few months later concerning the recently-introduced *Protection of Life (Ireland) Bill*[324] which Peel had passed in an effort to prevent any potential unrest in Irish rural areas as instigated by the Famine. The Bill stipulated the most severe penalties for anybody who might contemplate initiating any civil unrest or disobedience. One of the Bill's provisions, for example, included a punishment of fifteen years transportation for any Irish person who broke the strictly-enforced curfew then in operation in rural areas. Contrary to Peel's prognosis, the Famine years proved some of the least eventful in terms of civil unrest in Ireland during those decades of the nineteenth century.[325] Madden informed Smith O'Brien that he could use any of the documents he was enclosing, if they were of any benefit to his campaigning - i.e. "in his noble efforts against this atrocious Bill." The main document Madden was referring to here was a short essay he had written arguing against the provisions of the Bill, an essay in which Madden had underlined comments such as the following: "Should they not be successful, the Repeal Movement must make an onward movement." In case his comments were misunderstood in any way Madden also underlined the following statements: "The Association has not exhausted its peaceful powers of resisting downright tyranny, such as the violation of constitutional liberty intended by this wicked measure… "I do not point to any other means of redress which imply or necessitate violence." Madden obviously had some form of protest or peaceful civil disobedience in mind but the following passage in his document indicates that he was unsure really about what was the best approach to take:

> *The Repeal Association, if it limits its opposition to the measures that had already been put into operation against the Bill, will break the compact between it and the people and will never again regain it. The organisation of the country will be at an end - it will drag on a sickly existence for some months and then will fall to the ground like the Volunteer one after the Convention Act - a lumbering body of great bulk but of wasted energies and of withered heart and hope.*[326]

This document or "essay" which Madden sent to Smith O'Brien was actually a letter he had begun with the intention of getting it published. He had changed his mind halfway through realising that if it was made public under his name he would never have any hope of finding a decent job again. Madden did make the courageous offer to Smith O'Brien however - that he could attribute any quotes from the essay to him if it was necessary to do so for truth's sake - although he preferred if he did not do this. Madden's essay included an account of a killing he had witnessed in Ireland when he was younger and apprenticed to a chemist in the town of Athboy, County Meath. A rural youth had been murdered on that occasion by a local member of the gentry named Sir Francis Hopkins. It just so happened that the killer's son - also named Sir Francis Hopkins – was in the news at this same time because he had presided over a court hearing that sentenced a young Irishman named Brian O'Seerey to death by hanging - based on evidence that was extremely dubious to say the least. Madden wrote that he had never seen an injustice as blatant as this being committed in any foreign country which he had worked in – an injustice perpetrated, "under cover of legitimate authority…(and) with the connivance of the Viceroy's, the full knowledge of the Chancellor's and the silent sanction of the British Government." Smith O'Brien would not use the contents of Madden's letter, however. In fact, O'Brien never even got a chance to speak on the issue at all because a hasty vote was suddenly organised on the *Protection of Life (Ireland) Bill* which saw the Whigs, the Radicals, the Irish ministers and Disraeli's Conservative Protectionists all join forces to force the Tories from office and open the door again for the Whigs. The Whigs would stay in office after this for a full twenty years.

Madden remained in Portugal until October, 1846. Harriet and their young son Tom had left Lisbon the previous August. They travelled home on a small trading vessel which took three weeks to reach Liverpool. The entire family were re-united in Dublin in October, where they remained until the end of the year. While at home, Madden tried to help his old friend Dr. Miley in his efforts to heal the rift between John O'Connell and William Smith O'Brien. Some time prior to this Madden had introduced Smith O'Brien to Dr. Miley, informing O'Brien that Miley was a person who had new and innovative ideas as to how the friends of Ireland could lobby in relation to the Corn Act being proposed at this juncture. Dr. Miley wasn't a Smith O'Brien supporter however. His sympathies lay entirely with (Daniel) O'Connell, a fact which was a major impediment as regards any possible reconciliation between the two disputing factions. In fact Dr. Miley was a close personal friend of Daniel O'Connell's and even acted as his spiritual adviser for a time. O'Connell was very dependent on Miley as he became more elderly and actually sent him to Cahermoyle as his representative for a meeting with Smith O'Brien at one point.

While Miley was preparing for this meeting, he asked Madden to write him a letter praising this attempt at reconciliation between the two sides. A letter such as this might have an influence on Smith O'Brien seeing as Madden was in his "camp," Miley thought. Madden did as requested and wrote bemoaning the unfortunate disagreement that had torn apart the Repeal Association, an association that had once been both strong and united in purpose. Only the loss of one's soul could compare to the disaster that it would ensue if a resolution could not be found to the split that had torn the Association apart. Madden begged Smith O'Brien to do whatever he could to try and sort out the dispute, providing such a resolution was in accordance with his own honour and to the benefit of the country as a whole. He apologised for the fact that he himself could not attend the meeting in Cahermoyle as had been arranged but an important issue had come up which he couldn't explain on paper. Madden gave this letter to Dr. Miley and added a private note to Miley himself in which he included the following words. "In this negotiation I beg of you bear in mind that Mr. O'Connell has a great deal to atone for." It appears that this latter comment riled Miley because he never passed on Madden's "letter of appeal" to Smith O'Brien.

The negotiations in Cahermoyle went nowhere and having returned to Dublin, Miley made no attempt to get in touch with Madden ever again. Given his own political leanings and that the situation was so divisive, the choice of Miley as "mediator" was a poor one. Smith O'Brien didn't trust Miley and, rather than resolve the issue, he decided to leave the door open for a possible future debate on the issues that divided the Repeal Association members instead.[327] Before long it became clear that the split between the two factions was impossible to resolve. The political arrangement which some Irish Nationalists entered into with the Whigs was proof enough for Smith O'Brien that many politicians were more interested in putting their own personal interests before any "National" ones by ensuring that they received appointments in the new political administration. Smith O'Brien and the other Young Irelanders responded to this development by setting up a new political organisation which they titled the "Irish Confederation."[328] Unfortunately this organisation, too, was divided from the very first day of its foundation as John Mitchell, John Martin and Devin Reilly argued with the others about the direction it should take; these three men eventually broke away from the new organisation. Among this triumvirate it was Mitchell above anyone else, whose vision of Republicanism Madden found himself at odds with.

Given the hectic nature of the previous decade for Madden and his family, the first half of 1847 was particularly quiet. Madden, his wife Harriet, and their sons Thomas and Forde, moved to Paris at the beginning of 1847 where they all remained until Forde had completed his engineering studies at the age of nineteen. This period was unusual to a certain extent in that Madden seems to have given up his habit of letter-writing for a number of years. The fact that Ireland was in the throes of its worst ever national disaster probably explains why practices such as letter-writing were considered low on the list of priorities. The Maddens would almost certainly have kept up-to-date on developments as relating to the Great Famine through the press as the newspapers in Ireland, England and France included many articles describing the more horrific and gruesome events that occurred as a consequence of the Great Hunger. These included descriptions of chaotic food riots, hospitals that were overflowing with the sick and the dying, and lists of the clergy who had succumbed to fever. The poorer people of Ireland were generally mentioned only in statistical terms by the newspapers and other official sources of the time. *The Nation* accused the colonial government in Ireland of complicity in the murders of over two million people. While some newspaper articles about the Famine were quite brief and factual in nature, the discerning reader could still get a good sense of the horrific scale of this disaster in both human and social terms. In Skibbereen, County Cork, for example, the local court sessions dragged on interminably as it had to deal with over 4000 civil actions and 350 criminal charges as relating to the theft of cattle and sheep. Over seventy of the defendants found guilty in that court were transported overseas to other colonial outposts, a number that was insignificant, however, when compared with the hundreds of thousands of Irish people taking the "coffin ships" in an effort to escape starvation and disease. The Times reported that the Irish were leaving their homeland in such droves that an Irishman on the banks of the Shannon would soon be as rare a sight as a Native American in the United States.

One newspaper report that Madden was unlikely to have missed was the news that the Earl of Bessborough had died.[329] This report was followed a few days later by the news that Lord Clarendon, a man whom Madden was acquainted with, had slipped quietly into Dublin Castle and the government seat formally occupied by Bessborough. Only a short time prior to this Madden had consulted with Clarendon on the political situation in both Spain and Portugal and on the prospects of the Whigs in the forthcoming British election. No doubt the Irishman had sounded out Clarendon concerning his chances of securing a government post if the Whigs formed the next government. While there is no surviving documentation or correspondence indicating that Madden actually wrote to Clarendon requesting a job, it would have been strange if he hadn't written to every minister or official that he was acquainted with at this time. Before he left Lisbon, Madden was advised by Lord Howard de Walden to send a letter of application to Lord Palmerston who was responsible for the Foreign Affairs department, a department for whom Madden had previously worked. De Walden also wrote a letter to the same office recommending Madden for a post. One person whom Madden didn't bother to approach or lobby with regard to possible employment opportunities on this occasion was Lady Blessington. She was still smarting from the last barbed letter he had sent to her prior to his departure for Lisbon - "She was a little out of temper and I was not a little vehement, I believe, in expressing an opinion that those who belonged to the people, and came out of their ranks, should deal leniently with their faults and sympathise with their sufferings."

While there is a good chance that she would have dealt fairly leniently with her tenants in any event, Blessington's Irish tenants simply stopped paying their rents during the years of the Famine, struggling as they were to avoid starvation and death. That this coincided with a period where Lady Blessington had financial difficulties of her own was one of life's ironies. The rift between Lady Blessington and Madden was short-lived by all accounts. When she heard that he had been appointed Colonial Secretary for Western Australia by Lord Grey, Lady Blessington wrote to Madden congratulating him on his appointment. She told him that she had no intention of falling out with a friend as long-standing and decent as Madden. The Whigs had again done Madden an important favour. As Lady Blessington told Madden, Grey was someone who could see the decency in people and recognised a good and honest worker when he saw one.

Madden had built up a reputation as a decent and honest administrator as based on his previous postings. Madden's honesty meant that he was someone who could be trusted again with an important job. "I do not lightly form friendships", Lady Blessington said, "and when formed, I do not allow any differences in political opinions to interfere with them. I have known you too long and too well not to feel a lively interest in your welfare, however we may disagree on some subjects." She was sorry that his new posting would take him so far away from home but she had heard good things about the climate in Australia. She hoped that he wouldn't spend too many years in Australia and that Madden would return home healthy and happy again, in due course. She would be delighted if she could meet him sometime before he left for Australia so that she could convey her deepest respect and friendship to him in person. Her letter finished like this:

Count D'Orsay charges me with his kindness wishes for your health and happiness, and my nieces send you theirs. God bless you, my dear Dr. Madden.

Madden's new appointment was announced on the fifteenth of May, 1847. Early that same morning, Daniel O'Connell (known as "The Liberator") passed away in Genoa while on a pilgrimage to Rome. While Madden was relatively quiet in early 1847 in terms of letter-writing and public activity, he kept busy behind the scenes. For instance, while preparing for the long journey to Australia, he was writing a history book about the imposition of the Penal Laws against Irish Catholics. He left the manuscript of *The History of the Penal Laws Enacted Against Roman Catholics*[330] into the publishers in London with a note saying that he hoped to be on the high seas by the time the reviewers got their teeth into the new book. Madden dedicated the new book to Barney McCabe and he also included about twenty pages of an essay McCabe had once written about Daniel O'Connell for the *Tablet* in this latest publication. Madden credited Thomas Davis as the inspiration for his writing this new book. If there was an obvious criticism of this new book, it is that Madden included too many passages and essays from other books within a text that was overly-long. The new book had the appearance of being rushed. Barney McCabe returned the compliment – (that was Madden's dedication to him) - when he collated many of the stories that they had heard as boys from the "Poor Scholar" (Geraghty) who had stayed with them and dedicated this collection to Madden. It is clear that McCabe idolized Madden to a certain extent - "by that unflinching foe to slavery and oppression in every form."[331] Amongst other things, McCabe credited Madden with publicly challenging the oppressive effects of the Pawn System that the British had brought to Ireland.

Madden made a short trip home to Dublin before setting out for Australia. He was in the Pro-Cathedral when O'Connell's remains were received, having been brought in cavalcade across the city's streets on arrival from Italy. It was a very solemn and sad occasion and he was most likely also in attendance the following morning when Dr. Miley gave the funeral oration in praise of O'Connell in the same church. Madden probably felt the poignancy of this moment more deeply than many of the other mourners present as he must have felt that this might well be the last time that he would set foot in Ireland. As Barney McCabe noted in his writings at this period, the chances that Madden would return hale and hearty from his latest posting in such a far-off country were slim indeed.

Madden auctioned off about 1100 of his books in Dublin city in January, 1847. Amongst these books was a copy of Robert Emmet's *Colonel Templehoff's Military Treatises*, now held in the Royal Irish Academy, Dublin. Later again that year, a London book dealer was seen selling off other books from the collections of the "late (sic) Dr. R. R. Madden."[332] Presumably Madden was saving as much money as he could in order to buy a new house in Australia and set himself and his family on a steady footing over there. This last trip to Ireland before his departure for Australia found Madden in sombre mood regarding the future of his native country, however. "Ireland's fatal beauty," he wrote, "still clung to her like a curse but could not hide her chains. Her dependence on a conqueror had made of the land a Golgotha of graves."

Madden had been waiting and hoping for a new post for a long time but now that he had secured one, he felt uncomfortable and nervous about his decision to accept it. Hadn't Daniel O'Connell himself sensed exactly the same thing many years before – the irony that was O'Connell's resilience in his agitations against various aspects of colonial and religious repression, particularly from 1846 onwards – and yet the fact that his own family were reliant on jobs in that same colonial, administrative regime that they were so critical of! Wasn't it the bitter truth that no Irishman had ever secured a job in the colonial civil service unless he had first betrayed his own country to one degree or another?

In a private letter he wrote to Thomas Davis at this juncture, Madden opened up about his conflicted feelings with regard to working for the British establishment while at the same time objecting to the oppressive nature of that establishment as manifested in so many countries abroad. While Madden felt torn about working for the British, he was also convinced that it would only be to Ireland's benefit if more Catholic Irishmen such as he took jobs in the British civil service – infiltrating it form within. Madden was also able to salve his conscience to some extent by arguing that he was only re-accepting a job in the civil service that had been taken from him unjustly in the first place. Such "rationalizations" didn't cut much ice with the Young Irelanders, however. The Nation made no mention at all of Madden's acceptance of this new post – it was as if they were ashamed of it really – and some of the statements published by the *Nation* at this juncture must have made Madden very uncomfortable – the likes of the following, for example:

If any Repealers were ready to sell their principles for place, they would obtain it (said Smith O'Brien) and along with it the eternal malediction and everlasting scorn of their country.

If these words had any meaning then Irishmen had to abandon all thoughts of taking a job in the civil service of the day. The civil service was organised differently then when compared with today. Competition in the form of civil service examinations didn't exist then. Instead, people were appointed as "favours" or as based on the recommendations of different government ministers. The common belief was that the appointment of certain Irishmen to civil service positions in the colonies was a privilege given in lieu of proper constitutional freedom in that particular colony. Worse again, some of this "jobbery" and power of patronage in the civil service was considered a part-compensation for the poor salaries that the government ministers themselves were paid. In fact, William Gladstone himself had at one point considered it impossible to run an efficient parliamentary government according to a more modern, more equitable and democratic model as proposed on a number of occasions by those seeking to reform the system.[333]

It might appear strange to a modern reader that there were many people in high office at this juncture who felt that public competitions for civil service competitions would never work. One well-known public figure who felt that way, for example, was Anthony Trollope[334], who, somewhat ironically, may have been remembering his own entry to the ranks of the governmental administrators when he refuted the allegation that the public offices were filled with "the idle, the weak in mind, the infirm in body, the unscrupulous, the jolter heads, the ne'er-do-wells, the puny and the diseased."

While the controversies concerning the appointment process for public office were on people's minds in England, the situation was even trickier for the likes of Madden back in Ireland where *The Nation* was constantly emphasising the vices of "place-begging" and "place-taking." Just as Madden was leaving for Australia there was an ironic note in the press regarding another colonial appointment which must have come as a shock to Madden. The *Nation* reprinted a story from *The Pilot* which confirmed that Francis Brady, known as "a wise man and a clever lawyer" had been appointed Chief Justice in Newfoundland, an appointment described as follows:

We believe Mr. Brady really is a "prudent and clever" young man; but what is more to the purpose with the Whig Government, he is one of the Parliamentary Committee of the Loyal National Repeal Association of Ireland, and author of one of the published Reports. Conciliation Hall Repeal is unquestionably strong to the Colonies.[335]

Madden was at heart a repealer. His sympathies lay with the Young Irelanders as opposed to the Liberals. He had been upset when O'Connell described the men of 1798 as a useless rabble. He had defended their high principles and their bravery and was accused of extreme political bigotry by some of the prominent newspapers of the day as a consequence; his accusers maintained that his political opinions served to incite the Irish people to rebel against the government. And now this same man had been appointed administrator in one of Britain's colonies.

While many people were surprised that Madden had accepted such a post, there were others who must have been even more shocked that he was offered such a position in the first place. It is likely that many members of the then government had ambivalent feelings about Madden's appointment, given that the government was actually *in situ* for a year before the appointment was officially announced. What undoubtedly stood to Madden's benefit was his long association with the Whigs, the Abolitionist movement, and the ridicule he had suffered in a previous Whig administration as relating to the question of slavery in West Africa. As Lady Blessington had pointed out, the Whigs were repaying Madden for his loyalty in the past while turning a blind eye to his recent "shiftlessness" as relating, one assumes, to the nationalist question. Like others who were even more intimately associated with the Repeal movement than he was, it is likely that Madden had benefited principally from the system of patronage operated by that particular Whig government. The past was the past as far as the Whigs were concerned and provided somebody proved capable in their job, they were satisfied to appoint them. Madden's new post had two immediate consequences: it put a temporary halt to his political writings and it meant that a Catholic was now a member of the colonial administration in Western Australia for the first time ever. Previous to this - as Madden himself confirmed to the Vicar-General of the Dublin Diocese in September, 1853 - it was "Irish Orangeism for the interests of Orangemen" that had been the ruling ethos in this colony. Lord Grey had been very aware of this, Madden maintained, and "being determined to break down that Government of a faction sent out a Roman Catholic as secretary, the first Catholic ever appointed to that office in the Colonies - myself." There was no correspondence at all between the Young Irelanders and Madden upon his return from the Continent at the beginning of 1847. Neither did he accept any employment opportunities while back in Ireland, no matter how small. He did not write even one newspaper article which was a sign, perhaps, that he was deliberately distancing himself from public affairs with an eye to his new job in Australia. Philosophically, it would have been difficult for Madden to have continued along the same path as the Young Irelanders in any case.

In the final analysis, Madden was willing to settle for civil disobedience as a form of ultimate protest whereas the Young Irelanders had become more daring as time went on and were increasingly influenced by the violent and revolutionary ideas then current to France, Austria and Germany. Increasingly, the Young Irelanders began to examine the theory of armed struggle as a potential route towards a political resolution in Ireland. Some members began to discuss the possibility of creating a National Guard which would ensure Ireland's statutory independence from England while others discussed the necessity for the creation of an Irish Republic. These developments ensured a widening ideological rift between people like Madden and the Young Irelanders at this point. An even greater irony would unfold shortly after this in the vast continent that is Australia.

Madden received a warm welcome in his new post, administering what was one of Australia's largest regions while (almost contemporaneously), his former colleagues in the Young Irelanders, Smith O'Brien included, also found themselves in Australia - but under very different circumstances. The leaders of the Young Ireland movement arrived as prisoners to an Australian penal colony. They arrived as broken and disillusioned men, their rebellion in Ireland having failed to get off the ground in any significant way. Smith O'Brien put a brave face on the failure of their revolt by maintaining that Irish people would rather die of hunger at home than go into exile voluntarily by means of the emigrant ship, a choice which he himself had not been given. The reality was more painful again. While the vast majority of the Irish populace had nothing but respect for the high-principled stand taken by the leaders of the 1848 Rebellion, the truth was that they had neither the heart nor the energy for the fight: the Great Famine had broken them.

CHAPTER 11
A SPELL IN WESTERN AUSTRALIA

While Madden was full of enthusiasm for his new post, he found himself in the "wars" even prior to setting foot in Australia. Once again, he found himself at loggerheads with the Colonial Office, and, on this occasion, it was with regard to his conditions of employment. As had been the case in the past, the Colonial Office was penny-pinching in relation to his travel expenses. It was bad enough, Madden complained, that he would be stationed in a colony where the climate was particularly debilitating and where the salary was poor. But why hadn't the Colonial Office provided him with any money to pay the travel costs for his wife Harriet and their nineteen-year old son Thomas More? Their other son Forde was staying behind in Ireland where he had secured a new job. Madden's badgering of the Colonial Office paid off in the end as, after much negotiation, the office agreed to pay Madden 250 pounds towards the cost of the boat tickets for his wife and family. The three of them boarded the *Orient* in Cowes on the 27th of November, 1847. They were joined on embarkation by a group of 51 boys from Parkhurst Prison who were being transported to Australia for various crimes - described by Madden as: "grave offences such as robberies varying in amount some even to the value of 40 pounds." These boys, some of whom were younger than twelve years of age, were marched onto the boat singing - "God save the Queen", under the direction of the Prison Governor. Madden received a number of letters of farewell prior to the *Orient* leaving port including one from his old friend Barney McCabe:

> I am (he said) *tumbling in thought with you all on the rough seas, and shrinking with you in the cold cabin...and wishing I had you all back again and listening to Tom's laugh, and joining with you in railing against a wicked, nasty, scheming, plotting, insincere world. Doctor, we are not relatives, but excepting Forde and your sister, I doubt if you have one relation, but excepting Forde and your sister, I doubt if you have one relation in the world who has thought of you and yours so much since we parted as myself. You must know that until we see ach other again, I have laid down a rule that every Sunday after dinner your healths are to be drunk here...You will find by The News of the World of this day that I have referred to you - that I make you plead to save our unfortunate country from the spy system...the reorganisation of which...has commenced...Your book makes a very pretty volume...Need I tell you how proud I am of the dedication to myself...I am working as hard to have the book noticed as if it were my own. I hope before you go that you may be able to receive the Dublin Review with my article on it.*[336]

Another farewell letter was from Madden's son Forde. Tragically, this may have been the last letter his parents would ever receive from Forde, given that he would die unexpectedly only a short while later. Forde's letter, not unnaturally, included the latest news from the "home front" including various details about his new job as an apprentice engineer. Forde also thanked his father for all the sacrifices he had made on his behalf and promised him that all of his hard work would not be in vain. Presumably, Forde was referring here to the large fee of five hundred pounds which had been paid to Mulvany's firm to secure the apprenticeship. Forde couldn't wait to start work in his new firm and was confident that he would "learn the ropes" very quickly. He also sent his love to his mother and his younger brother. Madden felt very sad at having to leave Forde behind and tried to convey his emotions in verse-form. He had spent the bulk of his life moving from place to place and now he was setting out on yet another journey, one that would take him all the way across the Indian Ocean and onwards to Australia. He was a well-seasoned traveller, but, given the choice, he would still have preferred to remain in Ireland and be near his eldest son.

> *The wings of travel wearied, droop at length,*
> *The spirit soars not, it reserves its strength,*
> *For homeward flights where household gods have shrines,*
> *Idols for homage: and most radiant lines*
> *In that bright face of thine, my own brave boy*
> *With all its themes for me of future joy.*[337]

Little did Madden realise when writing the above lines that he would never see his son Forde again. The *Orient* spent seventeen days at anchor just off the Isle of Wight, a delay which provided Madden with the chance to get to know his fellow-passengers as well as to write some more poetry.

> *Rowley-powley all day long*
> *Pitch and toss, and then swing-swong;*
> *In cot or hammock all night thro'*
> *Sick and sad and sleepless too*[338]

The ship then travelled onto the port of Plymouth where it remained at anchor until the twenty-first of December, before setting sail for real. The first week of the journey was very rough with ferocious gales tearing the ship's sails apart and having "a sobering effect on the convict boys." They were approaching the Spanish Madeira before the weather became more pleasant - "In the course of a week from the depth of the winter and most tempestuous weather we were launched into the temperature of summer with cloudless skies, gentle breezes and a sleepy sea."

They passed close to the islands of Cape Verde where they spotted large groups of porpoises and grampi but little else of note seems to have happened until they reached the shores of Australia. The complete journey from Plymouth to Fremantle[339] took eighty-nine days in total - "the shortest and most propitious that our captain, an old East India commander, ever made." Their first sight upon arrival in Fremantle included the prisoners who had been sentenced to transportation being rowed ashore in large groups under a tropical sun which beat down on the occasional white-washed house that dotted the coast-line.

The local newspapers welcomed Madden to the colony with *The Inquirer* printing a fairly long article about the newly-arrived administrator on the twenty-second of March, 1848, an article which did not conceal the locals' unhappiness with the ruling local government and the then acting Colonial Secretary, George Fletcher Moore,[340] in particular. The newspaper had this to say about Madden:

We are sure that his advent will be hailed by all the settlers with feelings of unmingled satisfaction - so weary, so disgusted, are all the classes at the manner in which the interests of themselves and the colony have been treated by the present local administration...He comes amongst us a stranger, to local politics and what is better, to local prejudices, and will, we sincerely trust, exert that intellect it is manifest he possesses to the advancement of a colony which has been kept in the background solely by an adherence to antiquated opinions and a dogged perseverance in asserting the right to act in contradiction to the avowed sentiments of the public.[341]

While Madden was undoubtedly excited about his new job, the truth was that he couldn't have been appointed to a more difficult post. The West Australian colony was just twenty years old and was in terrible state, infra-structurally, administratively and economically. There were less than five thousand "white" people living in the colony at this stage, and this "settler" community included three women for every two men. Its main town was Perth with a population of just over 1000 people and Fremantle, a port-town situated on the banks of the Swan River about twelve miles from Perth was home to about 500 people. The settler population included three thousand Protestants and about three hundred Catholics. There had been a great deal of pessimism regarding the development of this colony from the first day of its foundation, a pessimism that appeared well-placed after many of the colony's initial settlers found the conditions too tough and returned home again. The colony had grown slightly subsequent to this initial set-back however and by 1835 settlers had set up camp in five places other than Perth and Fremantle. These settlers were sheep-farming and had also begun to raise horses.

A weekly newspaper had been set up and the Crown had leased six hundred acres for the use of these new settlers. The colony had shuffled along without major incident until 1842. By then the settlers had gained some say in the administration of their own affairs and tensions between themselves and the native peoples were on the decrease. Indeed, cooperation between some of the people native to the area and the settlers was so good in some cases that it was proposed that the local "natives" ought to be considered British citizens, something that began to happen in practice from then on. The population of the colony began to increase slowly but surely. An economic slowdown throughout many parts of Australia in 1842 brought this progress to an abrupt end however. On Madden's arrival to Fremantle the economy was in very poor shape with the colonists citing legislation governing the use of land and a lack of capital and workers to engage in new enterprises as the main reasons for the economic downturn. The real causes of the economic problems in Fremantle and nearby areas were more complex however. Imported goods were trumping exports from Australia at this point and a surfeit of available food meant that food prices were also in decline. The years 1845 and 1846 saw the (local) West Australian parliament warning the Colonial Office in London that the colony's decline could only be prevented if more settlers were transferred to live there - both monied settlers and settlers who were willing to work as labourers.

Only one of the recommendations made by the then local government seems to have been acted upon by the Colonial Office, however. This was the decision to transform the Western Australian colony into a penal settlement. This solution suited the Colonial Office perfectly as the colonial settlements in Eastern Australia were refusing to accept any more convicts at this stage and convicts could now be shipped to the region bordering the Swan River instead. As one would expect, Madden threw himself fully into his new administrative role.

> *There are many things* – (he says - in a note found amongst his papers), *that might make a thoughtful man pensive in the position I now find myself placed. A Colonial Secretary of Western Australia, who is a Catholic, an Irishman, a Liberal in politics, an official who has battled with abuses in other colonies and a bookish man into the bargain, who has written works which are distasteful to people who deem the Penal Laws salutary enactments, and the past policy of England towards Ireland a good one, is not likely to come into office with much prestige or many prepossessions in his favour to secure a fair stage for his intentions, or fair play, perhaps, for his acts. But I feel very little apprehension, though it is evident I will soon have many difficulties to meet, jealousies to bear up against, and formidable interests opposed to me. My trust is not in myself, nor in any friends or partisans, for I have none here. My entire confidence is in God. On entering on my duties in this colony I commit myself to His Providence. I beseech His*

goodness, that I may be enabled by His mercy to do what is right and just. With His help I will endeavour to deal justly with all persons; to make no sacrifice of truth or principle to gain the favour of any man, or to escape any censure, slander, or invective; to do my duty to the Government, and so to employ all my energies and faculties as to promote the interests of this colony; to protect the natives, and never to lose sight of the just claims they have on us for protection, enlightenment, and compensation for their lands and their labours. I pray to be so directed as never to turn the opportunities of office to the account of my private interests; nor any power it gives me, to the detriment of others. Lastly, to bear in mind that I am very liable to error, subject to many infirmities, and that it behoves me to be watchful over myself, and very considerate and charitable in dealing with others. Trusting in Thee, my God, for all my guidance and all my help, I enter on the duties of this new office without fear, presuming only on Thy sufficiency, and my hope in Thee, which has never failed me.[342]

Madden outlined this new crusading spirit of his within a month of his arrival in a letter he sent from Perth to his friend Sir James Stephen[343], the then Under-Secretary of State for the Colonies.

I entered on my duties as soon as possible, and count on being enabled to discharge them efficiently, looking neither to the right nor to the left, but aloft occasionally for that good help which enables a man to surmount all difficulties and impediments. I will trouble you with no long statement of those obstacles. This government has been for some time as a kind of patrimony or family property in the management of individuals here, who undertake to manage public affairs so as to spare the Governor too much trouble, and prevent his disturbing the dead repose in which it is the interest of a few official parties to keep things. That regime, which has depressed me all interest and energies but those of five or six persons, it is now sought to maintain. This I cannot acquiesce in; and hence I think it right in the beginning you should know this much, in order in the event of any representations being made calculated to prejudice me, that my silence may not be taken for acquiescence in the justice of the; but that whenever you think a defence on my part called for, you will be good enough to apprise me of that necessity.[344]

The phrase - "this I cannot acquiesce in" was a giveaway - i.e. that Madden was already in the thick of an ideological "battle", despite having just arrived to the colony - a battle in which he would ultimately come off worst. Madden's correspondence at this juncture indicates his usual impatience to set everything which he considered unjust to rights immediately, irrespective of the many innumerable obstacles that lay in his way.

His letters and notes also prove - if proof were needed - that despite Madden's undoubted energy and capacity for hard work - his personality wasn't really suited to the type of role he was now charged with. In fact, many of Madden's problems in Australia – and in his other colonial posts – seem to have stemmed from the fact that he was never really sure how much authority he could exercise in the role he had been given and within the British governmental machine generally. Ultimately Madden was only a cog in the governing apparatus, a government official through whom the Colonial Governor and the colony's Upper-Council could channel their decisions. Madden was never politically astute enough to bring other government officials "on-side" when he found himself to be in disagreement with their point of view, however. The ability to act as a mediator or to persuade people to adopt a particular political position was not one of Madden's strengths. In the final analysis, Madden failed to understand that - despite any idealistic rhetoric to the contrary - the Swan River colony was first and foremost "a capitalist speculation sanctioned by the Government."[345]

In essence, it was a business venture that would probably

be abandoned as soon as it became clear that rumours the French wished to colonize this part of Australia proved unfounded. The fact there were various British "pioneers" willing to take a risk in this part of the world on receipt of significant donations of land and British government guarantees of protection were enough to ensure that the British kept their "hold" on this particular region of their Empire. This method of land donation was the way that the Western Australian region had functioned from the earliest days of the colony there.

For instance, James Stirling, a Scotsman, had been a British Navy captain before being appointed Lieutenant Governor of the Swan River colony of the 1830s. He did not receive any salary for this appointment but was given a huge parcel of land - 100,000 acres - instead. The men who accompanied him in this initial venture - Frederic Chidley Irwin, Peter Brown, John Septimus Roe and George Fletcher Roe - were appointed to the positions of military commandant, colonial secretary, surveyor general and advocate general respectively. While there were other "settlers" appointed to prominent positions in that first colony - the colonial surgeon and the crown solicitor, for example - the aforementioned five formed a sort of an oligarchy in the new colony, this, despite the fact that, by 1848, when Madden had arrived, those deemed "unofficial" settlers were technically permitted to appoint four nominees of their own to the colony' governing council.

The colony's governor was the only individual with the power to instigate new legislation within the region, albeit that the English Parliament still reserved the right to agree or disagree with any new legislative changes. The various government officials could do as they wished within their own assigned regional districts as long as they ran any new initiatives or plans past the senior administrators back in London, however. There were, of course, certain periods when the governor was out of the region or on a visit to another part of Australia, or during those occasions when a new governor was being chosen. Unfortunately, the local regional administrators, a good many of whom were Irish Protestants, took full advantage of these periods of stasis to impose their own often-bigoted attitudes on the Catholics living in their jurisdiction. Unsurprisingly, the local Catholic population had little love for these administrators; nor did the remainder of the local population who belonged to neither religious camp within the colony and who were not considered members of the "Irwinite Clique" as the then ruling oligarchy was locally named. Madden spent just eight months in Western Australia but was able to enumerate at least nine different measures which he had instigated to counteract the misrule instigated by the ruling Irwin oligarchy. At the top of the list Madden placed the question of religious bigotry. He challenged the anti-Catholic prejudice of the ruling class and also did his best to defend the rights of the local indigenous Australian population. These were the two initiatives that he considered his most effective, as based on the relatively short period of time he spent in the West Australian colony. Madden didn't mean to imply that ordinary working-class Protestants and Catholics were at loggerheads with one another. Rather it was the case that Catholics weren't receiving the civil rights they that they were entitled to from the colonial government.

Emancipation for Catholics was still a very new development in most corners of the British empire and in Australia there were still many government administrators who thought Catholics should be happy with very limited civil rights if any - believing that "wherever the British flag is planted, there, by that very fact, the Protestant Church becomes the national and established fact." In reality, Catholics had very little say in government affairs in Australia until Father Therry[336], the priest seen as the founding-father of the Catholic Church in Australia, vociferously campaigned on their behalf. He lobbied Viscount Glenelg, the then Colonial Secretary in the government of Lord Melbourne. As a consequence of his lobbying, it was decided not to prefer one church over another in terms of government grants. While history would show that the Irish Catholic emigrant was blessed with a chameleon-like quality that enabled him or her to integrate socially in the "New World", no matter what new social and cultural milieu they found themselves in, this doesn't seem to have been the case as regards the Catholic population then in Australia.

Catholics were a small minority in Australia at this juncture and were still a relatively impoverished group. They were a group who were determined to achieve social advancement nevertheless and they had a good leader in Bishop John Brady[346] who led them from the front even if his guidance was sometimes misguided. Madden and he were of a similar age, and Brady was the first Catholic missionary leader ever to set foot in Western Australia, arriving there in September, 1843. Originally from County Cavan, he was the son of a small farmer and had received his education courtesy of a hedge school before leaving for France to study for the priesthood in a seminary for foreign missionaries. Brady spent nineteen years working as a priest in a French mission based on the island of Reunion where he did a great deal of excellent work. Brady was a living "saint" according to Archbishop Ullathorn, the cleric who originally brought him to New South Wales. In New South Wales, Brady was known to work extremely long hours, travelling the country in all weathers on horseback or by wagon, this despite being in poor health. The first issue that had brought Brady to greater public attention was when he criticized the Protestant population of the colony for refusing to contribute or help in any way with the construction of a new church which he was attempting to build there.

Having spent nineteen years in an entirely Francophone environment Brady had forgotten much of his English and as soon as this controversy was ignited the local Protestant population mocked him on the linguistic front, the implication being that he was just an uneducated "hedge priest" who was unfit for the position of Bishop within his own Church. Ullathorn came to Brady's aid however, and backed him in a controversy which became increasingly bitter and public. Claims, counter-claims and insults flew back and forth until the case eventually went to litigation. The local newspaper was brought to book over some of its comments and eventually went into liquidation as a consequence of its legal costs. When the diocese of Perth was officially set up a number of years later, the Holy See decided to reward Brady for his staunch defence of Western Australia's Catholics by appointing him Perth diocese's first Catholic bishop.

Ullathorn is said to have recommended this appointment to the Holy See, favouring Brady over the other main candidate for the post, Dr. Polding, the then Archbishop of Sydney. Polding was said to have been hurt by this turn of affairs and is alleged to have questioned Brady's experience and qualifications for such a prominent position. Time would prove Polding's concerns well-founded. Brady's health was quite poor by the time he arrived to take up his new appointment in Perth, accompanied by his two assistants, Father John Joostens, an elderly Dutchman, and Patrick Reilly, an Irishman who was also a teacher. Brady belied his physical frailty, however, by fulfilling an annual work schedule so punishing that many local government ministers and members of the Protestant majority community held him in admiration for. Brady had another side to his character however, one which appeared to hinder his pastoral and administrative efforts on many levels. He was a very headstrong and assertive character and could be dogmatic and unyielding in social and administrative negotiations when a more diplomatic approach would have ensured better results. He could also be defensive and over-sensitive at times, seeing insults where none were intended. He was also tried to impose these character traits on his Catholic flock and was constantly warning them to be on the alert for anti-Catholic prejudice just as he was. If Catholics sensed any hint of prejudice being directed at them they were to meet fire with fire and not retract an inch. While this was a useful approach at times it could also backfire badly, resulting in an increase in anti-Catholic sentiment rather than its opposite. Despite these particular character traits of his, Brady was initially very successful in his new post.

The then Governor of Perth, Governor Hutt, gave Brady free rein to build whatever schools, churches and presbyteries he needed and guaranteed Brady generous financial help for these projects under the Church Act, on the proviso that he reimbursed whatever initial outlays he incurred at the beginning of these different projects. The Catholics of the diocese were delighted with this progress and were overjoyed when the foundation stone of Perth Pro-Cathedral was laid in January 1844, an occasion when many of Perth's Protestants also expressed their congratulations and admiration to the local Catholic population. By the time Hutt finished his term as Governor[347], the atmosphere of religious toleration and respect had changed significantly however. Bishop Brady wasn't shy about expressing his disappointment with the new administration either. He complained that the new colonial administration in Western Australia was now impeding his various projects and the development of the Catholic Church generally.

The Church Act was no longer being implemented, Brady said, and various building projects and the upkeep of the Catholic clergy now had to be delayed or cancelled completely. While the new administration certainly wasn't sympathetic to Catholics, many of Brady's problems also lay closer to home. He had no business sense and a poor grasp of financial administration. The debts piled up quickly and his representative in London, a Benedictine named T.P. Heponstall was driven crazy trying to keep the expenditure relating to the diocese of Perth under some sort of fiscal control. A number of large bills remained unpaid and incurred penalties and interest of 20% annually. By 1845, Brady's debts had reached 2500 pounds which was a colossal amount of money for a small religious community to repay, especially considering the small Catholic minority were quite poor and economic and social conditions were difficult. Undeterred, Brady continued to build churches, schools and Missions on the edges of major towns but now his funding was reduced to whatever money the Archbishopric of Sydney could raise on this behalf. In 1844 Brady travelled to

Rome to be officially inaugurated as bishop. On his return from Italy he was accompanied by eighty new religious - including priests, nuns, deacons, and one lay-person, all of whom were assigned to parish-work in various parts of Western Australia. Two Spaniards among this group, Dom Joseph Mary Benedict Serra and Dom Rudesinda Salvado would found the first Benedictine monastery in the outback of New Norcia[348] where they hoped to convert the local Aboriginal population to Christianity.

The nuns who came out to Perth included six sisters and a novice and were from the Sacred Heart convent in Baggot Street, Dublin. Documents in the archive of the Sisters of the Sacred Heart describe how these nuns made the treacherous journey up the Swan River singing the Litany of the Virgin Mary as they went. There were hundreds of people waiting for the nuns when they finally arrived in Perth and a large crowd formed a procession with the Sisters at the quayside, accompanying them to the "humble cathedral, with walls unplastered and an unceilinged roof." A few days after their arrival the novice was officially inaugurated into this group of sisters in the Cathedral there - the first ceremony of its kind ever held in Australia - where the Bishop gave a beautiful sermon on the religious life and on the particular duties of the Mercy Order. The ceremony was so moving that "all present, even the officers of the Governor, were moved to tears." The sisters set up house in "a nice house in Perth, but between the Government House and Barracks and the Church of England." After a while the sisters found that there was no privacy in that quarter of Perth however, and they soon left this "grander" residence to live in three rush-covered shacks in another part of the city. Bishop Brady had actually miscalculated by bringing such a large group of clergy to Western Australia. The group was too big given the small population of Catholics in that region. In fact, Brady had accepted at face-value a report given to him in Sydney which put the number of Catholics in the Western Australia colony at 3000 people, when, in reality, the number couldn't have been much higher than 300. Brady probably had in mind the Aboriginal people of that region and the possibilities that some of these indigenous people - (which another of his reports estimated at 2 million, in that region alone) - might also convert to Catholicism and would need pastoral care in addition to the immigrant Irish. Bishop Brady had erred however in assuming that such a tiny population of Catholics could support such a large number of clergy and religious. It must be remembered that, unlike today, the local Catholic community had to provide for almost all of the earthly needs of these religious – including food, clothes and housing. Brady's difficulties worsened when the colony's Governor - (not unreasonably one must say) - refused to re-imburse the huge travel expenses of the nuns and priests who had come to Australia, something for which a precedent had previously been set. The Governor's coffers were depleted enough as things stood and the Governor was probably afraid of the reaction of some of the local Protestant churches who would view this influx of Catholic Irish religious as a threat to the special position they had held in the colony prior to this.

A Protestant religious minister attacked Brady in the press when the Irish bishop opened a new Catholic school in Fremantle, arguing that there were already adequate educational resources in the vicinity. The founding of a Catholic school was simply an attempt at proselytism according to the minister and the school would just be used to convert Protestants to Catholicism. At the same time as this "controversy" was playing out in the newspapers, lay members of local Protestant communities were blaming their own pastors for doing little to reinforce the Protestants "special position" before it was too late - especially now that the immigrant Catholics were making their presence felt. On a personal level, Bishop Brady was more than happy to live a life of frugality in a two-roomed shack with only the minimum to eat – with a view to easing his Church's financial burden in some way. The diocese's finances were seriously out of control at this stage however and such private cost-saving tactics on Bishop Brady's part made little or no difference. His debtors became increasingly frustrated at his clumsy handling of financial issues and his inability to repay the debt. Some of Brady's own employees also lost patience with him and brought him to court because they hadn't been paid their salaries. A local Catholic schoolteacher named Cafarelli refused to do any more work until he received the salary that was due to him and Father Powell, the Vicar-General, Brady had brought out from Ireland, left the diocese hurriedly, saying that he could do more valuable work in another region. Sensing a major crisis, Brady sent the two Benedictines, Dom Serra and Dom Salvado back to Europe to raise funds on behalf of the diocese. The complaints of the local Catholic population regarding the latent anti-Catholic prejudice of the Western Australian colonial administration had actually been one of the main reasons why Madden was appointed to the position of Colonial Secretary. Christmas 1846 saw the presentation of a petition to Queen Victoria signed by Bishop Brady and 158 Catholics of the Western Australian diocese. The petition set out the manner in which Catholics felt their religious rights were being ignored. Hundreds of people had already left the diocese of Western Australia according to the petition's signatories, fearing that they would never again see the appointment of a new Catholic priest.

The colonial administration now had only one intention as relating to the religious character of the diocese. This was to ensure that the colony remained a bastion of Irish Protestantism - "or, in other words, Orangemen; for they all are now of that hue or dye." "This most bigoted and prejudiced Council," would never give official recognition to Bishop Brady and his clergy and had gone back on the formal assurances the previous Governor had given the Catholic minority, particularly as relating to the issue of religious education for their children. The petitioners implored Victoria to investigate the administration of the colony in Western Australia so as to put an end to those self-centred and bigoted administrators whose blinkered vision and selfishness was tearing the colony apart. A response to this Catholic petition came from Earl Grey who referred to a statement that been made on the issue of religious equality a full twelve years earlier. It was not the intention of Queen Victoria's government that the authorities in any one of the British colonies should display a hostility to the Roman Catholic Church, Grey stated. It was a source of some sorrow to him, Grey added, that religious tensions were interfering with the peaceful co-existence of the people living in this small colony:

> ...the newly-appointed Governor Captain Charles Fitzgerald, (R.N.) would be made fully aware that it is the determination of Her Majesty's Government to require from those entrusted with authority in any part of Her Majesty's Dominions the most perfect impartiality in the administration of the Civil Government towards the adherents of different religions.[350]

Shortly after this correspondence had passed to and fro, Madden found himself appointed to the position of Colonial Secretary. One of the very first things he did upon his arrival in the colony was to try and improve this religious stand-off. Madden considered the crux of the religious "problem" to be the fact that Brady's office and title was not receiving due acknowledgement and respect from the civil authorities in western Australia. In an effort at improving this situation Madden invited Bishop Brady and Father Joostens to an official reception at the residence of the incoming Governor, Charles Fitzgerald, an Irishman who was originally from Kilkee in County Clare. Fitzgerald was an old acquaintance of Madden's, the former gaining his reputation as the captain of a naval ship named *The Buzzard,* before being appointed Governor of Gambia in 1844. His appointment to the position of Governor in Perth was a promotion for Fitzgerald and Madden must have felt happy to have found him coming to work for a fellow Irishman, the same man whom Madden had first introduced to the Anti-Slavery Commission in London, in 1840.

The Commission had been ecstatic that same day - given that Fitzgerald was the first British naval officer to take it upon himself to officially seize a slave ship travelling under the auspices of the American flag.[351] The official reception at the Governor's residence proved a great success - on the surface at least - with Fitzgerald issuing a great welcome to both Brady and Joostens. He told the two men that there was nothing that would make him happier than putting an end to their fears regarding the anti-Catholic bigotry then widespread in the colony. No sooner had the clerics departed however but Fitzgerald informed Madden that putting an end to the religious tensions would be a much more difficult problem than he had indicated to the bishop and his assistant.

A friend of Fitzgerald's had attended a Catholic religious event a few months prior to this where he claimed to have heard Bishop Brady criticise the government from the altar in "terms of violent invective, calculated to excite the people." Madden was surprised to hear this and said that he had never heard anything like that in any Catholic church. If he ever heard such a criticism of the government, Madden said, he would walk out of a church. Fitzgerald said that he had more than one witness who could testify to Brady's criticisms in the church and given that he was Governor, these comments had put him in an awkward position. Madden advised Fitzgerald that the best thing would be to inform the Bishop of the allegation that was being made against him so that he could have the opportunity to defend himself and issue a denial if the rumour was false. Fitzgerald agreed with this approach and Madden sat down to compose the private letter right away. Shortly after this, Madden received a response from Brady denying ever having made such an anti-government statement and saying that the rumour had been initiated by somebody maliciously.[352]

Despite this hiccup, there is no question that Madden's appointment was a big boost to the Catholic population of Western Australia. The Archbishop of Sydney, Dr. John Bede Polding, issued a warm welcome to Madden when he first arrived in Australia, congratulating him on being the first Catholic ever to hold such an important appointment on the Australian continent. "It is to me a subject of great consolation", he informed Madden, "that you occupy the place which in a colony opens the way to great good, and in no colony is a proper occupant for such a place more required than in western Australia." Polding was of course referring here to the poor Church-State relationship that then existed in Western Australia. The Church-State relationship wasn't the only one that was under strain at this point in time either. The relationship between Polding and Brady was also far from good. Apparently, Polding had sent at least four of five letters to Brady but had yet to receive any reply. Polding was also agonizing over the correspondence that would have passed between some of Western Australia's leading Catholics and Lord Grey and what these Catholics might be saying privately about the public "stand-off" between Brady and him. Privately, Polding told Madden that if he was able to do anything to heal the dispute between Brady and he - two parties "who to produce permanent good must go hand in hand" - that the Catholic community would be forever grateful to him. As Polding hadn't received any responses to previous letters he had sent Brady, he wasn't entirely clear what Brady's attitude to him now was. He therefore asked Madden if he could (privately) help him compose a short and pleasantly-worded note to Brady, in an effort to initiate a dialogue once more.

Polding's diocese was showing great signs of vitality at this point in time and the Catholic Church was growing quickly there. Many lapsed Catholics had begun practicing again and between six and eight Protestants were said to be converting to Catholicism on a weekly basis. "Yesterday", Polding informed Madden, "I administered Confirmation to nearly 650 persons - every one of the adults converts to our holy faith."[353] Included among this large group of coverts were two Anglican ministers. Polding had also recently ordained the first Australian-born prelate in the diocese - a man whose name (coincidentally!) was Daniel O'Connell - and there were many others then studying for the religious life in that same diocese. Polding asked Madden's help in ensuring that three priests from the Passionist Order who had come to Australia from Rome were able to complete their studies for the priesthood on Australian soil. The trainee priests in question had come to Australia to set up a mission amongst the Aborigines but had found themselves sent to a region where there were no Aborigines through "some muddling, mismanagement, self-will or self-seeking." Polding also mentioned to Madden how keen he was to secure the services of a renowned Benedictine priest and musician named Dom Salvado for the Sydney Diocese. This diocese was a place where the latter would have had great scope for his musical talents given that Sydney Cathedral then housed a high-quality organ costing nine hundred pounds – then lying idle.

Madden found himself in agreement with most of Archbishop Polding's observations concerning the situation of the then fledgling Catholic Church in Australia. He was also was diplomatic in his dealings with Brady. Little enough archival evidence survives concerning his contacts or correspondence with the Irish bishop but what is clear is that Madden forgave Brady many of his inadequacies and focused on the great work he was doing on behalf of Australia's Catholics instead, this despite frequent hostility and overt bigotry on the part of many of the then civic authorities Years later, when Brady faced possible censure by the Vatican, Madden wrote a testimony on his behalf to the Vicar-General of Dublin where he outlined Brady's bravery and determination against the odds. In this testimony he described how the Cavan man had courageously taken on virtually the entire local government of Western Australia by himself, this despite the fact that the vast majority of the governmental authorities were vehemently prejudiced against Catholics and Catholicism:

I found Dr. Brady battling for his mission, stoutly and sincerely, not always discreetly or effectually, with a set of unprincipled astute bigots in authority. But he established the mission and he maintained it in spite of them up to the time of my arrival. Without his pertinacity, and one would almost say daring, in confronting powerful opposition, in contending against adverse circumstances of the most formidable kind, the mission could never have been established. During the year that I remained in office, in the performance of his clerical duties - I mean administering the Sacraments, assisting at the altar, visiting the sick, promoting the education of the poor, rescuing their children and even adult Catholics from Protestant Churches (which had gone on to an enormous extent before the mission was established), in assisting the distressed, and, above all, in dealing charitably with poor natives - I can safely say that the conduct of Dr. Brady was most exemplary. He lives in a miserable hovel without comforts of any kind, on the simplest food; his diet was not only, to my certain knowledge, coarse and poor, but often scanty in the extreme. Dr. Brady had got so much into this mode of life that he desired no other for himself, and the belief seemed to have grown on him that all other persons in religion about him or connected with mission (however differently physically constituted) could have no other desire and were capable of living as he did. This was a great mistake, and it led to all the difficulties that took place.[354]

Madden arrived in Australia just as Brady decided not to bother pressing the Catholic position any further with the administrators then in office and to bide his time to see what kind of person the new governor turned out to be. Unsurprisingly, Brady had little good to say about these officials of the "Irwin Club", as he referred to them. Irwin, himself, had a very bad name among Catholics as a consequence of his various public pronouncements, many of which were overtly anti-Catholic. Prior to the appointment of Fitzgerald, Irwin was appointed *ad interim* governor, a position that made him the most powerful official in the colony and in full control of the colony's armed forces. As far back as the 1830s Irwin was known to have refused the Catholic soldiers in this force their meals if they did not attend Protestant religious services. While Brady was naturally more than willing "to go into the breach" on behalf of his Catholic flock, Madden counselled him to be diplomatic and not to get involved in the back-biting and gossip against the administration which was a normal aspect of colonial life but which was even more pronounced in a colony as small as Western Australia. Any complaint that was issued either directly or indirectly needed to be backed up with solid evidence, he warned Brady.

Brady clearly took Madden's advice as he refrained from using the occasion of Fitzgerald's official reception to complain about various incidents of anti-Catholic bigotry that had preceded the Irishman's arrival in the Governor's office and which were still ongoing. As if fearing a potential barrage of complaints concerning the anti-Catholic atmosphere then present in the colony, Captain Fitzgerald used the occasion to reiterate the promise which the London government had made with regard to the promulgation of religious tolerance in the colonies:

> ...to know no party save the inhabitants at large, without distinction of creed, country, or colour, giving to all their undoubted birthright as subjects of a Government that is the envy of the world, the utmost toleration, the fullest protection, and a just proportion of the means that may enable them to worship their God with the reverence and decorum usual in civilised communities, without let or hindrance, according to their consciences.[355]

Despite uttering these platitudes in public, Fitzgerald still remained a partisan Protestant behind the scenes. Within six months of this statement of appeasement to Brady he was informing Lord Grey that the Catholic prelate's over-exuberant defence of his community was defaming the Protestant population. As an example of this he cited Brady's propensity to send local Australian seminarians to Rome for their theological training. "Maybe we ought to do something similar", Fitzgerald mooted.[356]

Another person who wasn't a supporter of Brady was G.F. Moore, then the Attorney for the Crown. Brady was convinced that Moore had incited some of his own bishops to rebel against him by taking him to court when their subsistence costs hadn't been paid. That the bishops had done this despite the fact that Brady hadn't spent a penny on himself and had been waiting for the grant-aid from the local government which never materialised, only made Brady even more suspicious of Moore's motives. Moore wasn't a Catholic himself and was probably unaware of the bond that might exist in this era between Catholics and one of their most senior pastors. Ultimately, Moore had advised his clients to bring Brady to court only when every other means of redress had been exhausted.

The bishops weren't alone in expressing their frustration at the manner in which Brady had accumulated scores of unpaid bills. Three Frenchmen found themselves in court for attacking Brady's house in the middle of the night and issuing drunken threats to both Brady and his elderly Vicar-General Father Joostens. The three men in question held their ground in court however, saying that their intention in "blowing up the bishop" was simply to spur Brady into paying them various monies that were due to them. Anti-Catholic bias and prejudice were the source of most of Brady's other protests at this juncture. On one occasion, the Colonial physician named Ferguson prevented a priest from visiting a Catholic parishioner of his who was seriously ill, warning the patient that he would lose his right to medical treatment if he sought the spiritual ministrations of a priest. Another incident saw Brady being refused planning permission twice for a site where he wished to erect a new church building while another applicant, who had applied for the same site at a later date than Brady, was granted permission immediately. Subsequent to this incident, Brady made a complaint to the authorities, and following some enquiries by Madden, the authorities admitted that an irregularity had taken place on an administrative level. Ironic as it may seem, Madden found himself blamed for this irregularity – but blame wasn't attributed to him until after he had left his position of Colonial Secretary - conveniently enough![357]

While there was no shortage of hillocks or sandbanks in the vicinity where Brady had sought to erect the various religious buildings, the Catholics were also refused permission to have a graveyard in the area. To be fair to the Protestant officials who were making these decisions however, it couldn't have been easy for them to listen to Brady's evocations of Canon Law to explain why Catholics could not be buried alongside atheists, schismatics and heretics. Madden was on hand to provide Brady with additional moral and practical support now however as he himself, explained - "From the time of my arrival I took care that Dr. Brady and his mission were no more trouble or warred with. I got the mission encouraged and aided by the Government. I obtained grants from the Council for its schools, a burial ground, the right of visiting prisons etc."[358]

The Governor's private secretary, Walkinshaw Cowan was one public servant who refused to give any public recognition to Catholic priests or bishops or their offices. Cowan and others even went so far as to remove the words Rev. or Right Reverend from postal addresses or official documentation. Cowan paid the price for such churlish behaviour in the end however. Once Madden was satisfied that Cowan had acted in this manner, consistently, and over a long period of time, he arranged for Cowan to be transferred to another post. Bishop Brady expressed his satisfaction at this "wise and judicious" decision on Madden's part as relating to someone who was "so notoriously hostile to our body and myself." It is not clear what the then Governor thought of Madden's decision to transfer his private secretary to another post. If he was opposed to the decision, he certainly gave no indication of this. He simply reported Cowan's transfer to Earl Grey without further comment.

Education was the most contentious issue between the Catholic settlers and the local Protestant colonial regime. The Catholics expressed the wish that they be permitted to set up their own schools where Catholics could be employed as teachers, particularly as relating to the classes in religious instruction. If the local administration refused this, the next best thing that Catholics could hope for would be non-denominational schools, but schools which would be free of sectarianism and anti-Catholic sentiment - as were now on the increase back in Ireland. That the Catholics were right to argue their case is clear. A perusal of the local newspapers of the time indicates that anti-Catholic prejudice was quite common amongst certain sections of the Protestant ruling class there. A teacher writing to a local newspaper at this juncture outlined his pity for the Catholic settlers whom he described as "objects of aversion and pity", and a people for whom he felt an obligation to "expose the insidious errors of Popery." Such anti-Catholic rhetoric upset Brady a great deal, so much so that he and the other Catholic representatives withdrew from the local education boards. Brady refused to do business with people as bigoted as Colonel Irwin and Nash, irrespective of what hardships his Catholic flock would have to endure in the interim.

When this teacher's derogatory letter was shown to Madden he tried to extract some promises from the local education board that there would be some sanction taken against the teacher in question. Madden also satisfied himself that Catholic children would no longer be subject to Protestant religious instruction classes (Scripture lessons) in any of the board's schools and that similar occurrences wouldn't be repeated. The religious sisters who had followed Brady to the colony and who had set up small convents in both Perth and Freemantle were also a source of controversy on a number of occasions during Madden's term of office. On one occasion, for example, an army officer who had disguised himself as a woman sought "shelter" at one of the convents, falsely claiming to be suffering from some "affliction" or other.

This, and similar outrages, (said the bishop in a letter), have not only been allowed to be committed with impunity but was (sic) connived at during the administration of Major Irwin. I applied for redress to the Crown Commissioner, Major Irwin's brother-in-law but received no redress. The officers continued to annoy those excellent Sisters of Mercy, up to the time of their (the officers) departure for India.[359]

On Guy Fawkes Night,[360] 1848, a group of "local youths" gathered outside the convent in Fremantle with flags and tambourines in an effort to intimidate the nuns. The nuns complained about this incident to the local authorities and were aided in this complaint by the local Catholic bishop. The bishop saw in this "vile and offensive practice" the danger of nourishing and perpetuating in this impolite land... the feelings of animosity, hatred and ill-will from which Catholics suffered at home." This incident unexpectedly led to a more serious dispute when Peter Brown - who had once held Madden's position as Colonial Secretary, but was now the governmental representative in Fremantle - was refused entry to the convent there. He attempted to meet the nuns there so as to discuss the incident of intimidation that had occurred and to assure them of their future safety there. To complicate matters further, when Brown was refused entry to the convent, the young nun at the gate explained this refusal with a story which completely contradicted the report which her supervisor, the Bishop had just issued. Unsurprisingly, this irritated the Governor and he wrote a letter to "Madam, the Superioress" where he advised her to be prudent regarding the range of rumours then circulating in the colony.

The Governor also claimed that the Bishop had been misinformed about the entire incident; otherwise he wouldn't have spoken out or behaved in a manner that was so hostile to the government and a threat to public order. These claims on the Governor's part only served to incite the local bishop further and he lectured the Governor on basic manners and the sense of courtesy that was appropriate when speaking to the religious sisters. The bishop then tried to explain the context of the nun's response to Brown and he also reiterated the huge insult and distress that the religious sisters had suffered.

Madden tried his best to smooth over the whole controversy. He found out that Brown had actually visited the convent prior to receiving the Governor's instructions on what to do about the incident. This had led to much of the confusion and bad feeling in relation to the issue. Madden then passed on a copy of the Governor's letter to the Mother Superior and advised her to reflect on the issue "considerately and in a charitable, conciliatory spirit." Madden's advice was taken on board and Bishop Brady requested that he inform the governor "that this removal of a misintelligence over which he had no control could not be otherwise than most agreeable to them." That was the end of the matter, although Madden kept one document in his private papers which indicates that Brown had trusted him with a loan of 650 pounds - a fact which indicates the esteem in which Madden was held by some of the central figures within the colonial administration there. In spite of these successful diplomatic initiatives on Madden's part, there is no doubt that his activities were still a source of concern to the members of the Irwin Club (or the Irwinite Club as it was also known). Whatever concerns the Irwinite Clique may have had about Madden, they came to an end much sooner than they had anticipated; neither was it a religious issue that generated the most controversy in the end either.

It was the concerns which Madden expressed regarding the treatment of the Aboriginal communities in the colony that brought matters to a head in the end. These communities made up a large percentage of the overall population in the Western Australian colony, the majority of which were still nomadic. They formed a range of different cultural groups who varied in terms of dress and tradition, cultural groups united only by their religious beliefs - as based on totemic/animist beliefs - and the conviction that many of their communities were descendants of the same ancestor. Given his humanitarian interests, Madden would most likely have taken a personal interest in the situation of the Aborigines, irrespective of any instruction from London in this regard. As it happens, a set of directives had actually been issued from London regarding what type of relationship the administrators were expected to foster with the Aboriginal communities in the Western Australian colony. This is clear from Madden's own personal papers where he underlined sentences as relating to these directives in relation to the Aborigines.

The Governor of the colony was directed to engage with the Aboriginal communities so as to gain their friendship and trust. The Governor was also to present himself as their defender and counsellor, someone whom they could approach for help if the Aborigines felt that they were being discriminated against. This latter directive became a personal "sine qua non" for Madden who also took to heart the next section of the directive - "You will make it a chief and paramount duty to acquire an adequate familiarity with the native language, so that you will be able to associate with the Aborigines, enter into their plans and ideas, and thus gain an insight into their peculiar habits, manners and opinions." In the absence of any textbook for the study of the native Aboriginal languages, Madden began to compile his own glossary of useful words and sentences. He also took on board another instruction as issued to the Governor, directing him to do everything in his power to convince the Aborigines that the British administration intended treating them in a fair and equitable manner. Nobody would be permitted to oppress the Aborigines or abuse them in any way, provided, of course, that the Aborigines themselves accepted the laws and customs which the colonial administration was imposing across the colony. Madden immediately identified the contradiction which existed between these apparently noble precepts as handed down by the British government and the fact that the colonial's Supreme Council was passing a Bill which severely curtailed the most basic of the Aborigines' human rights. This Bill allowed the local justices summary jurisdiction over cases involving the Aborigines. Trial by jury was removed in these cases and the white settlers were also permitted to punish the Aborigines with whips if they felt like it, irrespective of whether the Aborigines in question were male or female. It was this duplicity and cruelty on the part of the British colonial regime in Australia that would eventually see Madden part ways with the colonial administration there. Governor Fitzgerald described the souring of this relationship in a report he forwarded to the Secretary of State and in a private letter which he sent to Benjamin Hawes, Stephen's replacement in the Colonial Office.

The colony's Supreme Council had met to discuss the implementation of the proposed (Aboriginal) Bill and whether its provisions were likely to be consistently abused. Madden announced that he was against the implementation of the Bill at that particular point in time. He asked that he be given the opportunity to compile a brief report outlining what he saw as the Bill's principal faults and that this review of the Bill could then be entered into the Council's minutes. A few days later Madden asked Governor Fitzgerald whether he could have copies of various reports compiled by Fitzgerald's predecessors in the colonial administration. Fitzgerald provided these reports "without much thought as to the purpose Mr. Madden wanted them for."

Various long and heated debates followed at subsequent meetings of the Supreme Council, however. Madden vigorously criticised the manner in which Colonel Irwin had run the local colonial government prior to Fitzgerald's appointment and Irwin responded by objecting to the inclusion of Madden's report - (concerning the proposed Bill as relating to the Aborigines) - in the Supreme Council's minutes. Irwin also complained that various confidential reports which he and Governor Hutt had sent to the Colonial Office had now been made public and misinterpreted. Ultimately, when Governor Fitzgerald realised that the entire Council, Madden excepted - agreed that criticisms of previous Governors be excluded from the minutes - he ruled that this is what should happen. If he had ruled otherwise, Fitzgerald claimed, then "a precedent fertile in future inconvenience" would have been set. Fitzgerald did however agree to forward a record of Madden's protest and Irwin's response to

Downing Street, a move which - (as he explained to Madden) - would ensure that the matter was brought to Lord Grey's attention. Fitzgerald explained his actions as follows:

> *This I had hoped would have satisfied Mr. Madden. He, however, when I had done speaking, replied in a most excited manner: "Sir, I resign my office into your hands, and I shall hold you personally responsible for any loss I may sustain." To this threat I replied: "Mr. Madden, you cannot hold me responsible for any loss I may sustain." To this threat I replied: "Mr. Madden, you cannot hold me responsible for the conscientious discharge of my duties as President of the Council." Mr. Madden replied that he thought he could when I was no longer in office. On the Council, adjourning, Mr. Madden asked me in what position he was to consider himself. I told him I considered him Colonial Secretary, but if upon reflection next morning he was still determined to resign, I would accept his resignation. When Mr. Madden called upon me next morning, I told him distinctly that I could not allow such conduct to me to pass without bringing it before Lord Grey's notice; and that my position must be indeed one of the fearful peril if I became liable to actions at law by every member of the Council from whom I dissented, and that I considered that his attempt the day before was one aiming to establish a reign of terror in the Council. It is but just to say that Mr. Madden saw at once his great error and expressed in the most candid manner his regret both then and before the Council for all that had passed. He then stated that he had been some time in very bad health and had suffered for some grievous affliction of mind at the death of his son and hoped that I would let him leave the Colony for a time. This request I brought before the Council, who aware of all he (had) suffered, advised my giving him the leave requested.*[361]

While this was an acceptable and a credible excuse, it nevertheless ill-became Madden to take refuge in it. Madden was sent for a medical examination and Ferguson, the Colonial Physician provided him with a certificate that declared him unfit for work. Madden subsequently sent a memo to Governor

Fitzgerald where he outlined in more detail the stress which had contributed to his poor health. He had only recently received news that his son Forde had drowned in a work accident in Ireland. Forde had died just prior to this, on the 29th of March, when he and a work colleague had drowned in the Shannon near Tarmonbarry while working on behalf of Mulvany's civil engineering firm on a navigational project there. The boat in which he and another young man named George Montfort had been travelling in had overturned and nineteen-year old Forde, had unsuccessfully attempted to save his companion - "The loss of a son, centre of all of my hopes - a finished man, entering on the world, of whom there was reason for a father to be proud and hopeful, and that loss, too, occasioned by a violent sudden death is a deep grief."[362].

The manner in which Madden received this tragic news could only have deepened his anguish. The ship transporting the mail from Singapore to Southern Australia had been battered by gales off the coast of Fremantle and the ship sunk without trace, its entire crew drowned in the process. By a strange twist of fate, the post-box carrying the news of Forde's death was swept ashore, and Madden had himself actually delivered this post-box to the authorities when next visiting Perth, little realising that the box included the news of his son's death. Forde's death was a terrible blow to both Harriet and Madden, a blow that was only partly assuaged by the large number of messages of sympathy which they received from Ireland, England and Australia. Madden's old friend William Beattie sent him a poem expressing his sympathy while the poet Thomas Campbell also wrote to the Maddens extending his sympathies.[363]

The Maddens would have received some consolation from the simple poem that a clerk in Mulvany's engineering firm, a twelve-year old boy named John Kielty - a boy who had been a good friend of Forde's - had forwarded to them:

> *Confide in God in prayer increase*
> *Of sinful thought beware;*

Be humble, and a friend of peace
And shun the proud with care.[364]

As was usual for him in such emotionally-charged situations, Madden put pen to paper and noted down some of his thoughts concerning the tragedy in verse-form, poems where he described his fatherly pride in his now-deceased son. He had always been very proud of Forde - "perhaps too proud, too confident, my own loved boy, in thee - "the complement and crown of all my hopes!" That their son's life might end so abruptly had naturally come as an enormous shock to both Madden and Harriet whose only real consolation lay in the strength of their religious beliefs and the conviction that their good-natured son was now happy in the company of the angels in Heaven. The same thoughts would provide solace to Madden four years later when he visited the place where Forde had drowned.

Beyond the bright stars and the glorious sun
With God on high is our boy.
He went up to heaven as undefiled
As he came from his Maker's hand
An angel of light is that spotless child
We have now in the spirit land.[365]

Fitzgerald, the Colonial Governor, may have been closer to the truth than he imagined when he attributed Madden's unhappiness in the colony, his "outspoken" statements, and his antipathy to Irwin to the fact that the doctor felt angry at the society which he saw around him in Western Australia. Madden was a kindly and diligent Colonial Secretary but the colony of Western Australia was the last place to which he should have been posted, according to Fitzgerald. It was unfortunate, he added, that Madden was the only "upper middle-class Catholic" in the whole of Perth and:

...his Bishop a Gentleman somewhat turbulent in disposition and over apt to magnify and enlarge on every little

circumstance, whether the act of the Government or of an individual, that could by any possibility be construed as offensive to his God or his Church, and consequently very prone to complain...Dr. Brady has stated to me, before Colonel Irwin, that he would agitate for the removal of the figure of the Cross from the cover of the Testament used in our Courts of Law as insulting to the Roman Church and that it had been done by Mr. Plunkett in Sydney. I merely observed to Dr. Brady - "My Lord, Roman Catholic Ireland has made no complaint on that subject, yet Mr. O'Connell saw the cross on the Bible used in the Courts of Law of that country."[366]

That particular anecdote demonstrated the extreme (and often illogical) nature of some of the religious tensions that existed in the colony. Fitzgerald recounted this anecdote to try and provide a flavour of the complex and often-poisonous atmosphere that existed in the colony then. Fitzgerald was honest enough to admit that the most frequent complaint which he received as Governor concerned the hostility to Catholics which had existed previously under Irwin's Governorship. In his letter to Hawes, Fitzgerald went on to explain the basis for the disagreement that had taken place between Madden and himself. The situation was so tense between the two men that Fitzgerald considered it better if neither he nor Madden had occasion to meet one another again for the remainder of the Irishman's stay in the colony. Madden himself had no great inclination to return to the colony but he couldn't possibly resign from this administrative position before securing another. Fitzgerald concluded his letter to Hawes by saying that he held no personal grudge against Madden but that a job in another colony such as Malta might be more suitable for him.[367] The memo which Madden prepared to send to London was long-winded but a good deal more biting than Fitzgerald's. His principal objection to the then colonial administration in Western Australia concerned the manner in which they were attempting to colonize the Aboriginal communities. Firstly, he said that the plans for "controlling" and oppressing the Aborigines - using a combination of corrupt law on the one hand and physical force on the other - had never been put before the Secretary of State in its fullness or discussed in any great detail.

If London understood clearly what was intended, Madden was certain there is no way they would have approved the measures then being taken against the Aborigines. This punitary and violent approach was being put forward initially on purely economic grounds as the colonial administration considered it more economical to punish the Aborigines physically through the use of whips and other physical violence than to imprison them. That the Aborigines themselves - given their nomadic tradition - would have preferred physical punishment to prison was also proposed to justify severe physical punishments. Neither of these two arguments was in any way morally sound or justifiable from Madden's point of view.

> *Economy should not affect principles of race relations,* (he said), *and even if the second ground were true, the Colonial government was supposed to be concerned with exercising civilizing functions towards the natives with which the flogging proposal was not in conformity. The lash had no civilizing effect on savage people; one might as well argue with the aboriginal custom of punishment by driving a spear through the fleshy part of the legs and thighs which the party punished might prefer to imprisonment, should be retained as being "Consonant with the wild notions of Justice an habits of retaliation and expiation of the natives" with which Colonel Irwin said he had entire concurrence.*[368]

The use of physical violence against a vulnerable population such as the Aborigines was disgusting and immoral, Madden argued, and it would do nothing to aid the spread of the Christian Gospel either. Education in the form of training - whether this involved the use of the spade, the saw, the axe or the plough was infinitely preferable to beating people into submission with implements of torture. Madden had travelled far more widely than Colonel Irwin ever had. He had lived in many different regions across the globe and it was his experience that the indigene never forgot the beatings he received from the white man. Indeed Madden had never seen such a violent approach - as was now being mooted in relation to the Aborigines - being advocated back in Britain or in the ranks of either the British Army or the Royal Navy. Such measures would never work in the long run. Neither would they save money for the Crown.

In fact, the opposite would most likely be the case. Using more punitive measures against the Aborigines would inevitably necessitate the expansion of the army and the police force. It had cost a full twenty million pounds to put an end to the punitive regime that had been imposed in the West Indies not so long before this, Madden argued and he also said that there was no way that the Secretary of State would have agreed to such anti-Aboriginal measures if he had realised that women were going to be punished in as equally brutal a manner as the men. Colonel Irwin had been careful to allude to "male offenders" only when he had argued the merits of the proposed Bill but the Bill specified that it was applicable to "any of the aboriginal race." This latter aspect of the Bill would, (in itself), have more than justified that these legal measures in relation to the Aboriginal communities be withdrawn and placed before the British Government for consideration once more. It wouldn't have been right anyway to base such a legal measure on the draft bill that was then under consideration. Given the draft had so many changes and amendments inserted into its text at this stage it was barely recognizable when compared to the document originally sent on to the Secretary of State for his approval. Madden took the opportunity presented by this controversy to discuss the attitudes and policies as relating to the Aborigines then current in the Australian colonies generally.

The colony of Southern Australia had been in Britain's

possession for twenty years by then. Initially the Aborigines had been treated as if they were British citizens who were subject to the same laws as other British people and thereby entitled to the same protections. Under the proposed Bill this situation would change radically, however, and the settlers would increasingly have it within their rights to oppress the Aborigines further. What was the intention behind this move towards a more oppressive policy in relation to the Aboriginal peoples, Madden asked? There was no rebellion there and no white man had been assaulted - indeed it had been a full seven years since a white man had been attacked with a spear. The Aborigines hadn't shown themselves to be averse to work nor had they been rebellious or troublesome in any way. As far as Madden see, relations between the Aborigines and the settlers in Western Australia had been reasonably good up till then. In spite of this:

> *Suddenly Colonel Irwin puts forward his measure which hands over the natives to flock owners whose stock may stray in the bush in a country which has no barriers, no fences and no boundaries, and no means of preventing their herds straying and being outstanding temptations to the starving natives. The only justification for a civilised people accepting the care of an uncivilized one is to bring the blessings and benefits of civilization - if this is not borne in mind the transaction becomes one of simple spoliation. The whites, in contrast with the natives, were often stock men of wild and reckless disposition and were situated where the law had no power to restrain them.*[269]

Irwin sent a rejoinder to Madden's memo cautioning the Irishman and telling him that it was not the Irishman's role to remind the Secretary of State about the rights and responsibilities that ensued from the Laws of Nature or the Laws of the Nation. As regards the actual implementation of such laws and theories, the Secretary of State was more than aware of how this had happened, given that he had received official reports from the colonial governors in this regard from the very first year of the colony's foundation. The Secretary of State had never found fault with any of the activities described in these reports, Irwin reminded Madden:

The protest, (he said), is marked throughout by a strain of personality towards myself as if I were the sole originator of a measure so obnoxious to the Secretary; I have simply submitted for Your Lordship's consideration a measure previously recommended by the great authority of Mr. Hutt, urgently and unanimously proposed by the Legislative Council and long and loudly called for by all classes of the community. It must be left to your Lordships to decide whether the sanction of an "eminently just and humane Governor", the unanimity of the Local Legislature, the general concurrence of all classes of the Colonists, and the experience derived from 18 or 19 years familiarity with the character of the local Aboriginal Race are sufficient to outweigh, he opinion of an individual opponent, the soundness of whose judgement may be appreciated by his own assumption that, after a residence here of 8 months, he is qualified to be the exponent of the sentiments on this subject of a larger portion of the enlightened settlers of this Colony than the advocates of this measure.[370]

When Madden was returning to England, Fitzgerald gave him an official and confidential document to pass onto the Secretary of State in addition to the protest-letter by Madden and the rebuttal to this as written by Irwin. In this private document, Fitzgerald informed Earl Grey that Madden had some very strange opinions as regards the way in which the Summary Jurisdiction Bill could be enforced. Fitzgerald considered Madden a generous and hospitable man, a man whose opinions he respected. Madden was inclined to forget about the concerns and rights of the colonists and settlers, however. The Supreme Council had already examined this issue, in detail, Fitzgerald said, as was clear from Colonel Irwin's clear-sighted memo. Whatever pre-conceptions he (Fitzgerald) may have held prior to this with regard to the Aborginal "issue," he would still go along with the viewpoints of those men who had already spent half of their lives living in Australia. Such settlers considered the proposed Bill a reasonable and egalitarian piece of legislation as applied to both the settlers and the indigenous Australians. Fitzgerald was in agreement with this view and considered the proposed Bill a more efficient legislative device with which to target law-breakers, a measure that would prove more effective and humanitarian when dealing with criminals than the system that was then currently in operation. Under the system then in use, criminals were sent onto the higher courts where a trial by jury was the norm, a system that involved significant expense. Implementing this Bill would mean that the legal costs incurred by the colony would be reduced by almost 90%.

The various legal changes that would accompany this new Bill would have little enough overt impact on the Aborigines, Fitzgerald opined, given that the most of the Aborigines had no understanding of the law anyway. All the Aborigines were afraid of was that they would be incarcerated, their greatest fear being the possibility of imprisonment on Rottnest Island.[371] For all of the aforementioned reasons, Fitzgerald now felt obliged to forward this proposed legal measure for discussion at the next meeting of the administrative council provided Earl Grey was in agreement with its provisions.[372] Madden left Australia on a vessel called the *Emperor of China* on the ninth of January, 1849 and the new Private Secretary to the Governor, a man by the name of Rivett Henry Bland replaced him - initially on a temporary basis. Madden was accompanied on this arduous return trip by his wife Harriet, his son Thomas More and two Australian Aboriginal youths who were going to Europe to study for the priesthood. One of these same youths allegedly belonged to a tribe that had still practiced cannibalism until very recently; the same tribe lived in the outback without any contact with the white man. In spite of the particular circumstances of his childhood, this youth had proven very capable both educationally and socially.

A few days prior to the departure of this group from Perth, a Catholic delegation led by Bishop Brady and Dom Salvado paid a special visit to Madden presenting him with a written memorial as subsequently published in appendix-form in the next issue of the local newspaper, the *Inquirer*. The newspaper editor's article claimed that Madden was not gone for good but was due to return again to the colony; his article also stated that many people were unhappy that the Irishman had left the colony at all. He was always a very fair and hospitable man and someone who was respected by rich and poor, the editor added. The accusation which was sometimes directed at him - that he was overly-sympathetic to his co-religionists the Catholics - just didn't add up. He had treated every societal class equally. This accusation of religious bias on Madden's part was most likely spread by members of the Irwinite clique, as it was certainly in their interest to do so.

The Catholic delegation which called on Madden to say goodbye to him on his departure used the opportunity to express their bitterness at the treatment they had received under the colonial administration prior to his arrival in Western Australia. The Catholics there had hardly had the opportunity to enjoy the definite improvement in their situation under Madden's tenure but now the Irishman was leaving again - for a year in the first instance. His departure made the Catholics very nervous as they were unsure what sort of a religious environment they face in the future. Matters would already have become more difficult for the Catholic population if a recent attempt on Governor's Fitzgerald life had succeeded. Madden left no description behind of his return journey from Australia. We can imagine that it was probably a fairly downbeat trip however given that Madden had a great deal of time on his hands to worry about where he might next secure a job.

Two points were immediately clear to him i.e. There was no way that he could return to the colony in Western Australia.

There was also no chance that he would ever be able to convince the colonial administration in Perth that his point of view was correct with regard to the Bill concerning the Aborgines and that the Colonial administration was treating the Aboriginal population badly. Unfortunately for Madden, his old friend Stephen had retired from his previous governmental position to take up a Professorship in Cambridge. Madden wasn't acquainted with Stephen's successor, a man by the name of Hermann Merivale.

The "word on the street" was that Merivale was even brighter than Stephen, a man who was acknowledged as a very intelligent and capable individual. Merivale was a Liberal who had abandoned a Chair of Political Economy in Oxford to take a post in the public service. On his return to England in May 1849, Madden left his baggage in his old lodgings at Panton Square, Haymarket and sat down to write a letter to Gordon Gardiner, the Assistant Under-Secretary in the Colonial Office, a man with whom he was acquainted. A copy of that letter has not survived but Gardiner's reply has, and it indicates to some degree what the contents of Madden's letter must have consisted of. Gardiner had received a copy of Madden's memo of protest against the Summary Jurisdiction Bill to which he could formally respond with whatever actions he saw fit. Gardiner "passed the buck" on this however saying - "I am sure you will not take it amiss when I say that I think I could hardly accept such a responsibility. He therefore returned Madden's protest to him and advised him to forward it directly to Lord Grey. When Grey received the letter of protest he also received an accompanying copy of Governor Fitzgerald's official report in addition to a lead sample as extracted from the Murchison river [373] The likelihood is that Lord Grey also interviewed any other government officials who could have helped him come resolve this dispute. In reality, as indicated in the London departmental files, there was very little interest at all in the Aboriginal issue. If the issue was discussed at all, it was done privately, and no references to it were made in any official correspondence. The clerks in the department were hard-nosed realists. Gardiner told Merivale that the tone of Madden's letter revealed more about the Irishman's nature than did any of the facts contained within his text, commenting that "Dr. Madden seems to have taken a higher view of his duties and responsibilities…"

> …than that which it is usual to attach to the position of a subordinate officer. The effects which he describes are perhaps not immaterial in a limited society which has received a very small infusion of strangers for some time past, and where there exists a very limited check on the executive government, where the officers are poorly paid, are extensive landowners and are obliged to improve their means by creating interest which may most probably often impede the fair execution of their duties. This letter appears to show sufficiently the impossibility in existing circumstances of the Governor and Colonial Secretary continuing to act in concert.[374]

Merivale placed these documents before the Colonial Secretary. He also alluded to Madden's observations regarding physical brutality towards Aboriginal women and that such brutality was not prohibited under the Summary Jurisdiction Bill; this was an aspect of the Bill which hadn't been highlighted prior to this. "Of course," Merivale added, "Dr. Madden's protest has brought the omission fully before the Legislative Council and therefore (as the New Ordinance is not yet prepared) it may be assumed that it will be remedied. "Still, it might be well to notice it in passing." Merivale also advised that the governor be fully briefed on the fact that Lord Grey abhorred the suffering endured by Colonel Irwin as a consequence of the unreasonable attack on his work by a fellow colonial official. Merivale also sought assurances that Madden's attack on Irwin's policies had not diminished Irwin's stature in the eyes of Lord Grey:

> As to Dr. Madden, said Merivale, I fear this correspondence too

plainly indicates what is to be expected of him. His intemperance of language so completely detracts from the value of his statement as to make it impossible to judge how much of truth there may be in the general vituperation if the colonists clear that he will not live on good terms with Governor Fitzgerald when he goes back; but I do not suppose his present conduct and writing will increase his chances of employment in another colony: while at the same time there does not appear to be any serious charge against him such as to forfeit his situation. I do not know that his letters requires more than the usual acknowledgement.[375]

Lord Grey added to this same memo, outlining his continued support for Colonel Irwin - "I suppose Dr. Madden will not relent, but this can only be learnt when his leave expires, and meantime he receives half-salary." These various commentaries on the controversy were promptly prepared and the document sent forward to Governor Fitzgerald made reference to Madden's inappropriate use of the reports compiled by various Governors prior to Fitzgerald's tenure in office. In December, 1849 Gardiner was reminding Merivale that Madden should long since have departed from England, if he intended returning to Australia for the ninth of January (1850), the date when the Irishman's period of leave came to an end. Neither man had heard anything from Madden however and Gardiner suggested that they ought to contact him to find out what his plans were - "There does not seem much probability", said Gardiner, "of his returning and it would, I am afraid, be an unhappy thing for the colony if he did, seeing how little probability there is of his acting cordially with the Governor."

Grey granted Merivale permission to send Madden a letter enquiring as to his future plans although they were privately hopeful that Madden wouldn't return to Australia in the near future.[376] On receiving this letter, Madden pointed out that his year's tenure would not be up until the day he was actually due to leave London again and he requested an extension to his holidays. This time extension was granted to him immediately. Merivale couldn't think of any reason why Madden should be given this extension to his career break other than the fact that he wasn't welcome back in the colony anyway - and this was as good an "excuse" as any to delay the Irishman's return there. "I certainly concur", Merivale said to Lord Grey, "in thinking that as far as the Colony is concerned, Dr. Madden is far better here than there. I should be sorry to do him an injustice, but, looking at all these papers, I think his absence no disadvantage." Grey agreed with this approach and Madden was informed that he could take another three months off provided he gave an undertaking that he would return to his post in Australia at the end of this period.

Madden's back was against the wall now. If he returned to Australia he would have to enforce Colonel Irwin's policies and measures, something which he was unable to bring himself to do. While the Bill would be amended now as a consequence of Madden's protests - the measures permitting the physical punishment of women were now omitted - the reality was that physical violence was now legally permissible and could be used against the Aborigines for the most minor of indiscretions. On the other side of the coin, Madden and his family would be left in a very precarious financial position if he resigned from his job. Madden requested extra time in order that he be allowed demonstrate to Lord Grey the unjust measures that were the cornerstone of this (albeit amended) Bill. If this extra time was not granted to him then he was left with no other option but to resign from his position - "reluctantly but most respectfully." Madden didn't consider himself in a position to place any further conditions on his re-instatement or to request a transfer to another job. He did mention his twenty years of hard work in a range of administrative positions in various different colonies and humbly requested that a job be found for him wherever the British administration saw fit to place him.[377] The Colonial Office delayed their processing of Madden's request to leave his Australian posting. Hawes opined that they should simply accept Madden's request and reply with "the general answer couched in civil terms" so as to enable the Irishman to secure another position reasonably quickly. Grey responded to Hawes' lead and agreed that it was better to accept Madden's resignation. He also suggested that they inform Madden that - while they wished him well - the scarcity of available jobs meant that he (Grey) could not guarantee him any new or alternative position.

A solution then occurred to Grey, one which would ensure that the position in Australia was filled, and Madden found further employment. He made enquiries as to who the Acting Secretary - then in the process of transferring to Western Australia was - and he was informed that it was a man named Henry Bland.[378] While Bland was now - in situ - in the Australian post, this did not mean that he or anyone else had a definitive claim on the Western Australian job. The appointment in Western Australia had originally been premised on Governor Hutt's advice that the appointee be sent out from Britain and have no strongly-held previous views as to the "local interests" that were a source of contention in the colony. Indeed, it had been Madden's perceived "neutrality" on both political and religious issues that had originally seen him as the preferred candidate for the post. Unfortunately for Madden, it had been his misfortune to find himself embroiled on arrival in the various tensions and disputes between the Catholics and the Protestants of the colony. This experience led Grey and Hawes to believe that Madden's replacement in Western Australia should be someone who was "immune" to – or outside these various religious factions and disputes. A resolution to this Western Australian "dilemma" which was to the benefit of both Madden and the Colonial Office was found in somewhat dramatic fashion when Merivale - presumably at the instigation of somebody more senior in the organisation - asked Gardiner to compile a written statement, the contents of which were based on previous correspondence as archived within the organisation. This statement outlined Madden's entitlement to favourable treatment in this particular situation. It was decided that Madden's request for a new job be looked upon favourably in order to acknowledge his campaign work against those aspects of the Summary Jurisdiction Bill that had been unjust and prejudiced against the Aborigines. Gardiner composed this statement as requested and included the following:

> *I apprehend the fact to be that, having been prominently opposed to the undue coercion of the coloured race during many years, he considered himself bound to make an active demonstration against the summary infliction of the law on the natives of Western Australia under any circumstances; and party feelings seem to have led him to show an unwarrantable history to Colonel Irwin.*[379]

This statement was followed by a letter - as had been proposed by Grey - where Madden's resignation from his Australian post was acknowledged and accepted. Grey followed this with a memo to Governor Fitzgerald informing him that C.N.J. Piesse[380] was now appointed to the position of Colonial Secretary for Western Australia. A raft of paperwork passed to and fro behind the scenes and this exchange of positions was organised. Madden was appointed Secretary to the Irish Loan Fund in Dublin Castle where he replaced Piesse. Piesse consulted with Madden and the former Governor, Governor Hutt, before his departure for Western Australia. Hutt advised Piesse to travel to Australia alone and to leave his daughters behind in Britain until they were a bit older. Subsequent to his consultations with Madden, Piesse requested that certain law books be forwarded to him in Perth. He realised that there were very few legal ordinances as relating to the colony actually written down, a situation which he was intent on improving. Earl Grey brought the whole transfer issue to a conclusion when he noted the following in the British departmental files: "Mr. Piesse is going a little beyond his province in these recommendations. Acknowledge and say that I consider it unnecessary to send either the books or the artillery."

At this point in the narrative, Madden leaves the colonial service, never to return. He never received any public acknowledgement for his work in Western Australia, unlike two of the men he had found himself at loggerheads with while working there. The town of Geraldson was named in honour of Fitzgerald and the river Irwin was named after Madden's nemesis. As far as we can tell, Madden didn't have much truck with honorary or commemorative titles such as these, although a number of journals in Ireland did highlight the fact that the Irish doctor had never received any recognition from the British government for all the work he had done in the various colonial outposts to which he had been assigned. (*Freeman's Journal*, 6 February, 1886; *Irish Sportsman*, 13 February, 1886). It goes without saying that the British colonial service was delighted to see the back of Madden and it would have gone completely against the grain for them to honour him in any way for the various jobs he had held throughout the years. Ironically, Madden kept involved to a certain extent in the various controversies relating to the Western Australian Church through the medium of letters after his return, this despite the fact that he was now living on the other side of the world! Bishop Brady had sent the two Benedictines Dom Serra and Dom Salvado back to Europe to raise funds for the development of the Church in Western Australia. The first fund-raising trip that the two Benedictines undertook went well but then the authorities in Rome decided to appoint Serra as Apostolic Vicar to Port Victoria, a location the British government had named as the site for a new colony of theirs. Bishop Brady was very disappointed when news of this appointment reached his ears and he came under further pressure from his debtors as they suspected that the funding gathered by Serra in Europe would now go to any new parishes set up in Port Victoria, rather than to them. His penury and his monies worries bore down heavily on Brady so that his health failed him both mentally and physically. Rome responded to this crisis by assigning Serra to Perth as coadjutor to Brady, where the Benedictine was now charged with administrating the financial affairs of this diocese. Salvdo replaced Serra in Port Victoria, to which he was now appointed as Bishop. Grey showed a great interest in all of these developments with Madden explaining to him that the Benedictines had been appointed to ensure that Brady's problems were sorted out once and for all. Grey was delighted to see Spaniards such as the two Benedictines, both of whom had a good background in agriculture, being given important positions in western Australia, as he felt that they were well-suited to the climate and terrain of the new colony.

Serra set to work sorting out the financial affairs of the Church in Perth. He received big monetary donations from his family back in Spain where he was also welcomed with open arms by both the ordinary people and the government ministers of the Spanish Crown on a return visit to raise funds. Indeed, the Queen of Spain was so impressed with Serra that she made one of her warships available in order to transport Serra and his fellow Benedictines on their return journey to Australia. She also personally appointed Serra a member of the Catholic Order of Isabella. On the eighteenth of October, 1849, Serra wrote to Madden. Serra was still under the assumption then that Madden would be returning to Perth, now that his year's holiday was up. The Spaniard told Madden about his new responsibilities and he asked Madden for a contribution that might help in the alleviation of debts accrued by Brady. These debts included debts based on land which Brady had bought and on which he intended founding a new college to educate new Catholic arrivals in Western Australia – amongst other things. In his letter, Serra added that he was sure Madden would do all that was in his power to help strengthen the Catholic faith in Western Australia and to help develop the Swan River mission further. Father Heponstall was also keeping Madden updated at this time on how many of Brady's bills he was continually being sent by various debtors in Australia.

The date of the last Bills I have seen was 11th May. I have paid two of this late: yesterday another for one hundred pounds of a prior date was communicated to me. The imprudence of such proceedings is to me quite incomprehensible. Every one of these Bills must have been returned to the Colony if Dr. Serra had not gone back.[381]

In December, 1849, Serra arrived in Fremantle accompanied by seven priests and thirty-two Christian Brothers and clerical students. Included in this group was Father Dominic Urquhart, an Englishman from the Trappist Monastery of the Holy Saint Bernard in Leicestershire, England. Urquhart and Serra had a serious falling-out with one another on the journey from Europe to Australia aboard a Spanish frigate and the two men would remain at loggerheads with one another for a long time afterwards. The omens were not good as they made their way from Fremantle to Perth. Brady hit it off with Urquhart straight away, a fact which was not that unusual given that the latter was the only English-speaker amongst the recently-arrived group. Quite soon after the group's arrival in Australia, Brady announced that he was appointing Urquhart his Vicar-General, an announcement which angered Serra no end. Serra immediately announced that he would leave Perth if Brady even considered appointing Urquhart to the position of Vicar-General; he also demanded to see the diocese's account books so that he could get a clear and immediate picture of the financial difficulties that needed to be sorted out. Brady had no account books to show him however and Serra was forced to note down whatever debts the Irish cleric could remember, a series of debts which Brady dictated to him verbally. It turns out that Serra had arrived in the colony at an opportune moment given that various debtors were on the point of bringing Brady to court in order to confirm that he was completely bankrupt. Serra ensured that the then enormous sum of three thousand pounds was repaid within the first fortnight. The people paid what was due to them included a schoolteacher named Tarlach Farrelly who was due payment for a full two years of teaching.

Serra paid Farrelly the amount which Brady claimed was due to Farrelly but that amount comprised only a third of the actual total which Farrelly was actually owed. Farrelly was forced to institute legal proceedings in order to recoup his losses and he brought Serra to court in an effort to gain full ownership of the cattle and the farm equipment that he had purchased on the behalf of the Mission in New Norcia. Ironically, Brady gave his backing to the schoolteacher in these legal proceedings as he had now made up his mind to ignore the authorities in Rome; he had also appointed Urquhart his Vicar-General.

This led to an ugly and complicated dispute between both bishops with Urquhart bringing Serra to court - with Brady as his witness in the retrieval of nine sovereigns allegedly loaned to Serra prior to this. Brady then summoned Serra before the Synod to publicly confirm that he was no longer an administrator or a coadjutor and when Serra refused to attend the Synod he was suspended from his clerical position, *ab omnibus sacris.* Serra then sent one of his Benedictine monks to Rome to report to the Holy Congregation Propaganda what was happening in the Perth diocese and to request that he be allowed to leave his position there. Serra also put an announcement in the local newspaper stating that neither he nor the Mission would be responsible for any debts which they had not personally incurred. Brady responded to Serra's challenge in a robust manner by issuing a strong rejoinder to Serra's letter and then sending a group of men armed with guns to New Norcia to take possession of the Mission there. Serra left the mission-house voluntarily so as to avoid further scandal but he also asked the local court to provide evidence of what had had happened to an upcoming commission of investigation in Europe. Brady immediately tried to frustrate this move on Serra's part. He secured a loan of 150 pounds and headed for Rome himself where he hoped to persuade the Vatican administration that Serra's presence in Perth was to the detriment of Catholicism there. Brady also visited London from where he sent Madden a letter. Madden, who was by then in Dublin, was given "the most heartrending accounts" which Brady was allegedly receiving from Western Australia even while in absentia.

> *Whilst the Very Revd. Father Urquhart was engaged in giving a regular course of instructions during the last Lent and well attended not only by Catholics but also by Protestants, Dr. Serra came from his monastery to Perth and thrown (sic) all the Catholic members into the deepest affliction by appealing to the Advocate General for his right to both spiritual and temporal jurisdiction over all and pronouncing suspension, excommunication, interdiction etc. etc. against Dr. Urquhart and Mr. Donovan and all who would not obey his orders. All this misfortune is now inflicted upon our dearly beloved children, and here we are without being able to give relief, waiting for the decision of the Holy See which I fear will be very long as we have a good deal of underhand jobbing and under workings, in and from religious bodied in Rome and elsewhere. May I beg you will see His Grace the most Reverend Dr. Murray and relate to His Lordship these painful accounts with what you know yourself relating to the lands and flocks of sheep etc. and how I have been involved in temporal matters by those very monks who are now disturbing the flock etc.* [382]

Brady told Madden that it would be no harm if he was to inform the Very Reverend Cullen[383] of what was going on in the diocese of Western Australia.

> *How could the spiritual direction of the convict settlement be placed in the hands of monks who could not speak English?*[384]

Brady sent Madden another letter, dated the nineteenth of July, 1850, from Weymouth, Portland[385] where Brady had gone to see off the next group of Catholic emigrants who were setting sail for Western Australia. In this letter Brady described how shocked and dismayed he was to discover that the hundred or so prisoners, pensioners and accompanying family members had no Catholic religious to minister to them on the long journey to Australia but would have to rely on the spiritual ministrations of a Protestant clergyman who was travelling with the party in a company which included his wife, his children and his three servants. Brady went on to describe how these emigrants would find no religious of their own denomination to welcome them reached Western Australia. Worse still, the man who could have made these emigrants feel at home in their new environment now found himself in Europe attempting to defend himself against the trickery and deceit of two Benedictine clerics and their allies in the Vatican.

As far as we can tell, Madden did nothing in response to Brady's various promptings. A few months later the Vatican issued a formal letter confirming Serra's position as Bishop of Perth and its neighbouring Missions. Serra immediately issued a formal letter to Urquhart, confirming this development and when he didn't receive a satisfactory answer from the Englishman, he wrote to him again. In this second letter Serra informed Urquhart that Polding was now the Principal Archbishop in Sydney and that a decree to this effect, as issued by the Pope, would be implemented irrespective of whether Urquhart accepted it or not. Serra also requested that Urquhart hand over the seals and the keys to the Cathedral and offered to pay Urquhart's return passage to England if he so wished. When there was still no response from Urquhart after a few days, Serra officially removed him from his priestly duties and followed this up with a series of notices and warnings. Urquhart eventually gave in and prepared to leave the colony. News filtered back to Australia that the then Pope, Pius the Ninth, had not minced his words at Brady's hearing in the Vatican. The Pope had criticised the poor administration of the Western Australian diocese's finances and the impudence of that Diocese's Synod in finding fault with the coadjutor whom he (the Pope) had personally appointed. On hearing this, Serra must have felt vindicated and he made certain to keep Archbishop Polding up-to-date on these various developments as they occurred in the Vatican.

Pope Pius the Ninth gave Brady permission to return to Ireland but was surprised to hear shortly after their meeting that Brady was intent on returning to Australia. Fearing a further continuation of the Western Australian debacle, the Pope immediately appointed himself Bishop of Perth and ordered Brady to return to Rome immediately. He charged Serra with the administration of the Perth Diocese - on behalf of the Holy See - and made it clear that if Brady contradicted his (the Pope's) instructions and returned to the region near Swan River, he would be stripped of his status as a bishop *ipso facto*. Unperturbed by these canonical admonishments, Brady returned to Australia, his ship docking in Fremantle, in December, 1851. Serra immediately went to see him and warned him of the harm which his return to Australia was likely to cause the Diocese. Serra reminded Brady that the Irishman no longer had any authority in that Diocese and announced that he would resign immediately if Brady could produce a document which countermanded the decree that the Pope had issued with regard to the future of the Diocese. Brady's response to this was to issue legal proceedings against Serra seeking compensation of 3000 pounds, a development which a local source described as follows:

> *The Catholic Community divided into two factions, the Serraites and the Bradyites. Some regrettable scenes occurred. Both sides requested the Governor to intervene; both published their defence of their views in the daily press; both took legal proceedings to establish their rights; both held separate services for their adherents.*[386]

This unfortunate situation continued until April, 1852 when the text of a recently-issued Papal Bull was reprinted in the *Inquirer* newspaper. This document indicated that the Vatican no longer recognised Brady as a Bishop, that Serra had now been appointed Apostolic administrator of the Western Australian diocese and that the faithful were asked to accept his authority from now on. Cardinal Franzoni, then Head of the Holy Congregatio Propaganda asked Polding to set up an enquiry into the troubled state of affairs that was the Perth diocese. Polding spent four months in the diocese and gradually improved matters there. One Sunday in July, 1852 Brady knelt before the altar during Mass and read out a statement where he promised to accept both the Pope's authority and the authority of his representative in Australia from then on. Brady also apologised publicly on the same occasion for the trouble he had brought upon the diocese. This apology didn't hold for too long however. The trouble re-ignited between both "factions" once more and Brady requested the local Civil Court to render null and void the statement of apology and acceptance which he had previously signed.

Polding had had enough by then, however, and he threatened Brady with excommunication, a move which finally brought the Irishman to his senses. Polding also "disciplined" a few Catholics - (supporters of Brady presumably) - who had written letters to the newspapers relating to the dispute and imposed a range of penances on them! That was the end of whole controversy. Over time, Serra was gradually accepted as the spiritual leader of the Diocese and the Pope's authority was accepted unequivocally so that Polding was able to report to the Vatican authorities that "all things are now in perfect peace." Brady, who was by then in very poor health, left the colony in August, 1852. The Vatican allowed him to keep his official title of Bishop of Perth and he went to live in Europe. He spent considerable periods of time in Ireland after this, where he often ministered in the Diocese of Kilmore[387] but it is not clear whether he ever met Madden again subsequent to his departure from Perth. Brady died in France in the month of December, 1872.

CHAPTER 12
EXILE'S RETURN: A JOB IN IRELAND

Madden's return from Australia was to coincide with the death-throes of the "dissolute" and wild-spending lifestyles of society "beaus" Lady Blessington and Count D'Orsay. These two members of the gentry had accumulated such massive debts over time that the courts were about to move in an effort to recoup them. A legal writ was issued against the pair, confirming that their residence Gore House was to be confiscated and its contents auctioned off to pay off various debtors. Madden attended this auction which was his last opportunity to view the house where he had experienced both kindness and suffering. Now that this fine house and its contents were to be sold off in their entirety, Madden only felt sadness at the ruin now visited on this once-grand establishment.

Renowned author William Thackeray, a personal friend of the family, attended the auction and he too felt both sadness and disgust at the sight of the house's furniture and belongings being sold off to the highest bidder. He described the buyers who filled the house's balconies and terraces at auction as brutes whom he wished to usher out of the house with the admonishment, "Sirs, be civil in a lady's room." Madden's described the scene as follows:

Every room was thronged. The well-known library salon, in which the conversations took place were crowded, but not with guests. The armchair in which the lady of the mansion was wont to sit, was occupied by a short coarse gentleman of the Jewish persuasion, engaged in examining a marble hand extended on a book. People as they passed through the room poked the furniture, pulled about the precious objects of art and ornaments which lay on the table. And some made jests. It was the most signal ruin of an establishment I ever witnessed. Here was a total smash, a crash on a grand scale.[388]

In reality, the ruin of Gore House had been on the cards for a long time. For a full twenty-five years prior to that fateful day Madden had witnessed unbridled spending and an opulence that shocked him beyond measure. What had surprised him more than anything else was the fact that this day of ruin hadn't arrived many years earlier. Almost a decade previous to this, for example, Madden had received a "begging letter" at his then home in Portugal from D'Orsay. The Count was in debt as usual and he asked Madden if he could help him find a buyer for a statuette of the Duke of Wellington[389] which he wished to sell.

Knowing full well that money problems had induced D'Orsay to make such a request, Madden had declined to get involved in the Count's latest attempt to raise cash. He wrote back to D'Orsay informing him that his principles forbade him from giving any recognition to Wellington or others who were "idolators of the war principle." On that particular occasion D'Orsay had been under the pressure to repay a debt of 125 pounds and had come up with the bizarre plan to sell this statuette in an effort to come up with some "ready cash." This wasn't the first time that D'Orsay had come up with various strange and eccentric money-making schemes. On different occasions, he had experimented with a number of unusual but unsuccessful business ventures including a bizarre scheme involving the exchange of cattle as opposed to the normal buying and selling of stock at fairs, and an attempt to create gold from a mix of cheap metals. At one point, he even invented a strange contraption which allegedly prevented accidents on the railway line.

Lady Blessington died suddenly just a few weeks after the auction at Gore House and the rumour went around that she had committed suicide. Madden found no truth in these rumours, however, and opined that she had probably died from a broken heart, having seen her once-great house go to rack-and-ruin. Of far greater personal concern to Madden than these scurrilous rumours was the fact that Lady Blessington, though baptised a Catholic, had apparently strayed from the faith over the years. At one stage Madden had felt brave enough to take up his pen and proffer her with spiritual advice. On that occasion he had admonished her for her lack of seriousness with respect to her religious duties and reminded her that her faith was much more important than any fame or worldly glory, or any joy of a temporal nature which might be gained from the intellect or from the company of intellectual people. He also gently chastised her on the inherently false nature of her extra-marital relationship. Lady Blessington's private papers were donated to Madden after her death and he later recalled searching for his letter of admonishment in these same papers. He never did find that letter but nevertheless had a strong feeling that his heartfelt advice to her had not gone entirely unheeded.

Lady Blessington had been in the habit of attending Sunday Mass with her husband while he was alive. She continued this practice after his death although Madden's suspected that she did so out of habit as opposed to any deep-felt adherence to the regulations of the Catholic faith. Subsequent to her death, D'Orsay confirmed that Lady Blessington had continued to attend Mass regularly right up until her death. D'Orsay also told Madden that it was his belief that Lady Blessington had always remained a Catholic in the "privacy of her own heart." Whenever she visited Paris, it was her habit to attend Mass every Sunday in the Church at Madeleine where she was normally accompanied by another member of her immediate family. In later years Madden would also recall the deathbed conversion of Lady Blessington's own father, Edmund Power, as an example of the way in which people's attitude to their faith became more serious as they neared their death. Her father had abandoned Catholicism twice and had been no stranger to violence – he was accused of murder at one stage during his life - a killing which he was probably guilty of. Despite a life of dissipation and violence, the dying Power had found his only solace in the Catholicism that he had been baptised and reared in. He had been bedridden for a while before his death, Madden noted, a fact which had given him the opportunity to reflect on life's "big questions" and it was then that he had decided to return to Catholicism once more. Madden visited Paris, on business in 1852 where he rekindled his friendships with Beranger and de Lammenais again. The three men discussed the recent *coup d'etat* that had taken place in France and the reasons for the failure of the constitutional system in that country. Madden's papers note that, while on this visit, he witnessed Napoleon – a man whom he referred to as a "man-mystery" - receiving a salute from a squadron of soldiers one day. The most poignant scene he recalled from this French visit was his last sight of D'Orsay, however:

He burst out crying when I entered the room, and continued for a length of time so much affected that he could hardly speak to me. Gradually he became composed, and talked about Lady Blessington's death, but all the time with tears pouring down his pale face for even now his features were death-stricken. He said: "In losing her I lost everything in the world. She was to me a mother, a dear dear, dear mother, a true loving to me." While he uttered these words he sobbed and cried like a child. And referring to them he again said, "You understand me, Madden." I understood him to be speaking what he felt; and there was nothing in his accents, in his position, or his expressions (for his words sounded in my ears like those of a dying man) which led me to believe he was seeking to deceive himself or me...

...I turned his attention to the subject I thought most important to him. I said, among the many objects which caught my attention in the room, I was very glad to see a crucifix placed over the head of his bed; men living in the world as he had done were so much in the habit of forgetting all religious feelings. D'Orsay seemed hurt at the observation. I then plainly said to him "The fact is, I imagined - or rather supposed - you had followed Lady Blessington's example, in not giving up your own religion, in seeming to conform to another more in vogue in England." D'Orsay rose up with considerable energy and stood again, and, pointing to the head of the bed, he said "Do you see those swords?" pointing to two small swords which were hung over the crucifix crosswise. "Do you see that sword to the right? With that sword I fought in defence of my religion. I had only joined my regiment a few days, when an officer at the mess-table used disgusting and impious language in speaking of the Blessed Virgin. I called on him to desist; he repeated the foul language he had used: I threw a plate of spinach across the table in his face; a challenge ensued; we fought that evening on the rampart of the town; and I have kept that sword ever since."[390]

Whatever strange antics were going on here, Madden never attended another meeting of the Famine Relief Fund's General Committee. Madden's return to Ireland had coincided with a pivotal era in Irish history. The Repeal Association that had been so vibrant at one time was now on its last legs. A reporter for the *Saunders' Newsletter*[391] gave a poignant account of the Association's final meeting, a gathering which took place in Conciliation Hall, in an article entitled "Finis Hiberniae." Samuel Law, the only member of the Committee who was present, had addressed the meeting at the instigation of John O'Connell. He outlined the precarious position the Association now found itself in given that its weekly income had seen a drastic fall from a high-point of 3500 pounds when the Association was at its apex to the meagre sum of five pounds a week, a sum which only barely covered the rent for the meeting hall. O'Connell suggested that the Association disband until it was guaranteed enough support from followers in the Irish populace and it was a viable entity again. This proposal was passed without a single dissenting voice. The correspondent with the *Saunders' Newsletter* described the final moments of the Repeal Association as follows:

The audience, which was scanty, withdrew. An old lady who sat in the gallery was the last but one to leave the Hall. She uplifted her eyes and hands towards heaven, and remained for a moment in an attitude of prayer or amazement at the mutability of human affairs. She sadly and pensively retired upon one of the forms. In the Hall sat an elderly and rather care-worn man, in bankrupt circumstances. His very bad hat was slouched over his eyes; his head drooped, and his chest was supported by a stick. He was almost stupefied by the dread reality. When all but himself had withdrawn he arose, and silently and mournfully walked out in the street.[392]

The Nation had also had a story at this juncture that Donal O'Connell, the "Liberator's Son," had been appointed as Queen's Counsel in Para, Brazil. This rumour was followed by another in the same newspaper just a few months later which claimed that Maurice O'Connell, another of the "Liberator's" sons, was in line for an even better job closer to home:

We are in a condition to announce - (said the Nation, on the 13th of July, 1850), that the Whig Government have provided for another O'Connell. The honourable member for Tralee has got a promise of the Collector-Generalship of Taxes for Dublin, with a salary of 800 pounds a year. Hurrah for Repeal! Long live Conciliation Hawl![393]

A week later, a sarcastic reference was made to Smith O'Brien in the newspaper the *Galway Vindicator*, a reference that would have left Madden feeling uncomfortable no doubt:

> *While the descendant of a gallant line wears the chains of exile at the Antipodes, Maurice O'Connell is booked for the office of Collector-Generalship of Customs in Dublin in Dublin - (said the paper).*[394]

By now, Madden had settled into his new job, in an office that was located just inside the main gates of Dublin Castle. He had completely severed his links with the Young Irelanders at this stage having disapproved of the rebellion of 1848; he was against such an armed revolt in principle. The annual general meeting of the *Celtic Society* which met in 1850 in the Royal Irish Academy was a good example of the fault-lines which had developed at this stage in the remnant of the intellectual rump that was the Young Ireland Movement.

This meeting saw the Marquis of Kildare, the Rev. Thomas Farrelly, James Frederick Ferguson, Richard Madden M.D. and the Viscount of Kildare, James S. Close, all elected as members of the Royal Irish Academy (R.I.A.) Council where they replaced Charles Gavan Duffy, Samuel Ferguson, Denis F. McCarthy, John F. Mitchell and Robert Tighe. The *Nation* announced these changes in the membership of the Celtic Society in a brief statement but made no other comment on the issue. One of the most interesting aspects of Madden's biography is the "behind the scenes" story of how he managed to secure his job in Dublin Castle. The official British government "line" was that Madden had formally resigned from this post in Western Australia on the ninth of January, 1850, a date of departure which was then extended by seven weeks to the first of March. As of that date, Madden was unemployed although Lord Grey had wished him the best and expressed his hope that Madden might someday find employment in the Colonial Office again, if and when a vacancy arose. This was the "official" position of the government but the real story was not so straightforward. The reality behind this "official" rhetoric was much more positive as regards the possibility that Madden might secure another governmental job. In actual fact, Madden had been party to the official statement as released by Lord Grey while simultaneously putting in place a swap arrangement with Charles Piesse, the Secretary of the Loan Fund Board, a government section which was based in Dublin. Madden's own *Memoirs* provide do not provide any explanation as to how an intellectual - with a known penchant for the writing of "rebellious" literature and a track record as an "awkward individual" and "campaigner" on a range of issues as relating to the Colonies - nevertheless managed to secure a job in a place such as Dublin Castle. Madden's personal papers do go some way towards explaining how the Irishman had circumvented these "issues" so as to secure this post on home soil, however:

> *This was so far effected that I had a promise of Piesse's office, and I exerted successfully all my influence in the Colonial Office to get Piesse appointed to mine. In this state of things, Piesse informed me my appointment to his was office was determined on, but that it was indispensable I should write a private letter to his friend and relative, Matheson, of the Secretary's Office, that I had no intention, if appointed, of writing any work similar to the "United Irishmen's History." I did not conceive I ought to have been called on to write any such letter. I wrote, however, the letter of which this is a copy and was appointed.*[395]

The following was the letter which Madden sent to C. Matheson Esq., First Clerk in the Chief Secretary's Office.

My dear Sir,
    My object in desiring to obtain home employment and to relinquish for it my office, in a distant land, of Colonial Secretary, is simply this. Many months have not elapsed since a grievous domestic calamity fell upon me, the loss of a son, the centre of all my hopes, in his 19th year, by a sudden and

untimely end on the river Shannon.

This young man of great scientific acquirements which I had made no small sacrifices to obtain for him thus perished on the Government works of the Shannon, conducted by Mr. Mulvany, with whom I had placed him as an articled pupil at the period of my departure for Australia. My ambition does not extend now beyond the land in which the remains of my beloved child are buried.

I take no part in politics, I have never belonged to any political society, nor have I written my work intended or calculated to lead to violence, insurrection or rebellion. To do so would be against my principles, and all my experience would be against that course. I have seen many rebellions and several revolutions, in Spain, Portugal, Italy and Greece; in the East and in the West. I have watched their results as a man of some observation and plain common sense might be supposed to do, and I may add, have not seen any good arise from them to the people of those countries where such civil wars have taken place.

I hope that humanity and justice would have been served by the anatomy of a rebellion, like that of '98 in Ireland, by laying bare the machinery of secret conspiracy, the perfidy, cupidity and truculency that stalk in its paths; the brutality, intemperance, cruelty and ferocity masked under a show of zeal either for order or religion, that are to be found in the agency of the subordinates of authority, entrusted with power, against the opponents, real or suspected, of government in such bad times, when society, stirred to its lowest depths, sends that which is vilest to the top, all its scum to the surface, and no small quantity likewise of spurious patriotism, of froth and foam, bubbling up from the ferment that is going on there.

I have reason to know that my work called The Lives and Times of the United Irishmen was so understood by the present Earl St. Germains (then Lord Elliott) when he filled the office of the Chief Secretary of Ireland. His Lordship has spoken of that work to me when he I had the honour of partaking of his hospitality in the Phoenix Park, and on one occasion when I spoke of the simultaneous appearance of an official report of mine on African Affairs, and a newly published series of the work in question - and observed - "My Lord, I fear you will think I have too many irons in the fire", - his Lordship replied - "I did not say that nor do I think so." The latter words, too, being spoken with marked emphasis.

It is hardly needful to say, should I obtain employment here, as I hoped to have done through the strong recommendation of my friend and relative, the late Mr. Wm. Murphy, the useful friend, let me add, of British interests in Ireland, as understood by all liberal Governments in Ireland since that of the Marquis of Wellesley - writings of mine on political subjects must cease.

I desire to live in peace, "milli et muses" in as far as any business I am employed on may allow me, in my own land, and the muses I speak of are not these which Tyrtans invoked or Thomas worshipped.

With such inclinations my leisure would have other occupation than the preparation of any other editions of those works of mine which have treated of politics even of past times.

I perhaps ought to have observed to you that this work of mine The Lives and Time of the United Irishmen, appeared in 3 series at different periods. The first series was published in 1842, the second series in 1843, and the 3rd series in 1846 and the last volume of this series was offered for sale separately in the spring of 1847. It was subsequently to all these dates that Earl Grey conferred on me the appointment of Colonial Secretary in Western Australia, the date of it gazetted in the London Gazette of May 15th 1847.

If the title of that work be taken as an indication of objectionable opinions, so must be that of my late friend Dr. William Cooke Taylor - The History of the Civil War in Ireland and that also of Mr. Moore - The Life of Lord Edward Fitzgerald.

Dr. W.C. Taylor moreover (now for the first time I divulge that which has hitherto been a secret as far as I am concerned) was the writer of that very striking Introduction to my first series of the United Irishmen, extending to 37 pages. He was, moreover, the writer of one of the most remarkable Memoirs in the 2nd Series of that work -"A Memoir of Counsellor Sampson."

Nay, the work would never have been published if it were not for poor Taylor's special recommendation of it to an English publisher as the enclosed copy of a letter of his on that subject to a London bookseller will show you. May I ask was Dr. William Cooke Taylor one of "Les Classes Dangereuses" of authors - though he did write of Irish Wars and Rebellions? Except to the small faction that clings tenaciously to an effete tolerance that has been the bane of the British interests in Ireland, Dr. Taylor did not seem of this class; and further, let me observe, if I was of that category, I should not have had the friends who have interested themselves in me, or any application of mine for employment.

Yours,

R.R. Madden

Madden had to swallow a good deal of pride to write such a letter, but swallow it he did. His humility "paid off" in the end when he was chosen to become the next Secretary to the Loan Funds Board. Madden must have felt very relieved when he received the letter confirming his appointment in this new post, as it was really "a make or break" situation for him and his family, especially given that there was no way that he could ever return to the "hornet's nest" that was the Australian job. The Irishman received a good number of congratulatory letters from family and friends when the news of his appointment because public knowledge. His old friend James Stephens was one of the first to congratulate him. He wished Madden well on having negotiated the various storms that he had encountered thus far in his career so as to finally secure a "berth" in his native land. Stephens played down any influence he may have personally brought to bear on Madden's securing of the Dublin job and told Madden his decision to resign from the Australian job had been the correct one. While Stephens undoubtedly knew the real reasons for Madden's departure from Western Australia he preferred to concentrate on the "mundane" or "domestic" reasons why Madden's return to Ireland was a good thing.

> *The most difficult questions in casuistry, (he wrote), are those which relate to the order in which rival duties are to be preferred to each other. But I cannot doubt that the parental duty, especially in a case such as yours, is the highest which you owe to any fellow-creature, next after the duties of conjugal life; that your boy has an absolute right to your personal care; that therefore you have not the right to put half the world between you and him; and that you have still less right to take him with you to the other side of it, and to bring him into contact with the present colonists there, unless, indeed, his actual subsistence depended upon it. Therefore, just sit quietly down in this anxious land, do what you can to enlighten and improve it, and ten years hence, when the boy shall have become a man, migrate with him to the ends of the earth, if such shall then be his pleasure and yours.* [396]

"Sitting quietly down" would never have been an aspect of Madden's make-up however. He began quietly researching the lives of the United Irishmen again in spite previous statements to the effect that he was finished with that type of research. The difficulties he had encountered over the years in a number of administrative roles had rendered him more politically astute also. From now on, any time he was presented with a political or administrative impasse, he made certain that he made his governmental superiors aware of the situation immediately, rather than attempting to deal with the problem himself. Within a short time, he had mastered the essentials of the post, although he would discover once again that his initial impressions of the job were not entirely accurate. Unknown to him, he had taken up his new role just as the Irish Loans Fund Board was going through a difficult patch in its development. In fact, Piesse was leaving the Loan Board to escape the serious mess that he had created, as became clearer to Madden in due course.

To understand the evolution of the "Loan Fund" system it is necessary to go back to its beginnings in the eighteenth century when Dean Jonathan Swift[397] first set up the Loan System in Ireland. He had instigated the system on behalf of Dublin's poorest tradesmen so as to protect them when economic conditions were particularly difficult. Swift had also overseen the implementation of the system, tramping Dublin's toughest streets to personally oversee the repayment of the loans. Prior to Swift's death another Charitable Loan Fund had been set up, this time based on the annual profits which the Dublin Musical Society made from their Fishamble Street Music Hall.

This latter loan fund system had fallen apart by 1823 however and Parliament had passed an Act in that same year authorising each individual guild of tradesmen to put in place their own Charitable Loan funds including systems of additional interest - as imposed in the case of non-payment. Unfortunately this new system gave rise to many illegal and corrupt practices and an amended version of the Act was passed a decade later in 1863, an act which ensured that the Loan Fund Board would monitor the funds of different tradesmens' guilds. Another similar act followed in 1838 and in 1843, the various laws relating to the management of these loan funds being amalgamated and standardized in the eyes of the law. A few years prior to the amendments of 1843 Piesse had spoken in optimistic terms about the Loan Fund system although his enthusiasm was probably somewhat "forced" and false in nature:

It is hard to say to what class of the community the Loan Fund system affords most benefit, whether to small dealers, with whom it forms at once a capital for outlay, and a deposit bank for weekly receipts: or to the tradesmen of various denominations who, by getting a sum in hand, are enabled to purchase on cash terms the material of their trade or tools; or to the small farmer, to whom it acts as additional capital to supply any temporary deficiency, or enable him to hold over produce for better markets. To the labourer, the Loan Fund is invaluable as affording capital for the annual purchase of his pig. The low wages obtained by this class put it almost out of their power to save a sufficient sum for this purpose, without being tempted by their continual necessity to encroach upon it.[398]

By the early 1840s the Irish Loan Fund also had a serious competitor for the first time, one that was making them quite nervous. This was a body known as the Irish Reproductive Loan Fund Board an umbrella group that was based on a range of smaller groups which had evolved in London during the early 1800s to aid the poorer farmers of Ireland. Some of the smaller groups which were by now subsumed into the Irish Reproductive Loan Fund Board had specialised in small-money loans to individuals involved in farming, fishing or the purchase of particular equipment as relating to those industries. In 1823, the London government, under the auspices of the Irish Reproductive Loan Fund, had collected 300,000 pounds as relief aid for those rural Irish areas they referred to as the Congested Districts in an effort to ease the hardship and starvation that was widespread in these areas.

Two decades later, when the tragedy that was the Great Famine caused devastation and death on an unprecedented scale throughout the whole of Ireland, the Board in London had given all of the money they had raised to the Viceroy of Ireland instructing him to spend it on whatever relief schemes he saw fit, provided he had the prior approval of the State Treasury to do so. Over time it became clear that to the Dublin-based Irish Loan Fund Board that the "Reproductive Loan Funds" were being spent only irregularly, however, and it therefore made a big effort to try and get these funds assigned to its control. The Dublin-based Irish Loan Fund Board failed in this attempt however, the Londoners having so much political power that they managed to get a paragraph which had been inserted in the 1843 Bill - giving the Dubliners a certain amount of administrative control over the funds - removed. In addition to this the London Board managed to get this now-omitted section of the Bill changed so as to include a strong admonition to Dublin - warning Dublin to stay out of its affairs completely. As a consequence of these long-running tensions between the two Loans Boards, the Irish Viceroy and the State Treasury unsurprisingly decided to keep the two organisations separate from one another, this despite the fact that both organisations were engaged in the same business and were, in reality, in competition with one another. In 1842 the number of associations that were under the stewardship of the Irish Loans Fund Board had increased to 300, the highest number that they would ever reach. By 1845, this number had fallen to 255.

The years of the Great Famine saw the number of loans taken out reduced by a quarter of a million pounds, with less than a million pounds-worth of loans taken out in total. Many depositors lost faith in the different associations and withdrew their money as they emigrated from Ireland. The mis-management of funds in many associations generated doubts in the minds of investors and while the Board was keen to shut down these associations, they were still reluctant to allow other new Associations set up given that their monitoring and control of these Associations left a lot to be desired.

The Board openly acknowledged these administrative problems in the Annual Reports produced in 1851 and 1852, Madden's first two years as Secretary to the Board. In fact, these two Annual Reports requested that a Government Parliamentary enquiry be set up to investigate irregularities in the Loans Process so that the Government could see for itself the extent of the mismanagement problem that then existed. The year 1854 saw Sir. John Kingsmill resign from the Board because of his dissatisfaction with the Board's mismanagement and the lack of adequate regulation and implementation of the laws relating to Loan

Funds and processes generally. Madden, as one would expect, was one of the principal people "behind the scenes" who was pushing for an investigation. In the interim, and while waiting for his request to be assessed, he tried as best he could to improve matters "on the ground" as relating to the whole Loans process. Only a handful of people worked in the Loans Fund Office, including two clerical officers, one of whom earned an annual salary of eighty pounds a year while the other earned fifty pounds. The other two people employed by that office were Madden himself and an inspector who was paid the same salary as Madden but who had to cover his own travel expenses.

The actual committee which comprised the Board of Directors of the Loans Fund was "top-heavy" with a full thirty members - as was frequent with such Committees. While the Loans Fund Board officially comprised thirty members, the fortnightly meeting of the Board never saw more than three of these members - a bare quorum - in attendance. Those in attendance were either the members who lived in Dublin or close to Dublin, or who had a vested interest in the meeting's order of business. These Board members received no payment for their attendance at meetings, meetings that were frequently long-winded and involved "going through the motions." Most meetings involved Madden going through the minutes of the previous meeting and confirming what had been decided on the previous occasion. These fortnightly minutes were - to all intents and purposes exactly the same from one meeting to another - i.e. a description of the confused state of the Loans Fund finances as a consequence of mismanagement and dishonesty. A good number of the associations operating under the Loan Fund's auspices were collapsing and their investors' monies were being squandered as a consequence. One of the first decisions Madden made in his new job was to place a number of statements before government indicating that depositors had lost the (then-enormous) sum of 27,000 pounds - since 1843 - the year that the Loans Fund Act had been implemented.

These statements also indicated that many associations

were increasing their incomes through unjust methods including unduly large fines and interest rates based on customers' pre-payments, membership applications and application forms. When these various "charges" were added to the original loan charges, the interest rates went way beyond a level that Parliament would have deemed appropriate. The interest rates on customer accounts sometimes reached as high as 20% or 25%. Worse than this, the Loans Fund Board was powerless to control the actions of managers and the administrative staff of the associations or to impose a standardized approach country-wide. There weren't enough inspections of these associations' activities taking place and the Board had no power to implement its own fairly generalised regulations as relating to the activities of the same associations.

All that the Board could do was write to the various associations warning them that their licences would be revoked if their behaviour was deemed irregular. More often than not, however, the Associations simply ignored these warnings from the Board and continued with their illegal business practices. Many of the administrators working in these associations were very corrupt and siphoned away money for their own personal use. As Madden would discover, a good number of the Associations which had fallen apart during the years of the Great Famine had not collapsed simply because they had misappropriated the savings of the wealthier farming class. In many cases the associations' clerks had stolen the money of the depositors, stashing it away only to later claim that their depositors had died, disappeared into the Poorhouse or emigrated to America.

The bitter truth was that the Loans Fund Board had lost whatever control they had once exerted over the associations during Piesse's tenure as Secretary to the Board, partly because of poor management on Piesse's part and partly because the other Board members found it easier to absolve themselves of any responsibility, assigning blame for the entire mess to Piesse alone. Madden had spoken openly and forthrightly on all of the problems which had plagued the Loans Fund Board when giving evidence to the Select Parliamentary Committee instigated in March, 1855. He was the first witness to give evidence to the Committee and the most important.

The country is beginning to rise from its depression, (he said to the Committee), the energies of the people require not only to be aided and encouraged but directed in the way of advancement of material interests...The Loan Fund system has the peculiar advantage over that of the Savings Bank; it keeps its deposits in circulation in the country where the earnings of its industrious poor have been invested by them. Increase the public confidence in the Loan Fund Institution and the capital in it will be largely increased.[399]

Madden prepared a detailed written summary for the occasion, a summary which he presented to an Irish Parliamentary representative and civil servant named French on the Committee so that the latter could base his initial questions on this document. As one would expect from Madden, he began his summary by outlining the historical background to the Loan Fund system and its initial implementation in Ireland. He referred to a number of European lending models and mentioned a similar-type Loan Fund system then operating in Italy. This was the Banco dei Poveri, which had seen its beginnings in a one-time rivalry between two religious orders - i.e. the Franciscans and the Dominicans - and the subsequent evolution of banking systems in both Lombardy[400] and Holland. The Select Committee didn't spend very long deliberating. Within a few months, it had compiled a report outlining the principal reasons for the failure of the Loans Fund System in Ireland, as it then operated.

The Committee identified two principal reasons for the collapse of so many Associations. One was the devastation that Ireland suffered in 1847 "which the altered circumstances" of Ireland render it improbable...will recur." The second failure the Committee identified was the improper and inefficient management of the various associations and the necessity to amend the laws pertaining to the management of these associations.

The Committee commended Madden on his work and made a number of recommendations. None of these recommendations was ever implemented subsequent to this however, irrespective of how often they were referenced in the many reports produced on behalf of the Loans Fund Board, in the years following Madden's report. The income of the Loans Fund Board went into an irreversible decline from 1860 onwards and the Board was forced to sell off various investments to pay its administrative costs. By 1874 the associations' monies then in circulation had fallen to a total of 523,000 pounds as compared with a figure of 1,875,000 pounds in 1845. This decline was explained with reference to the slightly improved status of the poorer Irish "labouring class" and the gradual growth in investment banking in Ireland. The status of the Loans Fund Board continued to fall in later years while Madden was secretary to the Board and the government appeared unconcerned with remedying the situation. Madden expressed his incredulity at the Government's lack of interest in the Loans Fund Board on many occasions, but to no avail. The Government's position never changed and the Loans Fund Board decline continued subsequent to Madden's eventual departure from the post.

By the early 1900s the number of associations had fallen to fifty and the Board was on its last legs. The Board was eventually subsumed into the Department of Agriculture in 1915. His work for the Loans Fund Board gave Madden the opportunity to witness at first-hand the pitiful conditions that existed throughout much of Ireland in the decades immediately subsequent to the Great Famine. The barony of Longford, the Shannon side of which had once been home to the Madden family, had seen its population halved by death, disease and emigration.

> *I travelled for miles along the Shannon valley, (he says), without meeting a peasant or a cottage with a roof left on it, and grass grew over many a once happy homestead. I heard no more the*

children's merry laughter; or the peasant's song: naught but the wild bird's cry or the raven's cawing in the woods - too truly was the Celt gone with a vengeance. The famine of 1846 and the following years, fever, the vandalism, of absentee landlords and the crowbar evictions had done their job. Between 1846 and 1850 more than one and a half millions of Ireland's peasantry were swept away. In every part of Ireland I found the same sad state of affairs. The country towns were depeopled and poverty-stricken. The Poor Houses and hospitals were crowded beyond their capacity. And more than once I had seen emaciated corpses in the ditches.[401]

In Ballinrobe, County Mayo, the local parish priest had handed Madden a list of 2000 people who died as a consequence of starvation and eviction from their smallholdings. Another issue which Madden became aware of very quickly was the spread of proselytism and the "Soupers."[402]

Mission schools, orphanages, and soup kitchens were established everywhere, and Scripture readers were to be seen busily occupied with the work of prosleytism, holding in one hand a steaming soup bowl, in the other a bible, recantation of Popish errors being the price of these tempting viands, gazed at so wistfully by many a dimmed and dyed eye.[403]

Madden had personal experience of the effects of this proselytising drive by some Protestant groups and the engrained resistance of many Catholics to its effects:

I was driving across the country in the vicinity of Ennistymon, wrapped in a warm cloak, when my attention was attracted by the car's driver "O, mister, look at those poor creatures asleep in the snowdrift." I sprang from the car and approached the bank where they lay. One of them I found to be unconscious, the other dead. This is a sequel to an eviction.

Both parents were dead, and the children were on their way to the workhouse, when overcome by hunger and fatigue, they lay down in the ditch. I had the surviving boy brought to a nearby hotel, and when he recovered his senses he cried out in a tone of terror "Let me away - this is not the workhouse. I must go to the workhouse." When I enquired why he seemed so much frightened, and so anxious to go away from the comfortable room where he lay close to a good fire wrapped in warm blankets, he replied earnestly, "Because I promised my dead mother never to go to the Mission house. I won't stay here with the soupers now. You are very kind and good, sir, but you are a souper and I won't stay.[404]

In the incident described above, Madden had done his utmost to reassure the boy that he was in fact now in a workhouse and not in a Mission house as he suspected. The boy had only been fully reassured however, when he saw Madden talking to a Catholic priest, the day after the good doctor had found him in the snow. Madden and the boy kept in touch with one another by letter for many years after this. On that visit to Ennistymon, County Clare, Madden had ended up staying in the area for longer than he had intended, due to the necessity for him to give testimony at the local Coroner's Committee. The day after he attended the Coroner's Committee and described the deaths he had witnessed, he also visited the church adjacent to the old monastery in Ennistymon, a visit which left a lasting impression on him.

The church was crowded with people and Madden had never seen such a public exhibition of religious devotion as he witnessed on that occasion. The crowd was so large that many people lined the streets outside the church or knelt in prayer on the graves of their relatives. A large proportion of the people in attendance were now homeless, having been evicted from their smallholdings, and some were so weak with the hunger that they had actually crawled some of the way to the church as they no longer had the strength to stand. These people's public expression of religious faith and devotion would leave a lasting imprint on Madden's mind, particularly as many of the people listening to the sermons in the church that day were only hours away from death themselves. In Nenagh, County Tipperary, the few street traders still in operation had lined the street with hundreds of newly-made coffins, in anticipation of the sales that were inevitable. In the market-house there Madden saw a widow and her five children stretched out keening alongside the body of the dead woman's husband.

A few hundred people a week were dying in the poorhouse in Nenagh and Madden collected samples of the black, inedible rye-bread that was being fed to the poor there and sent it to the Department of the Poor Law in Somerset House.[405] Madden also contacted any of his Parliamentary friends who were in any way influential and impressed upon them the terrible nature of the crisis that Ireland was experiencing. He also regularly "canvassed" the ministers whose responsibility it was to ease the suffering of the Irish people but met with little success. As most of these government ministers were themselves members of the landlord class, they had little sympathy for the tenants who were then dying in their droves, and did nothing constructive to improve their situation. Members of parliament who professed to hold liberal views now stood full-square behind the then-colonial government whose policy was to do nothing. It was Madden's view that the government's reluctance to do anything to save the people was actually a deliberate and "unspoken" policy of wiping out significant proportions of the "lower-class" Irish.[406]

On every side, the manifestations of a people's ruin are before them, in those roofless houses, newly levelled walls, patches of ground round them recently rooted up; they are to be seen in the emaciated forms, the falling limbs, the shrivelled, haggard, sharp-set features of people perishing for want of food; they are to be noted in the dull eye, void of all expression, lustre, animation and intelligence; in the mournful, listless stolid look of stupefaction nay, even in the lank hair, the bony fingers, the sunken chest, the pinched-up belly, the flattened truck; in the swollen extremities - in the whole air and aspect of those squalid, sickly, almost exanimate poor creatures, the homeless outcasts whom the owners of the soil have doomed to die, as surely as if they consigned them to the gallows, or put them to the sword.[407]

Madden also witnessed the horrific sight of a family being evicted from their cabin in Bantry, County Cork. While on his way to the scene of the eviction Madden heard a crying sound coming from a nearby wood. He searched the trees where he found a middle-aged man lying on the grass. The man was moaning, his face twisted in the death-throes of fever. When the man spotted Madden coming towards him, he crawled across the ground, placed his back against the tree and turned to face the doctor, his gaze fierce and challenging. The man initially thought that Madden was the sheriff from whom he was fleeing. The frightened man's sole concern at this point was to die somewhere where he couldn't hear the cries of his own children - children who were already keening their mother who had just died. Madden explained to the man that he was a doctor and a stranger to that part of Ireland and that he had only heard about the eviction that day by chance. He helped the feverish man to his feet and they made their way to the cabin of a local fisherman where he explained to the people there how to care for the sick man. He then made his way onwards to the scene of the eviction. Madden was there when the Sheriff's men arrived to evict the tenants. The leader of this eviction group proceeded to read aloud from a document outlining the legal conventions which preceded the eviction itself. When the man finished speaking, Madden took the opportunity to step forward and plead that the eviction be stopped on humanitarian grounds. He reminded the eviction party that the inhabitants of the house were either dead already or would probably be dead very shortly, given that they were all stricken with fever. The man-in-charge responded to Madden by asking him his name and informing the doctor that he didn't care who he was - that the law would take its course. Powerless to prevent what was happening, Madden lost his temper and called the Sheriff's men "a gang of legalised murderers."

While groups such as the sheriff's men were bad enough it was the landlords who authorised such evictions that were the worst of all. These landlords and their friends in government sickened Madden, who identified Lord John Russell and Lord Clarendon as particularly culpable for their roles in cruelties similar to the eviction he witnessed then in the Bantry countryside. When he was finished shouting Madden was arrested and the eviction proceeded. He was later released without charge and when he returned to the inn where he was staying, Madden handed the landlady - who was herself quite poor - some money, and requested that she provide the evicted tenants with lodgings. The woman refused to accept his money however. Did this gentleman honestly think that she would accept money in order to cover the lodgings of a group of evicted people? Instead, the landlady sent her daughter out with a horse and cart to transport the evicted tenants to her inn where she looked after them for a number of years after these events as generously as she would members of her own immediate family. Madden also called on the local parish priest - a kindly man - who sold his horse to help support the evicted people. As Madden later recalled that the priest was himself exhausted and weak with sickness, partly as a result of his own constant attendance at the houses of the dead and the dying. The priest accompanied Madden to the fisherman's college where he gave the dying runaway the Last Rites and comforted him with the news that his children now had a roof over their heads. That priest was to die himself within a few months of these events, struck down by the same fever that killed so many clergy and non-clergy alike.

1850 was to prove an auspicious year for Madden as he found himself in "hot water" with the Colonial government in Ireland only months after being appointed to his new post in that same administration. On the nineteenth of August, 1850, the *Freeman's Journal* published the first in a series of anonymous articles - signed with the letter "X" - concerning the condition of the Irish poor - the starvation and fever then rampant throughout the country, the deplorable conditions of the Poorhouses, and the poor state of the "Union"[408] in Kilrush, County Clare – then one of the most deprived regions in the country. Madden's travels had taken him to this small town where he had witnessed a particularly gruesome sight, one which he could never erase from his memory. A group of horse-drawn carts - (now minus their horses) - were lined up outside the gates of the Poorhouse. Stretched prone on each cart were old men and women in filthy rags who looked like they were already dead and younger people who were so weakened by fever and dysentery that they were even unable to raise themselves into a sitting position. These miserable creatures had requested that they be transported to the poorhouse where they might receive food, medical help or even be assigned a coffin or a grave. "Yes," one dying person had informed Madden in a weak and barely audible whisper – "to receive a coffin, sir… It is better to be waked and coffined in the Poorhouse than to have the dogs eat you in the ditch."

Aside from the impassive people lying on the carts, there were also crowds of people hunkered down outside the Poorhouse walls waiting to be called in. Inside the walls, the Poorhouse yard milled with people who shouted and pushed against one another every time the Poorhouse doors opened. The same people who had once been petrified of ending up in the Poorhouse were now practically beating the doors down in an effort to be admitted, now that they were reduced to eating the grass in the fields. Not only were these people skeletally thin but they also carried the stench of death.

Famine has its odours - rank and heavy - its loathsome mouse-like smell. You may scent its victims as you pass along the road where - in the ditches - they are huddled together, pining away…[409]

Those who were homeless died quickly once the cold and the rain took its toll. Despite their decrepit state, Madden was amazed how the sick and the dying showed no thirst for revenge against their colonial masters and were resigned to their fate – "O Merciful Mary", one woman said to him, "don't mourn the dead or the dying" The Son of God knows what is best for each of his children." He heard another elderly man whisper the following: "Let us forgive one another in the same way that we will soon seek forgiveness ourselves." Another woman tried to comfort her dying child with the following words – "You just wait and see child. The angels will transport you to the Heavens, my love, to a place where there is no longer any hunger or cold." The child couldn't stop crying however, and moaned – "I am too tired to travel there, mother; do you think the angels will carry me there?" Madden witnessed all of these unfortunate cases and he did what he could medically-speaking for the worst cases that he came across. Complete chaos reigned inside the front door of the Poorhouse where the Poorhouse administrators "tested" each of the new applicants to see whether they fulfilled the criteria for admission. Despite the chaotic scenes that surrounded them, the administrators were required to judge each individual applicant on his/her "merits" bearing in mind their duty to "balance the books." This decision involved taking into account the needs of each of these desperate applicants as set against the rights of local rate-payers whose rates supported the maintenance of the Poorhouse.

    Madden outlined the peculiar circumstances these poorhouse administrators now found themselves in as they tried to deal with hundreds of cases in as calm a manner as possible, while the crowds milled about them moaning and crying and beseeching that they be accepted as poorhouse residents. Madden recalled hearing the haunting voice of an eleven-year old child screaming out above the multitude and pleading with his mother not to abandon him there. "Oh, Mammy, mammy, don't leave me mammy, I won't stay here without you. Oh, Mammy, love, you wouldn't leave me in this place?"

Madden estimated that there were at least 1000 people gathered in the vicinity of the Poorhouse on that particular day with a total of 819 people securing admittance. Each widow with two or more children was allocated a handful of yellow meal. £7.7.3 or less than 3 and a ½ pence per person was the cost of this allocation or subsistence relief, as distributed to a total of 533 people on the day that Madden was in attendance. Those people unfortunate enough not to secure admittance to the Poorhouse had slept in the sheltered hedges that skirted the road outside in the shadow of the market-house. Madden's enquiries in Kilrush revealed that more than 5000 people in that vicinity alone were already residents of the Poorhouse by then or staying in the "temporary Poorhouses" that had sprung up within the vicinity of the "official" Poorhouse there.

The people were being admitted to these temporary poorhouses more quickly than they had been previously, a process made speedier by the fact that more people than ever were dying. One of the local authorities with whom Madden spoke stated that it cost an average of just eight pence to keep an adult alive for the duration of one week! This subsistence diet did not include any meat, vegetables or milk. Instead, the principal subsistence food consisted of black, hardened bread that was made from an inedible combination of barley and rye. The local doctor had requested that, at the very minimum, each of the poor be provided with milk as a preventative against disease and death. His words had gone unheeded however, and many people were dying even while in receipt of the bread ration.

While malnutrition was one of the primary causes of starvation and death, so too was disease as a consequence of the severely-crowded conditions people were now living in. Men, women and children who had come to the Poorhouse seeking admission were now crowded into whatever lodgings could be found for them and disease spread quickly as a consequence. In one local school which was doubling as a temporary Poorhouse, the children were indoors all day long except for a few minutes in the morning when they were allowed down to a small river at the rear of the school to wash their feet. Their sleeping quarters were very cramped with a low-hanging roof and the children slept three to a bed. Every morning two of the children carried those who had died the previous night outside, placed them in makeshift coffins and buried them in close-knit rows that bordered a deep hollow at a corner of the local graveyard. It was rare that a relative would ever attend the burial and when the disease and starvation reached its apex it became difficult to identify one body from another.

One would have imagined that Madden's first letter to the *Freeman's Journal*, in which he described the dreadful ravages of death and disease that he had witnessed, would have been enough to incite the authorities to take action against Madden in order to silence him. This was particularly true given that the editor of the *Freeman's Journal* stated it a pity that there were no other men like "X" in Ireland – men who were willing to truthfully describe what the Irish people were suffering in order to pressurise the "guardians" of society into taking immediate action. By the time Madden's sixth letter appeared in the *Freeman's Journal*, the government were very angry and it wasn't long before it had discovered who the "anonymous" letter-writer known as "X" really was. Madden soon received a letter from Under-Secretary Redington informing him that the Viceroy had heard that "an official with a connection to the Government" had been making enquiries regarding conditions in the Poorhouses of the Kilrush "Union" area.

A quick comparison between the short notes Madden had entered in the visitor's books of these Poorhouses and the letter published under the signature "X" in the *Freeman's Journal* indicated that the letter-writer was most probably one and the same person. The Viceroy was now asking through his intermediary - Redington - whether there was any truth in the rumour that Madden had undertaken an unofficial information-gathering exercise in the Kilrush poorhouses, while using his governmental and administrative post as a "cover."

If these facts were admitted, Madden would have acted improperly, first, in seeking information ostensibly as a person, "connected with the Government;" and secondly, while withholding it from the Government, in having communicated the result of his inquiries to the public through an anonymous communication to a public journal. Charges of a most serious nature had been made against the administration of the Poor Law, which, if communicated by Madden, should properly have been made to the Government in order that they might be examined and considered.[410]

Madden responded to Redington's enquiry by letter from his address in Rathmines. He admitted that he had visited the Kilrush Poorhouse in County Clare but stated that he had never once claimed that this visit was in any way official or Governmental in nature or that it had any connection with his work on the Loans Fund Board. If the Government so wished, Madden could provide proof of this as he still had a transcript of the letter with which he had introduced himself to one Poorhouse official he had spoken to while in Kilrush. If the Viceroy requested this transcript, Madden was quite prepared to supply it. Madden's letter continued as follows:

To the next point of enquiry, not in the way of any absurd bravado, but in a grave and sober spirit, I reply that the letters signed "X" which appeared in the Freeman's Journal of the 6th of March, etc., were written by me, and that I still respectfully adhere to the opinions and statements then published. I did not originally collect the information contained with the intention of publishing it; but when the facts stated connected with the Poor Law Management in Ireland came to my knowledge, I thought that the interests of humanity would be promoted by giving publicity to them.[411]

Madden was quite open about his intentions in making public the information he had gathered. He had been just about to publish the notes from his Kilrush visit in their entirety, but decided not to do so on receiving the Viceroy's letter.

And now that I am fully aware, as I regret I was not before, that the strictures in question might be regarded in a light I certainly never contemplated, I will take care to abstain from giving any publicity to them or any similar matters in future...[412]

Madden offered to present all of his notes relating to the Kilrush visit to the Viceroy:

...with infinitely more alacrity than I would give them to the press...Finally, sir, I would beg to have it stated to His Excellency that the subject of Poor Law Management in Ireland is one that I regard not as any political or polemical matter in the public discussion of which it may not now be permissible for me to take part, but as a great and urgent question of humanity from an interest in which none can be debarred. And hence I trust that even if I should have fallen into any technical contravention of official usage by my action in this matter, perhaps His Excellency will be pleased to think that this departure from routine procedure was of a character which anyone who had long been engaged in the cause of outraged humanity abroad, as I have been, might, under the present appalling circumstances here, very naturally fall into.[413]

The week following this correspondence, Redington requested that Madden forward his "Poorhouse notes" for examination by the Viceroy. Madden then sent the Viceroy a detailed statement regarding the Poorhouse conditions in the various County Clare districts he had visited and how the implementation of the Poor Law was (or was not) being implemented in that county. In his *Memoirs* Madden points out that a subsequent governmental enquiry into the matter simply confirmed much of what he had reported and when various measures were finally implemented to ease the starvation crisis, the result was an almost immediate improvement in mortality rates. No official sources survive to indicate whether Madden was investigated any further as to his "extracurricular" and "activist" activities although he did receive a firm "rap on the knuckles" from governmental sources at this time including:

> ...*a stern demand and warning to desist from further uncalled for interference with matters they deemed more prudent to have concealed than published. Nevertheless, although I knew only too well, and soon fully realised, the effects of my proceedings, as far as regarded my own prospects, now irretrievably ruined by my persistent exposure of Irish grievances, I would not be deterred in my efforts to seek some redress for the wrongs of my suffering fellow countrymen.*[414]

It may be significant that Madden never received any salary increase in his government-sponsored Loans Fund post subsequent to this incident, despite spending many long years in the post. The 300 pounds a year which he continued to receive was a much smaller amount than others received who were in similar-type Government jobs. There is no doubt that Madden did his best to help as many Irish people as he could during the Famine years. His wife Harriet often mentioned to her friends the lengths to which Madden's generosity extended for many years subsequent to the worst ravages of the Famine. He gave away any spare money he had to the poor, sold off any jewels or paintings which they possessed, and regularly donated whatever bedclothes and food was in the house to the many starving and dispossessed people who called on them. Harriet herself was also well-known for her generosity to the poor but even she found herself exhausted attempting to cope with the crowds of people seeking temporary accommodation whom Richard had brought back to their house while he attempted to secure new and more permanent lodgings for them. Madden was also particularly kind to the "remnants" of 1798 who were still living. He was particularly friendly with Anne Devlin[415] a woman who had been strikingly beautiful in her youth. She was a niece of Michael Dwyer[416] and her brother and a number of her cousins had been strong supporters of Robert Emmet. When Emmet first built his house in Butterfield Lane it functioned as an impromptu headquarters for both he and the other leaders of the 1803 rebellion. Anne Devlin's father had appointed her the unofficial "lady of the house" whose job it was to coordinate the movements of the rebels who came and went on a regular basis. In fact, it was to this very house that Emmet and a number of his supporters had first retreated when the 1803 rebellion failed. Anne Devlin had suffered as a consequence of her support for the rebels as she was tortured by yeomen who wished to find out where Emmet was hiding while he was "on the run." The yeomen had even attempted to bribe her into revealing Emmet's whereabouts. "And you accepted their money from them, of course?" Madden had joked, on first getting to know Devlin in 1842. "Take their money, is it? Robert's blood money. No chance. I threw it back in their faces", Devlin responded. In fact, she was imprisoned in Kilmainham Jail where she was left in solitary confinement for long periods in the hope that she would change tack and turn informer.

When Madden came to know her many decades later she was living in a converted horse's stable in St. John's Lane, Dublin and most of the local people were completely unaware of the pivotal role this elderly woman had once played in some of the most defining historical events of their native country. Although she was elderly, Anne Devlin had to work as a washerwoman to make ends meet and to support her family, which included her husband Campbell and a daughter who was still living with them. Madden realised on first meeting her what a mind of historical information Anne Devlin was and she was a big help to him when he was writing his "life" of Emmet. On one occasion she and Madden even visited the house in Butterfield Lane which had once been the unofficial headquarters of the Young Irelanders. It was only shortly after her death that

Brother Luke Cullen helped Madden research the pivotal role which Anne Devlin herself had played in the events relating to the 1803 Rebellion. Madden also learned of her personal bravery and the way she had staunchly stood by her man, Robert Emmet, both while he was "on the run" and while he was incarcerated in the weeks before his death. "The day will come", he said, "when the name of Anne Devlin…will be spoken of with feelings of kindness not unmixed with admiration."

As with many of the "background people" in the fight for freedom, Anne Devlin never received any recognition for the important role she had played in the Irish struggle. She was completely forgotten about when she grew old – except for the people like Madden who would visit her regularly each time he returned to Ireland. He often gave her some money to help her as she was in such straitened circumstances. As Devlin's living conditions worsened in her old age, Madden even organised a collection for her through the pages of the Nation – although this collection only brought in the fairly meagre sum of four pounds. Devlin's husband died and her sight severely declined so that she was almost blind. Devlin's daughter who was in very poor health was entirely reliant on whatever income her mother could earn. As the years passed Devlin's family became even poorer. She died in September, 1851 and was buried in the pauper's plot in Glasnevin. Unknown to most people, Madden paid to have Devlin re-interred in a better grave that was in the section of Glasnevin Cemetery where Daniel O'Connell is buried. He always had a Cross and an inscription erected above her grave.

Madden's spirits had risen initially when the movement for "Tenant's Rights" had gained traction in Ireland; he felt certain that it was an opportunity for the Protestants of Northern Ireland and the Catholics of the South to join forces around a common aim. His spirits must have been dashed later, however, when he heard about Lord Russell's letter of submission – "the Durham Letter" as it was known. The Catholic Church in Britain had changed the parish and diocesan system that it had operated in generations previous to this. Instead of functioning as bishops *in partibus infidelium,* as had been the case before, Catholic prelates were now given authority to direct only those Church affairs that were local and specific to them.

Long-engrained anti-Catholic prejudices raised their heads once again and anti-Papist rants became commonplace. Russell wrote a letter to the Bishop of Durham to coincide with Guy Fawkes Day where he accused the Pope of being an enemy of Britain. Russell also raised the old accusation that Catholics were a superstitious lot, and used this excuse to bring in the "Ecclesiastical Titles Bill." According to this legislative decree no Catholic Prelate would be permitted to hold any title, ecclesiastical or otherwise, anywhere within the jurisdiction of the United Kingdom. This move on the British Government's part angered the majority of the populace in Ireland and the spark of sectarian tension was ignited in a number of British cities where the Catholic, immigrant population was a large one. A large anti-Catholic riot took place in Stockport near Manchester in the north of England. The Catholic side of the divide decided to strengthen its position by making as many strategic links as it could with other "like-minded" bodies. The "Tenant Leaguers", under the stewardship of Gray, Gavan Duffy and Lucas soon joined forces with the Catholic Protection Association that had been formed by the Irish representatives of the Liberal Party in Westminister. This small group of politicians were nicknamed the "Irish Brigade" or the "Pope's band". This group had a certain amount of political clout since the then British Government was reliant on their votes to stay in office. Indeed, this group withdrew their support and the Government duly fell and a General Election was called for February, 1852.

This election had all the bearings of a religious crusade, of course. The clergy lobbied the people hard and it was primarily through their efforts that 48 new people were elected to parliament, the bulk of who were committed to maintaining a stance that was independent of the English government until the Irish people were given their civil rights. In fact, these Irish

MPs now held the balance of power in the new parliament now that Lord Stanley and the Tories were in office. One of the new breed of "independent" Irishmen who stood for election was Madden's nephew Willie Cogan from County Kildare. His election literature announced that not only was he against the Orangemen but that he also would have nothing to do with any Whig politicians either. He had hated all of the anti-Irish measures adopted by the previous government with a passion and had never accepted any of these measures as laid down by the previous incumbents to power. Strangely, no-one stood against Cogan in that election in Kildare; not that you would have thought that he had "the run of the town" on voting day in Naas, County Kildare, however. The British military presence was very heavy on General Election day by all accounts:

A squadron of the 7th Dragoon Guards patrolled the town; two companies of the 60th Rifles and a large posse of police filled the area in front of the Court House, and the galleries of the building, normally crammed by the electors of the county were crammed with policemen, armed with carbines. (Freeman's Journal)[417]

Given his job, Madden could not now be seen to have any overt involvement in public affairs, particularly if this involvement had any political implication. He remained involved on the periphery of the political scene nevertheless. We know that he spoke out against slavery in the company of John O'Connell at an Anti-Slavery Public meeting held in the Rotunda on a wintry night in February, 1853.[418] We know too that he was involved with the group over whom Lord Charlemont presided and whose aim was the erection of a memorial in honour of Thomas Moore. Madden's "behind the scenes" influence on public affairs can be felt on a number of other fronts also. In 1852, for example, he was in James Haughton's house in 35 Eccles Street, Dublin, for a committee meeting of the campaign to free William Smith O'Brien and his allies from prison, the men eventually being released in 1856. Smith O'Brien would later enjoy

Madden's "biography" of Robert Emmet while recuperating from his prison experiences. Madden's continued letters on the conditions he had witnessed in Kilrush increased public dissatisfaction with the government, and the "anonymous" verses he continued to publish must have been a source of ongoing satisfaction to him personally. Poems such as the verse below appeared frequently in print:

> *A cartload a day of the poorhouse dead,*
> *Is trundled away from the mansion dread,*
> *To the trench which yawns for the lowly slain*
> *In these swordless wars of a Whig campaign.*[419]

and the following:

> *… but hush!*
> *Oh, speak not of Christ and His*
> *Law in Kilrush!*[420]

Madden wrote the following "as directed" at the British Prime Minister himself:

> *Lord John Russell's gone to bed,*
> *Says the Shan Van Vocht;*
> *And he is dreaming of the dead,*
> *Says the Shan Van Vocht.*
>
> *He is troubled in his dreams*
> *With a famished people's dreams,*
> *And his brain with phantom teems,*
> *Says the Shan Van Vocht.*
>
> *They have laid our peasants low*
> *Says the Shan Van Vocht*
> *And they cared not for their woe,*
> *Says the Shan Van Vocht.*
> *But before the living God,*

They shall answer for their blood
And their pauper-killing code,
Says the Shan Van Vocht.[421]

By 1852, the Whigs had lost whatever semblance of respect they had previously held amongst Irish Nationalists, as indicated in the following excerpt from the *Nation*, published in February, 1852:

The most villainous administration that ever marred Irish affairs is hopelessly foundered. We thank God heartily for their downfall. Old and bitter enemies fill their places. But if it were Satan himself, instead of Scorpion Stanley, who became Premier of England, the change would be a welcome one for the Irish people.[422]

The government which followed the Whigs proved even more ruthless in relation to the quashing of Nationalist aspirations however. This government comprised a coalition of Liberals and the followers of Robert Peel[423] and included among its junior ministers, John Sadlier and William Keogh, two leaders of the Catholic Protection Association. At the time, it was commonly rumoured that the new Archbishop of Dublin, Cardinal Cullen and some leading members of the clergy had privately given their blessing to the involvement of these two leading Catholics in this government. Rumour had it that the Catholic hierarchy preferred that Keogh and Sadlier be involved with this government rather than other Catholics such as Gavan Duffy and Lucas - the latter was editor of the Catholic newspaper, the *Tablet* and had converted from Protestantism.

These latter men were mistakenly considered to be as anti-clerical as many Nationalist intellectuals on the Continent - or so rumour had it. Public disaffection with this perceived approach on the part of the Catholic hierarchy increased however when both Sadlier and Keogh were appointed to ministries in this government, appointments which led to a split in the Irish Independence Party. Worse was to follow for the Irish Nationalist cause, however. There was further upheaval when the Irish bishops fell out with those Nationalist leaders who had sympathy for the Catholic position. Those Irish Nationalists who had been ignored by the Catholic hierarchy found their leadership ranks decimated when Lucas died suddenly and Duffy emigrated to Australia, a country in which he would eventually be elected to the position of Prime Minister of the State of Victoria.

Political considerations and the usual broken promises aside, it made sense at this time for the British government to appoint Sadlier as Lord of the Treasury. Sadlier was extremely wealthy, albeit that he had allegedly gained the bulk of this money through "shady" dealings – i.e. appropriating the savings of thousands of County Tipperary farmers and shopkeepers who had deposited money in the bank he owned. It looked good - "on paper" at least - to appoint somebody who had been praised by the Irish Catholic bishops, who spoke up for Catholics in Westminster, and who had spent a good deal of his fortune on the set-up of the two Catholic newspapers then in Ireland - *The Daily Telegraph*[424] and *The Weekly Telegraph* newspapers which were under the patronage of the Cardinals of Dublin and Westminister respectively. These two newspapers were, of course, founded as competitors that would reduce the influence of the *Tablet* and the *Nation*. Madden's old school friend, Barney McCabe, was actually the editor of the *Daily Telegraph* and moved back to Ireland from England when the paper was set up there. McCabe, a decent man, would become depressed in later life having discovered that Sadlier had committed suicide and had also been defrauding the customers of his bank for decades. That Sadlier had been dishonest and a fraud for much of his life came as quite a shock to McCabe, who had placed Sadlier on a pedestal in his newspaper columns for many years, listing him alongside the Pope as the two great Church authorities Irish Catholics could look up to. The fact that Sadlier had ended his life on Hampstead Heath by ingesting poison was a sad and sordid reality that McCabe found difficult to accept.

Sadlier had exhibited a ruthless streak throughout his life however, even if he had managed to keep this side of his personality hidden from less-astute observers. Just two years prior to his death, he had managed to have an election opponent imprisoned on false pretences in the middle of the Irish General Election.

Sadlier was forced from office during that General Election but just a few weeks prior to his death, rumours began to circulate that his bank in Tipperary was on the point of collapse – this as a consequence of years of financial fraud and the mismanagement of funds. Even then, most people assumed that these rumours only referred to a minor financial hitch as between head office and the regional branches of the bank. It was only subsequent to Sadlier's death that the local people realised the full extent of the huge fraud which had taken place. It was then that the bank's customers came in from their rural villages only to find the doors of the Tipperary branch locked against them. Believing that the money was still hidden in the vaults of the bank, these unfortunate investors got picks and shovels and began digging their way into the bank - only to find that there was nothing there. A minor riot took place that evening in Tipperary town - but this wasn't the worst of it.

The Tipperary branch of Sadlier's bank had also held a good deal of the accounts of the "poor law unions." As all of this money had disappeared the unions were unable to feed the poor who were dependent on them for some time. Various railway companies, mortgage companies and other banks were also horrified to find that Sadlier's bank had collapsed and the losses soon totalled 1,250,000 pounds. Some of Sadlier's friends were also implicated in the fraudulent activities of the bank and these people left the country in a hurry before legal proceedings could be instigated against them. Sadlier's one-time parliamentary colleague William Keogh was not - initially at any rate - tainted by his friendship with Sadlier in any way. In 1855 he was appointed Ireland's Attorney-General. He was appointed a judge subsequent to his term as Attorney-General but after this his life took a downward spiral culminating in a death as sudden and tragic as Sadlier's.[425]

The *Weekly Telegraph* went into decline at this juncture too (the daily edition of the paper had ceased publishing at the beginning of 1853) and McCabe resigned from his editor's post. Newspapers such as the *Weekly Telegraph* hadn't succeeded in wiping out their competitors but the competition for market-share had left its mark on these other newspapers nevertheless. The *Nation*, for example, was edited initially by John Cashel Hoey and a few years later by the brothers, A.M. and T.D. Sullivan, and while it would always remain a paper that was political and radical in content, its tone was never as radical or anti-establishment afterwards as it had once been. It would consistently oppose the rise of secret organisations such as the Fenians for instance, this in spite of the fact that the general mood of the Irish people had shifted increasingly towards a more revolutionary stance. This change of mood had come about primarily because the Irish were now sick of the political trickery and accommodation of the likes of Sadlier and Keogh.

Madden himself seems to have become somewhat cynical and depressed with regard to the "National Question" at this time also. When asked to speak on behalf of election hopeful, Sir Campion Domville in April, 1857, he replied that - while he might have been personally well-disposed towards Domville - he preferred not to speak at such events anymore. Madden had seen so much abuse of the "token" Irish position in the British parliamentary system - much of it for personal gain - he had come to the conclusion that Ireland would be better-off without any representation at Westminister.[426]

> *It is better, I think, to be underrepresented than misrepresented. The legal candidates for posts of honour and preferment, aspiring young barristers devoted to the country and its creed while on the hustings, but who, once they enter Parliament, pursue their own aims and schemes and objects there...I have hitherto abstained from exercising the election franchise and voting for any candidate, Whig or Tory, and I see no reason to take another course now.*[427]

Madden also advised a friend who was interested in publishing his own memoirs "to show them to some friend, one in whose judgement, whose fidelity to you, sterling honesty and staunch devotion to Irish interests (he could rely) - not Whig interests, mind you, nor Tory interests." When Disraeli went forward for the General Election of 1861, Madden sent him a pamphlet on the history of the "Orange Institution" in Ireland and the legal status which had bolstered its position in Ireland through the generations.

The subject is worthy of your most anxious attention and affects the interests of your party most materially. The whole power of the Whig party in Ireland has its origin and being in the supposed connexion of your party with Orangeism, Disabuse the Roman Catholic people of Ireland promptly of that opinion...and you may count on their support at the next election...[427]

Disraeli seems to have ignored Madden's advice and the Whigs stayed in power until 1866, much to Madden's disgust. When his relative James Murphy invited Madden to holiday with him on the Continent, Madden refused, such was his despondency at the direction in which Ireland was being taken.

Don't talk to me of going to Italy, or Spain, or Switzerland. I have not fallen, but tumbled headlong down into the sere and yellow leaf of life. I will never go abroad again - except on one long journey which will be the last of a life of wanderings..."It's all mighty fine, Father Austin," as the sweep going to be hanged said to his spiritual comforter - my old friend Father Austin of John's Lane Friary - "for you to be talking to me all the joys of Paradise. I want to stay where I am." So do I, Master Jem. But take a hint, if you do go to foreign parts, come back speedily, for if you do not - and God in His wrath, for the punishment this unfortunate land of ours, should leave the Whigs much longer in office - perhaps you will not have a country to come to...In very sober sadness and seriousness, my strong conviction is that this country is going to utter ruin, and that a terrible policy is being pursued by our rulers...[428]

Unsurprisingly, Madden turned down all offers to stand for Parliament himself.

CHAPTER 13
MADDEN'S LITERARY CAREER TAKES A PROLIFIC TURN

The first decade he spent working for the Loan Funds Board saw Madden's literary output at its most prolific. He published two short books in 1852 and early the following year he wrote a two-volume scholarly tome of more than nine hundred pages in length - *The Life and Martyrdom of Savonarola* (1854). He was barely finished with this research when he started writing his detailed biography of Lady Blessington which he completed and published in 1855. This biography had only just gone to press when he began writing his own memoirs, a project which he never brought to fruition. He would later abandon his memoirs to research the phenomenon then referred to as the "phantasmata,"[429] and publish a book entitled *Phantasmata* in 1857.

Madden's interest in spirituality and Catholicism, in particular, never waned during these years of writing and publishing. July, 1854 saw him writing under a pen-name in the *Dublin Evening Post* and warning the newspaper's readers that many mobs of Orangemen were as out-of-control and violently anti-Catholic as ever, with Catholics still being murdered on a regular basis in Northern counties such as Tyrone and Antrim. In the following year he was writing under his own name for the *Freeman's Journal* and describing various attempts at the proselytism of "the pagans" - i.e. the Catholic Irish - which he had witnessed at the end of Dun Laoghaire pier in south County Dublin. These open-air sermons were - "a new apostle to the gentiles from the sister kingdom" and an insult to Catholicism and its clergy. The sermons were spoken by "a white-choked gentleman of an unwholesome aspect, a bilious temperament, strong in the lungs and uncomfortable in the spirit"; and Madden warned the Irish police to keep a close eye on these "itinerant fanatics and sanctimonious firebrands" before they began to harass local communities on a continual basis. Large chunks of Madden's tome on Savonarola took the form of long quotations, paragraphs as collated from other published and unpublished sources and then collected together.

While much of Madden's material for this book had previously been published in different forms and in a diverse range of sources, the writing of this book nevertheless took up a good deal of his time. Most of his sources were in foreign languages, Italian in particular, and Madden had to find all of these references, and then translate them, and organise them into a coherent structure. To the modern-day reader this book appears an indigestible and "heavy-read" but at the time of its publication the book sold well and even went into a second edition. Madden's dedication to Gladstone,[430] himself an author (he wrote a book entitled *The State in its Relations with the Church* (1838) and a member of the Liberal Party at this point in time, is an interesting aspect of this book. The Church/State nexus was the main theme which motivated Madden in this latest research. In one section of his book Madden compared the views of Gladstone and Savonarola on the best way to integrate Christian values with good government and the systems of the ruling class. What Madden was almost certainly not aware of at this point was the fact that Gladstone had changed his philosophical position as outlined in *The State in its Relations with the Church* (1838) quite soon after completing the book. At the time that Madden was compiling this book, Protestants generally claimed Savonarola as one of their own and as a pre-Lutheran visionary of sorts. This view of Savonarola also tended to find acceptance among Catholics of this era, many of whom considered Savonarola a schismatic, a heretic and someone who had fallen outside the Catholic fold. Madden's opinion of Savonarola was very different however. His researches led him to the conclusion that Savonarola was one of the leading thinkers of the 15th century and that he was actually one of the brightest jewels in the Catholic intellectual pantheon. Madden's musings on Savonarola's life led the *Quarterly Review*[431] to pose the following question:

> ...how far it would tax theological subtlety to reconcile the excommunication and murder of Savonarola by one infallible Pope and his canonization by another.[432]

The past century has tended to confirm Madden's view of Savonarola's seminal role in the development of Catholic social thought. Rudolfi who wrote a detailed biography of Savonarola[433] in 1959 admitted that he had been sceptical of his subject initially but had changed his mind over the course of time, eventually concluding that Savonarola was a leading visionary and thinker. A review of Rudolfi's book in the *Manchester Guardian*, immediately subsequent to its publication echoed similar sentiments.

> ...that reading the record of this passion, it is impossible not to sympathise with the widespread movement to have Savonarola officially canonized in Rome.[434]

The critics of the *Quarterly Review* went easy on Madden on this occasion as compared with some of his previous publications. While they praised his biography of Savonarola in general terms, they still found fault with him as relating to a number of minor textual errors. For instance, Madden had expressed his surprise that Savonarola's *Trionfo della Croce* (1901) had never been translated into English. The reviewers of the *Quarterly Review* had located an English translation which had been published in 1661, however. In the introduction to his next biographical work entitled *The Literary Life and Correspondence of the Countess of Blessington* (1855) Madden felt it necessary to "justify" the fact that Countess Blessington had selected him as her "official" biographer. Why had he been chosen as her biographer when there were so many other highly-qualified literary people who could have been chosen for this honour? Apparently, Countess Blessington's close friends had met up shortly after her death in order to select the most appropriate person to write her literary biography and had decided on Madden. Madden presumed that they had chosen him because he had been a close friend of hers from the earliest days of her literary career and the fact that she had always placed such trust in him both as an honourable man and as a friend. Other than Count D'Orsay, there was no-one who once had as close a friendship with Blessington as Madden had. She had related her life story to him in detail, on more than one occasion, and may have done so with half-an-eye on the possibility that it might one day see publication. Madden's biography was based on a combination of the Countess' private papers, his own reminiscences of her and any other information he could source.

The result was a somewhat bizarre and unevenly-written work, an enormous tome comprising three volumes and over 1500 pages. The book was far too long of course. Half a volume would have been more than enough to outline the main incidents in Countess Blessington's life. Its verbose style and content aside, Madden's book included much important information that would have been permanently lost if Madden hadn't undertaken the biography. His accounts of the various gentry who once visited Gore House are of much interest. Madden seems to have had a great deal of respect for Lord Brougham[435] who was a regular visitor to the house, partly because both men held similar opinions with regard to issues such as Catholic Emancipation[436] and the Slavery question. Madden also regarded Brougham as one of the leading intellectuals in the then British establishment. Madden's biography went into some detail on the manner whereby Countess Blessington had started out on her literary and editing work in 1832, the year when she experienced her first serious financial difficulties. Madden described Blessington as an "embarrassed elegant", someone who wrote prodigiously, producing much that was of poor quality in the process. Just after it was published, Madden described her first novel - *The Repealers* (1833) as the worst of all her literary works:

> From all Irish political novels, including *The Repealers* the English public may pray most earnestly to be delivered.[437]

Madden's biography of Lady Blessington sold well and even went into a second edition. Its popularity wasn't enough to save it from the knives of the more acerbic literary reviewers however. In addition to the criticisms of various literary reviewers, poet Walter Savage Landor[438] wrote to the *Athenaeum* to correct some references which had been attributed to him personally. Another writer and historian Edmund Lenthal Swift followed this with a letter to the same journal a fortnight later where he complained that a full five pages of Madden's biography covered the genealogy of his (the Swift) family, but that each of these pages was error-ridden.

> *My brother Dean Swift...did not quit Ireland in '98 without returning thither. On the contrary he "returned" in 1799, remained there several years, revisited it several times, and is now "to be heard of" at his residence in Dublin. It may be that his '98 politics were not unlike those which have since that period helped many an Irish patriot into place and preferment; but whatever they were, they did not "compromise" me either with a Protestant Government or with my comrades in*

"The Lawyers' Corps"...Finally I was not educated at Oxford: and I can confidently assure Dr. Madden, not only that I did not "die in my great trust about seven years ago," but that I am at this moment inter vivos, his and your very humble servant.[439]

The *Athenaeum Review*[440] (3 February, 1855) summed up Madden's biography of Countess Blessington in three terse words - "an embarrassing book." A review of the book by literary critic Michael Sadlier was shorter, but was equally as critical as the review which appeared in the *Athenaeum Review:*

The three volumes of this work are indispensable to any study of the life of Lady Blessington. Dr. Madden had all the documents and information available at the time, and undoubtedly set out to do the very best he could for a woman of whom he was genuinely fond. Unfortunately, the discretion necessary at the time he wrote and, even more disastrously, his own genius for disarrangement and prolixity, turned what should have been a treasure house of original material into a heart-breaking jumble of repetitions, irrelevancies, inaccuracies and self-contradictions.[441]

Madden had a habit of sending a copy of each book that he wrote to Sir James Stephen, who reciprocated his friendship and loyalty. As a friend of his, Stephen felt it his duty to provide Madden with his own personal "reviews" of his two most recent books - i.e. the Savonarola and Blessington biographies. Stephen told Madden that the Blessington book included a good deal of padding and gossipy, irrelevant-type material, but that this was to a certain extent unavoidable, given the very public social life that Countess Blessington had lived. She hadn't lived a life of sacrifice or heroism. Nor was much of what she had written of lasting value. While he didn't say it in as many words Stephen didn't consider that Madden's tome had been worth the enormous effort he had put into it. The move from the Savonarola book to the Blessington one had also been quite a leap in terms of subject matter, Stephen added. Only a Celt such as Madden could have had the audacity to jump from one subject to a completely unrelated one in the space of just a couple of weeks. Stephen also told Madden that he felt he hadn't really done justice to a subject and a personality as formidable as Savonarola.

Madden had indeed written a biography of Savonarola, Stephen explained, but the central figure in the biography had been somewhat obscured by a vast quantity of un-related and overly-verbose material. This additional material, while it provided an interesting description of the era in which Savonarola had lived, shed very little light on the man himself. A more appropriate biography would have been a much shorter book, a book which assumed that the reader already possessed a certain degree of background information on the society and background which had shaped Savonarola and his thinking. Stephen made one other very relevant point. Irrespective of the book's weaknesses, the truth was that the prejudiced society in which they then lived meant that a biography of a leading Roman Catholic figure - (even if it had been written by a literary biographer as renowned as Bossuet, for example)[442] – would never receive universal acceptance among the higher echelons of British and Anglo-Irish society. Stephen included his various opinions on the two biographies in a long letter he wrote to Madden, a letter which he composed when the Crimean War was the most common subject of conversation for many people in both Britain and Ireland:

> *One is hurried on with the current of events, like a moth feeding on the lining of a railway carriage on an express train, and as little able to arrest them. Meanwhile, both you and I have, of God's mercy, the direction of our pens...The newspapers say you are to have H. Newman among you as head of your new college - an excellent choice if learning, ability, vigour of mind, and exquisite power of language were the only essential qualifications.*[443]

While he may have meant well with his comments on the biographies, Stephen was essentially unable to view the issues of the day from a Catholic perspective - as indicated by the above quote. This is hardly surprising given that Stephen was a sincere and faithful Protestant, one who was proud of his place within the British establishment – at Cambridge University where he then held the Chair of Modern History. Stephen considered himself to be a broad-minded person, a liberal person given the social and religious divisions and constraints of his era. His opinion of himself has a certain grain of truth in it - especially if one considers that he regularly joked with Madden that he was willing to put up with him despite the fact that the Irishman was a Papist, a Jesuit and a bigot - all rolled into one!

We are travelling different roads under different guides, (he said to Madden). May it be to the same home, and then we shall understand these mysteries better.[444]

Stephen's description of Madden as a bigot was not the first time that the Irishman had been placed in this category. In 1847, the Vicomtesse de Fitz James had asked Madden to help raise financial subscriptions on behalf of a Protestant school whose pupils were educated free-of-charge. He sent the book of subscriptions back to her however, in addition to politely outlining the basis of Catholic belief. Any money the Catholics had, they needed to spend it on building their own schools, he explained. There were also other occasions when Madden had felt duty-bound to defend his own spiritual beliefs and Catholicism in general. In 1851, he attended a dinner in Blackrock, south Dublin, where the guests began to discuss the Cross of Cong[445] then in the possession of Lord Cloncurry.[446]

Cloncurry jokingly announced that he was thinking of constructing a shrine at the base of the Cross. A female guest then announced that she would never worship at the foot of any Holy Cross. Madden did not take these anti-Catholic jibes lying down and immediately responded to the woman who had made the comment about the Holy Cross, advising her that she could do a lot worse than pray at the foot of a Cross. As he had done many times previous to this, Madden decided to put pen to paper to explain his spiritual and philosophical beliefs. He wrote a letter to Cloncurry where he outlined his belief in the doctrines of Catholicism and explained the central theological tenets of Catholicism as clearly as he could. His father and mother had educated him in the precepts of the faith, Madden explained, and the truths they had inculcated in him were firmly imprinted on his soul. To denigrate Catholicism's traditional beliefs as was then fashionable in "high society" was a tragic and prejudiced attitude on the part of those same people who often claimed to be broadminded or liberal in outlook. While jokes incorporating religious prejudice might appear somewhat insignificant at first glance, they nevertheless had a serious affect on the wider Catholic population as regards their self-identity and their representation by others.

Madden was well-aware that many ordinary Catholics had been swayed by anti-Catholic propaganda to the effect that it was somehow unseemly for educated Catholics to follow more traditional rituals such as pilgrimages and prayers before icons and statues. This view had gained currency "since that ghostly statesman and spiritually-minded Minister, Lord John Russell, has denounced the practices of my Church as superstitious mummeries calculated to enslave the intellect and debase the soul." While the snide arrogance of the colonial elite with respect to Catholic practice did not embarrass him in any way, Madden considered the anti-Catholic bigotry of the Orange Order in a different category completely. The Orange Order were so prejudiced against Catholics that they even looked forward to inhabiting a section of Heaven that would be for them only, an area that would ensure their segregation from their fellow Christians i.e. the Catholics. You could not find anyone who was more tolerant of other religions than he himself was, Madden said. Some of his best friends were Protestants, he explained, and one of his own grandparents had been a Protestant and an Englishman to boot. Madden's wife Harriet, the mother of his own children was an Englishwoman who had been raised as a Protestant. Madden was indebted to a Protestant minister who had helped him gain an education when he was young and poor. There was no way that anybody could accuse him of being a bigot, Madden reiterated. In truth, his whole life was a testament to the importance of tolerance and the necessity to rid society of bigotry and prejudice of any form. Cloncurry's response to Madden was quite brief. He too had clung to his parents' views on religion for the best part of fifty years, Cloncurry explained, and he also had never changed those views. The most depressing thing about religion in Cloncurry's opinion was the manner in which God's gift to the world had been twisted by so many men so that it became a source of unhappiness and bigotry. Cloncurry then scurrilously implied that Madden had been party to deliberate prosleytism himself, a reference to the fact that Madden's wife Harriet had converted from Protestantism to Catholicism many years before.

This gave offence, (he said to the priest from his own parish). The next time I dined there a Protestant clergyman, the editor of an Orange newspaper, took occasion to condemn strongly Archbishop Cullen's doctrines. I expressed some doubt of the justice of that condemnation. The gentleman referred to the ultramontane dogma of the Catholic Church regarding the exclusive salvation of its members. I said I believed every tenet of the Roman Catholic Church, but did not believe that the particular tenet referred to was rightly interpreted by the gentleman who addressed me; that no enlightened Catholic believed, or was called on to believe, that those out of the Roman Catholic Church in what was called invincible ignorance of its truth, would not be judged by the law they were under the obligation of accepting...I saw there was a desire to misunderstand me. I ended the conversation by saying "I am acquainted with a Quaker in Birmingham. Wherever his spirit shall be in the other world, I would not be sorry to be in its company."[447]

Cloncurry's insinuation was a real "cheap shot", given that virtually all of the religious prosleytism then taking place in Ireland involved organised "conversion" campaigns on the part of various Protestant groups who were "targeting" Catholics. That Madden was acutely aware of this phenomenon is clear from his personal papers amongst which is a collection of memoranda and correspondence between a Catholic chaplain to Richmond Prison[448] and himself, where the continuous attempts of the prison officers to forcibly convert their Catholic prisoners was discussed at some length. Prosleytising groups were rife in the poorest districts of Ireland's major cities, where some Protestant sects - often referred to as "Soupers" mounted intense campaigns to "tempt" the poorer Irish away from Catholicism. Some Catholics changed their religious affiliation on a temporary basis returning to their original denominations when the immediate benefits of "conversion" had come to an end. William Le Fanu[449] recounted a somewhat bizarre anecdote concerning this phenomenon in his best-selling book about Irish life - *Seventy Years of Irish Life* (1893) where he described an elderly widow visiting the local Protestant Minister, and requesting that she be admitted into the Protestant Church.

"Sir, I would like to convert from Catholicism and become a Protestant," she said. "And why do you want to convert?" the minister asked her. "Well sir," she said, "I hear that you give everyone who converts a blanket and a leg of mutton." "Do you mean to tell me that you would sell your soul for a blanket?" the Minister asked incredulously. "Oh no, I wouldn't do that, sir. I would have to get the leg of mutton."[450] The minority of Catholics who converted to Protestantism at this juncture included such well-known public figures as the novelist William Carelton,[451] the two Mortimer brothers and Samuel O'Sullivan, all of whom became Protestant ministers. All of these individuals were very talented in their own right. Mortimer is remembered as the central protagonist in *Travels of an Irish Gentleman in search of a Religion* (1833) as written by Thomas Moore and the follow-up to this book - *Guide to an Irish Gentleman in search of a Religion.* Samuel O'Sullivan, the editor of the latter of these books was a regular contributor to the *Dublin University Magazine*[452] and it was he whom Madden suspected of writing a number of anonymous and very critical reviews of the *Lives of the United Irishmen,* which had appeared in that magazine. Not only did the O'Sullivans convert to Protestantism, they also joined the leading archaeologist, Reverend Caesar Otway and twelve other Protestant Ministers who would spend the next twenty years - i.e. from the period of Catholic Emancipation down to the 1860s - actively attempting to proselytize Catholics. They had huge financial resources to support them in this prosleytism drive, so much so that a Protestant lawyer from London once quipped that each individual soul converted from Protestantism to Catholicism must have cost the proselytisers in the region of 100,000 pounds! These Protestant sects were determined to "save" the Irish from Catholicism and the overtly-bigoted manner in which they discussed Catholics and Catholicism would shock most modern-day readers:

> *There sits the Pope (said the Reverend Alexander R. Pollock in a lecture in the Rotunda) in 1854, kept in his chair by a foreign force...a puppet, yet a Lord...the ruler and originator of world-wide movements the full extent of which I believe to be known to none but those ministers of secrecy and those agents of deadly plotting who hold their dark seats in the chambers of the holy office...Nevertheless if the pope were to go out unattended by soldiery for a single hour, he would be brought back to the Vatican assuredly a corpse...Adored as a God, he is yet the mark of a hundred murderous stilettos...Look at the broadcloth which adorns the priest's backs - why, the gloss of it is something to startle you on their approach. Look to the horses which they ride about the streets...the whole style of Romish ministers shows*

organisation. It shows that the enemy is marshalling...The chapels are now styled the "Parish Churches"...Dr. Cullen is "The Archbishop of Dublin." Dr. Cantwell won't pay the Income Tax except he is allowed to designate himself "the Bishop of Meath..." While Rome is growing in arrogance here, and gathering in some converts in another land, she is in reality gaining no strength...her losses in Ireland testify to the rottenness of her system when examined by the light of reason and scripture.[453]

The Rev. Pollock finished the above speech with two catchphrases - one for his flock - *No Dissension* - and one for the Catholics whom he hated - *No Surrender*. When contrasted with sentiments such as the above, Madden's defence of Catholicism in his correspondence with Cloncurry and others was so mild in tone, that it didn't even bear comparison. Along with the vast majority of Catholics in Ireland, Madden found an everyday existence as then circumscribed by the Protestant minority difficult to stomach. The winds of change were already beginning to blow, however.

By the 1850s Gladstone had already recognised that the attempts of the Church of Ireland to become Ireland's national (established) church had failed. There had been more Protestants in Ireland in the sixteenth century than there were now in the nineteenth century and these statistics spoke for themselves. Twenty years later Gladstone would "dis-establish" the Protestant Church of Ireland - in Ireland. Madden's medical qualifications were given further public acknowledgement in 1855 when he was elected a "fellow" of the Royal College of Surgeons in England. Six Fellows of the Royal College of Surgeons officially attested to the fact that Madden was a qualified physician with the highest moral and scientific credentials. On the surface of it, it seems a strange move on Madden's part to seek election as a Fellow at this stage of his life. He had practiced very little as a medical doctor during the course of his working career and the vast majority of his publications had no connection with the medical field. It seems likely that his real reason for seeking this fellowship was the fact that he had begun a new research project, a pseudo-scientific book he would entitle *Phantasmata* (1857). The medical qualifications "FRCS England" as listed after his name would appear much more authoritative on this book's front cover alongside his other qualifications. *Phantasma* was published on the first of January, 1857 by the publisher Newby.

As one had come to expect of Madden, it was a giant book comprising two volumes and over one thousand pages. The first volume included a discussion of some of the mental illnesses that were common throughout Europe between the fourteenth and the seventeenth centuries. It also discussed various aspects of astrology and some of the beliefs concerning evil spirits then common in both Britain, Ireland and on the Continent. Madden covered a range of subjects as relating to mysticism and theosophy including Swedenborg and his publications, the visions of Blessed Theresa[454] and various traditional aspects of Christianity as relating to Portugal and Spain. The final chapter of Vol. 1 was given over to the phenomenon then referred to as witchcraft monomania. The second volume of *Phantasmata* covered subjects as wide-ranging and diverse as epidemic monomania, Jansenism[455] and the "voices" which Joan of Arc had heard. Madden's analysis of Joan of Arc,[456] her saintliness and the unusual phenomena which she had claimed to experience led Madden to much the same conclusion as regards the verification of these phenomena - as the Catholic Church would decide upon many years later - and which led to the canonization of Joan of Arc.

> *Previously to her captivity, (he wrote), I am not aware of any marked peculiarity in her mental constitution which would lead to the conclusion that her agency might not have been within the scope of Divine Providence, for the accomplishment of a design whose aim was the deliverance of a nation from a foreign enemy, and the humiliation of its oppressors. To come*

to this conclusion, it is not necessary to believe that Jeanne D'Arc had daily intercourse with saints and angels. It is only essential to believe in the justice of that design, and being of such a kind that it appeared to have been promoted by her, that her motives and actions corresponded to the exalted mission persumed to have been assigned to her; that she believed in it; that the purity of her life was a guarantee for her integrity; and finally, that she performed acts which served to attest her pretensions to powers not ordinarily given to persons of her age, sex and condition.[457]

The late 1850s was a period when Madden was particularly consumed with medical and scientific subject matters but the source of his enquiries also had a strong personal dimension. His son Tom suffered from severe chest problems which were a frightening reminder to Madden of the tuberculosis which he himself had suffered as a child. In fact, his son had such difficulty with his breathing that Madden sent him to live in the warmer climate of the Continent for two winters in a row.

In February, 1858, Tom was living in Malaga, Spain, where he was visited by his cousin James Murphy, who was from Mount Merrion in Dublin. Madden's personal papers don't give any indication of how sick Tom was at this juncture but the very fact that his father turned to poetry to describe his feelings is probably indicative of the fact that the young man's parents were afraid that he might die. Madden also composed poetry at other "emotional" moments in his life, such as the time when their son Tom left the bosom of the family to begin his third-level studies in 1854.

On that occasion Madden also selected a small section of text from the Book of Tobias[458] which consoled him at this emotionally-charged time: "And the angel said to: I will watch over him now and bring him back safely to you once more." Madden composed a payer based on the above quotation:

Oh Jesus ever pitiful, to whom
The young, the simple and the poor are dear!
Jesus who condescended to become
Of such the friend and the companion here.
Give this dear child of ours we part with now
Some Guardian Spirit's guidance on his way
To shield his youth and innocence...[459]

    A short while prior to this, Madden had compiled a collection of poetry by a number of well-known authors, a collection which was published by Duffy after Madden's death. *In Memoriam* (nDé) included a short introductory note where Madden outlined how appropriate these poems were for anybody remembering those people who were close to them, and who had recently died. Twenty poems in the collection were written by Madden himself while a number of well-known contemporary poets wrote the remainder - including Mrs. Hemans, Gerald Griffin, Percy Bysshe Shelley, E.B. Browning and Madden's long-time friends Tom Campbell and Willie Beattie.

CHAPTER 14
THE SECOND EDITION OF THE *LIVES*

Ireland was in a very bad position, both socially and politically by the mid-point of the nineteenth century. Gavan Duffy had emigrated and Lucas was dead, while G.H. Moore had lost his seat in Parliament. The few politicians who purported to have an interest in Ireland tended to put their own personal interests and wealth first while the Irish "question" remained very low on their list of priorities. In 1858, a Conservative minority assumed control of the British Parliament and the Irish situation worsened. One by one, the Irish Parliamentary representatives gave their support to this new Conservative Government, after which they promptly split into two factions - those who were either for or against the Reform Bill. The Irish Independent party went into a decline while the Irish Republican Brotherhood[460] began to come to prominence. The aim of this group - known colloquially as the Fenians – was to instigate a revolution that would see the foundation of an independent Ireland, a republic independent of Britain. Some of the members of this new revolutionary group had been among the rebels who had fought in the failed rebellion of 1848. Prominent members of the Fenians included James Stephens Michael Doheny, Thomas Clarke Luby, John O'Mahony, John O'Leary and Charles Kickham.

Two former rebels whom the Fenians tried to "bring on board" in this new organisation but who declined to join were Meagher and D'Arcy McGee. Mitchell joined up reluctantly, although he had serious misgivings about the potential of this new group to instigate any radical change.

As long as England was at peace with other countries, both within its Empire and outside it, Mitchell thought Ireland had no chance of gaining its freedom. Mitchell was also somewhat suspicious of organisations like the Fenians, because he disapproved of the fact that all of its members were sworn to secrecy, himself included. D'Arcy McGee's objections to the Fenian Movement were more philosophical in nature. As with Gavan Duffy, his preference was for the path of constitutional nationalism rather than military rebellion. Meagher, for his part, had no objections to the principles of Fenianism or the concept of a secret society. The reason he didn't join up had more to do with personalities and the fact that he didn't get on with Stephens and a number of other senior members of the Movement. Smith O'Brien was another major political figure who did not embrace the Fenians. Having been released from prison, he began working at the *Nation* newspaper where he joined John Martin, P.J. Smyth and John Blake Dillon in objecting to the Fenians and what he perceived to be the dangerous and secretive nature of the new Movement. Despite the Fenian Movement's failure to attract all the members of the failed 1848 Rebellion into its fold and in spite of the Church's constant denunciation of the new Movement's aims, the Fenian Brotherhood spread rapidly throughout Ireland. Under Stephen's tutelage, the new Brotherhood evolved quickly along similar lines as the secret societies with whom Stephens had previously been involved on the Continent.

In reality, the Movement proved far from secret in its initial stages, however. In fact, the opposite was the case, and for a group purporting to be a secret society, it could be said that the Fenians suffered from "over-exposure" in its earliest days. The general public were awash with talk - some of it just rumour, but much of it accurate - regarding the new Movement. It wasn't long before all of this information officially found its way into the public domain through the medium of the newspapers. The newspapers of the day also gave considerable coverage to the speeches and activities of the Fenians in America, where the movement had some of its strongest support, both ideological and financial. In 1861 the Movement received an enormous symbolic boost when the body of Terence Bellew McManus[461] was brought home to Ireland. McManus, who died in prison in England was one of the leading revolutionaries of the 1848 Rebellion and had always been a firm believer in the use of military force to achieve Irish independence. His funeral was an enormous public event, this despite the fact that the then Archbishop of Dublin Cardinal Cullen[462] had refused to allow a funeral ceremony for McManus to be held in any Dublin church. In spite of this ban, at least 50,000 Fenians followed the cortege to the cemetery while a similar number of people lined the streets of Dublin to pay their respects. Talk of revolution and "taking the fight to the English" was in the air once more, as a new generation of Irish talked of throwing off the shackles of oppression once and for all. The U.S. was then witnessing its own bloody struggle with the American Civil War in full rein, and the Irish were observing developments in that country closely, courtesy of the regular "dispatches" that came back from the large Irish Diaspora that had emigrated to America both during and after the Famine. The Irish fought in large numbers on both sides during the American Civil War and many of those who survived were well-trained militarily by the time the conflict was over. This generation of newly-arrived Irish had bitter memories of the Ireland they had let behind, memories which included widespread starvation and the battering-rams of eviction. Many of these Irish-American soldiers and officers prayed that the American Civil War would finish sooner rather than later, so that they could amass a new military force which would return to Ireland and secure its freedom. Bizarre as it may seem to a modern-day reader, a large force of American-based Fenians actually attempted to initiate a take-over of Canada in May, 1866.[463]

The Fenian Movement in Ireland went from strength to strength until about 1864 when John Blake Dillon, a Nationalist figure who had been on the sidelines for a number of years, decided to found a new National organisation to pursue the route of Constitutional Nationalism as opposed to armed revolt and violence. Dillon's intention was to develop a new movement that would receive the blessing of the Irish Catholic hierarchy and work closely with the English Liberals. He had always objected in principle to the use of violence for the achievement of political ends and had vociferously opposed the failed rebellion of 1848, when preparations for this Rebellion had been at the planning stage. He had displayed his loyalty to the Nationalist endeavour of 1848 however by taking up arms with the other rebels and fighting alongside them in Killanaule.[464] Dillon's Nationalist credentials were enhanced further by the fact that he was forced into exile for eight years as a consequence of that rebellion. In reality Dillon faced a mammoth task in drumming up support for this new group - titled the National Association - given the fact that the Fenians were still very popular in Ireland and the bulk of the Irish populace were very cynical of the benefits which pursuing the political route (solely) could bring. They had already witnessed decades of political negotiation and trickery, all of which had achieved very little in terms of progress. Consequently, the Irish people were very sceptical of any possible political involvement with either the Whigs or the Liberals. Only one English member of parliament - John Bright[465] - seems to have been held in a certain esteem by the Irish populace at this juncture. This was partly because of the independent nature of Bright's political and personal views - but more importantly - because he had consistently displayed a strong empathy with the subjugated Irish. Sensing an opportunity, Dillon decided to invite Bright to a national meeting in Dublin, both to boost his newly-founded National Association and to garner support amongst those Irish impressed by Bright's credentials. The invitation to Bright was welcomed in most quarters. The Conservative newspapers, not unnaturally, were an exception to this. They took the cynical tactic of inciting the Fenians to "break up" this meeting, a ploy which the Fenians did not pursue. Ironically, Bright and a group of his supporters were physically attacked subsequent to a meeting for working-class men in the Mechanics Institute, but it was a group of Orangemen who were responsible for this attack.

The National Association's first national meeting was well-attended and a success, although Dillon tragically never lived to see it. He died suddenly of cholera only a few weeks prior to the meeting. His death was a big blow to the newly-formed National Association and to Madden who had always been a close friend of his. Madden had known Dillon from the earliest days of his political involvement. Theirs was a lifelong friendship that had cemented around the same time as the political meeting in the Phoenix Park where Dillon, Davis and Duffy decided to found what would become one of Ireland's most influential broadsheets ever - i.e. *The Nation*. Madden had been struck from the very beginning by Dillon's commitment to Ireland and the great energy he devoted himself to every cause which he threw himself into. From the very first occasion that he had heard Dillon speak at a meeting - a meeting organised by the Board of Works in Glasthule, south Dublin - Madden had been impressed by Dillon's noble demeanour and the confident and eloquent way in which he spoke. Madden had considered Dillon a courageous and refined individual, one who "had loved his country, if not wisely but too well." His commitment to the Irish cause had been put to the test on many occasions and he had suffered, both on the personal and the public levels, on behalf of his native country. Although forced to spend the best part of a decade in exile, he had yet returned to help the Irish cause in whatever way he could:

> I who long knew and loved and honoured him, saw him breathe his last with that emblem of salvation in his hand, the hope of which through Christ was in his heart. He was a man indeed

most worthy of being loved and honoured. He had the happiest combination of intellectual gifts, of social qualities, of manly, earnest, straight-forward views, of tolerant opinions, of kindly feelings, all the gentleness of a woman's nature in alliance with the firmness of a character constituted for the accomplishment of heroic purpose. He loved his country well, but he loved his religion better. He was a lawyer and a sound one, he was a liberal in the true sense of the word, but he did not think it ungenteel or unprofessional, or unworthy of acceptance in what is called good society, either Catholic or Protestant, to make any apologies for being, as the French say, foncierement Catholique. John Dillon thought it one of the greatest blessings of his life to possess a firm faith in all the doctrines of his Church...[466]

Madden's description of Dillon's personal traits were most likely a "template" of what he considered the exemplar of a "true" Irishman. It comes as no surprise to find that Madden was involved on the periphery of the National Association, as set up by his recently-deceased friend. Madden had made it his business to meet English MP John Bright when he had visited Dublin for the Association's first nationally-organised meeting. While in Dublin, Bright had stayed in the house of James Haughton in Eccles Street and it was here that Madden called to him on a number of occasions. The two men already knew one another quite well as they were both members of the Anti-Slavery Movement. 1865 saw a rebellion by the colonised population of Jamaica where large numbers of people were killed by the British authorities. The disturbances on the island were so violent that at one point there was talk of sending a Commissioner of Enquiry to the island to investigate the circumstances and causes of the Rebellion. Madden heard this and recommended himself as a potential candidate for such a post. After all, he already had previous experience of living in Jamaica and knew the island reasonably well, albeit that this knowledge had been gained many years previously. Madden made clear to Bright that he wasn't attempting to use his friendship with him as a lever with which to be appointed to such a position. If he was honest about it, he explained, the post with the Loans Fund Board which he had held for the previous fifteen years was a fairly "dead-end" job. He had little enough work to do in the job and the post held little importance in the greater scheme of things. The three hundred pounds which was being mooted as a salary for the proposed Commissioner of Enquiry would have been sufficient to satisfy a man such as himself, a man who was getting on in years and who had little in the way of career ambition left. The enquiry in Jamaica could probably be completed within the space of twelve months and there might be a possibility that his son would be permitted to take his place with the Loans Fund Board for this short period. Madden's son, Thomas More was twenty-seven years of age by then, and was highly-regarded as a doctor. Madden outlined this proposition of his in a letter to Bright and mentioned to him that he could pass this letter onto Lord John Russell if he saw fit to do so - "He is not without knowledge of me", he added. Madden's proposal did not lead to anything however. Thomas More's job prospects turned out better than Madden had anticipated when he had written that letter. Madden's son secured a job as Assistant Doctor in the Rotunda Hospital, Dublin and Madden also handed over the family home at 9 Great Denmark Street to Thomas before he and Harriet moved out to live in the suburbs outside of Dublin. Madden and Harriet settled in Blackrock, south county Dublin, in a house titled "Frascati" - a house that had once been owned by Lord Edward Fitzgerald.

In 1865 Madden moved onto another address at 1 Vico Terrace, Deilginis, before finally settling at 4 Ballygihen Avenue, Glasthule - also in south county Dublin. All three of these addresses had in common that they were in close proximity to a particularly scenic coastal area, on the edge of Dublin Bay. Moving from Dublin city centre had necessitated that Madden sell off another large batch of his books, and so, for the second time, a public auction was held where Madden's personal library was sold off, a sale which the *Freeman's Journal* [467] described as "the most remarkable sale of books that has taken place in Ireland for many years." Over 3500 books were listed on the sales catalogue including manuscripts and monographs as diverse as British secret service reports, collections of letters and the personal papers of some of the leading United Irishmen. Included too was the original typescript of a compilation of songs and music as written by George Moore, a compilation which had originally been sent to a publisher named Power. Also included amongst Madden's vast collection was "The Blessington Papers", a collection which wasn't sold on that particular occasion. Madden's personal papers indicate that he had made a number of attempts to set up a meeting with British MP, Bright during the 1860s, a meeting which never came to pass. Madden's intention had been to lobby Bright in order that the Englishman would sustain his interest in the Irish "question", this despite the vicious physical attack Bright had suffered in Dublin at the hands of a group of Orangemen in 1864. Madden corresponded with Bright by letter and apologised to him for the violence he had suffered while visiting Ireland for the meeting of the National Association. Bright could be forgiven for thinking that all of the Irish were uncivilised and out of control given the injuries he had sustained at the hands of this Orange mob.

    As Madden explained to Bright, the only excuse for such reprehensible behaviour was that it was a direct result of seven hundred years of British oppression and misrule. When a people were denied their freedom for so many centuries they were also stripped of a good deal of their human dignity and self-respect. The slave had no option but to resort to lies, flattery, dishonesty and treachery. Madden also advised Bright that it was time for the Church of Ireland to be dis-established as Ireland's "official" religion and that the "Land Question" needed to completely resolved in a manner that would see a cessation in the huge rates of eviction and emigration then prevalent in

Ireland. If an English parliament proved unable to resolve these questions, then an Irish Parliament would have to take the lead. The "Home Ruler" was breaking out in Madden once more! Political matters aside, Madden proved as tenacious as ever - (as *foncierement Catholique*) - in his defence of the rights of Catholics and the ongoing struggle against Protestant intolerance. His personal papers from this juncture include many examples of his personal and public defence of Catholicism. The following two examples relate to the 1860s but are typical of the type of letters Madden wrote. In 1862, a committee organised the erection of a memorial in honour of Daniel O'Connell in Ennis, County Clare but discovered that it had a surplus of money available for the project. A suggestion was then made that a "national" memorial be erected in memory of the "Liberator" in Dublin city centre instead.

Madden discussed this suggestion with Dr. Gray, the then editor of the *Freeman's Journal* and a group of O'Connell's old friends at a dinner organised by P.V. Fitzpatrick the chairman and treasurer of the Tribute Committee. Gray hurried back to his desk after the dinner to write a newspaper article announcing that any further subscriptions for the Ennis memorial would now go to fund the national memorial which still stands in Dublin city centre today. In the September, 1862, issue of the Freeman's Journal, Madden contributed an essay where he praised the political career of the "Liberator" - the man who had scrapped the Penal Laws from the Statute Books. Madden also opined that the Irish nation should ensure a statue of O'Connell begun by the well-known sculptor George Petrie many years before be completed, and that that it be erected in a prominent location as a further expression of respect on the part of the Irish people. Madden continued as an active member and fund-raiser for this Memorial Committee until its work was completed. He also kept a close eye on any public expressions of anti-Catholic bigotry then prevalent among members of the Royal Dublin Society - a society of which he himself was a member from the year 1853 onwards. This

Society's upper echelons comprised members of the Anglo-Irish Protestant Ascendancy, an elite group who had refused membership to the Catholic Archbishop of Dublin, Dr. Murray in the 1830's. Three decades on and the same prejudice was still firmly entrenched. This anti-Catholic atmosphere insured that the number of Catholics permitted membership of the Society be kept at just 10% of the total, while virtually all of the Society's senior positions and organising committees were occupied by members of the Protestant Ascendancy class. One issue relating to the Society which irked Madden was the "false" Sabbath which ensured that the Flower Gardens of the Royal Dublin Society remained closed to the public on the one day of the week that the ordinary people of Dublin could visit them for relaxation. By June, 1863, Madden saw no change occurring in the Society's attitudes and regulations and he resigned his membership, a fact which he publicly explained in an article published in the *Evening Post* of July, 1863. His son Thomas followed his example two years after this and also tendered his resignation from the Society. Thomas resigned in protest at the results of an election organised under a recently-revised Constitution of the Society which continued to sustain a system of political apartheid organised along religious lines. The departure of the Maddens meant that all seventeen of the remaining Society members were Protestant, only two of whom were Liberals.

    The questions of religious secrecy, nepotism and political chicanery were all subjects of much debate in British literary and intellectual circles at this juncture also. Charles Dicken's periodical *All the Year Round* included an essay in July, 1861, for example, confirming the *Monita Secreta Societatis Jesu* or the Secret Directives of the Jesuits, which had recently been published and made publicly-available for the first time in Paris. Of course, this wasn't the first time that the newspapers and periodicals of the day had been fascinated by aspects of the Monita. This latest essay claimed that on each occasion the Monita had previously been printed, the Jesuits had managed to get their hands on every print copy and hide it before the Monita became publicly knowledge. The essay also alleged that the president of each house of Jesuits was under strict instructions to keep this list under lock-and-key and to reveal its contents only to a very small number of other Jesuit priests. The Monita allegedly included instructions on how to court favour with royalty, important members of society, and even rich widows who might be recruited as supporters of the Jesuit Order. As always, Madden was quick into the breach and wrote a riposte to this essay which he sent to Dickens himself. His riposte included a list of facts which countered virtually every allegation the original essay had made, thereby proving that the essay was comprised of a melangé of stereotype, fantasy and hodge-podge – a melangé which Madden described as:

...collecting materials for a faithful history of a very memorable period in the annals of British imperial rule and for a record of some of the most remarkable men that Ireland ever produced.[468]

Madden felt certain that the essay had been published without Dicken's say-so, but as he explained to Dickens in his letter of protest - the very fact that the essay accused the Jesuit Order of crimes as serious as murder, lies, treachery and hypocrisy - meant that it was incumbent on Dickens to publish his letter. The periodical refused however and responded with the claim that there was nothing in Madden's letter that refuted the original essay's allegations. Neither did they wish to initiate a controversial and troublesome controversy in their letters' page, they added. Madden forwarded a copy of this correspondence to the *Dublin Review* a publication that were quite happy to publish his list of historical facts and which also supported Madden's viewpoint. The editors of the *Dublin Review* also pointed out that the response Madden had received from *All the Year Round* reflected badly not only on that periodical but on Dickens himself.

On his initial appointment to the Loans Fund Board many years before, Madden had made a conscious decision not to publish any further material relating to the United Irishmen for fear that it would cause him difficulties in his job. How he managed it is not entirely clear but Madden did succeed in publishing a second edition of the *Lives* – about 2500 pages in all! – between 1858 and 1860. Incredibly, he also managed to ensure the publication of this second edition without drawing the wrath of the authorities on himself. His interest in this turbulent period of Irish history had clearly never waned, as he, himself, duly acknowledged:

> ...collecting materials for a faithful history of a very memorable period in the annals of British imperial rule and for a record of some of the most remarkable men that Ireland ever produced.[469]

Most of the longest-surviving members of the United Irishmen were dead by the 1850s, the decade that Madden had quietly spent preparing this second edition of the book, a fact which had made it more difficult for Madden to gather useful material for this, the updated edition of the *Lives*. He had been extremely thorough in his search for sources however and had managed to unearth a good deal of new and valuable material for the purposes of this book. Included amongst these sources were the private papers of Major Sirr and Lord Cornwallis, acquisitions that enabled Madden flesh out the personal motives and strategies of many of the principal protagonists of his narrative. A good example of this process occurs in the volume relating to the life of Wolfe Tone where Madden recounts how Lord Kelwarden, the Senior Justice of the King's Bench, gave the order to arrest Sandys, - one of the three Wardens who had terrorised the population of Dublin in 1798 – because he had not submitted to the writ of *Habeas Corpus*.[470]

The bloodthirsty and undisciplined reign of terror Sandys had visited on the Irish of the final decades of the eighteenth century had always disgusted Madden and one senses a note of righteous indignation in his description of Sandy's last days on this earth. A man whose word had once been a source of fear and loathing now lay on his deathbed, sick, undignified, and abandoned even by his closest friends.

> He died in abject misery, squalor and most grevious suffering, about 1811, for several weeks previously to his decease hardly with the necessaries of life, deserted by all his friends, and...labouring under one of the most revolting cutaneous diseases to which humanity is liable...an example and a warning instance of the unerring aim and condign terrors of the Divine retribution, which those who enter on violent courses and inhuman procedures, however countenanced by authority, would do well to ponder on.[471]

Madden couldn't resist describing what he saw as the "Divine retribution" that had also been visited on Sandys sister, a "comeuppance" which he himself had witnessed one day in a Dublin street. A woman who had once been a "society beauty" and a leading socialite of the colonial ruling class had found herself reduced to beggary in old age. Madden had seen her swathed in a tattered old black dress while she sat on the steps outside a house in Dublin's Great Charles Street, begging for alms. Madden had initially been too frightened to consider producing a second edition of the Lives, especially since he feared the possible loss of his job with the Loans Fund Board. Ironically, it was that same job that enabled him to view documents that he would otherwise never have had access to. In actual fact, his friends and contacts in the Civil Service were able to provide him with copies of private papers, which he would never have been able to access if he had still been a cog in the public service apparatus himself. He managed to draw on sources as diverse as handwritten documents relating to pension entitlements for both the Civil Service and in relation to various leading political figures. He also somehow got access to a good deal of documentation relating to the British Secret Services, documentation that was normally kept under lock-and-key in the library of the Secretary-General, in Dublin Castle. From today's perspective, it seems quite amazing how Madden managed to secure access to such sensitive documentation. This documentation enabled him to make public a good deal of confidential information that proved embarrassing to the Ascendancy ruling class of his day. For example, he was able to demonstrate the way in which the owners of the *Freeman's Journal* - the Harvey family, a member of whom had been married to Henry Grattan – received a regular pension from the British government. This money wasn't "blood money" technically-speaking, as Madden explained. Rather, they were payments designed to keep one newspaper in business while destroying others.

In addition to his writing Madden kept up his work on the humanitarian front, whenever it possible. At one point, he wrote a letter to the British Prime Minister Lord Derby - the man who had given him his first job as a justice of the peace, in Jamaica – requesting clemency for two Fenians – Thomas F. Burke and John McCafferty who had been sentenced to death for their part in the Fenian rebellion.

The remission of that awful penalty would tend to promote the true and permanent interests of the Imperial government in Ireland and the higher interests of justice, mercy and humanity and, not least, the high estimation in which the best of English sovereigns, our present gracious Queen, is held.

Other letters appealing for clemency (including one written by Madden's friend and fellow-abolitionist James Houghton) were also written to the British government on behalf of these two condemned Irishmen at this point. A delegation of well-known people also visited the Viceroy arguing the case for the two Fenians. Irish primate Cardinal Cullen also appealed for clemency and the death-penalty was eventually rescinded for both men. In September, 1867, Madden similarly wrote to Disraeli asking for a reprieve from the death penalty for Allen, Larkin, O'Brien, Maguire and Condon. He requested that his views on the "the impolicy and inexpediency of carrying out the death sentences" be taken on board, explaining that:

These are solemn truths soberly considered by one who has no sympathy with Fenians or Fenianism, no object to promote, no interest to serve, save the objects and interests of justice and humanity.

Apart from such humanitarian concerns, Madden continued the "double-game" he had played for many decades. At the same time as he was appeasing those whose loyalty was to the English Crown, he was simultaneously hunting the records that would undermine the history of the Colonial government's rule in Ireland. In 1866 Madden purchased a batch of private papers sent to one-time Viceroy Lord Carlisle[472] by people who had claimed that Carlisle owed them political "favours." Madden tracked this collection of letters to a clothes shop in Cork where the shopkeeper, named Mrs. Kelly, sold them to him for the enormous sum of thirty shillings. This file of letters had at one time been in the possession of John Hatchell who had been Private Secretary to the Viceroy for Ireland between the years 1863 and 1864. Just a few years after this, Hatchell, who was by then living on the Continent, had been instructed to give up his house in Dublin and he sent a message to his auctioneer to sell off the house's furniture and contents. Hatchell had obviously forgotten about these letters and would have been quite shocked if he had heard that the same letters had ended up in Madden's possession.[473]

Madden continued to be as prolific as ever in terms of his writing and he would publish three more books before the 1860s were out - i.e. *Irish Periodical Literature* (1867); *Galileo and the Inquisition* (1863) and *Exposure of Literary Frauds and Forgeries Concocted in Ireland* (1866). *Irish Periodical Literature*

(1867) was a book that he had spent a full five years preparing and he dedicated it to Gladstone because of "the earnest disposition uniformly manifested by him to promote the interests of Ireland." The timing of this book's dedication was quite appropriate given that Gladstone was then on the point of dis-establishing the Protestant Church in Ireland. This book provides an introduction to the various types of newspapers and periodicals that were published in Ireland between the end of the seventeenth century and the middle of the nineteenth century as well as a range of biographical notes concerning the various editors and columnists who wrote for these publications. As with previous publications by Madden, the book was quite a weighty tome, albeit that the information it contained was organised in a reasonably coherent and logical fashion. Madden did include a somewhat long-winded introduction - (a full 82 pages long!) - to the book - where he gave an overview of England's dealings in Ireland during the previous few centuries. Madden also included a good number of appendices to the book many of which appeared to be as unconnected with the main subject matter of the book as ever! One appendix, for example, discussed the inscription on the tombstone of Francis Higgins[474] the infamous spy, an inscription which Madden described as "something unequalled in the history of sepulchral literature."[474b] The Higgins, this inscription referred to had been, in Madden's view:

> ...one of the quaintest scoundrels in Irish history, a man who could betray human beings with facility and boast that, when his Government-subsidised paper died, it would not be of dullness.[475]

The book *Galileo and the Inquisition* (1863) published by two Catholic publishers - one based in London and one in Dublin - was in some ways an "apologia" for the Catholic Church and a response to a number of published essays by two medical doctors - Sir. Benjamin C. Brodie and T. J. Pettigrew - where they were critical of the Catholic Church. These essays claimed that the Catholic Church was against science and was so blind to the potential of modern science that no intelligent person could realistically be a believer in Catholicism. Brodie claimed that the Catholic Church had tortured Galileo because he had made public a verifiable scientific fact while Pettigrew alleged that the Church was attempting to suppress medical knowledge and that the institution refused to give her blessing to its practitioners and researchers. While Madden's book didn't respond to Pettigrew's claims to any substantial extent, he did take up on Brodie's allegation. Madden argued that Catholic Cardinals and Popes had, in fact, accepted the theory regarding the circular nature of the earth and its neighbouring planets a long time before Galileo's announced his theory publicly. It was also an exaggeration to allege that Galileo had been tortured, Madden claimed.

In truth, Galileo's "punishment" had only consisted of a few weeks confinement in a comfortable house where he was instructed to pray the Penitential Psalms. Brodie had claimed that Galileo remained unsurpassed as a scientist, a fact which made the Catholic Church's "censorship" of his views even more scandalous. Madden countered this claim by arguing that it was Galileo's pride that had first initiated the difficulties between himself and the Inquisition. Galileo had refused outright to accept the theory which Copernicus had willingly agreed to many years before. Instead, Galileo had begun analysing the question of the earth's rotation from a Scriptural point of view and had made a dogmatic controversy out of something which was simply an accepted opinion as relating to the Natural Law. According to Madden, it was Galileo who had instigated the controversy and the tension with the Inquisition and not the other way around. Madden only assigned a very brief portion of his book to the controversial Galileo "question." The remainder of the book was taken up with diverse subjects as relating to religion, politics and cultural affairs. He was as staunch as ever in his defence of Catholicism and the one controversial issue which he dealt with in some detail was the Inquisition and the documentary evidence that existed relating to this dark period in the Church's history. The Vatican was regularly criticised in this era for its refusal to publicly release its archive of documents relating to the Inquisition. Madden argued however that it might not have been possible for the Vatican to release the documents relating to this historical period since many of these documents weren't in the Church's possession anyway. Ironically many of these documents were now held in various parts of the world by members of the British colonial establishment! In 1862, for example, Madden had himself examined 55 volumes of these bound (quarto) papers and 12 (unbound) volumes as held in Trinity College Dublin. The French too had taken some of the documents relating to the Inquisition when they were in the Roman archives in 1798, although some of these documents were later returned in 1846. Just three years later the French (or the Garibaldis) had plundered the archive in Rome again, however.

There is no property in umbrellas, books and pamphlets, and a great number of persons who would not like to be called thieves act on that notion.[476]

An Irish (Protestant) minister, the Reverend Richard Gibbings had bought a large number of these Roman documents while living on the Continent, documents which he later re-sold to Trinity College Dublin. Madden had had an opportunity to view these documents courtesy of the Irish Antiquarian Doctor Todd. There were no papers relating to the Galileo case amongst these documents but Madden's investigations revealed the manner whereby "the plundered archives" had been misquoted and deliberately manipulated when previously in the possession of Gibbings to incite anti-Catholic sentiment. Gibbings virulent anti-Catholicism had led him to write three books which purported to be based on these documents, but which were really a selective manipulation of the sources.

Gibbings first book was titled *Were Heretics ever burned alive at Rome?* (1852) while the sub-heading to his second book was the longwinded - *The Case of a Minorite Friar who was sentenced by Saint Charles Borromeo to be walled up, and who, having escaped, was burned in effigy* (1853). Gibbings had deliberately mis-translated and mis-interpreted the facts in each of these three publications so as to further his own agenda, Madden claimed.

As an example of such mis-interpretation, Madden had given the following sentence instructing that the accused as charged by the Inquisition's jurors be subject to a detailed cross-examination *al rigoroso essame* had been deliberately mis-translated by Gibbings to read as follows: - "should be subjected to an examination by torture,"a torture which Gibbings further interpreted as signifying "torture with whips." Gibbings account of a Minorite friar who was accused of heresy was another questionable account which Madden identified. The friar's punishment had involved being kept imprisoned or "walled-up" in a place where he had to repent of his sins and where he could confess to his sins once each week. Unsurprisingly, Madden pointed out the incongruity between being apparently "walled up" and the possibility of attending Confession with a priest. As regards Pietro Carnesecchi, his punishment - as assigned to the Roman Governor for implementation - was termed "due chastisement" - with the provision that none of the prisoner's blood was spilt and that there was no danger of death.

The Inquisition's documents never mentioned what form of "chastisement" the Governor had decided upon in the end yet Gibbings had interpreted this punishment as indicating that Carnescchi had been burnt alive! Madden returned to the Galileo "question" as an aside at this juncture and pointed out that Catholics were under no obligation to defend the "case" that had been taken against Galileo, for the simple reason that there was no substantial "issue" worthy of debate.

I know full well they would never have been adopted by the Pontiff, Urban VIII, if they had not been forced upon him... [477]

Galileo's critics had consisted primarily of mathematicians and those religious who believed his theory contradicted the Scriptures. The Church had never made any public pronouncement condemning Galileo's theory - of this Madden was absolutely certain. The Inquisition had undoubtedly discussed the Galileo "question" but the Inquisition had also been mistaken in many of its judgements and Catholics were under no obligation to accept the veracity of any judgement as pronounced by the Inquisition. The third book which Madden published during this decade (the 1860's) dealt with a completely different religious topic. Books such as *The Moral Sayings and Prophecies of Saint Colmcille* (n.d.), publications purporting to describe the visions of Saint Patrick and Saint Brigid and the prophecies (Coiril mhic Croineain and Ultan of Leitrim - (whoever these characters were!) - had proved incredibly successful amongst gullible (or poorly educated) sections of the Irish Catholic population in previous decades.

Madden set out to prove that many of these popular titles comprised a melangé of unproven myth and superstition. Many of the aforementioned books had acquired a stamp of legitimacy because of the claim that Irish scholars extracted this material from ancient manuscripts after which it was translated into English by churchmen such as the Reverend M. Taafe. Madden did the public a service therefore when he highlighted the superstitious claptrap that formed the basis of much of these publications and refuted many of the claims that passed as "fact" in these same publications. Madden's criticism of these publications came in the form of a series of essays entitled *Exposure of Literary Frauds and Forgeries concocted in Ireland*, published in 1866.

As an example of the way this superstitious nonsense infiltrated the public domain Madden referred to a series of letters which had passed between his old friend Barney McCabe, the then editor of the *Dublin Weekly Telegraph* and Nicholas O'Kearney the author of a "silly" collection of poems that were published in 1856. As part of this correspondence O'Kearney had given a ridiculous but funny account of the manner in which the fairies had taught him to read Irish -(albeit that O'Kearney had been quite serious about his claim at the time!). While Madden didn't speak or read Irish himself he had close friends who did and with whom he could verify any material that was in the Irish language. Despite his linguistic abilities and literary interests, there is no indication that Madden ever made any attempt to learn Irish although he once told a journalist[478] that he would gladly abandon all the other European languages he was fluent in, if only he could read and speak the Irish language. Madden was well-acquainted with a number of the leading Irish-language scholars of his era including John O'Donovan, George Petrie, William Reeves and Eoghan O'Curry -all of whom he knew through their association with the Royal Irish Academy. These scholars helped Madden with any material that he needed to have translated from Irish into English. Madden was particularly friendly with O'Donovan who was not in the best of health by then and was attempting the difficult task of editing the Brehon Laws[479] for publication in a modern format. Despite their close friendship, O'Donovan and Madden still had their disagreements, disagreements that may have had their roots in the similarities of temperament as much as anything else.

O'Donovan was as honest and "direct" an individual as Madden - when the moment required. Madden and he discussed the relative merits of *The Book of O'Hara* O'Donovan dismissed one of the poems in the book i.e. *Eire Nocht* (Éire this night) as a "recent forgery" and a poem that was "absurd, barefacedly silly, impertinently spurious and unworthy of credit." The poem's translator explained that five of the poem's quatrains referred to subjects as "wide-ranging" and apparently "unconnected" as the Protestant clergy who held control over Catholic church buildings, railway carriages, the Irish political scene subsequent to Daniel O'Connell's death and even the temperance work of Father Theobald Matthew. Despite his reservations about reproductions of publications such as *The Book of O'Hara*, O'Donovan, as with other Irish language scholars of this era, was reluctant to be drawn into any public controversy on such issues. Such a low-key approach was anathema to Madden of course, a man who was never shy to voice his disapproval of anything which he thought might promote superstition or weaken people's religious faith in any way. In Madden's view, the *Book of O'Hara* was simply:

> ...a farrago of absurdities conglomerated without connexion, order, or arrangement, concocted for sordid persons who speculate with no less audacity than success on the ignorance they cater for, and impiously assign their fabrications to an origin that for them has nothing sacred or saintly in it.

Books such as this simply pandered to superstition and hocus-pocus, and while the prophecies the book cited were undoubtedly "favourable" to Catholics, the compiler and publishers of such books really only had one thought in mind i.e. making money.

> ...as a Roman Catholic, who loved truth better than any paltry temporary advantage gained by practising on the credulity of any portion of my co-religionists, to expose the delusion.

The same year as Madden voiced his reservations about such publications, Cardinal Cullen made a public pronouncement warning his flock to be discerning about such books and to be alert:

> ...against certain superstitions and prayers...and also against so-called prophecies, which have been foolishly attributed to the illustrious St. Columbkille, though they are the invention of later years.[480]

CHAPTER 15
THE END OF THE ROAD

Madden felt very unwell at the beginning of 1869. He took to his bed unsure as to whether he would ever be well enough to leave it again. W.J. Fitzgerald informed Madden's other friends that the chronicler or United Irishmen was very weak and was unlikely to live much longer. Fitzpatrick also made the following assessment of Madden's work, an assessment that was only slightly effusive, if the truth be told – "One rarely finds a talent for painstaking accuracy and enquiry combined with such a vigorous style of composition. Dr. Madden possesses the former gift but is sadly deficient in the latter"[481] Madden rallied however, and it wasn't too long before he was back on his feet again. He had become increasingly frail and had given up any writing or research which was overly-demanding or which might sap his energies. Like many elderly people, Madden found himself reminiscing on the past a good deal at this juncture and considering the hopes and dreams of his own generation and the generation which had preceded his, sometimes in the form of poetry Had anything really changed in Ireland during the course of his own lifetime? Had the Act of Union made any significant difference to the hopes and dreams of his father's generation, for example? Madden's personal papers as relating to this time indicate that he was remembering all his forebears and friends in turn. In his mind's eye he was back again in the year 1815 and recalling his relatives and their opinions regarding what the then proposed Act of Union might herald for the Ireland of that period.

Among the people he imagined debating the terms and conditions of this proposed political development were his father, Edward Madden, the hotelier Johnny Power, former hawker John Corrigan, Jimmy Griffin (the man they had nicknamed "Hopper"), little sulky Con Crotty, John Tolerton, the good-humoured chemist Dr. Brady, Keogh, the coffin-maker from Cooke Street – and many others. Where were the dreams of all of these people now? Had any of their hopes for the Ireland they loved been fulfilled yet?

Age and infirmity did little to hinder Madden's productivity with respect to literary and cultural matters. At the end of 1869 he oversaw the handover of Tom Moore's personal library which was presented to the Royal Irish Academy (RIA)[482] by the well-known publisher Thomas Newby. Madden had always enjoyed the environment that was the R.I.A. and the intellectual camaraderie that went with it. He became increasingly disillusioned with the ethos of the R.I.A. and some of its leading members as he great older, however. He considered some of them to have had more interest in their own political and social standing than they did in anything relating to Irish culture.

Madden indicated to the Academy that he wished to resign his membership and only changed his mind when Samuel Ferguson asked him to reconsider. Madden seems to have had a great deal of respect for Ferguson as indicated by the following:

Dearest friend, Madden said, I have held you in high esteem for many years and my respect for you is of such a longstanding nature that I will not refuse your advice in this matter. I will do whatever you recommend as the best course of action.[483]

Madden also attended the meetings of the Todd Memorial Committee at this juncture and was part of a delegation which visited the newly-appointed Irish Viceroy, Earl Spencer. He doesn't seem to have been invited to the levée, although his son Tom, who was one of Dublin's most highly-regarded medical doctors by now, did attend. The following year saw Tom involved in a scheme to build ambulances - later donated to France to help their wounded in the then war between Germany and France. The French government would later present Tom with an honorary award for this work, an award that Madden senior was particularly proud of, given the long association between his family and France. Madden's health was quite poor again in 1870. His mortality looming, he was keen to finish his autobiography and told one of his relatives that he would finish it if he lived for two more years.

Incredible as it may seem, Madden would live for a further sixteen years and yet he never did get to complete that autobiography of his. In addition to his autobiography, Madden had many other concerns at this juncture. He was still working as normal in his post based in Dublin Castle but because he wasn't entitled to any pension the Loans Fund Board found it difficult to request that he retire from this position. Madden also badly needed the 300 pounds a year he earned, an annual income that had remained unchanged for many years at this stage. Despite his age, Madden was still more than capable of completing his daily work as the job had become less busy over the years. In fact, the most difficult aspect of his job was the daily trek to and fro between his house and Dublin city. In 1868 he rented a house on Vernon Terrace, at the end of Booterstown Avenue. From this house he could see the railway station, Howth Head and the Irish Sea. His next-door neighbour was Thomas Scratton, Secretary to the Catholic University, a man who had moved to Dublin to work under Newman's tutelage. Madden remained an enthusiastic traveller despite his advancing years and used the Irish railway system a good deal as indicated by the following anecdotes.

One winter's day I was in a second-class carriage train in the company of two other people. Opposite me sat a vivacious and somewhat-aggressive widow while right next to me was a former British Army officer who had spent a good deal of his career in East India. This man initiated a discussion on the customs of the Orient. I had a heavy cold on that particular day and pulled down the carriage window which was closest to me. The widow pulled the window down again immediately however and gave me a dirty look when I began coughing. When I noticed what kind of a mood the widow was in, I turned to the retired military man beside me. "I spent a good deal of time in the Orient myself", I said to this man. "There is one custom they practice in India, which I approve of myself. This is the custom of burning the widow.[484] *Without glancing at myself or the ex-soldier, the widow murmured to herself – "That is one of the most brutal things I've ever heard about."*[485]

This second story is included in the *Memoirs* and Leon Ó Broin also heard it from Kate Leech, the landlady of the Vernon Terrace property when Ó Broin was living in Madden's former house. Mrs. Leech remembered seeing the elderly Madden and his wife Harriet walking arm-in-arm to Mass when they were still living there. She also remembered that the house was full-to-overflowing with papers, paintings and books and that Madden's poor wife Harriet was tormented with the large amount of items her husband continued to collect. Not only were the rooms bursting at the seams with books and papers but even the stairs was dangerous to negotiate given the amount of papers placed there. There was so little space left in the house at one stage that Madden had to play tricks on his family to "smuggle" any new books into the house. He would have any new purchases delivered to a local rail station. As soon as they arrived at the rail station and his wife had left the house Madden would stand out on the front steps and wave to one of the porters at the rail station, thereby indicating that it was safe for the porter to deliver the books to him.

> *Five hundred times at least, I've said -*
> *My wife assures me - I would never*
> *Buy more old books: yet lists are made,*
> *And shelves are burdened more than ever.*
>
> *Ah that our wives could only see*
> *How well the money is invested*
> *In these old books, which seem to be*
> *By them, alas, so much detested!*
>
> *'Tis better in the past to live*
> *Than grovel in the past lively,*
> *In clubs and cliques, where placemen thrive,*
> *And faction hums, and drones rank highly*

Madden remained as firm as ever in his convictions and beliefs. He admired the alcohol abstinence campaigns of both James Haughton and well-known Carmelite Father Spratt greatly. Alcohol and violence/war – these were the two questions which continued to exercise Madden greatly and which he considered most responsible for the misery of the world as it was then.

He was as active as ever in the promotion of Irish or Nationalist-related scholarship. He gave strong encouragement to Sir Samuel Fergsuon[486] when he hesitated regarding the publication of his *Lays of the Western Gael* (1888). Ferguson was nervous that there was too much of a political slant to his poetry.

> I was greatly afraid, when you read those poems to me, that you might be deterred from publishing them. For your sake, but above all, my dear Ferguson, for the sake of this dear land of ours, under all its miseries so deserving of all our love

and of all that we can do for its honour, I rejoice in the publication of them.[487]

On the other hand Sir. J. Bernard Burke, the Ulster King of Arms approached him asking to borrow a copy of a thesis and some papers referring to various State trials. Madden refused, in a strongly-worded letter of reply. He suspected that Burke was really attempting to borrow these items on behalf of J.A. Froude[488] who was then writing a history of Ireland. Burke's brief reply to Madden's "outburst" was conciliatory and indicates that Madden's suspicions were probably correct.

I need hardly tell you there is no tract or trial in my possession that is not at your service. But for the use or service of the man James Anthony Froude, the eulogist of the monster Henry VIII, the champion of his hard-hearted daughter Queen Elizabeth, the reckless defamer of the unfortunate Queen Mary of Scotland, the very recent proclaimer of the inexpediency of any measures of conciliation in favour of Catholic Ireland - I have no tracts, trials or information. I have never read any historical works of a man so perverted in mind, so utterly regardless of truth in dealing with historic facts, as the author of the History of England...I look upon him as so unscrupulous an opponent of all that is worthy of praise or pity in those who have suffered for it, that I could not bring myself to aid or assist him in any of his pursuits.[489]

If he was mistaken in his hunch that the requested papers were for Froude, Madden said that he apologized for his abruptness or candour. The response that he received from Burke indicates that Madden's hunch was almost certainly a correct one.

My dear Madden, I honour and respect your motives. You are, and have ever been, an honest politician, a staunch patriot, and what I value especially, a kind-hearted friend.[490]

Madden continued his "behind the scenes" lobbying for the cause of Irish independence until his very last days. His personal papers at this juncture show him writing to leading intellectuals such as Sir William Wilde to argue the Nationalist viewpoint with regard to the Irish "question." Madden told Wilde that it suited Britain well to keep the Irish people divided along religious lines, a division that ensured they didn't unite against the real enemy.

> *I am an old man now, and cannot hope to see an Irish parliament; nevertheless I feel convinced that in a not very distant day my native land shall be again as:*
>
> *Great, glorious and free,*
> *Fairest flower of the earth, brightest gem of the sea.*[491]

The final decade of Madden's life did see more discussion of the notion of a "home" (Irish Parliament), than at any other period during the course of Madden's long life. While the deaths of the "Manchester Martyrs"[492] and other Irish rebels, generated huge Irish Nationalist sentiment and forced Gladstone to give serious consideration to the Irish "Question", it wasn't enough to signal any radical change in British colonial policy as relating to Ireland.

The Manchester Martyrs "controversy" had been a catalyst for the arrival of a young Protestant landlord named Charles Stewart Parnell on the Irish political scene at the same time as the elderly Tory lawyer Isaac Butt took control of the Home Rule Association. When Butt died in 1879, Parnell became the leader of what was titled the "New Departure", an alliance of both radical and conservative elements that saw in the hardships of rural Ireland a wonderful opportunity to achieve the aims of the Irish National Land League. The essential aims of this League were twofold – to put an end to excessive rents and to transfer ownership of Irish land from the landlords to the cottiers. Christmas 1885 saw a General Election in Ireland, after which Parnell assumed control of the House of Representatives.

Gladstone saw this as the moment to initiate some political change in Ireland and he introduced a Home Rule Bill in April, 1886, just a few short months after Madden's death. Some of the Liberal elements in the Government rebelled against the proposed Bill and thereby ensured its failure. The fact that the Bill was mooted in the first place had signalled a seminal shift in British policy towards Ireland, however, and it was now only a matter of time before some form of self-government was permitted in Ireland.

Despite these advances in relation to the Irish "question" it is interesting that Madden found it increasingly difficult during his last years to convince all of his family of the merits of the Irish Nationalist position. While Madden and his nephew Willie Cogan were good friends right up until the doctor's death, for example, they no longer saw "eye-to-eye" politically anymore. When the controversy over the "Land Question" erupted, Cogan's political popularity declined sharply and he lost his Westminster seat to a member of Parnell's Party. Cogan then retired from public life, to all intents and purposes. His appearance one day on the rostrum at a Unionist political rally in Leinster House, a rally which denounced the very possibility of any secession between Ireland and England, demonstrated how far from Madden's Nationalist position Cogan had travelled. His last years saw Madden as eager as ever to bring souls to the Church. Christmas, 1870 saw him writing to his old friend Willie Beattie to discuss the merits of a religious book which Madden was himself particularly fond of.

> *I haven't forgotten,* (Madden said), *that I spotted a copy of Thomas á Kempis' great oeuvre on the shelf in your house. You offered to give me that book as a present but I refused at the time – without ever explaining why I'd refused. I'll explain myself now and I'll mention something else which is close to my heart while I'm on the subject, a matter I won't ever raise again. I refused to accept a copy of "The Imitation of Christ" on that occasion because the thought came into my mind that*

one day this might be of great interest to my dear friend Beattie and might bring him closer to the faith of the book's author. From that time onwards, not one Sunday went by that I didn't say a prayer at the Holy Sacrifice of the Mass that my good friend would join me in the Roman Catholic fold. I trust you won't be annoyed with my comments here, and to be perfectly honest Beattie, it wouldn't bother me if you were annoyed with me...!

Beattie died in 1875, without ever taking the spiritual step which Madden had hoped for. Whether a crippling financial setback he had suffered not long before his death had anything to do Beattie's passing, we will never know. An insurance company with which Madden had saved the huge sum of 7000 pounds collapsed and its investors – including Beattie, Madden and others – were "cleaned out." Beattie never told his friends anything about what had happened although he had to cut down on the grants he donated to various charities so that his annual donations came to the sum-total of 300 pounds. Right until the end, Madden was quick into the breach if he felt the Catholic Church was being unjustly attacked. The year 1873 found him protesting by letter regarding an advertisement in the Dublin-based newspaper *The Irish Times* for a forthcoming lecture entitled "The Decline of Popery in Italy; Bablylon, Ancient and Modern; and the God of Rome Eaten by Rats." Advertisements such as these emanated from a place Madden referred to as:

That cobweb-covered, dingy-looking emporium in D'Olier Street, better known as the Bethel, sacred to tract-selling and Cant.[493]

Madden was also, at this point, seeking a publisher for a book about the Jesuits he had initially begun writing a full thirty years prior to this when he was living in Portugal. The principal subject of this book was his attempt to trace the decline of this once-powerful religious order in Europe. Madden's researches amongst the primary sources in the various Continental libraries (e.g. in Lisbon, Paris) revealed to him the extent to which the aristocracy of countries such as Portugal had been persecuted (and sometimes killed) because of their association with the Jesuits. This scenario had unfolded in Portugal, for example, where the Jesuits, and those members of the aristocracy who were perceived to be supporters of theirs, were put to death, for attempting to remove Don Joseph, the King of Portugal from his throne. Madden had put this project and the research papers he had gathered all those years ago on the "back-burner." More recent events had made the subject relevant again, however. Madden had heard about the anti-Jesuit campaign which was then being waged in Prussia, a campaign which had also received the backing of 22 members of twenty-two members of the British House of Representatives in Westminster, in addition to a number of elected Lords.

More disturbing than this again was the fact that the British government had promised to bring in a proposal at its next parliamentary session recommending that all religious orders be removed from both Britain and France in accordance with the provisions of the Emancipation Act, 1829. Madden was hopeful therefore that his book would highlight those attributes of the Jesuit Order which promoted organization, truth and faith. He was honest enough to admit that he, himself, had not personally been very sympathetic to the Jesuits at the outset of his researches. His sympathies had lain more with the spiritual vision of Pascal[494], particularly his *Lettres Provinciales*,[495] a work which he had initially had a huge admiration for. The many hours he had spent tracing the history and development of the Jesuits had changed his mind however. His initial suspicions regarding their alleged propensity for temporal power and their perceived "worldly" motives had now been allayed. Madden dedicated this latest book to a Jesuit friend of his, Father Joseph Lentaigne and to the London-based publishing company which published the fruits of his various researches. His dedication included the following words.

> I compromise no truth in the vindication of much calumniated Jesuit Order.[496]

Despite his advancing years, this book was as monumental a work as any of Madden's previous publications. The book was more than 1000 (royal octavo) pages in length and Madden himself arranged to buy fifty pounds-worth of the books, copies to distribute amongst his closest friends. The first sixty pages of the book had already been printed when a row took place between Madden and the publishers. Printing was suspended and the book would never actually see the light of day in published form. In fact, the manuscript of this book would be sold in its entirety only at the auction of Madden's effects, an auction which took place after his death. Madden's longevity – as compared with many of his peers – meant that he found himself increasingly isolated in his old age. His personal papers for 1873 indicate his happiness on receiving a visit from one of his friends from the old days, a man who had also been granted the robust health that ensures longevity. Charles J. Matthews was still "incredibly youthful-looking" (Ó Broin, 352) and they spent the day relating past events and discussing people who were long dead. The day after his visit, Madden sent Matthews a copy of a letter that he had written to Count D'Orsay in Naples many years earlier – on one of those occasions that Madden had found himself "mediating" in some personal dispute or other. Madden's letter recalled some of the correspondence he had had with Lady Blessington over the years and concluded as follows:

> I will make another attempt, (he said), to see you before you start, for I greatly fear I may never again have that pleasure. Out of my own family there are not many I entertain the same

strong feeling of regard for that I do for you. And now don't get into a passion with me my old friend when I remind you we are both men on the verge of eternity and it behoves us both to bestow, not a little, but a great deal of our leisure time and thoughts on Eternity, of which hitherto both you and I have thought too little.

Madden's personal papers for the late 1870s see him recording the increased infirmity that accompanied his old age in addition to various aspects of Irish current affairs which then grabbed his attention. He noted with interest, for instance, a newspaper report concerning a man named Edward Burn Madden, who had been charged with threatening to assassinate the English Queen. He also remained in contact with his friend Barney McCabe, and both men swapped "stories" on the various ailments that now afflicted them in their old age – as indicated by this extract from one of McCabe's letters:

To the frost, my rheumatism and my bad sight have confined me to the house ever since I called upon you. I am afraid to stir as long as the paths are slippery...I send on the next page some doggerel. Perhaps you may guess upon whom or on what occasion it was written.[497]

Madden's reply to McCabe describes the bouts of gout and lumbago he regularly suffered. His declining energy meant that he had been forced to give up his literary work and his book-collecting activities. Madden was always kind to anybody who had fallen on hard times. He used his influence to help out some of his neighbours including the widow and daughters of the novelist Michael Banim[498] who had suffered many financial difficulties subsequent to the novelist's death. Poor health had forced Banim to give up his position as postmaster for Kilkenny, an appointment which the Earl of Carlisle had originally arranged for him. Banim and his family moved to Booterstown to live on an allowance from the Royal Literary Fund, but he died there just a year later. He got to know Madden well prior to his death, the Maddens regularly inviting the Banims to dinner in their house. It upset Madden to see how poor the Banim family became after Michael Banim's death and he used his "contacts" to secure a Civil List Pension from Disraeli[499] on behalf of Mrs. Banim when her huband Michael pre-deceased her. Madden's "connection" in the Government who helped him arrange this matter was the Undersecretary T. H. Burke, an official who would later be stabbed to death by *The Invincibles*.[500] Banim's family were very fond of Madden and considered him a very accomplished individual – in addition to being a well-travelled person and a leading writer.

In 1880, Madden added to his long list of cultural accomplishments when he was elected to the Society for the Preservation of the Irish Language, founded just three years earlier. May, 1880 saw him retiring from his job with the Loans Fund Board, a job which he had held since 1850. The *Freeman's Journal* of the twentieth of March, 1880 explained the reasons for his retirement as twofold – his long years of service and the heavy workload which had now become a burden to him, given his age. Madden's innate honesty precluded him from drawing down a salary for work that he was no longer able to complete. He was now 82 years of age, a milestone that saw him receive a retirement gratuity of 1200 pounds, a payment that was spread out over the four years following his retirement. Ironically, Madden would only live four years longer anyway. He had always held to the philosophy of earning his living *sudor mentis*, as he would say himself and now that this was no longer possible, he felt it time to relax and spend more time on spiritual matters. His personal papers for the last few years of his life note him resolving to devote more time to prayer and devotional work. He now also had more freedom to read the huge quantity of books that were piled from floor to ceiling in his house. While he always welcomed any of his friends with open arms, he preferred to pass his time in the company of his wife Harriet, their children, and their grandchildren. Madden seems to have had a particular way with children who reciprocated his kindness and when his-seven-year-old granddaughter Beda (the daughter of Madden's son Tom) - a girl Tom referred to as "our dear little angel child"[500] - died in June, 1882, it was as much a blow to her grandfather as it was to her parents. In the midst of this tragedy, Madden found consolation in the words of faith Beda herself had uttered shortly before her death – "Goodbye…I am gong to God."[501] Madden also records that he found solace in the words of the Psalmist: *For though I should walk in the midst of the shadow of death I will fear no evil, for thou art with me.* Madden also occasionally turned to poetry as came closer to the last months of his life, composing verses such as the following:

> *Come to me, my good God, in mercy's guise.*
> *To soothe and comfort, gladden these dim eyes,*
> *With the bright vision of Thy Glory, Lord,*
> *Revealed in Christ, in Him to be adored.*[502]

An essay published in the *Freeman's Journal* on the occasion of his retirement highlighted how Madden's gentle nature and kindness had made him a respected friend to many. The *Journal* expressed the hope that when the Viceroy came to fill the position (in the Loans Fund Board) that Madden had vacated, he would appoint a worthy successor who would do his best to promote Irish interests in the same way that had Madden had done. A man named John Norwood was appointed as Madden's replacement and when Norwood died in 1884, the job went to a man named P.J. Smyth, a man who died suddenly after just a few weeks in the job. This Smyth was the same "Nicaragua Smyth" whom John Mitchell made reference to in his *Jail Journal* (1913). As Mitchell himself admitted it was a sad end to Smyth's struggles in the cause of Irish freedom that he found himself forced to accept a government job as a consequence of his family's straightened circumstances. As he said at the time:

> *Poor as I was, surrounded by difficulty as I am, had I but*

myself to think of, I would have sunk into my grave officeless. All that I once had has been sunk for Ireland. I do not regret it. As I have loved my country, so to her I freely and willingly and un-grudgingly gave my all. I have accepted this appointment for the sake of my wife and children, who are dear to me. I harness myself for their sakes, so let a generous people judge me.[503]

In the summer of 1880 a man named Doctor T.A. Emmet, a grand-nephew of Robert Addis Emmet and Thomas Addis Emmet, arrived in Dublin to research a book about the United Irishmen and (particularly) the role played by his own relatives in the Movement. He was keen to meet Madden, having corresponded with him by letter for many years. Madden, for his part, tried to help the American doctor in whatever way he could, this despite the fact that his memory was not what it had once been. Madden proved very helpful to Dr. T.A. Emmet in his genealogical researches and brought the American to visit many of the places which had a particular association with the younger doctor's famous forebears.

The local authorities became suspicious of this illustriously-named American and his intentions and Emmet soon found himself being tailed by the police. When he attempted to take a photo of the court-room in Green Street where Robert Emmet had given his famous speech from the dock, the police prevented the American from doing so. Madden advised him to return again on a Sunday when the police presence was likely to be less-organized – something which the American duly did. He then slipped the doorman a sovereign and took the photo he needed.

For several days, (Emmet later wrote), I had taken Doctor Madden out in an open landeau, with the photographer and instruments upon the box alongside the driver. I, as usual, was under police observation, but Doctor Madden, who had resided out of the city for some years, and the photographer were too much for them, and as they could not determine what devilry or treason I was up to, I was advised to leave next day.

Dr. T. A. Emmet would afterwards recall two memories of his research with Madden in Ireland, both of which had made a lasting impression on him. The first was the unfortunate damage that had been done to the death masks of the rebel leaders executed after the 1798 Rebellion. Madden had purchased a good number of these masks which had been made by the well-known sculptor George Petrie[504] immediately after the executions, many years prior to this.

These masks had been kept in a stables behind Madden's house but one rainy day when he was at a loose end, his manservant had decided to pass the time by applying white paint to these dark-looking death-masks! The second abiding memory of Dr. Emmet's was his final farewell to Madden. He would later recall his last glance at this "poor old gentleman" who had tears in his eyes and the words – "I fear we shall never meet again" - on his lips. Despite his great age and his infirmity, the American Emmet would later say that he had never met anyone that made such a lasting impression on him as Madden did.[506] On the twenty-fifth of October, 1882, Madden sent his last letter to his son Tom, who had a house in Merrion Square and who was by then one of Dublin's best-known medical surgeons. His handwriting was weak but still very legible.

> I am a troublesome old father to you. The bath chair has just come to hand. It is the very thing I wanted...Since I first spoke to you about getting one for me my loss of power in the lower left limb has greatly increased and become evidently and obviously an evil never to be got rid of. So I must never expect to be able to surmount it without the use of the chair moved by a manservant...I have not the slightest expectation of ever recovering the use of my right leg again. The disease is obviously extending from the right kidney to the joint of the

right thigh. And that it is incurable I have no doubt. So God's will be done and borne with as patiently as it can be...

Madden rallied once more and was soon able to do without the wheelchair. In January, 1886, he suffered another serious "turn", however, one from which he would never fully recover.

Your father is quite unable to walk, (Harriet said to Tom). He was near falling down yesterday with pain and weakness. He is taking very little to eat - yet was angry when the man and I and the servants said it was impossible for him to go to Church...Where is the merlin chair that we had years ago?[507]

Tom bought a special chair and had it delivered to Booterstown but Madden refused to leave his bedroom or make use of the chair. Madden's wife Harriet wrote as follows to her son on the Wednesday, the day following the delivery of the chair.

On my return home today I found that your father had just got to bed. The poor man fell off his chair having insisted on the man rolling up a rug and putting it behind his back. (I suppose thinking it would relieve the pains in the loins he was suffering from.) The great roll of rug filled up the chair...and a slight movement of course caused his fall in his very enfeebled state. You may fancy there was no little difficulty in raising him from the floor and he went at once to bed...He had a couple of hours sleep afterwards, but is very feverish since he woke...[508]

Harriet continued to send messages and telegrams into Tom who lived in the centre of Dublin. By Friday Madden was "a little easier but wandering" and the next day the doctor told Harriet:

...that your father seemed less suffering but much weaker than yesterday...the nurse has been out from eleven and not returned...perhaps she won't come back. She ought not to

stay out when she engages to attend a very sick person. Father Gaussen called to see your Father. He is a good priest...I am something better, will not go out...tomorrow...Doctor said no immediate danger but no one could say positively.[509]

By the following Monday afternoon:

...the doctor saw your father. The poor man would not allow him to examine him so he could do nothing for him.[510]

Madden doesn't seem to have seen "eye-to-eye" with the local doctor and he refused to listen even when the local priest – a Father Gaussen – explained that this doctor was equally as good as Sir Francis Cruise, a doctor with whom he had been acquainted for many years. In addition to being his family doctor for many years, this Sir Francis Cruise shared similar cultural and spiritual interests with Madden. He was an acknowledged expert, for instance, on the well-known spiritual book *The Imitation of Christ* (1639)[511]

The family eventually found it easier to send for Cruise who pronounced Madden's condition as very weak. Cruise informed both Harriet and Madden's manservant Edward that he was now in a very poor state both mentally and physically and was unlikely to live very much longer. Cruise also told Harriet that he would speak to her son Tom concerning the drawing up of a certificate which would confirm that Madden was no longer capable of arranging his financial affairs or signing official documents. Father Gaussen came into the room then and said that he would administer the Last Rites to Madden as soon as Tom was informed of his father's condition. A letter written by Harriet at this juncture indicates that everyone in the family was doing whatever they could to bring comfort and solace to the dying Madden.

May the good God relieve him and give us the grace to do our best for the poor sufferer and grant him and us all the grace of *a happy death and everlasting bliss...*[512]

The fact that the weather was particularly bad at this juncture only added to Harriet's worries. Lizzie Cogan came out from Dublin city to visit her uncle and fell awkwardly in the snow while stepping from the tram, an accident which made Harriet increasingly worried about Tom's regular journeys from Dublin city centre. Lizzie Cogan was shocked at the deterioration in her uncle's health as compared with the last time she had seen him. Madden himself knew that the end wasn't far off and told Lizzie as much. He told her that he would never see her again and said his goodbyes to her before she left his sick-room. Madden seems to have made one final rally as indicated by the next batch of telegrams sent by Harriet to Tom. The doctor had seen a small improvement in Madden's condition and announced that he was now likely to live for another few days.

The Thursday of that week was a peaceful one with Madden's breathing improving slightly. He died the next day, however – on Friday the fifth of February, 1886. His funeral took place on the following Tuesday and he was buried in the old cemetery in Donnybrook after Requiem Mass in Booterstown parish church. His funeral was a very large one with the cortege over a mile long. No major political figures of the era attended although this wasn't surprising given that Madden had outlived almost all of his own contemporaries. The end of that decade would see people beginning to acknowledge Madden's seminal role as a catalyst for research into the 1798 era, in particular.

The 1898 commemorations of the 1798 rebellion brought Madden's name into the public sphere once more and the seventh of February, 1898 saw a big crowd in attendance at Madden's grave. This crowd, the majority of them young men, laid wreaths and floral tributes on Madden's grave. Some of these same young men would later be active in the national uprising of 1916. The men represented many different local and regional Nationalist groups, all of whom were titled with the same names that had littered Madden's voluminous historical works. Representatives of the following groups were recorded as being in attendance that day by the *Daily Independent* of the ninth of February, 1898 – Wolfe Tone, Michael Dwyer, Lord Edward Fitzgerald, Oliver Bond, James Orr, Napper Tandy and the Sheares brothers to name but a few. Madden was buried in his family's grave beneath the cypress trees which he himself had transplanted from Napoleon's grave in San Helena, a full forty years earlier.[513] The following words which Madden had chosen and dictated in his will were inscribed on his grave – "A Man who loved his Country."

Two years after Madden's death, his wife Harriet also passed away and she was buried next to him. While Harriet had remained in the background throughout most of Madden's "public" career, she had always been his most loyal friend and supporter. She had backed him through every controversy and difficulty he had encountered during the course of his "often-turbulent" political life. In addition to this, Harriet had made no small contribution to his prodigious literary and historical output. In addition to looking after their children she had re-written literally millions of words for Madden's various publications. Apart to having "the patience of a saint" she was widely-acknowledged as someone whose kindness to rich and poor was legendary. Harriet remained mentally lucid until the very last moments of her life.

The *London Times* gave an accurate account of Richard Madden's life in its obituary page with no trace of hyperbole. Of all the books he had written the *Times* correspondent praised *The Life and Martyrdom of Savonarola* (1854) for its style and historical interest and *The Connexion of the Kingdom of Ireland and the Crown of England* (1845) as historical research that was as useful a tool then as it had been when first published. *The Irish Times* included an article praising Madden's role as a public servant, his literary accomplishments, and his expertise as a book collector. The *Freeman's Journal* had a long essay highlighting the "rigid and unscrupulous straightforwardness of his work on behalf of enslaved black peoples" and also referred to his political courage in circumstances where he often found himself without any allies at all. As with the London Times, the Freeman's Journal chose Madden's The Life and Martyrdom of Savonarola (1854) as his best books. Articles concerning Madden's death also appeared in a number of other newspapers and journals at this time and included praiseworthy comments such as the fact that his job with the Loans Funds Board had been "below the standard of his merit." Many articles referred to his generous nature and the fact that he was always very happy when he was doing a favour on behalf of someone else. Unsurprisingly, the Nation highlighted his work on the Lives of the United Irishmen as that which would always keep Madden's memory alive. Even if had written nothing else the Irish nation was forever indebted to Madden because of the long hours of valuable research which Madden had spent on this project, the newspaper said.

> From the first to last Madden did not allow his own position as a Government Official to deter him from his earnest justification of the men who had endeavoured in perilous times to overthrow British tyranny in Ireland.[514]

An article in the Irish Monthly recalled some less publicly-known examples of Madden's integrity as an individual. Father Matt Russell (C.I.)[515] wrote that Madden really displayed the true extent of his generous nature on his marriage to Harriet Elmslie, the daughter of a Protestant landowner man named John Elmslie. With that marriage Madden had inherited a large plantation in Jamaica. He could have sided with the slave-holders but instead he had taken the part of Clarkson and Wilberforce, both of whom were then campaigning for the abolition of slavery. It was this same streak of honesty and uprightness that had made him take a stand on behalf of the men *who rose in dark and evil days to right their native land* rather than taking the easy route as most government officials in a similar position would have done.

The basic moral decency that was at the core of Madden's

being was highlighted by Raymond Postgate in his autobiography of Robert Emmet, published in 1931. While this "impetuous and venerable medical man" had been susceptible to the occasional erroneous statement throughout the course of diplomatic and literary career, it was nevertheless the case that:

> ...his honest personality chimed through his work and his zeal had rescued the memory of the United Irishmen that would assuredly have perished otherwise.[516]

The enormous personal library which Madden had carefully collated over the years was carefully catalogued and auctioned after his death. Apart from books, newspapers, journals, theses and autographed letters, his collection also included death masks, portraits, painted statuettes and all sorts of ancient artefacts. This is not to mention the archives of Blessington and Mountjoy and the various manuscripts Madden had written which had never been officially published. The fact that this very valuable and diverse library collection was broken up and sold off on the open market was a tragedy for Ireland as many valuable resources were bought by private collectors and disappeared to unknown locations.

Amongst the most valuable items Madden had held in manuscript form was a copy of the *Annals of the Four Masters*, a copy, some of which was in James Clarence Mangan's handwriting. Madden's manuscripts had also included original issues of the Trinity College, Dublin Historical Society publications for the years 1801-1804 and a valuable history of the Orange Order that had yet to see publication. The history and development of the Orange Order had always been a subject of interest to Madden and the loss of this manuscript was very unfortunate. The manuscript was actually purchased at auction by Tim Harrington, a Parnellite member of Parliament and one-time Lord Mayor of Dublin but was re-auctioned again subsequent to Harrington's death - after which it isn't clear what happened to it. Some of the papers auctioned after

Madden's death ended up in the libraries of the Royal Irish Academy, Trinity College Dublin, the National Library of Ireland and the library of Dublin Corporation.

A publishing company named Swan, Sonnenschen and Co. purchased some of Madden's handwritten manuscript material, material which they later published alongside an editor's note by J. Bowes Daly[517]. Daly's introduction to this book alluded to Madden's old failing as relating to the excessive accumulation of material. Daly states that he initially intended publishing Madden's work "word-for-word" with no cuts or edits. Before long, however, he was forced to abandon this plan because of the "mass of extraneous matter, repetitions and unnecessary detail", Madden's original manuscript had included. Other miscellaneous and fascinating papers that were auctioned off included a large file of material relating to the "Spottiswode Conspiracy."[518] Spottiswoode had led a committee that had raised money to organise against Daniel O'Connell's followers in 1837. A subsequent parliamentary enquiry discovered that Northern Ireland's Orangemen who had publicly displayed their allegiance to the Queen had in fact been covertly agitating for the young and well-liked Queen Victoria to be sidelined and replaced by Ernest, King of Hanover. Ernest had a reputation for "immorality" but his position as Head of the Orange Order meant that the Order's members turned a blind eye to this aspect of his personal history.

The full story of the Spottiswoode Conspiracy had yet to be revealed in the public domain by the time of Madden's death, but he had acquired the documents relating to this episode from William Francis Finn, a man who was related to the O'Connell family by marriage. A large raft of personal papers as relating to Madden's own personal and literary interests were also sold on the open market at the auction held subsequent to Madden's death. Luckily, these documents had been bound into hardcover volumes by Madden's son Tom and they eventually made their way into a number of Irish archives which can be consulted today. Today, these various volumes are distributed between two archives – i.e. the National Library of Ireland and the collections of the Diocesan College of Clonfert, located in Ballinasloe, County Galway.

REFERENCES

CHAPTER 1 - MADDEN'S YOUTH

1 - Madden, R.R. (1891) *The memoirs (chiefly autobiographical) from 1798 to 1886 of Richard Robert Madden* - (Edited by his son Thomas More Madden). London: Ward and Downey.
2 - Tone. T.W. (1827) *Memoirs of Theobald Wolfe Tone / written by himself; comprising a complete journal of his negotiations to procure the aid of the French for the liberation of Ireland.* London: H. Colburn.
3 - James Napper Tandy (1740 –1803) was a well-known Irish rebel leader. A Dublin Protestant, Tandy attended a Quaker boarding school in County Kildare after which he worked as a small tradesman. He became a member of Dublin Corporation where he denounced municipal corruption and proposed a boycott of English goods in Ireland, in retaliation for the restrictions then imposed by the British government on Irish trade. Tandy joined the Whig club founded by Henry Grattan and, along with Wolfe Tone, was a key figure in the foundation the *Society of the United Irishmen* in 1791. He became the first secretary of this new organisation and helped moved the organisation in a direction of rebellion as influenced by then French revolutionary thinking. Under pressure for his increasingly "anti-government" activities he moved to Paris in February 1798 where he joined with a number of other prominent Irish political figures – Wolfe Tone amongst them – in planning a rebellion in Ireland with the help of the French. As part of the 1798 rebellion, Tandy sailed a corvette he'd been given by the French government from Dunkirk to Ireland. Subsequently arrested in Germany, Tandy was imprisoned until April, 1801 when, on the reprieval of his death sentence, he was allowed to live in exile in France. Napper Tandy is still remembered in a number of well-known ballads as sung in Ireland, *The Wearing of the Green* and *The Spanish Lady*, amongst them.

4 - Likely to be an invented "mythological" name for an imaginary place in Ireland.

5 - Dónal O'Sullivan Beare (1561–1613) was reputedly the last leader of the Gaelic O'Sullivan clan in southwest Ireland during the seventeenth century. In 1602, a combined force of Irish and Spanish soldiers was defeated by the English at the Battle of Kinsale, a loss which signalled the end of the Gaelic way of life. Absent from the siege because he was meeting with Hugh O'Neill in the north, O'Sullivan gathered together his remaining followers, including women and children, and left the southwest for a more receptive environment amongst the Gaelic chiefs of the North. His long march north has been immortalized in song and tradition. In the northern counties, O'Sullivan tried to organize a Gaelic resistance along with the Gaelic chiefs in that region. He later went into exile in Spain.

6 - Charles Lever (1806-1872) was born in Dublin, in 1806. He was educated at a number of private schools and at Trinity College, Dublin where he took a degree in Medicine, in 1831. A well-known practical joker and adventurer, he travelled to Canada on an emigrant ship while still an unqualified surgeon. He hiked through various backwoods in Canada and even found himself affiliated to a tribe of Native Americans at one point. On qualifying as a medic, he worked as a doctor in both Counties Clare and Derry and was involved in Irish literary circles. During the mid-1800s he wrote some very highly-regarded books which excelled in their accounts of military conflict - including *Charles O'Malley* (1841), *Jack Kimton* and *Tom Burke of Ours* (1843).

7 - Ó Broin (1971, 16)

8 - Ó Broin (1971, 17)

9 - Originally named after a Danish Bishop St. Michan's Church is believed to have been founded in the late eleventh-century by the Danish community then resident in Oxmanstown on the northside of the River Liffey.

10 - Thomas Moore (1779 –1852) - referred to as "Tom Moore" in Madden's narrative - was an Irish poet, singer, songwriter, and entertainer, now best remembered for the lyrics of *The Minstrel*

Boy and *The Last Rose of Summer.* Born in Dublin, he was one of the most popular composers and entertainers of his day and his ballads were published as *Moore's Irish Melodies* (more commonly titled *Moore's Melodies*) in 1846 and 1852. Moore's success ensured that he also travelled extensively and played concerts in countries as varied as Bermuda, Canada and the United States.

11 - George Petrie (1790 – 1866) was an Irish painter, musician, antiquary and archaeologist. Petrie's writings on early Irish archaeology and architecture were considered of great significance in their day, in particular his *Essay on the Round Towers of Ireland*, published in 1845. Between 1833 and 1843 he worked for the Antiquities division of the Irish Ordnance Survey.

12 - (See R. Myles - *An Apostle of Catholic Dublin* (1944: 129-30).

13 - Botany Bay is situated just south of Sydney Harbour and acts as Sydney's industrial port. From the early 1800s the British colonial regime in Ireland began to transport Irish political prisoners landed to Australia and New South Wales, they were kept imprisoned west of Sydney in Paramatta, or in Botany Bay.

14 - Ó Broin (1971, 20).

15 - The Records of the Chancery of England, known as the Master of the Rolls, is the second most senior judge in England and Wales, after the Lord Chief Justice.

16 - Correspondence of Daniel O'Connell I, 59.

17 - Lord George Gordon (1751- 1793) was a British politician after whom the incident known as the "Gordon Riots" of 1780 were named. In 1779 he appointed himself head of the Protestant associations which he organised an in attempt to have the Catholic Relief Act of 1778 repealed. On June 2, 1780 he fronted a mob which marched from Saint George's Fields to the Houses of Parliament in order to present a petition against (partial) Catholic Emancipation. Once the mob reached Westminster the "Gordon Riots" began.

18 - Ó Broin (1971, 23).

CHAPTER 2 - IN EUROPE, TURKEY AND THE MIDDLE EAST

19 - Madden, Memoirs, p.18.
20 - Lord Charles Murray-Aynsley (1771–1808) was an English dean. In 1803 he was appointed Dean of Bocking, in Essex and on one occasion, he entertained King Louis XVIII of France and his followers there when they visited England.
21 - Madden, *Memoirs* pp. 20-21.
22 - Madden, *Memoirs* p. 28.
23 - Ó Broin (1971, 30).
24 - The Levant is a traditional description for the region that is the Eastern Mediterranean but it was also frequently used as a geographical term denoting a large area of Western Asia as formed by the regions bordering the eastern shores of the Mediterranean. The Levant included Lebanon, Israel and the Palestinian territories, Syria, Jordan, and occasionally Cyprus, Sinai, and parts of Iraq.
25 - Sadlier, *Blessington D'Orsay – A Masquerade*, p. 26.
26 - Leslie *Mrs. Fitzherbert* p. 50.
27 - Duffy *My Life in Two Hemispheres*, p. 125.
28 - Alfred Guillaume Gabriel, known as the Count D'Orsay (1801–1852) was a French amateur artist, dandy, and *bon viveur*. Born in Paris, he was the second son of Albert Gaspard Grimaud, a Bonapartist general. In 1821, he turned against his own Bonapartist inheritance when he joined the French army of the restored Bourbon monarchy. It was the following year, while stationed at Valence on the Rhone that he came to know Charles Gardiner, the first Earl of Blessington and his wife, Marguerite, also known as the Countess of Blessington, after which the trio became firm friends. In 1823 he met renowned poet George (Lord) Byron at Genoa, and the published correspondence of the poet from this period includes many references to D'Orsay's artistic gifts and accomplishments and his peculiar relationship with the Blessington family. After the death of Lord Blessington in 1829, the widowed Marguerite, (Countess of Blessington), a prolific novelist by profession, left Ireland

for London where she lived with D'Orsay, initially at Seamore Place and later, at Gore House ,a place which acquired a reputation as something of a *salon* for the most fashionable literary and artistic elements in London society. D'Orsay was also a talented painter and sculptor.

29 - Throughout the Middle Ages, Constantinople was considered the imperial capital of the Roman Empire (the Byzantine/Eastern Roman Empire, the Latin Empire and the Ottoman Empire). In 1930 the city was officially deprecated in favor of the Turkish name Istanbul.

30 - *Dragoman* was an official title as assigned to the person who functioned as an interpreter, a translator and an official guide between Turkish, Arabic, and Persian-speaking countries in Middle Eastern and Europe consulates and trading posts at this time. The position of dragoman came to prominence during the years when the Ottoman Empire was at its height.

31 - Ó Broin 1971, pp. 36-7.

32 - Ó Broin 1971, p. 39.

33 - Ó Broin 1971, p. 39.

34 - "Pasha" or "pacha" was a term denoting a person of high rank within the political system of the Ottoman Empire.

35 - Ó Broin 1971, p. 41.

36 - Ó Broin, 1971, 42.

37 - Ó Broin, 1971, 42.

38 - Ó Broin, 1971, 42.

39 - Ó Broin 1971, p. 43.

40 - Madden *Memoirs*, 40.

41 - Lady Hester Lucy Stanhope (1776–1839) was the eldest child of Charles Stanhope, the third Earl of Stanhope – and by his first wife, Lady Hester Pitt. She is remembered by history as an intrepid traveller in an age when women were discouraged from being adventurous. A good number of books have been written about Hester Stanhope's adventures including her own memoir – *Memoirs of the Lady Hester Stanhope* published in 1845.

42 - Ó Broin 1971, pp. 44.

43 - Ó Broin 1971, p.45.
44 - Ó Broin 1971, p.45.
45 - Ó Broin 1971, p.45.
46 - Ó Broin 1971, p.46-7.
47 - Ó Broin 1971, p.48-9.
48 - Ó Broin 1971, p.46-7.

CHAPTER 3 - THE PUBLICATION OF MADDEN'S FIRST BOOK

49 - Sir Moses H. Montefiore (1784-1885) was one of the most famous British Jews of the nineteenth century. Montefiore was a financier, banker, philanthropist and Sheriff of London. Born in Livorno, Italy, he began his career as an apprentice to a firm of grocers and tea merchants, but later emigrated to London. He was a very successful businessman but after retiring in 1824, he devoted his time and fortune to civic responsibilities and interests. An inveterate traveller, he visited many countries in the Middle East. He focussed his philanthropic efforts on alleviating the poverty and persecution of the Jews in a wide range of countries.
50 - History has it that Croesus (595 BC – c. 547? BC) was the king of Lydia from 560 to 546 BC and until his defeat by the Persians in about 547 BC. An extremely wealthy and powerful man, the fall of Croesus had a profound impact on the Hellenes, even providing a fixed point in their calendar. In Greek and Persian cultures the name "Croesus" became a synonym for a wealthy man and this signification carried over into the English language.
51 - Ó Broin (1971, 51) describes how this marriage didn't work out and provides as a possible explanation the theory likewise posited in Doris Longley Moore's (1961) *The Late Lord Byron: Posthumous Dramas*; London: J. Murray – that the bride was only a "decoy" whose presence legitimated d'Orsay's position within the Blessington household, Lady Blessington having been assured that the marriage with the young bride would never actually be consummated.
52 - The *Encumbered Estates Act* (1849) was an element of the British response to increased land agitation and Fenian violence on the part of the Irish tenant class and a simultaneous growth in nationalist feeling throughout Europe. The sale of many Irish lands and estates by debt-ridden and (primarily) absentee landlords subsequent to the passing of the Encumbered Estates Act led to some improvement in the conditions of the Irish tenants. The

"new" landlords tended to be resident in Ireland and were not as prone to charging exorbitant rents as excessive as those previously imposed by the "absentee" class.

53 - John Philip Kemble (1757–1823) was an English actor. Born into a theatrical family in Prescot, Lancashire he was the eldest son of Roger Kemble, actor-manager of a touring troupe. His elder sister Sarah Siddons achieved fame with him on the stage of the Theatre Royal, Drury Lane. Kemble took a lead role in many Shakespearian plays during the course of his career.

54 - Cited in Willard Conneely *Count D'Orsay*, 115.

55 - Cited in Richard Robert Madden *The Literary Life and Correspondence of the Countess of Blessington*; (Volume I); New York: Harper 1855, 433.

56 - Apoplexy is an outdated medical term, which can be used to mean 'bleeding' in a cerebrovascular accident. When used in a non-medical sense it tends to mean a state of extreme rage or excitement.

57 - Cited in Richard Robert Madden *The Literary Life and Correspondence of the Countess of Blessington*; (Volume II); New York: Harper 1855, 342.

58 - Cited in William Beattie - *Life and Letters of Thomas Campbell* (Volume III) – (1850, 104).

59 - The Monks of the Screw was the name of an Irish drinking club active in the period between 1779 and 1789. It was also known as the Order of St. Patrick. The "screw" in the title was a reference to the corkscrew used to open bottles of wine. The group was founded by John Philpot Curran, a well-known Irish lawyer and orator. The members of the club were mainly lawyers or politicians in the Irish parliament, the majority of who were liberal in their political leanings and supporters of the *Irish Patriot Party*.

60 - This remarkable novel was titled *Anastasius, or Memoirs of a Greek Written at the Close of the Eighteenth Century*; London: John Murray (1819).

61 - Sir Francis Burdett (1770-1844) was an English reformist

politician. In Parliament he soon came to prominence as a staunch opponent of William Pitt the Younger, and as an advocate of popular rights and an agitator for reform.
62 - Cited in Marion Lockhead *John Gibson Lockhart*, 105.
63 - Madden, R. R.*The Infirmities of Genius* (1833).
64 - *Quarterly Review* 1833 p. 60.

CHAPTER 4 - JAMAICA AND THE ANTI-SLAVERY MOVEMENT

65 - Ó Broin, 1971, 63.
66 - Ó Broin, 1971, 65.
67 - Ó Broin, 1971, 63.
68 - Ó Broin, 1971, 63.
69 - Ó Broin, 1971, 66.
70 - Ó Broin, 1971, 68.
71 - Colonial Office Papers (CO) Public Record Office London (137/192).
72 - Ó Broin, 1971, 70.
73 - Ó Broin, 1971, 71.
74 - Colonial Office Papers (CO) Public Record Office London (137/193).
75 - Ó Broin, 1971, 72.
76 - Ó Broin, 1971, 72.
77 - Ó Broin, 1971, 72.
78 - *Anti-Slavery Papers*, Rhodes House, Oxford. (RH: Mss. Brit. Emp. S 22, G.4).
79 - Ó Broin, 1971, 74.
80 - Ó Broin, 1971, 74.
81 - Ó Broin, 1971, 74.
82 - Ó Broin, 1971, 77.
83 - William James MacNeven (1763-1841) was an Irish-American doctor and writer. He studied initially in Prague before completing his medical studies in Vienna, Austria, in 1784. This same year he returned to Dublin to practice as a doctor. He became involved with the United Irishmen at this time also and was arrested along with a group of men including Lord Edward Fitzgerald, Thomas Addis Emmet, and his brother Robert Emmet in March, 1798, and confined to Kilmainham Jail. He was later transferred to another prison in Fort George, Scotland where he remained until 1802, after which he was freed. He went into exile in France and when his attempts to secure French troops from Napoleon for another uprising in Ireland came to nothing, MacNeven set sail for America in 1805.

84 - Ó Broin, 1971, 78-9.

85 - Ó Broin, 1971, 79.

86 - Henry Phipps, (First Earl of Mulgrave) (1755–1831) was a British soldier and politician. Lord Mulgrave joined the army in 1775 and rose to the rank of General. His army career coincided with the American Revolutionary War. He was Foreign Secretary under William Pitt the Younger between the years 1805 and 1806.

87 - Sir Lucius O'Trigger was a character in a five-part comedy of manners first performed in 1775. The play titled *The Rivals* was written by Richard Brinsley Sheridan, an Irish-born playwright, poet and politician, a man who was at one time the long-term owner of the London Theatre Royal in Drury Lane. A later (re-worked) version of *The Rivals* became a standard play in the repertoires of many nineteenth-century theatre companies in both Britain and the U.S.A.

88 - Valentine Brown Lawless (1773–1853), the second Baron Cloncurry was an Irish politician and landowner. He lived in Ardclough, in County Kildare. Lawless is said to have been involved as an organiser with the United Irishmen and during the rebellions of both 1798 and 1803, although the extent of his involvement is unclear. What is certain is that Lawless was imprisoned in June 1798 on suspicion of treason in London and was held in the Tower of London until March 1801. After his release, he went to Paris and then onto Rome, where he remained while Robert Emmet's rebellion was in progress. Emmet's biographer Ruan O'Donnell surmises that he was earmarked as a member of the new Republican Government in-waiting. He returned to Ireland in 1804 and became more conservative politically in later years. He supported the campaign for Catholic Emancipation but did not support Daniel O'Connell in his campaign for Repeal. Lawless was granted a British peerage in September 1831 a few days after the coronation of William the Fourth.

89 - Lord Edward FitzGerald (1763-1798) was born in County Kildare, Ireland. He joined the British Army in 1779 and served in the American Revolutionary War and was seriously wounded at the Battle of Eutaw Springs in September, 1781. In 1783, he returned

to Ireland to become involved in political life. In Parliament Fitzgerald associated with the small opposition Irish Patriot Party group as led by Henry Grattan. Fitzgerald visited Paris in October 1792 where he lodged with Thomas Paine and where he took up the doctrines of the French Revolution with great enthusiasm. He was dismissed from the army and the House of Commons and in 1796 he joined the United Irishmen, who by now had given up as hopeless the path of constitutional reform. In 1796 he travelled to the Continent where Wolfe Tone was organising a new uprising with the support of the French. In 1797 Fitzgerald's role as military organizer for the United Irishmen in Kildare was denounced at the same time as the English government imposed martial law in Ireland. A reward £1000 was offered for information leading to Fitzgerald's capture and an informer named Magan disclosed Fitzgerald's hide-out. Badly-injured while attempting to escape the soldiers who came to arrest him, Fitzgerald was taken to Newgate Prison, Dublin where he was denied proper medical treatment. He died from his wounds on the fourth of June, 1798, just as the rebellion raged outside on the streets of Dublin.

90 - Cited in P.S. O'Hegarty *Ireland under the Union 1801-1922*, 271).

91 - James (Jemmy) Hope 1764 – 1847) was a United Irishmen leader who fought in the 1798 and 1803 rebellions against British rule in Ireland. Influenced by the ideals of both the American and French Revolutions, he joined the Society of the United Irishmen in 1795 and quickly established himself as a prominent organiser. He was elected to the organisation's central committee in Belfast and was close to other leaders such as Samuel Neilson, Thomas Russell, and Henry Joy McCracken. He was finally forced to flee Dublin after the failure of Robert Emmet's rebellion in 1803 and he returned to the North.

92 - From a copy of a letter in the then (1971) possession of historian T.W. Moody – cited in Ó Broin (1971, 82).

93 - Ó Broin 1971, 82.

94 - Sir George Grey, (1799-1882) was a British Whig politician. He held office under four Prime Ministers, Lord Melbourne,

Lord John Russell, Lord Aberdeen, and Lord Palmerston. One particularly noteworthy aspect of his political career was the fact that he served three times as British Home Secretary.

CHAPTER 5 - CUBA, ABOLITIONISM AND THE CASE OF THE "AMISTAD"

95 - Ó Broin (1971, 85) – Ó Broin mentions that he sourced this information regarding these different African tribes in Lloyd, C.C. (1968) *The Navy and the Slave Trade*; London: Frank Cass and Co.
96 - Ó Broin (1971, 86).
97 - Sarah Curran (1782-1808) was the youngest daughter of John Philpot Curran, an eminent Irish lawyer. She was Irish rebel leader Robert Emmet's great love. Curran's father disapproved of Emmet as a suitor and their courtship was conducted through letters and secret meetings. In 1803, the couple became engaged in secret but the rebellion of that same year destroyed any chance they had of making their union a more permanent one. Sarah Curran contracted tuberculosis and died aged just 26. She is buried in Newmarket, County Cork.
98 - Ó Broin (1971, 87).
99 - Robert Fulton (1765-1815) was an American engineer and inventor who is widely credited with developing the first commercially successful steamboat. In 1800 he was commissioned by Napoleon Bonaparte to design the Nautilus, which was the first practical submarine in history.
100 - Ó Broin (1971, 88).
101 - Lit: "A hell of immorality."
102 - Ó Broin (1971, 91).
103 - *Foreign Office Papers* (FO. 84/221); Public Record Office, London.
104 - Ó Broin (1971, 92).
105 - Ó Broin (1971, 93).
106 - Ó Broin (1971, 93-4).
107 - *posada* – Spanish: *dwelling, lodging, boarding-house.*
108 - Captain Edward Windham Harrington Schenley, a British army officer.
109 - Foreign Office Papers (FO 84/136), Public Record Office, London.

110 - Ó Broin (1971, 96).

111 - Ó Broin (1971, 96).

112 - *Foreign Office Papers* (FO. 84/216);Public Record Office, London.

113 - Ó Broin (1971, 97).

114 - Ó Broin (1971, 97).

115 - *Foreign Office Papers* (FO. 84/217); Public Record Office, London.

116 - Cited in W. Owens *Slave Mutiny*; New York: J. Day Co. 1953: 38-9.

117 - N.P. Trist to John Forsyth, 9 September, 1839, *Department of State Records*. US Archives, Washington.

118 - Ó Broin (1971, 101).

119 - *La Amistad* (meaning "Friendship" in Spanish) was a ship which became notable as the scene of a revolt by African captives being transported from Havana to Puerto Principe, also in Cuba. On July the second, 1839, Sengbe Pieh led fifty-six fellow African captives (fifty-two adults and four children) - all of whom were being transported aboard this schooner - in a revolt against their captors. The Africans took control of the ship in July 1839 but were captured off the coast of Long Island by the forces of the United States Revenue Cutter Service. A long-running court case then ensued regarding the status of this African group given that the importation of slaves to the US had been made illegal in 1808. This schooner subsequently became a potent symbol for various worldwide campaigns to abolish slavery. On appeal, the case of *The Amistad* reached the US Supreme Court. In 1841, this Court ruled that these African people had been illegally transported and held as slaves, and the captives were duly freed.

120 - Cited in W. A. Owens *Slave Mutiny* 1953, 133-6.

121 - Cited in W. A. Owens *Slave Mutiny* 1953, 104.

CHAPTER 6 - MADDEN'S RELIGIOUS "CONVERSION"

122 - Ó Broin(1971, 105).
123 - Ó Broin(1971, 107-8).
124 - Ó Broin(1971, 108).
125 - Ó Broin(1971, 108).
126 - Ó Broin(1971, 108).
127 - Ó Broin(1971, 108).
128 - Ó Broin(1971, 110).
129 - Ó Broin(1971, 112).
130 - Ó Broin(1971, 112).
131 - Ó Broin(1971, 112-113).
132 - Ó Broin(1971, 113).
133 - Ó Broin(1971, 113-114).
134 - Ó Broin(1971, 115).
135 - Bellamy, Joseph (1841) *True Religion delineated ... in two discourses ...* London: T. Ward & Co.
136 - Ó Broin(1971, 115).
137 - 1844, known as the "Year of the Lash" saw an uprising of black slaves in Cuba. Referred to as the *Conspiración de La Escalera* (Conspiracy of the Ladder), the Cuban authorities brutally suppressed this rebellion.
138 - Antoine Henri de Bérault-Bercastel was a French priest and Catholic historian. He was born in Lorraine in 1720 and died about the year 1794 at Noyon, also in France. His most important work was entitled *Histoire de l'église* (lit: "History of the Church"), the various volumes of which were issued in Paris between the years 1778 and 1790.
139 - Joseph Sturge (1793–1859) born in Gloucestershire, England was a Quaker, an abolitionist and a political activist. He founded the British and Foreign Anti-Slavery Society and campaigned throughout his life on issues such as pacifism, working-class rights, and the abolition of slavery.
140 - *Anti-Slavery Papers*, Rhodes House, Oxford. (RH: Mss. Brit. Emp. S 22, G.18).
141 - Royal Irish Academy (RIA) Papers (24.0.II)-

142 - Aubrey Thomas de Vere (1814–1902) was an Irish poet and critic.

143 - Thomas Clarkson (1760– 1846), abolitionist, was born in Cambridgeshire, England. He became a leading campaigner against the slave trade in the British Empire. He helped found the Committee for the Abolition of the Slave Trade. In 1807 the lobbying of this group helped the passage of the Slave Trade Act of 1807, which officially ended the British trade in slaves.

144 - Sir Thomas Fowell Buxton (1786-1845) was an English MP, brewer, abolitionist and social reformer. He helped found the Society for the Mitigation and Gradual Abolition of Slavery (later the Anti-Slavery Society) in 1823 and took over as leader of the abolitionist movement in the British House of Commons after William Wilberforce retired in 1825. His efforts were rewarded in 1833 when slavery was officially abolished in the British Empire.

145 - Richard Davis Webb (1805-1872) was an Irish publisher and abolitionist. In 1837, he, James Haughton and Richard Allen founded the Hibernian Antislavery Association James Haughton and Richard Allen. Webb was one of the Irish delegates present at the 1840 Anti-Slavery Convention in London, a convention which attracted hundreds of people from the United States. The Irish delegation included Webb, Richard Allen, and Daniel O'Connell.

146 - Theobald Mathew (1790-1856), an Irish temperance reformer, popularly known as Father Mathew was born in Thomastown, County Tipperary, Ireland. The movement with which his name is still associated began in 1838 with the establishment of the Total Abstinence Society. The "promise" to abstain from alcohol indefinitely was referred to as "The Pledge."

147 - Ó Broin(1971, 118).

148 - Ó Broin(1971, 118).

149 - In December, 1839 Pope Gregory XVI issued *In Supremo*, an apostolic letter which condemned the slave trade in the strongest possible terms. The Pope's pronouncement set off a major debate both inside and outside the Catholic community in the United States, in particular.

150 - Ó Broin(1971, 119).
151 - Ó Broin(1971, 119).
152 - John Mitchel (1815-1875) was an Irish nationalist activist, solicitor and political journalist. A leading member of the Young Irelanders and the Irish Confederation, he became a public voice for the Southern American viewpoint in the United States during the 1850s and 1860s. His *Jail Journal* is one of Irish nationalism's most famous texts.
153 - Harriet Beecher Stowe (1811-1896) was an American abolitionist and writer. Stowe's novel *Uncle Tom's Cabin* (1852) depicted life for African-Americans under slavery. This book was one of the first "bestsellers" written in English and was read by many people throughout the English-speaking world. The book proved very influential and brought the anti-slavery movement centre-stage as a political issue.
154 - James Haughton (1795–1873) was a social reformer and a temperance activist. He was born in County Carlow, Ireland but settled in Dublin, where he became a corn and flour merchant in partnership with his brother William. Although educated as a Friend, he joined the Unitarians in 1834, and remained a strong believer in their philosophical tenets for the remainder of his life. He supported the anti-slavery movement at an early period and took an active part in it until 1838. When the movement promoting the (anti-alcohol) "pledge" initiated by Theobald Mathew got under way Haughton was one of its most devoted activists.
155 - Ó Broin(1971, 120).
156 - *The Tablet* is a Catholic international weekly review published in London. Throughout its history it has had many influential literary and intellectual contributors to its pages, Evelyn Waugh, Graham Greene, Pope Benedict XVI (as Cardinal Joseph Ratzinger) and Pope Paul VI amongst them. Launched in 1840 by a Quaker convert to Catholicism, Frederick Lucas, the *Tablet* is the second-oldest surviving weekly journal in Britain after *The Spectator*.
157 - Ó Broin(1971, 121).

158 - John Philip Kemble (1757-1823) was an English actor. He was born into a theatrical family, his elder sister Sarah Siddons achieving fame with him on the stage of the Theatre Royal, Drury Lane, London His other siblings, Charles Kemble, Stephen Kemble, Ann Hatton and Elizabeth Whitlock all enjoyed success on the stage. In November, 1781 he obtained what was considered a "star" role in Dublin, Ireland making his first appearance there – in the role of Hamlet. Another of his most successful roles was as Raymond in *The Count of Narbonne*, a play adapted from Horace Walpole's novel *Castle of Otranto*.

159 - The Shrine of the Holy House (Santuario della Santa Casa), is a Catholic place of pilgrimage in Loreto, Italy. Loreto is situated in the province of Ancona.

160 - Ó Broin(1971, 121).

CHAPTER 7 - THE ANTI-SLAVERY CAMPAIGN ON THE GOLD COAST

161 - Tyre is a city located about fifty miles south of Beirut in the Southern Lebanon.

162 - John Blake Dillon (1814-1866) was an Irish writer and politician who was one of the founding members of the Young Irelanders. In 1842, he met Charles Gavan Duffy, with whom he and Thomas Davis founded *The Nation* newspaper. He was also an active member of Daniel O'Connell's Repeal Association a group which advocated the repeal of the Act of Union (1800) as between Great Britain and Ireland.

163 - Thomas Campbell (1777– 1844) was a Scottish poet chiefly remembered for his sentimental poetry dealing specially with human affairs. He was also one of the people who put together a plan for the foundation of what later became the University of London.

164 - The *Morning Herald* was an early daily newspaper in Britain. Founded in 1780 by the Reverend Sir Henry Bate Dudley, former editor of The Morning Post, it was initially deemed a liberal newspaper as aligned with the Prince of Wales. Later, it would change its political sympathies and become aligned with the Tories. The *Morning Herald* closing in 1869.

165 - James Beattie was a Scottish philosopher and poet who spent his entire academic career as Professor of Moral Philosophy and Logic at Marischal College in Aberdeen. His best known philosophical work, *An Essay on The Nature and Immutability of Truth in Opposition to Sophistry and Scepticism* (1770) is a harsh critique of the scepticism of David Hume, which he saw as a moral danger to society. The *Essay* was very popular, and led to an audience with King George III, as well as an annual pension. Beattie's other major work was his *Elements of Moral Science* (2 volumes, 1790, 1793) which includes, among other things, an impassioned argument for the abolition of slavery.

166 - Ó Broin(1971, 127).

167 - The *Morning Chronicle* was a newspaper founded in 1769 in

London, England. It continued publishing under various owners until the year 1862. It was most notable for having been the first employer of renowned novelist Charles Dickens. This newspaper also published a range of articles by Henry Mayhew, articles which were later collected and published in book form *as London Labour and the London Poor* (1861).

168 - The second creation of this title came in the British Peerage of June 1838 when Constantine Phipps, 2nd Earl of Mulgrave KG was granted the title of Marquis of Normanby. Phipps was a noted politician of the day and served as Lord Lieutenant of Ireland and as Home Secretary.

169 - John Russell (1792-1878), the 1st Earl Russell and known as Lord John Russell before 1861, was an English Whig and Liberal politician who served twice as UK Prime Minister. Born into the upper echelons of the English aristocracy, he was the grandfather of Bertrand Russell, the mathematician, philosopher and political campaigner.

170 - Sir James Stephen (1789–1859) was the British under-secretary of state for the (British) colonies between 1836 and 1847. He was instrumental in implementing the slavery abolition act. Highly-regarded as a scholar, administrator and with a deep knowledge of legal issues Stephen regularly wrote a series of articles for the *Edinburgh Review*, the first of which (about abolitionist William Wilberforce) appeared in April 1838. In 1849 he was appointed Regius Professor of Modern History at Cambridge.

171 - Ó Broin(1971, 130).

172 - Ó Broin(1971, 132).

173 - Ó Broin(1971, 132).

174 - Letitia Elizabeth Landon (1802-1838) was a nineteenth-century English poet and novelist, better known by her initials L. E. L.

175 - Ó Broin(1971, 135).

176 - Ó Broin(1971, 13).

177 - Ó Broin(1971, 136-7).

178 - *Colonial Office Papers* (CO. 267/170); Public Record Office, London.

179 - William Lamb, 2nd Viscount Melbourne (1779-1848), was a

British Whig statesman who served as English Home Secretary between 1830 and 1834 and Prime Minister of Britain between 1834 and 1841. The city of Melbourne in Australia is named after him.

180 - Ó Broin(1971, 137).

181 - Edward Henry Stanley (1826-1893), known as Lord Stanley from 1844 to 1869 was a British statesman. He served as Secretary of State for Foreign Affairs twice, from 1866 to 1868 and from 1874 to 1878. In March 1848 he unsuccessfully contested the borough of Lancaster, and then made a long tour in the West Indies, Canada and the United States. He later made a brief tour of Jamaica and South America. In 1852 he went travelling again, this time to India. In 1858, Stanley was made the Secretary of State for the Colonies. That same year he had charge of the India Bill in the House of Commons and later became the first Secretary of State for India.

182 - Ó Broin(1971, 137).

183 - Ó Broin(1971, 137).

184 - Banjul (formerly Bathurst), officially titled the *City of Banjul*, is the capital of The Gambia. This city is situated on St Mary's Island (Banjul Island), where the Gambia River enters the Atlantic Ocean. Banjul takes its name from the Mandé people who gathered specific fibres on the island, which were used in the manufacture of ropes. In 1816, the British founded Banjul as a colonial trading post and as a base for the suppression of the slave trade. It was initially named Bathurst after Henry Bathurst, the then secretary of the British Colonial Office. The city's name was officially changed to Banjul in 1973.

185 - Ó Broin(1971, 140-141).

186 - Robert Vernon (1800–1873), known as Robert Vernon Smith until 1859, was a British Liberal Party politician. In 1830 the Whigs came to power in Britain under Lord Grey when Vernon was appointed a Lord of the Treasury (government whip), a post he hold until July, 1834. He served as Under-Secretary of State for the Colonies between 1839 and 1841.

187 - Ó Broin(1971, 145).

188 - The Slavery Abolition Act 1833 was an English Act of Parliament which abolished slavery throughout most of the British Empire

(with the notable exceptions "of the Territories in the Possession of the East India Company," the "Island of Ceylon," and "the Island of Saint Helena.")

189 - Ó Broin(1971, 146).

190 - The Niger expedition of took place in 1841 and 1842 and involved three British iron steam vessels journeying to Lokoja, at the confluence of the Niger and Benue rivers, in what is modern-day Nigeria. It was mounted by British missionary and activist groups, with the backing of the British government. Among the main supporters of the expedition was the Society for the Extinction of the Slave Trade and the Society and for the Civilization of Africa, set up in 1839 by Thomas Fowell Buxton. The crews of each of the three steam vessels suffered a high mortality rate from disease.

191 - Sir Francis Burdett was a member of the Burdett family of Bramcote. Educated at Westminster School and the University of Oxford, he travelled a good deal as a young man and witnessed the early days of the French Revolution in Paris. In 1796, he became MP for Boroughbridge. He became prominent as an opponent of William Pitt the Younger, and as an advocate of popular rights. A politician whose popularity was high amongst the British public, he denounced the war with France, the suspension of the Habeas Corpus Act and the conditions of British prisons during this era.

192 - The *Morning Chronicle* was a newspaper founded in London, England, in the year in 1769. It published under various different owners until 1862.

193 - John Easthope, MP (1784-1865) was an English politician and journalist. Originally a clerk in a provincial bank, Easthope moved to London to make his fortune. He became a stockbroker and a politician and in 1834 he bought the *Morning Chronicle* newspaper. He later sold his interest in the newspaper on his retirement from parliament in 1847.

194 - Ó Broin(1971, 148).

195 - Royal Irish Academy (RIA) Papers (24. 0. 9.)

196 - Ó Broin(1971, 149).

197 - Royal Irish Academy (RIA) Papers (24. 9. 9.)

CHAPTER 8 - *THE LIVES OF THE UNITED IRISHMEN*

198 - John MacHale (1791-1881), born in Tubbernavine, County Mayo, Ireland, was the Catholic Archbishop of Tuam and an ardent Irish Nationalist. He campaigned for many years in an effort to secure Catholic Emancipation, legislative independence from Britain and greater justice for tenants and the poor. He was also vigorous in opposing the anti-Catholic system of public education implemented under colonialism.

199 - Maynooth is a university town in County Kildare, Ireland. It is home to a branch of the National University of Ireland and is Ireland's main Roman Catholic seminary.

200 - Daniel O'Connell (1775–1847), known to many as "The Liberator", was an Irish political leader during the first half of the nineteenth century. He campaigned for Catholic Emancipation—the right for Catholics to sit in the British parliament at Westminster Parliament and for the repeal of the 1800 Act of Union between Great Britain and Ireland.

201 - Campaigning for Catholic emancipation and greater autonomy from Britain Daniel O'Connell announced 1843 as the "Year of Repeal" and began organising what the *London Times* called 'monster meetings' throughout the country. In County Meath it was estimated that one "monster meeting" saw three-quarters of a million people assemble on the Hill of Tara.

202 - Despite that fact that O'Connell ensured the enormous crowds who attended his "monster meetings" were orderly and peaceful, the colonial government grew concerned that violence might ensue. Sir Robert Peel, the then British Prime Minister went on the offensive and outlawed the next proposed "monster meeting" due to be held in Clontarf, Dublin on the eighth of October 1843. O'Connell called off the rally beforehand but he was still arrested and charged with conspiracy. He was sentenced to a year's imprisonment and a fine of 2,000 pounds.

203 - Irish rebel leader Robert Emmet's speech, given on the eve of his execution by the British authorities. He was executed in

Thomas Street, Dublin.

204 - John Philpot Curran (1750–1817) was an Irish orator, politician and wit, born in Newmarket, County Cork. The son of James and Sarah Curran, he studied law at Trinity College, Dublin and continued his legal studies at the King's Inns and the Middle Temple. He was called to the Irish bar in 1775. A liberal Protestant, he opposed the illiberal policies of the colonial government in Ireland. He also opposed the Union with Britain and defended several leading members of United Irishmen accused of high treason, Wolfe Tone, Napper Tandy, The Sheares Brothers and Lord Edward Fitzgerald amongst them. He was appointed Master of the Rolls in Ireland in 1806, following Pitt's replacement by a more liberal cabinet.

205 - On the twelfth of March, 1798, information provided by Reynolds led to the seizure of a number of leading Irishmen at the house of Oliver Bond. Lord Edward FitzGerald who was also a leading rebel was not arrested for his part in the conspiracy on this occasion.

206 - Madden Collection TCD Library, 477, Trinity College Dublin.

207 - Ó Broin(1971, 159).

208 - Ó Broin(1971, 159).

209 - Ó Broin(1971, 160).

210 - Thomas O'Hagan (1812-1885), Lord Chancellor of Ireland, was born in Belfast, the son of a trader. He became an Irish Queen's Counsel in 1849. His support for the maintenance of the Union with Great Britain and his appointment to the positions of Solicitor-General for Ireland (1860) and Attorney-General (1861) lost him the support of the Nationalist party in Ireland. In 1868 became Lord Chancellor of Ireland in William Gladstone's first ministry.

211 - Robert Stewart, (1769-1822), better-known as Lord Castlereagh was a British statesman. Castlereagh was leader of the British House of Commons between 1812 and 1822. Early in his political career, he was appointed Chief Secretary for Ireland and was ruthless in putting down the Irish Rebellion of 1798. He was also a central figure in securing the passage of the Irish Act of Union in 1800.

212 - Ó Broin(1971, 161).
213 - Ó Broin(1971, 161).
214 - The Invincibles were a secret society and insurrectionist group.
215 - Ó Broin(1971, 162).
216 - Samuel Neilson (1761-1803) was one of the founder members of the Society of United Irishmen and the founder of its newspaper the Northern Star. Neilson was indicted for high treason and held in Kilmainham Jail with other state prisoners for the duration of the doomed rebellion outside. After Oliver Bond and the Sheares brothers were executed Neilson and the other remaining prisoners agreed to provide the British authorities with details relating to the organisation of United Irishmen and how their plans for the rebellion had materialized. They did this in order to avoid the death penalty. Once the rebellion was over Neilson and the other prisoners were transferred to Fort George in Scotland and in 1802, they were exiled in various European countries. Neilson was initially deported to Holland but he later made his way to America where he died suddenly in August 1803.
217 - Walter Cox was born about 1770. He was the son of a Westmeath blacksmith and a hanger-on of the revolutionary United Irishmen. He proved faithless to both to Irish rebels and to the British Government, however. In 1797 he established the *Union Star*, a magazine which was nominally in the interests of the United Irishmen, but which was later repudiated by them.
218 - Charles Cornwallis, (1738-1805) was a British Army officer and colonial administrator. He was one of the leading British generals in the American War of Independence. He also served as civil and military governor in both Ireland and India. In both countries he oversaw the implementation of major legislative changes which made Britain's grip on its colonies even more secure – for example, the Act of Union in Ireland and the Permanent Settlement in India.
219 - In 1784, Francis Higgins (better known as the "Sham Squire") took over the running of *The Freeman's Journal*, the oldest nationalist newspaper in Ireland. Founded in 1763, this newspaper

had identified strongly with the politics of radical eighteenth century Protestant patriot/politicians including Henry Grattan and Henry Flood. This changed completely from 1784 onwards once the newspaper came into Higgins control. History has it that Higgins was the informer who disclosed the whereabouts of Lord Edward Fitzgerald - and who additionally took a much stronger pro-British view in the decades after the 1798 Rebellion.

220 - Ó Broin(1971, 163).
221 - Ó Broin(1971, 163).
222 - Ó Broin(1971, 167).
223 - These crypts are in Christchurch Cathedral, Dublin.
224 - Nicholas Daniel Murphy (1811 – 1890) was an Irish politician from County Cork. He was elected MP for Cork city in the British Parliament and represented this constituency as a Liberal between 1865 and 1880.
225 - Ó Broin(1971, 167).
226 - James Dowling Herbert, b. Dublin 1762/3, d. Jersey (Channel Islands) 1837. Artist, revolutionary, art dealer and writer, James Dowling Herbert was the son of James Dowling, an ironmonger in South Great George's Street. He was an assistant to the American painter Gilbert Stuart and finished some of the paintings started by Stuart when he worked in Ireland before leaving hurriedly for the US in 1793 to escape his creditors. James Dowling Herbert was implicated in the 1798 rebellion, after which he changed his name from Dowling to Herbert. James Dowling Herbert painted portraits of several of the leaders of the rebellion as well as a picture of the capture of the Irish revolutionary Lord Edward Fitzgerald.
227 - Ó Broin(1971, 167).
228 - Ó Broin(1971, 169).
229 - Cited in *Sir Francis Burdett and his Times*; (1931, 158).
230 - Ó Broin(1971, 171).
231 - Ó Broin(1971, 171).
232 - James Clarence Mangan (1803-1849) was one of Ireland's leading nineteenth-century poets.

233 - Sir Samuel Ferguson (1810-1886) was an Irish poet, barrister, antiquarian, artist and public servant. One of the most important Ulster-Scot poets of the nineteenth century his interest in Irish mythology greatly influenced the poets of the "Celtic Twilight", William Butler Yeats amongst them.

234 - Pierre Jean de Beranger 1780-1857) – was a widely-acclaimed nineteenth century French songwriter.

235 - (Letter from Madden to de Vere dated - 7 February, 1861).

236 - The "Spirit of the Nation" (1843) series was a collection of poems and ballads originally published in *The Nation*, and printed by James Duffy for the editors. It sold at sixpence a copy and a second part was issued a year later, in 1844.

237 - James Connolly (1868-1916) was an Irish socialist leader. Born in Edinburgh, Scotland, to Irish immigrant parents he began working at a very young age. He played a role in Scottish and American politics in addition to his involvement in Irish public and political life. He was executed by the British for his leadership role in the Irish Easter Rising of 1916.

238 - Ó Broin(1971, 172).

239 - See *University Review* Jubilee Issue, 85.

240 - Sir Charles Gavan Duffy (1816-1903) was an Irish nationalist and (later) an Australian politician. He was the eighth Premier of the Australian state of Victoria. Along with Thomas Davis, and John Blake Dillon, Duffy helped found the Irish newspaper *The Nation*. This newspaper was active in the campaign for Irish independence from Britain and as relating to Land Reform and tenants' rights. Duffy was the *Nation's* first editor. He was also a leading figure on the Irish literary scene of his day and edited *Ballad Poetry of Ireland* (1843) and a range of other works on Irish literature. In 1852 Duffy was elected to the House of Commons for New Ross, County Wexford. Despairing of the likelihood that Irish independence would come any time soon, Duffy resigned from the House of Commons four years later and emigrated to Australia with his family.

241 - William Smith O'Brien (1803-1864) was a leading Irish Nationalist, a British MP and leader of the Young Irelanders. Convicted of

sedition for his role in the Young Irelander Rebellion of 1848, his death sentence was commuted to deportation to Van Diemen's Land (Tasmania) in Australia. In 1854, he was released on the condition of exile from Ireland, and he lived in Belgium for two years. In 1856 O'Brien was pardoned by the British government. He returned to Ireland but was never active again in politics.

242 - *Manuscripts of Madden, Smith O'Brien and Luke Cullen*, National Library of Ireland, Dublin. – (Manuscript: 5758).

243 - The "Repeal" question was taken up by the Repeal Association, an Irish political movement with a mass membership as set up by Daniel O'Connell. The primary aim of the Repeal Association was to campaign for the repeal of the Act of Union of 1800 between Great Britain and Ireland and to ensure full Catholic involvement in the political process.

244 - Ó Broin(1971, 173-4).

245 - Ó Broin(1971, 174).

246 - The Marquis de La Fayette French pronunciation: (Marie-Joseph Paul Yves Roch Gilbert du Motier), (1757-1834) was a French aristocrat and military officer. Lafayette was a general in the American Revolutionary War and a leader of the Garde Nationale during the French Revolution. In the American Revolution, Lafayette served as a major-general in the Continental Army under George Washington.

247 - Duffy, Charles Gavan (1895) *Short life of Thomas Davis, 1840-1846*; London: T. Fisher Unwin; Dublin: Sealy, Bryers and Walker.

248 - *Manuscripts of Madden, Smith O'Brien and Luke Cullen*, National Library of Ireland, Dublin. – (Manuscript: 2644)

249 - Ó Broin(1971, 176).

250 - Ó Broin(1971, 177).

CHAPTER 9 - *THE LIVES OF THE UNITED IRISHMEN*: THE REVIEWS

251 - William Pitt the Younger (1759-1806) was one of the leading British politicians of the late eighteenth and early nineteenth centuries. He became the youngest ever British Prime Minister in 1783 when he assumed this role aged just 24. He left office in 1801 but was appointed Prime Minister again in 1804, a position he continued to hold until his death two years later. He was also the Chancellor of the Exchequer throughout his premiership. He was known as William Pitt "the Younger" to distinguish him from his father William Pitt "the Elder" who had also served as British Prime Minister at one time. William Pitt "the Younger's" tenure as prime minister was dominated by a number of major events in Continental Europe, including the French Revolution and the Napoleonic Wars.

252 - The Beresford family traced their ancestry to Englishmen who had been part of James the First's invasion to Ireland. Their estate at Curraghmore near Waterford, southern Ireland was large and consisted of about 100,000 acres of land.

253 - Ó Broin(1971, 179).

254 - The *Spectator's* review of the 2nd of July, 1842.

255 - Ó Broin(1971, 180).

256 - Ó Broin(1971, 180).

257 - Charles James Lever (1806-1872) was one of the most highly-regarded Irish novelists of the nineteenth century.

258 - On the twenty-seventh of January, 1827 a public meeting was held in County Cavan to announce the formation of the New Reformation Society, the aim of which was to re-double efforts at converting all of the Irish people to Protestantism.

259 - Ó Broin(1971, 181).

260 - Ó Broin(1971, 181).

261 - Ó Broin(1971, 182).

262 - Ó Broin(1971, 183).

263 - Ó Broin(1971, 184).

264 - Ó Broin(1971, 184).

265 - In March 1797, Thomas Reynolds, a relative of Lord Edward Fitzgerald and Colonel of the United Irishmen for Co. Kildare tipped off the authorities that the Leinster Directory of the United Irishmen would be meeting at Oliver Bond's house in Dublin. Ten provincial delegates and two members of the United Irishmen's Supreme Executive were arrested. The only senior figure of the Leinster group who managed to evade arrest was Lord Edward Fitzgerald. Immediately following this, the colonial administration in Ireland declared martial law and searches, hangings, and floggings became commonplace.

266 - Founded in 1763 by Charles Lucas, the *Freeman's Journal* identified with a number of radical eighteenth-century Protestant patriot-politicians including Henry Grattan and Henry Flood. The *Journal*, as it was more commonly-known was frequently read to large gatherings of Irish people in villages and towns by those who were literate within the local population – i.e. primarily Catholic priests and local teachers.

267 - Ó Broin(1971, 185).

268 - Ó Broin(1971, 185).

269 - Trinity College Dublin (TCD) *Madden Manuscripts: 43.*

270 - Theobald Wolfe Tone eloped with Dublin woman Martha Witherington while both were still students. Martha changed her name to Matilda, on Wolfe Tone's request. Further information on this can be sourced in: T.W. Moody et al. (eds.) (2007) Tone, Theobald Wolfe *The writings of Theobald Wolfe Tone, 1763-98. Vol. 3*; Oxford: Clarendon Press

271 - Ó Broin(1971, 186).

272 - Ó Broin(1971, 186).

273 - Ó Broin(1971, 187).

274 - Thomas Addis Emmet (1764-1827) was the elder brother of executed Irish rebel leader Robert Emmet. In addition to working as an Irish and American lawyer and politician, Thomas was also a senior member of the United Irishmen during the 1790s. He emigrated to the US as a young man and was New York State Attorney General between the years 1812 and 1813.

275 - Ó Broin(1971, 187-8).
276 - William McCabe was the son of Thomas McCabe, watchmaker and the part-owner of a cotton mill in eighteenth-century Belfast. He was a noted radical, and came to prominence in 1786 when he vigorously opposed plans by the city's merchants to fit out ships for the transportation of slaves to the penal colonies. Thomas McCabe was also one of the original group who had founded the Society of United Irishmen in October, 1791. His son William was a political organiser for the United Irishmen and involved with the production of its newspaper, *The Northern Star*. In 1794 he and his colleagues were taken to court for publishing seditious material, after which William moved south to Dublin. He is reputed to have inducted many thousands of new members into the United Irishmen. He died in Scotland in 1821.
277 - Captain Bartholomew Teeling (1774-1798) was one of the leaders of the United Irishmen during the rebellion of 1798. Educated in Lisburn, County Antrim and at Trinity College Dublin, he arrived in Ireland with French troops as Chief Aide de Camp to General Humbert. Teeling was captured by the English at the Battle of Ballinamuck and executed for treason.
278 - Ó Broin(1971, 189).
279 - See Helen Landreth (1948) *The Pursuit of Robert Emmet*; UK: McGraw-Hill.
280 - See Brian O'Higgins in the *Wolfe Tone Annual*, 1953, 16.
281 - Henry Peter Brougham, (1778–1868) was a British statesman who became Lord Chancellor of the United Kingdom. As a young lawyer based in Scotland Brougham helped to found the Edinburgh Review in 1802. He was a regular contributor to this same journal.
282 - Edward Granville Eliot (1798-1877), styled Lord Elliot from 1823 to 1845, was a British politician and diplomat. He followed Peel to Ireland where he served as Lord Lieutenant of Ireland in Lord Aberdeen's coalition government.
283 - Ó Broin(1971, 190).
284 - See Madden, R.R. *Memoirs* 1891, 205-6.

285 - Ó Broin(1971, 191).
286 - The Battle of Aughrim was the decisive battle of the Williamite War in Ireland. It was fought between the Jacobites and the forces of William III on twelfth of July, 1691. The battlefield was located near the village of Aughrim in County Galway and it proved one of the bloodiest ever fought on Irish soil – over 7,000 people were killed.
287 - Ó Broin(1971, 191-2).
288 - Ó Broin(1971, 193).

CHAPTER 10 - IN PORTUGAL FOR THE *MORNING CHRONICLE*

289 - Mary Ann McCracken (1770-1866) was a social reformer. She was born in Belfast, the sister of the Irish rebel Henry Joy McCracken, who was executed in Belfast following his role in the Battle of Antrim in June 1798. As with her brother, Henry, Mary Ann held radical beliefs which extended not just to the politics of the day, but also to a range of social issues including poverty and slavery.
290 - See M. McNeill *Mary Anne McCracken,* p. 302.
291 - Ó Broin(1971, 196).
292 - Ó Broin(1971, 197-8).
293 - Ó Broin(1971, 198-9).
294 - Blessington cited in Ó Broin 1971, 199.
295 - Ó Broin(1971, 199-200).
296 - Sydney Charles Buxton (1853-1934) was a British Liberal politician of the late nineteenth-century. Between 1892 and 1895, Buxton served as Under-Secretary of State for the (British) Colonies.
297 - Thomas Clarkson (1760-1846) was a noted abolitionist, was born at Wisbech. From Cambridgeshire, England he helped found the Committee for the Abolition of the Slave Trade, a group which campaigned for and achieved the passage of the Slave Trade Act of 1807, an Act which ended the British trade in slaves.
298 - Lewis Tappan (1788-1863) was a New York abolitionist who worked to achieve the freedom of the illegally enslaved African community aboard the *Amistad.* Contacted by Connecticut abolitionists soon after the *Amistad* arrived in port, Tappan ensured that the African captives had very good lawyers acting on their behalf, a fact which proved to their benefit once the case went before the United States Supreme Court. It was after reading a biography of William Wilberforce that Tappan began his quest for abolition in the United States.
299 - The *Anti-Slavery Reporter* was founded in 1825 by Zachary Macaulay, a Scottish philanthropist who devoted most of his life to the anti-slavery movement. At the age of 16 he was sent to

Jamaica, where he eventually became a plantation manager. He was very unhappy with the injustices being perpetrated against the people being kept as slaves in that country.Under Macaulay and subsequent editors, *The Anti-Slavery Reporter* campaigned vigorously for the abolition of slavery throughout the world.

300 - Perhaps the best-known of the Cabral brothers was Pedro Álvares Cabral a Brazilian Portuguese born circa 1467 and who is believed to have died around the year 1520. He was a Portuguese nobleman, military commander, navigator and explorer. In the latter capacity he undertook the first substantial exploration of the northeast coast of South America, claiming these territories for Portugal.

301 - Royal Irish Academy (RIA) Papers - 24.0.1.

302 - Ó Broin(1971, 205).

303 - Ó Broin(1971, 206).

304 - Ó Broin(1971, 206).

305 - Ó Broin(1971, 206-7).

306 - Ó Broin(1971, 207).

307 - Ó Broin(1971, 207-8).

308 - Francis Tregian the Elder (1548–1608) was the son of Thomas Tregian of Wolvenden of Probus, Cornwall and Catherine Arundell. A staunch Catholic, he inherited a number of substantial estates on the death of his father. In 1576 Tregian provided a "safe house" for a Catholic seminary priest, Cuthbert Mayne, who passed as his steward. On the eighth of June 1577, the Sheriff of Cornwall, Sir Richard Grenville surrounded the house with a large body of men and arrested both Tregian and Mayne. Mayne was executed later that year while Tregian, who was also condemned to death, had his sentence remitted to one of imprisonment. He was incarcerated at Windsor and in a number of other London prisons for a full twenty-eight years until he was finally released by King James the First. Having been pardoned by King James the First, Tregian left for Madrid, where he enjoyed a pension from King Philip III of Spain. He died in Lisbon.

309 - Blessed Cuthbert Mayne was an English Catholic martyr. He was born circa 1543 and was put to death in Cornwall, on the twenty-ninth of November, 1577.

310 - The youngest daughter of John Philpot Curran, an eminent Irish lawyer, Sarah Curran (1782-1808) was the Irish rebel Robert Emmet's great love.

311 - Thomas Campbell (1777-1844) was a Scottish poet chiefly remembered for his sentimental poetry dealing specially with human affairs. He was also one of the initiators of a plan to found what would eventually become the University of London.

312 - Campbell, Thomas *Literary Sketch-Book* (1824).

313 - Ó Broin(1971, 211).

314 - The Charitable Bequests Act was introduced by Sir Robert Peel in 1844, in an attempt to win over moderate support amongst the Catholic Irish. The Act enabled Catholics to leave money and other possessions in their wills and to the Catholic Church. The act therefore made local parish priests less dependent on their local parishioner for financial support.

315 - Ó Broin(1971, 212).

316 - John Dillon (1851-1927) was a leading Irish campaigner on the question of land reform. From Dublin originally, Dillon was also an Irish Home Rule activist, a nationalist politician, and a British MP for more than thirty-five years. He was the last leader of the Irish Parliamentary Party.

317 - John O'Connell (1810-1858) was a son of the Irish Nationalist leader Daniel O'Connell and his wife Mary. He followed his father as a MP and a leader of the Repeal Association.

318 - The Corn Laws were import tariffs designed to protect corn prices in Britain (then termed the United Kingdom of Great Britain and Ireland) against competition from less expensive foreign imports specifically between the years 1815 and 1846. The tariffs were introduced by the Importation Act of 1815 but were repealed again in 1846. These laws were often viewed as examples of how the British attempted to limit "free trade" and monopolize crop trading at this period. Interestingly, while the Act referred to "corn" it did not specifically refer to maize, but was a "catch-all" term for all types of grain and cereal crops.

319 - Thomas Francis Meagher (1823-1867) was a leading Irish nationalist and leader of the Young Irelanders in the 1848 Rebellion.

On being convicted of sedition, he was initially sentenced to death but this sentence was later commuted to transportation for life to Van Diemen's Land, Australia. In 1852 he escaped from the penal colony there and made his way to the United States He made a new life for himself in New York where he studied law and worked as a journalist. He also travelled throughout the US presenting lectures on the Irish cause. On the outbreak of the American Civil War, Meagher joined the U.S. Army and rose quickly to the rank of brigadier general. He was most notable for leading the Irish Brigade, a brigade which recruited and sought support among Irish immigrants for the Union.

320 - The Lord Lieutenant of Ireland (also known as the Viceroy or (earlier) the Lord Deputy) was the head of England's colonial administration in Ireland in the years prior to 1707. The holder of this office was the British King's representative in Ireland.

321 - Sir Thomas Nicholas Redington (1815-1862) was an Irish administrator, politician and civil servant. Born in Oranmore, County Galway, Ireland he received his education at Oscott College and at Christ's College, Cambridge in England. As he was a Catholic, however, he was not eligible to graduate with a degree. He went into politics and represented Dundalk in the British parliament between the years 1837 and 1846. He was a Liberal by political persuasion. On 11 July 1846 he was appointed under-secretary of state for Ireland. He was also a member of Sir John Burgoyne's famine relief commission in 1847 and worked hard to alleviate many of the worst affects of the Famine. He died in London in October, 1862.

322 - Ó Broin(1971, 215).

323 - *Manuscripts of Madden, Smith O'Brien and Luke Cullen*, National Library of Ireland, Dublin. – (Manuscript: 1499).

324 - *The Protection of Life and Property (Ireland) Act* 1871 was one aspect of the special emergency legislation that had been applied to Ireland by the British parliament in Westminster during the course of the nineteenth and early twentieth centuries. This Act was also known as the *Westmeath Act*. The Act permitted the arrest and detention without trial of persons reasonably suspected of

membership in a secret society.
325 - *The Great Famine* (1957, 138).
326 - Ó Broin(1971, 216).
327 - D. Gwynn *Young Ireland and 1848*, (1949, 88).
328 - The *Irish Confederation* was an Irish nationalist independence movement, established on the thirteenth of January 1847 by members of the Young Ireland movement who had seceded from Daniel O'Connell's Repeal Association.
329 - Earl of Bessborough is a title in the Peerage of Ireland. It was originally created in 1739 for Brabazon Ponsonby, 2nd Viscount Duncannon, who had previously represented Newtownards and County Kildare in the Irish House of Commons. In 1749 he was given the additional title of Baron Ponsonby of Sysonby, in the County of Leicester, England a title which permitted him a seat in the British House of Lords.
330 - *The History of the Penal Laws Enacted Against Roman Catholics* London: Thomas Richardson and Son, 1847.
331 - A *Grandfather's Story Book*, 211.
332 - From a reference, in the Bodleian Library, Oxford.
333 - See article "Civil Service Reform 1853-5" in *Public Administration* Spring 1954.
334 - Anthony Trollope (1815-1882) was one of the most successful and prolific English novelists of the Victorian era. Some of his best-loved works, collectively known as the *Chronicles of Barsetshire*, revolved around the imaginary county of Barsetshire. He is one of a small number of Victorian novelists whose popularity has continued unabated into the modern era. In 1841, he took up a post vacated by a postal surveyor's clerk from the west of Ireland. Trollope based himself in Banagher, County Offaly although his work consisted largely of inspection tours throughout the counties of Connacht. He married and took up another job in Clonmel, County Tipperary. A few years later he moved back to England on a permanent basis.
335 - *Nation*, 25 September 1847, 809.

CHAPTER 11 - A SPELL IN WESTERN AUSTRALIA

336 - Ó Broin(1971, 228-9).

337 - Ó Broin(1971, 228).

338 - Ó Broin(1971, 229).

339 - Fremantle is a port city in Western Australia. It is located nineteen kilometres southwest of Perth, the state capital, at the mouth of the Swan River on Australia's western coast.

340 - George Fletcher Moore (1798-1886) was a prominent early settler in colonial Western Australia, and one of the key administrators in the ruling colonial elite there. In addition to his work for the British colonial administration he was also an explorer who carried out a number of expeditions into parts of Australia which had not been documented by the settlers prior to this. He wrote a book recording some of the language of the Australian Aborigines in the Perth area.

341 - Ó Broin(1971, 229).

342 - Ó Broin(1971, 231).

343 - Sir James Stephen (1789–1859) was the British under-secretary of state for the colonies between the years 1836 and 1847. He was instrumental in implementing the slavery abolition act.

344 - Ó Broin(1971, 231).

345 - E.A. Benians et al. *Cambridge History of the British Empire*, Vol. 7 VII, 1933, 212.

346 - Father John Therry (1790-1864) was an early Roman Catholic priest in Sydney, Australia. Privately educated at St Patrick's in Carlow, Ireland, he was ordained a priest in 1815. On hearing that Catholic convicts in Australia needed a priest to minister to them, he let it be known that he was willing to work there as a missionary. On 5 December 1819 he set sail for Australia along with another priest, the Rev. P. Connolly. They arrived in Sydney on the third of May, 1820. Connolly would move to Tasmania for his religious work whereas Father Therry remained in the Sydney area. Despite much hostility from the British colonial administration, Father Therry did enormous work on behalf of the Catholics in New South Wales.

347 - Charles Grant, First Baron Glenelg (1778-1866) was a Scottish politician and colonial administrator. In 1811 Grant was elected to the British House of Commons as Member of Parliament for Inverness Burghs. He was appointed Lord of the Treasury in December, 1813 a position he held until August, 1819, when he became Chief Secretary for Ireland and a Privy Counsellor. In April 1835 he became Secretary of State for War and the Colonies. His term of office was difficult and controversial.

348 - John Hutt (1795–1880) was Governor of Western Australia between 1839 and 1846. Born in London, both John Hutt and his brother William were closely involved in the establishment of the colony in South Australia. Originally recommended for the position of first Governor of South Australia, he was instead appointed to succeed Sir James Stirling as Governor of Western Australia. He took up this post in January 1839 and resigned it almost a decade later, in 1846. Politically-liberal in outlook, Hutt's attitude to the Aboriginal peoples of Western Australia was quite different to that of Stirling and most previous settlers and administrators. Relations between the settlers and the Aborigines had deteriorated badly in the final years of Stirling's reign with Stirling attempting to oppress the Aboriginal peoples through the use of brutality and force. Hutt, in contrast, implemented a policy of protecting the rights of Aborigines, and providing education for their communities wherever possible.

349 - New Norcia is a town in Western Australia. It is located about eighty miles north of Perth, along the Great Northern Highway. It is the only monastic town in Australia.

350 - Ó Broin(1971, 238).

351 - *Anti-Slavery Reporter*, 15 July, 1840.

352 - *Royal Irish Academy (RIA) Papers*, 24, NI.

353 - H.N. Birt. *Benedictine Pioneers in Australia* II, 1911, 140.

354 - See P. Moran (1897) *History of the Catholic Church in Australasia*; Sydney: Oceanic Publishing Co., – (cited in Ó Broin 1971, 241).

355 - H.N. Birt, *Benedictine Pioneers in Australia*; London: Herbert &

Daniel, 1911. Vol. 2, 145.

356 - Colonial Office Papers – London: Public Record Office (CO 18/49).

357 - Colonial Office Papers – London: Public Record Office (CO 18/49).

358 - See P. Moran (1897) *History of the Catholic Church in Australasia*; Sydney: Oceanic Publishing Co., – (cited in Ó Broin 1971, 243).

359 - Ó Broin(1971, 245).

360 - Guy Fawkes (1570-1606) belonged to a group of English Catholics who planned the failed Gunpowder Plot of 1605. Born and educated in York, his mother married a recusant Catholic on the death of her husband at a young age. Fawkes later converted to Catholicism and left for the continent, where he fought in the Eighty Years' War on the side of Catholic Spain against the Protestant Dutch. He later travelled to Spain to seek support for a Catholic rebellion in England an attempt which was unsuccessful. He later met Thomas Wintour and the two men returned to England where Wintour introduced Fawkes to Robert Catesby, a man who was then putting in place a plan to assassinate King James I and restore a Catholic monarch to the English throne. The plotters became synonymous with the "Gunpowder Plot", an event which has been commemorated with bonfires in certain parts of England ever since the year 1605. The plot failed and Guy Fawkes was executed for treason.

361 - Ó Broin(1971, 248).

362 - *Colonial Office Papers* (CO), Public Record Office, London, 18/49, Paper 3870.

363 - W. Beattie (ed.) *Life and Letters of Thomas Campbell*; London: Edward Moxon (3 volumes) - Volume III, 120).

364 - Ó Broin(1971, 250).

365 - Ó Broin(1971, 251).

366 - Ó Broin(1971, 251).

367 - *Colonial Office Papers* (CO), Public Record Office, London, 18/50 Paper 3900.

368 - Ó Broin(1971, 252).

369 - Ó Broin(1971, 253).

370 - Ó Broin(1971, 254).

371 - Rottnest Island is located eighteen kilometres off the coast of Western Australia, near Fremantle. This island was inhabited by Aboriginal people as far back in history as 30,000 years ago. From 1838 onwards the colonial administration in Australia sent Aboriginal prisoners to Rottnest Island. The place was used as penal settlement for Aboriginal people between 1838 and 1931, except for the six years between 1849 and 1855. Many of the Aboriginal men imprisoned there were incarcerated for offences as minor as hunting livestock, burning the bush or digging vegetables. Rottnest Island was also used as an internment camp for German prisoners during both World War I and World War II.

372 - *Colonial Office Papers* (CO), Public Record Office, London, CO 18/48, Paper 3805; CO 18/50, Paper 3900.

373 - The Murchison River is the second longest river in Western Australia. It flows for nearly 500 miles, from the southern edge of the Robinson Ranges to the Indian Ocean at Kalbarri.

374 - *Colonial Office Papers* (CO), Public Record Office, London - CO 18/52.

375 - Ó Broin(1971, 257-8).

376 - *Colonial Office Papers* (CO) – (18/150) - Public Record Office, London.

377 - *Colonial Office Papers* (CO), Public Record Office, London - CO. Papers 3805-3870, 3900, 4012.

378 - Henry Bland (1811-1894) was a public servant and a company manager. He arrived in Western Australia in August 1829 and in December was appointed superintendent of government stock at York. In 1831, Lieutenant-Governor (Sir) James Stirling asked him to lead an expedition through the Darling Range and establish a government farm at York.

379 - Ó Broin(1971, 260).

380 - Frederick Henry Piesse (1853–1912) was a farmer, businessman and a politician, who is credited with much of the early development of the region around Katanning, Western Australia.

381 - Ó Broin(1971, 262).
382 - Ó Broin(1971, 264).
383 - Paul Cullen (1803-1878) was a Roman Catholic Archbishop of Dublin who became the first Irish Cardinal. He played a leading role in ushering in the devotional revolution experienced in Ireland throughout the second half of the nineteenth century and much of the twentieth century.
384 - Ó Broin(1971, 264).
385 - In Dorset, England.
386 - Ó Broin(1971, 266).

CHAPTER 12 - EXILE'S RETURN: A JOB IN IRELAND

387 - This Catholic diocese straddles the border between the Republic of Ireland and Northern Ireland, and includes almost all of County Cavan.
388 - Ó Broin(1971, 268).
389 - Arthur Wellesley, 1st Duke of Wellington (1769–1852), was a noted Irish-born British Army officer and statesman. He is most famous for his part in the defeat of Napoleon Bonaparte at the Battle of Waterloo.
390 - Ó Broin(1971, 270).
391 - *Saunders Newsletter* was a newspaper published in Ireland for more than a century. It ran from between the years 1755 and 1879. In 1777 it became a daily newspaper. Primarily concerned with commercial and business interests, its tone was moderate although it was at heart pro-colonial-Government and anti-Catholic. Its articles did not exhibit the same anti-Catholic bitterness and virulence as that shown by some of the Orange press, however.
392 - Ó Broin(1971, 273).
393 - Ó Broin(1971, 273).
394 - Ó Broin(1971, 274).
395 - Ó Broin(1971, 275).
396 - Ó Broin(1971, 278).
397 - Jonathan Swift (1667-1745) was an Anglo-Irish satirist, essayist, political pamphleteer, poet and cleric who became Dean of St. Patrick's Cathedral, Dublin. He is best remembered for books such as *Gulliver's Travels, A Modest Proposal, A Journal to Stella, Drapier's Letters, The Battle of the Books, An Argument Against Abolishing Christianity*, and *A Tale of a Tub*. One of the foremost prose satirists in the English language, Swift also wrote a good deal of poetry.
398 - *Manuscripts of Madden, Smith O'Brien and Luke Cullen*, National Library of Ireland - 4467.
399 - National Library of Ireland - (4469).
400 - Lombardy is one of the twenty regions of Italy.

401 - Ó Broin(1971, 285).
402 - Souperism was a phenomenon which appeared during the great tragedy that was the Irish Potato Famine. Various Bible societies set up schools in which starving Roman Catholic children were fed, while also being subjected to religious instruction in the tenets of Protestantism at the same time. The people who set up these Bible societies were generally reviled by the many Catholic families who had to choose between their religious faith and starvation. People who converted for food or "took the soup" were known as "soupers", a derogatory term that was used in Irish public discourse well into the 1870s.
403 - Ó Broin(1971, 285).
404 - Ó Broin(1971, 286).
405 - Somerset House is in Lorrha, County Tipperary, Ireland.
406 - Ó Broin(1971, 287).
407 - Ó Broin(1971, 287).
408 - The term "Union" here refers to the Union poor law workhouses which were commonly-found in many nineteenth-century Irish and English towns during the nineteenth century.
409 - Ó Broin(1971, 289).
410 - Ó Broin(1971, 291).
411 - Ó Broin(1971, 292).
412 - Ó Broin(1971, 292).
413 - *Office of the State Papers* (OSP), O.2271/339; O.2350/339; O.2510/339) 29.
414 - Ó Broin(1971, 293).
415 - Anne Devlin (1780-1851) was an Irish republican who acted as housekeeper to rebel leader Robert Emmet. She was also a cousin of two leading United Irishmen, Michael Dwyer and Arthur Devlin.
416 - Michael Dwyer (1772–1825) was one of the leaders of the United Irishmen who fought in the 1798 rebellion.
417 - Ó Broin(1971, 299).
418 - *Anti-Slavery Advocate*, VI, 45.
419 - Ó Broin(1971, 299).
420 - Ó Broin(1971, 299).

421 - Ó Broin(1971, 299-300).
422 - Ó Broin(1971, 300).
423 - Sir Robert Peel (1788-1850) was a British Conservative statesman who served as Prime Minister of Britain between December 1834 and April 1835, and again between August 1841 and June 1846. While working as Home Secretary, he helped develop the modern concept of the police force. As a consequence, police officers in Britain became known as "bobbies", a name which is still in use today while in Ireland they became know as "Peelers", a term which has fallen into disuse. As Prime Minister, Peel's most notable act was his repeal of the Corn Laws.
424 - The *Daily Telegraph* is a daily morning newspaper distributed throughout Britain and internationally. The newspaper was originally founded 1855 as the *Daily Telegraph and Courier.*
425 - See C.G. Duffy (1886) *The League of North and South: an episode in Irish history, 1850-1854*; London: Chapman and Hall., 375-6.
426 - Ó Broin(1971, 303).
427 - Ó Broin(1971, 303).

CHAPTER 13 - MADDEN'S LITERARY CAREER TAKES A PROLIFIC TURN

428 - Ó Broin(1971, 303).

429 - The Dictionary defines the archaic word "phantasmata" (phan-tasm) as:

    1. an apparition or spectre.

    2. a creation of the imagination or fancy; fantasy.

430 - William Ewart Gladstone (1809-1898) was a British Liberal statesman. In a career lasting over sixty years, he served as Prime Minister of Britain four times (1868–1874, 1880–1885, February–July 1886 and 1892–1894). He also served four terms as Chancellor of the Exchequer.

431 - See *Quarterly Review*, Volume XIX, June, 1856.

432 - Ó Broin(1971, 306).

433 - Ridolfi Roberto (1959) *The Life of Girolamo Savonarola;* (translated from the Italian by Cecil Grayson) London: Routledge.

434 - Ó Broin(1971, 307).

435 - Henry Peter Brougham (1778–1868) was a British statesman who became Lord Chancellor of the United Kingdom.

436 - Catholic Emancipation, once referred to as "Catholic relief" was a process which took place in both Britain and Ireland over the course of the late eighteenth century and the early decades of the nineteenth century whereby many of the restrictions on Roman Catholics which had been introduced by the British Act of Uniformity, the Test Acts and the Penal laws were gradually reduced and removed.

437 - Ó Broin(1971, 308).

438 - Walter Savage Landor (1775-1864) was an English writer and poet.

439 - Ó Broin(1971, 308).

440 - *Athenaeum Review* (3 February, 1855) The *Athenaeum* was a literary magazine published in London between 1828 and 1921. It had a reputation for publishing the very best writers of this era.

441 - Ó Broin(1971, 308-9).
442 - Jacques-Bénigne Bossuet (1627-1704) was a French bishop and theologian, renowned for his sermons and orations. He is considered by many to have been one of the most brilliant orators of all time and a masterly stylist of the French language.
443 - Ó Broin(1971, 309).
444 - Ó Broin(1971, 310).
445 - The *Cross of Cong* is an early twelfth century Irish Christian ornamented processional which was made for Tairrdelbach Ua Conchobair (d. 1156), King of Connacht and High King of Ireland. The cross was moved from Tuam, County Galway to Cong Abbey in Cong, County Mayo. It is from this area that the Cross takes its name.
446 - Lord Cloncurry (Valentine Brown Lawless) (1773-1853) was an Irish politician and landowner. He lived in Ardclough, County Kildare.
447 - Ó Broin(1971, 310).
448 - Richmond Barracks (Prison) was located in north (inner-city) Dublin.
449 - William Le Fanu worked as a Commissioner of the Irish Board of Works and published his book of reminiscences *Seventy Years of Irish Life* in 1893. His brother Sheridan Le Fanu was a famous Gothic writer of his day.
450 - William Le Fanu *Seventy Years of Irish Life* (1893, 158).
451 - William Carleton (1794-1869) was a well-known Irish novelist of the eighteenth century. Despite receiving a very basic education – his father was a farmer's labourer and Carleton's education came by way of various hedge schools. A good description of one of these schools occurs in one of Carleton's best-known works *Traits and Stories of Irish Peasantry* (1836).
452 - The *Dublin University Magazine* was an independent literary cultural and political magazine published in Dublin from 1833 to 1882. It began life as a magazine focused on political commentary but as the years went on it became increasingly devoted to literature.
453 - Ó Broin(1971, 312-313).

454 - Saint Teresa of Ávila (1515–1582) was a prominent Spanish mystic and writer of the Counter Reformation. A Carmelite nun she was a leading contemplative and is a Roman Catholic saint.

455 - Originating with the writings of the Dutch theologian Cornelius Otto Jansen, Jansenism was a theology and a movement which appeared during the period of the Counter-Reformation and after the Council of Trent (1545–1563). This theology placed a heavy emphasis on concepts including original sin, human depravity, the necessity of divine grace, and the theory of predestination. Jansenism was condemned as a heresy by Pope Innocent X in 1655.

456 - Saint Joan of Arc, (Jeanne d'Arc) sometimes referred to as "The Maid of Orléans" (1412-1431) is considered a national heroine of France and a Catholic saint and martyr. She was burned at the stake while just nineteen years of age.

457 - Ó Broin(1971, 314).

458 - *The Book of Tobias* (more commonly known today as *The Book of Tobit*) is a book of scriptures that is part of both the Catholic and the Orthodox biblical canons.

CHAPTER 14 - THE SECOND EDITION OF THE *LIVES*

459 - Ó Broin(1971, 314).

460 - The Irish Republican Brotherhood (IRB) was a secret oath-bound fraternal organisation dedicated to the establishment of an "independent democratic republic" in Ireland during the second half of the nineteenth century and the early decades of the twentieth century. It's counterpart in the US became known as the Fenian Brotherhood or the "Fenians."

461 - Terence Bellew MacManus was a radical Irish rebel who participated in the Young Irelander Rebellion of 1848. He was sentenced to death for treason but he had several others had their sentences commuted to life imprisonment and transportation. In 1849 he was transported for life to Van Diemen's Land in Australia. Three years later MacManus escaped after which he made his way to the United States. He died in 1861.

462 - Paul Cullen (1803-1878) was a Roman Catholic Archbishop of Dublin. He was the first Irishman to be prelate ever appointed an Irish Cardinal.

463 - American-based members of the Fenian Brotherhood attempted an uprising in Canada when they launched a series of raids there in the first week of June, 1866. The purpose of these raids was to seize the transportation network of Canada, with the idea that this would force the British to exchange Ireland's freedom for possession of their Province of Canada. The biggest of these raids, known as the "Battle of Ridgeway" saw the Fenians briefly capture Fort Erie and defeat a Canadian force at Ridgeway.

464 - Killanaule is in County Tipperary, Ireland.

465 - John Bright (1811-1889) was a well-known Quaker who was also a British Radical and Liberal statesman. He was associated with Richard Cobden and the formation of the Anti-Corn Law League. A staunch critic of British foreign policy, he sat in the House of Commons between the years 1843 and 1889.

466 - Ó Broin(1971, 318-319).

467 - *Freeman's Journal* – (21,11,1865).

468 - Ó Broin(1971, 322).

469 - Ó Broin(1971, 322).

470 - *Habeas corpus* (Latin meaning "you may have the body" [i.e. the subject person under detention]) is a writ, or legal action, through which a prisoner can be released from unlawful detention. The remedy can be sought by the prisoner or by another person coming to his aid. Although the concept of Habeas corpus originated within the British legal system, it is now used in a wide number of other countries throughout the world.

471 - Ó Broin(1971, 323).

472 - Richard Southwell Bourke (1822-1872), styled Lord Naas between 1842 and 1867 and also known as Viceroy Lord Carlisle was a statesman and prominent member of the British Conservative Party. A member of the Anglo-Irish aristocracy he was from Dublin, Ireland.

473 - Manuscripts of Madden, Smith O'Brien and Luke Cullen. National Library of Ireland (NLI) Numbers 403 and 8503.

474 - Francis Higgins was the chief Government spy master within the British colonial administration in Ireland and was largely responsible for the successful infiltration of the United Irish movement.

474b - Ó Broin (1971,338).

475 - Ó Broin(1971, 338).

476 - Ó Broin(1971, 339).

477 - Ó Broin(1971, 341).

478 - The journalist in question was a daughter of the then well-known Irish novelist Michael Banim. Madden's comments were made in an article published in the *Evening Telegraph* of the 20th of October, 1890.

479 - The Brehon Laws were the early Irish statutes that governed civil life and politics in Ireland during the Gaelic period. One of the oldest forms of law in Northern Europe, they suffered a decline during the Norman invasion of 1169, but saw a resurgence again in the thirteenth century. They survived in parallel with English law throughout most of Ireland until the seventeenth century.

480 - See *Royal Irish Academy (RIA) Papers* - XII, 132.9, 342.

CHAPTER 15 - THE END OF THE ROAD

481 - *National University of Ireland.* Manuscripts of John Matthews, 5762.

482 - Sir Samuel Ferguson was the President of the Royal Irish Academy in the late-1860s.

483 - M.C. Ferguson (1896) *Sir Samuel Ferguson in the Ireland of His Day*, Edinburgh: W. Blackwood, II, 205-7.

484 - A reference to the Sati tradition once practiced in India.

485 - *Royal Irish Academy (RIA) Papers* - 24.0.10).

486 - Sir Samuel Ferguson (1810-1886) was a well-known Irish poet who also worked as a barrister, an antiquarian, an artist and a public servant. He is considered one of the most important Ulster-Scot poets of the nineteenth century and was noted for the incorporation of Irish historical and mythical themes in his poetry.

487 - Ó Broin(1971, 347).

488 - James Anthony Froude (1818-1894) was a well-known English historian of the nineteenth century. In addition to his history work he was also a novelist, a biographer, and the editor of *Fraser's Magazine*.

489 - Ó Broin(1971, 347-48).

490 - Ó Broin(1971, 348).

491 - Ó Broin(1971, 348).

492 - The "Manchester Martyrs" were William Philip Allen, Michael Larkin, and Michael O'Brien – all of whom were members of the Irish Republican Brotherhood, an organisation dedicated to ending British rule in Ireland. They were executed for the murder of a police officer in Manchester, England, in 1867. Their deaths became a cause celebre throughout the world and a rallying point for Irish people and their supporters who wished to see an end to British rule in Ireland.

493 - Ó Broin(1971, 350).

494 - Blaise Pascal (1623-1662), was a noted French mathematician, physicist, inventor, writer and Catholic philosopher.

495 - The *Lettres provinciales* (Provincial letters) are a series of eighteen letters written by French philosopher and theologian Blaise Pascal under the pseudonym Louis de Montalte. They

were written during the throes of a controversy which occurred at this juncture between the Jansenists and the Jesuits. Pascal's Lettres were in defence of a friend of his, the noted Jansenist Antoine Arnauld who, in 1656, was condemned by the Faculté de Théologie at the Sorbonne in Paris for views that were deemed heretical. Pascal's *First Letter* is dated January the twenty-third, 1656 while the Eighteenth Letter is dated March the twenty-fourth, 1657. A fragmentary or unfinished Nineteenth letter is often included with the other eighteen.

496 - Ó Broin(1971, 352).

497 - Ó Broin(1971, 353).

498 - Michael Banim (1796–1874) was the brother of the more well-known John Banim, a leading eighteenth-century Irish novelist. Michael and John Banim wrote a number of books together and it is therefore difficult to ascertain how many novels or part-novels Michael actually wrote. Michael Banim was the principal author of *Crohoore of the Bill-Hook* (1848), *The Croppy* (1828) and *Father Connell* (1842)

499 - Benjamin Disraeli (1804-1881) was a British Prime Minister, parliamentarian, Conservative statesman and literary figure. He served in government for three decades, twice as Prime Minister of Britain. Disraeli played an important role in the creation of the modern Conservative Party subsequent to the Corn Laws schism of 1846.

500 - The Irish National Invincibles, normally referred to as "The Invincibles" were a radical splinter group of the Irish Republican Brotherhood (IRB). They were active in Dublin during the decade that was the 1880s, in particular.

501 - Ó Broin(1971, 354).

502 - Ó Broin(1971, 354).

503 - Ó Broin(1971, 354).

504 - Ó Broin(1971, 355).

505 - George Petrie (1790 – 1866), was an Irish painter, musician, antiquary and archaeologist whose life and artistic career spanned the first half of the nineteenth century.

506 - See T. A. Emmet *Incidents of my Life*; New York and London: G.

P. Putnam's Sons (1911, 347).
506 - Ó Broin(1971, 357).
507 - Ó Broin(1971, 357).
508 - Ó Broin(1971, 357).
509 - Ó Broin(1971, 357).
510 - Ó Broin(1971, 358).
511 - *The Imitation of Christ* by Thomas à Kempis(1639).
512 - Ó Broin(1971, 358).
513 - See "The Search for Madden's Grave" in *Studies*, May, 1961.
514 - Ó Broin(1971, 361).
515 - C.I. is an acronym for the Church of Ireland. The Church of Ireland is an autonomous province of the Anglican Communion. It operated seamlessly across the border between the Republic of Ireland and Northern Ireland.
516 - Postgate, Raymond W. (1931) *Robert Emmet*; London: M. Secker.
517 - Madden. R.R. (1888) *Ireland in '98: sketches of the principal men of the time / based upon the published volumes and some unpublished Mss of the late Richard Robert Madden*; edited by J. Bowles Daly. London: Swan Sonnenschein, Lowrey.
518 - See *Correspondence of Daniel O'Connell* – edited by W.J. Fitzpatrick II, (1888, 124).

SELECT BIBLIOGRAPHY

MANUSCRIPTS

Anti-slavery Papers. Rhodes House, Oxford (RH)
Royal Irish Academy (RIA)
British Museum: Gladstone Papers
T.W. Moody Private Papers - Trinity College Dublin (TCD)
Colonial Office Papers (CO). Public Record Office, London.
Foreign Office Papers (FO). Public Record Office, London.
Madden's bound volumes and papers, Garbally College, Ballinasloe and the National Library of Ireland.
Manuscripts of Madden, Smith O'Brien and Luke Cullen. National Library of Ireland. (NLI)
Office of State Papers (OSP)

PRIMARY SOURCES CONSULTED

R.R. Madden (1835) *A Twelvemonth's Residence in the West Indies*; London : James Cochrane and Co.

R.R. Madden (1855) *Countess of Blessington: diaries, memoirs, etc.*; London: T.C. Newby.

R.R. Madden (1841) *Egypt and Mohammed Ali*; London: H. Adams.

R.R. Madden (1866) *Exposure of Literary Frauds and Forgeries concocted in Ireland*; Dublin.

R.R. Madden (1863) *Galileo and the Inquisition*; London: Burns and Lambert.

R.R. Madden(1867) *The history of Irish periodical literature...* London: Newby.

R.R. Madden (1849) *Island of Cuba: Its Resources and Prospects*; London, Dublin: C. Gilpin; J. B. Gilpin.

R.R. Madden (1887) *Literary Remains of the United Irishmen of 1798*; Dublin: J. Duffy, 1887.

R.R. Madden (1847) *History of the penal laws enacted against Roman Catholics*; London: Derby.

R.R. Madden (1857) *Phantasmata, or Illusions and fanaticisms of protean forms*; London: Newby.

R.R. Madden (1845) *The Connexion between the Kingdom of Ireland and the Crown of England*; Dublin: J. Duffy.

R.R. Madden *The Life and Martyrdom of Savonarola*; London: Newby (1853).

R.R. Madden (1843) *The Slave Trade and Slavery*; London: J. Madden and Co.

R.R. Madden (1846) *The United Irishmen: their Lives and Times*; Dublin: J. Duffy.

R.R. Madden (1833) *Travels in Turkey , Egypt, Nubia and Palestine, in 1824, 1825, 1826 and 1827*; London: Whittaker and Treacher.

SELECT REPORTS

Reports of Commissioner of Inquiry on West Coast of Africa (1841-1843).

Report from the Select Committee on Loan Fund Societies (Ireland) 1854-1855.

SELECT NEWSPAPERS AND PERIODICALS

Anti-Slavery Advocate	The Nation
Daily Independent	Old Dublin Review
Dublin Evening Packet	Quarterly Review
Dublin Evening Post	Saunder's Newsletter
Dublin University Magazine	The Spectator
Evening Telegraph (Dublin)	The Tablet
Freeman's Journal	The Times

OTHER SOURCES CONSULTED

Beattie, W. *Life and Letters of Thomas Campbell*; London: Hall, Virtue and Co., 1850.

Berndt, R.M. and C.H. (1953) *The First Australians*; Sydney: Ure Smith

Birt, H.N. (1911) *Benedictine Pioneers in Australia*; London: Herbert and Daniel

Dickson, C. (1944) *Life of Michael Dwyer*; Dublin : Browne and Nolan

Duffy, C. G. (1895) *Short Life of Thomas Davis, 1840-1846*; London: Dublin: T. Fisher Unwin; Sealy, Bryers & Walker

Duffy, C. G. (1898) *My Life in Two Hemispheres*; London : T.F. Unwin

Duffy, C. G. (1886) *The League of North and South. An episode in Irish history. 1850-1854*; London: Chapman and Hall

Duffy, C. G. (1843) *The Spirit of the Nation*; Dublin: James Duffy.

Crowley, F.K. (1960) *Australia's Western Third*; London : Macmillan and Co.

Edwards, R.D. and Williams, D. (1956) *The Great Famine; Studies in Irish History, 1845-52*; Dublin: Browne and Nolan

Emmet, T.A. (1915) *Memoir of Thomas Addis and Robert Emmet, with their ancestors and immediate family*; New York: Emmet Press

Emmet, T.A. (1911) *Incidents of my Life*; New York; and London: G. P. Putnam's Sons, (1911)

Ferguson, M.C. (1896) *Sir Samuel Ferguson in the Ireland of his Day*; Edinburgh: Blackwood

Fitzpatrick, W.J. (1892) *Secret Service under Pitt*; London; New York: Longmans, Green

Fitzpatrick, W.J. (1869) *Sham Squire*; Dublin: London - W.B. Kelly; Simpkin, Marshall, and Co.,

Gwynn, D. (1930) *Daniel O'Connell*; London: Hutchinson

Gwynn, D. (1949) *Young Ireland and 1848*; Cork: Cork University Press

Le Fanu, W.R. (1893) *Seventy Years of Irish Life*;

London: Edward Arnold

Leslie, S. (1928) *Mrs. Fitzherbert*; London: Benn

Lloyd, C. (1949) *The Navy and the Slave Trade*; London; New York: Longmans, Green,

Lockhead, M. (1954) *John Gibson Lockhart*; London: John Murray

MacManus, M.J. (ed.) (1945) *Thomas Davis and Young Ireland*; Dublin: The Stationery Office

McCabe, W.J. *(1852) A Grandfather's Story Book*; Dublin: James Duffy

McNeill, M. (1960) *The life and times of Mary Ann McCracken, 1770-1866*; Dublin: A. Figgis.

Moran, P.F. (1897) *A History of the Catholic Church in Australasia*; Sydney: Oceanic Publishing Co.

Ó Broin, L. (1951) *Miss Crookshank agus Coirp Eile*; Baile Átha Cliath: Sáirséal agus Dill (1951)

Ó Broin, L. (1958) *The Unfortunate Mr. Robert Emmet* Dublin: Clonmore and Reynolds

Ó Broin, L. (1967) *Charles Gavan Duffy*; Dublin : James Duffy

O'Donoghue, D.J. (1896) *The Life of William Carleton*; London: Downey

Owens, W.A.(1953) *Slave Mutiny*; London : Peter Davies

Postgate, R. (1931) *Robert Emmet*; London: M. Secker

Ronan, M.V. (1944) *An Apostle of Catholic Dublin: Father Henry Young*; Dublin: Browne and Nolan Ltd.

Sadleir, M. (1933) *Blessington D'Orsay - A Masquerade*; London: Constable and Co.

LEON Ó BROIN

Leon Ó Broin (10 November 1902 – 26 February 1990) was an Irish Civil Servant, writer and playwright, who wrote many plays, stories and historical works in both English and Irish. He was born in Dublin. He joined Sinn Féin and Fianna Éireann while still at school. He was imprisoned in 1921 and 1922 and afterwards joined the Free State army as a non-combatant. In 1924 he was the first Administrative Officer appointed by the new Free State civil service, where he worked mainly in the Department of Finance. He was Secretary of the Department of Posts and Telegraphs from 1948 to 1967.

MÍCHEÁL Ó HAODHA

Dr. Mícheál Ó hAodha works at the University of Limerick. He has published many books in Irish and English on various aspects of Irish culture and particularly Irish migrants and migration and groups considered to be "outsiders" or on the margins of Irish society including: *The Turn of the Hand: A Memoir from the Irish Margins* (with Mary Warde) (2010); *Insubordinate Irish: Travellers in the Text* (2011). Two recent books are *An Scáileán Mór: Aistí Scannánaíochta* (2014) and *The Glen/An Gleann: Recollections from a Lost World* (2014). His books have been published with Manchester University Press, Peter Lang, Irish Academic Press, Rowman, Mercier, Arlen House/Cló Iar-Chonnachta, Liffey Press, Coiscéim amongst others.

Made in the USA
Charleston, SC
12 March 2015